Archibald M'Kay

The History of Kilmarnock

Archibald M'Kay

The History of Kilmarnock

ISBN/EAN: 9783337328054

Printed in Europe, USA, Canada, Australia, Japan

Cover: Foto ©ninafisch / pixelio.de

More available books at **www.hansebooks.com**

THE HISTORY OF KILMARNOCK.

BY

ARCHIBALD M'KAY,

AUTHOR OF "RECREATIONS OF LEISURE HOURS," "INGLE-SIDE LILTS," ETC.

THIRD EDITION, REVISED AND ENLARGED.

> Low in a *fertile* valley spread,
> An ancient borough reared her head;
> Still, as in Scottish story read,
>   She boasts a race,
> To every nobler virtue bred,
>   And polished grace.
>   BURNS.

KILMARNOCK:
ARCHIBALD M'KAY, KING STREET.
M.DCCC.LXIV.

TO

SIR JOHN SHAW, BART,

WHO HAS ALWAYS EVINCED A LIVELY INTEREST

IN

THE PROSPERITY

OF

KILMARNOCK,

HIS NATIVE TOWN,

THIS WORK,

ILLUSTRATIVE OF ITS HISTORY,

IS RESPECTFULLY DEDICATED.

PREFACE TO THE SECOND EDITION.

IN submitting to the public this Edition of the HISTORY OF KILMARNOCK, the Author may state that, by the favourable reception given to the work on its first appearance, he has been induced to publish it in its present revised and enlarged form. He trusts that the original matter introduced into various parts of the text, together with the many illustrative foot-notes that have been added, will render it still more deserving of general patronage.

He must acknowledge, however, that, from the difficulty of obtaining accurate information, he has been sometimes obliged, especially in the early part of the narrative, to give only a mere outline instead of a complete picture; but even that outline, affording, as it does, an idea of the appearance of the town and the social condition of the inhabitants, at a comparatively remote period, cannot fail to prove generally interesting.

Of the various members of the Boyd Family a more lengthened account might have been given; but this would have extended the volume beyond its proposed limits. The eventful career, however, of the unfortunate last Earl of Kilmarnock has been traced at some length, partly from its singularly pathetic interest, and partly from its close connection with an important period of Scottish history.

For the same reasons, the sufferings of the Covenanters in Kilmarnock and its neighbourhood have been briefly noticed. Their struggles and trials, it is true, are already widely known; but to have passed them over in silence would have been at variance with the spirit of the present volume, the object of which is to chronicle, in a concise yet faithful manner, the principal incidents and traditions connected with the locality.

An abridged translation of the Charter by which the town was erected into a Burgh of Barony, and several other interesting papers, that could not be conveniently woven into the text, have been given in the form of an Appendix.

The Author may add, that, should this Edition be found to contribute still further to the information or entertainment of his fellow-townsmen, and others interested in the historical associations of the district, he will not regret the pains he has taken, or the time he has expended, in the composition of the work.

116, KING STREET, KILMARNOCK,
June 1, 1858.

PREFACE TO THE THIRD EDITION.

THE Second Edition of the HISTORY OF KILMARNOCK experienced a favourable reception, and was soon out of print; hence the Author was led to prepare the work again for publication.

He may state that he has endeavoured to make it more worthy of public acceptance. The original text—the greater part of which is retained—has been carefully revised, and many new details, illustrative of the olden time, have been introduced. These details, several of which have not been hitherto published, have been collected from authentic sources, and are interspersed throughout the work as nearly as possible in chronological order. The narrative also embraces the principal matters of interest connected with the more recent history and progress of the town.

Several papers of a miscellaneous description, not formerly embodied in the work, are inserted in the Appendix; and a copious general Index, which was a desideratum in the former editions, has been supplied.

The Portrait of William, Fourth Earl of Kilmarnock, given as a Frontispiece, has been engraved from a rare contemporary print, and is believed to be an accurate likeness.

124, KING STREET, KILMARNOCK,
August 15, 1864.

CONTENTS.

CHAPTER I.
Antiquity of the town—origin of its name, &c., ... 1

CHAPTER II.
Dean Castle described—its associations, &c., ... 11

CHAPTER III.
Origin of the Boyds, and notices of the early members of the family, ... 19

CHAPTER IV.
Lord Soulis—notices of the Boyds *(continued)*, ... 25

CHAPTER V.
The Covenanters, ... 38

CHAPTER VI.
The Covenanters *(continued)*, ... 50

CHAPTER VII.
Charters granted to the town—Rebellions of 1715 and 1745-6, ... 60

CHAPTER VIII.
The Earl of Kilmarnock at the Battles of Falkirk and Culloden — taken prisoner—tried and sentenced to be executed, ... 7½

CHAPTER IX.
Behaviour of the Earl after his sentence—his execution, &c., ... 79

CHAPTER X.
Appearance of the town about 1750—its trades, public buildings, &c., ... 93

CHAPTER XI.
Pastimes of the people—the fairs, Kings' birthdays, &c., ... 106

CONTENTS.

CHAPTER XII.
Religious character of the inhabitants—violent induction of the Rev. William Lindsay, ... 119

CHAPTER XIII.
Early Schools and Schoolmasters—the Academy and other educational institutions, ... 134

CHAPTER XIV.
First Dissenting Churches—notices of their ministers, ... 149

CHAPTER XV.
Letter-press printing introduced—notice of John Wilson—Burns and his Kilmarnock patrons, ... 159

CHAPTER XVI.
Commercial Statistics—disastrous fires—fearful calamity in the Low Church, &c., 172

CHAPTER XVII.
Public improvements—Town Hall—old road through the town from Glasgow to Ayr, ... 184

CHAPTER XVIII.
First Kilmarnock Periodicals—Sketches of James Thomson, John Burtt, and John Kennedy, ... 192

CHAPTER XIX.
Dean Park meeting for Parliamentary Reform—Radical movement of 1819-20, 200

CHAPTER XX.
Statistics—the Cholera—Kilmarnock Newspapers, &c.—Sketch of Robert Crawford, ... 209

CHAPTER XXI.
King Street United Presbyterian and other Churches, ... 218

CHAPTER XXII.
The Shaw Monument—Memoir of Sir James Shaw, ... 227

CHAPTER XXIII.
Astronomical Observatory—Sketches of Thomas Morton, Professor Robert Findlay, Francis G. P. Neison, Thomas Y. M'Christie, and Professor James F. W. Johnston, ... 234

CONTENTS.

CHAPTER XXIV.
The Fine Arts—Sketch of James Tannock, &c., ... 245

CHAPTER XXV.
Poetical writers—Sketches of John Ramsay, Marion P. Aird, Alexander Smith, &c., &c., ... 252

CHAPTER XXVI.
The remarkable Inundation of the 14th July, 1852, ... 260

CHAPTER XXVII.
Literary Institutions—Masonic Lodges, &c., ... 275

CHAPTER XXVIII.
Recent Improvements—Commercial and other Statistics, &c., ... 281

APPENDIX.

I.—Charter by James VI, erecting the town into a Burgh of Barony, 1591, ... 299
II.—Kilmarnock Lands, ... 302
III.—The Town Green, and the Rights and Titles of the Burgh, ... 303
IV.—The Kilmarnock Coat of Arms, ... 306
V.—The Furniture of Dean Castle in 1611, ... 308
VI.—Cleaning the Streets in 1735, ... 309
VII.—"The Red Steuart," 310
VIII.—"Rabbling the Minister," 310
IX.—Fastern's E'en, ... 311
X.—Progress of the town since 1816, ... 312
XI.—Clubs, ... 314
XII.—The Snow-storm of Saturday, 3rd March, 1827, ... 315
XIII.—The Churchyards, ... 316
XIV.—Extracts from the old Kirk Records, ... 316
XV.—The Juggs, ... 317
XVI.—List of the Magistrates, Treasurers, Provosts, and Clerks of the Burgh of Kilmarnock, from 1695 till 1863, ... 318
INDEX 323

HISTORY OF KILMARNOCK.

CHAPTER I.

It is opportune to look back on old times and contemplate our fathers.
SIR THOMAS BROWNE.

THE origin of Kilmarnock, like that of many other towns of importance, is involved in considerable obscurity, and scarcely any thing illustrative of its ancient history can be gathered from the various statistical works in which it is mentioned. That it is a place of great antiquity, however, seems to be the general opinion. It is stated by some writers that, so far back as the year 322, it was the residence of a St Mernoc or Marnock. Here, according to tradition, he founded a church, and hence, in all likelihood, the origin of the town; for those who were seeking or had enjoyed his holy instructions would naturally incline to settle at or near the hallowed scene of his labours. It is also said that he was interred here within the precincts of the ground he had consecrated. From the same Saint the town has evidently derived its name, which, as shown by the Celtic word *Kil*, signifies the cell, the church, or the burial-place of Marnock.

The very early date, however, assigned to the time of St Marnock is doubtful; and it is more probable that he settled here about the end of the sixth or the beginning of the seventh century, when some of the early teachers of Christianity, who had been educated at *I-colum-kill*, under St Columba, established places of religious worship in different parts of our island.* But there is no account, we believe, on which reliance can be placed, regarding the Church of Kilmarnock prior to the twelfth century. The author of *Caledonia*, whom we shall afterwards quote on the subject, states that it belonged of old to the monastery of Kilwinning, which was then founded; and Pont, who seems to have perused the records of that monastery, says, "it was bulte by the Locartts,† Lords of it (meaning the barony), and dedicat to a holy man, Mernock, as vitnesess ye records of Kilvinin Abbay."

Kilmarnock, for a long time after the death of him from whom its name is derived, must have been a mere hamlet, for we find no trace of it in history until near the time when the noble family of the Boyds became possessors of the lands; and even then it is spoken of as a territory, and not as a town or village. It is mentioned by Barbour, in his *Life of Bruce*, as one of the places through which the English knight, Sir Philip de Mowbray, fled, after being defeated by Douglas, somewhere in the district of Cunningham, about the year 1306:

> "Therefore the ways forth took he then
> To Kilmarnock and Kilwinnyne,
> And to Ardrossan after syne," &c.

To trace the course of the progress of Kilmarnock, even from this time, would be almost impossible. The Town Books extend no farther back than 1686, and, consequently,

---

* See Dr Smith's *Life of St Columba*.

† The Locartts here mentioned are supposed to have been vassals of Hugh de Morville, an Anglo-Norman Baron, who founded the Monastery of Kilwinning, and who "obtained a grant of the extensive and valuable bailiweck, or great Barony of Cunningham."—*See Notes on Pont's Cunningham, by John Fullarton, Esq. of Overtoun.*

throw no light on the subject.* We may infer, however, that besides the Church of the good old Saint, the many natural advantages of the place, such as its somewhat sheltered, yet healthy situation, together with the stream of the Marnock gliding through it, and the Irvine meandering at a short distance, would all tend to make it a favourite place of residence, as the more peaceful arts began to be cultivated. Regarding the particular site of the first houses of the town we are also left in uncertainty. The most likely supposition is, that they were scattered around the ancient Chapel dedicated to St Marnock, which was no doubt situated near to or on the identical spot now occupied by the Low Parish Church. The narrow lane in the immediate neighbourhood, called College Wynd, is, or rather, lately was, one of the most antiquated streets of the town, and derives its name, we believe, from being the site of some Educational Institution in the olden time; one of its old-fashioned tenements is still pointed out by aged persons as having been a school-house of some importance.† In the same lane is another old building, said to have been the *Manse*, and behind

---

* The first entry in the Register of Baptisms is dated 6th February, 1644.

† Since the above was written, we have been favoured with extracts from various letters respecting Kilmarnock in past times, written by William Gregory, Esq., Virginia, to his brother here, James S. Gregory, Esq., Registrar. One of these extracts corroborates the above statement regarding the name College Wynd. Mr Gregory says: "At the north end of the Wynd, and the north-west corner of the Kirk-yard, stood an old house (it may be standing yet), the walls of which belonged to the College, and in it probably were educated some of your west country worthies—Boyd of Troch-rigg, and, perhaps, his kinsman, Zachary Boyd, and others. The College was burnt down about the middle of last century. My father attended there at the time, but was too young to be examined regarding the fire; however, I have heard him say that John Glen (whom I remember) was brought before the Bailies and examined as to what he knew about the fire. John answered that he 'kent naething about it, as he and Rab Elshender were making clay men in the Kirk-yard at the time.' The Collegians used the Church-yard at that time as a play-ground." It is said that the name of the last teacher in the College Wynd School was Mushat. As corroborative of Mr Gregory's conjecture respecting Zachary Boyd we may state that, according to *Chambers's Encyclopædia*, that eminent divine was educated at Kilmarnock.

it is what was called the Glebe Land. The first Bank, too, of which the town could boast, and which was a branch of the Bank of Scotland, was in the adjoining alley, called Low Church Lane;* and, assuming these statements to be true, it is not improbable that this now unfashionable quarter was the nucleus of Kilmarnock. Grange Street, which is near to College Wynd, and which was at one time called the *Clay Mugs*, from the circumstance of a pottery having been in the place, is also, we believe, one of the ancient *neuks* of Auld Killie. Strand Street, in close proximity to the Church, has likewise the appearance of considerable antiquity, and in all probability, was one of the earliest streets of the town. Though now chiefly occupied by the poorer classes, it was the residence of some of the more wealthy families during the last century. We may suppose, too, that the Cross, where stood the corn mill of the parish till the year 1703, would be partly occupied with houses at a comparatively remote period; its appearance, so late as the beginning of the present century, before King Street and Portland Street were formed, was old and antiquated in the extreme. But of this afterwards.

The first notice of any consequence which we have of Kilmarnock, and more especially of the extent of its population, at an early date, is in a document, given in Chapter X, respecting the appointment of a priest or clerk for the parish in the year 1547. The parishioners who took part in that election amounted to about three hundred; and as they, in all likelihood, comprised the whole, or nearly the whole, of the heads of families at that time in the parish, it may be inferred that the population was little more than fourteen hundred—a number which appears very small when we consider that the parish of Fenwick was then included in that

* Statement in 1858 of two respectable townsmen, the one upwards of 90 years of age, and the other between 70 and 80.

of Kilmarnock.* Of course the document furnishes us with no idea of the aspect of the town in regard to its streets or buildings; but it is worthy of remark, that the most of the names attached to it, though different in their orthography, are such as are common amongst us at the present day. The following are the various surnames arranged alphabetically from the document mentioned; and as the number of each is also given, it will be observed that the prevailing names were Brown, Smith, Boyd, Paton, and Adam:

Adam,..............11	Fulton,..............4	Nevine,..............3
Allan,..............3		Norvell,..............2
Andro,..............4	Gemyll,..............6	Nychole,..............1
Angus,..............1	Gilmure,..............5	
Arnot,..............2	Gray,..............2	Pally,..............4
Auchenloss,..............6		Pawtoun,..............12
	Halkhill,..............1	Patrick,..............1
Bar,..............1	Harbartsoune,..............1	
Blakwod,..............2	Harper,..............8	Quhyte,..............6
Black,..............1	Hillhousa,..............3	
Boill,..............1	Hobkyn,..............1	Rankyne,..............1
Boyd,..............15	Howay,†..............1	Robisone,..............1
Borland,..............3	Holmes,..............1	Ross,..............4
Brokat,..............1	Hog,..............7	
Brown,..............20		Schaw,..............2
	Kendy,..............1	Smyth,..............16
Calderwood,..............1	Kirkland,..............1	Steele,..............6
Campbell,..............1		Stesen,..............1
Chalmer,..............1	Lauchland,..............4	Stevinsone,..............1
Cochrane,..............1	Lowdoun,..............3	Strauchand,..............1
Craig,..............2	Lowry,..............3	
Cranfurd,..............2	Lymburnat,..............4	Tailzeour,..............8
Credy,..............2	Lyndsay,..............4	Tanathhill,..............9
Crux,..............7		Tempeltoun,..............1
Cunyngham,..............5	Masoun,..............2	Thomson,..............3
Curry,..............5	Miller,..............8	Tod,..............1
Cuthbertsoune,..............1	Mure,..............2	Torrence,..............1
	Mychell,..............1	
Dickey,..............5	Myll,..............1	Wallace,..............8
Duncane,..............2		Warnock,..............3
	Nasmyth,..............1	Wilsoun,..............2
Findlay,..............4	Neill,..............2	Wright,..............1
	Wylie,..............6	

* Fenwick was disjoined from the parish of Kilmarnock in 1642.
† Probably in Lochgoin, ancestor of the author of the *Scots Worthies*.

Timothy Pont, about sixty years after the time spoken of, namely, in 1609, visited the town when making a survey of Cunningham, and, in his own quaint manner, thus describes it: "Kilmernock-toune and Kirk is a large village and of grate repaire. It hath in it a veekly market, it hath a faire stone bridge over the river Marnock vich glydes hard by the said toune, till it falles in the river Irving. It hath a pretty church from vich ye village, castell and lordschipe takes its name. . . . The Lord Boyd is now Lord of it, to quhosse predicessors it hath belonged for maney generations. In this church ar divers of ye Lord Boydes progenitors buried, amongs quhome ther is one tombe or stone, bearing this inscription and coate, Hic Jacet Thomas Boyde Dominus de Kilmarnock qui obiit Septimo die mensis Julii 1432, and Johanna de Montgomery eius spousa. Orate pro iis."*

In another old work, entitled *Northern Memoirs*, written by Richard Franck,† in the year 1658, we have an interesting glimpse of the town as it then appeared. We suspect, however, that the picture is rather extravagantly drawn; at all events, it reflects no great credit, in some respects, on the memory of our ancestors. After describing the town as "an antient corporation, crowded with mechanicks and brewhouses," and as a place, "through the midst of whose crazy,

---

* In the books of the Irvine Presbytery, the following notice occurs regarding Lord Boyd's tomb: "At a visitation at Kilmarnock, 19th June, 1649, anent ane superstitious image that was upon my Lord Boyd his tomb, it was the Presbiterie's mynd that his Lordship sould be written to that he wold be pleased to demolish and ding it doun, and if he wold refuse, that then the Presbiterie was to take a further course." This appears to have been in accordance with an Act of Parliament, passed a few years previously, for "abolishing monuments of Idolatrie."

† Franck was a native of Cambridge, and is supposed to have served as a Captain in a cavalry regiment, under Oliver Cromwell. Like old Izaak Walton, he was a devoted angler; and he was making a fishing tour through Scotland when he visited Kilmarnock. A limited edition of his *Memoirs* was published in 1821, with notes, &c., by Sir Walter Scott.

tottering ports, there runs a river replenished with trout," the writer says: "Step into her dirty streets, that are seldom clean but on a sun-shiny day, or at other times, when great rains melt all the muck, and forcibly drive it down their cadaverous channels into the river Marr, whose streams are so sullied then, that the river loses its natural brightness, till the stains are washed out, and so become invisible. All which to examine, is enough to convince you that the influence of planets is their best scavenger. . . . These inhabitants," he proceeds, "dwell in such ugly houses, as, in my opinion, are little better than huts; and generally of a size, all built so low, that their eves hang dangling to touch the earth. . . . And that which is worse than all the rest, is their unproportionate, ill contrivance. . . . Not one good structure is to be found in Kilmarnock; nor do I remember any wall it has, but a river there is, as I formerly told you of, that runs through the town; over which there stood a bridge so wretchedly antient, that it's unworthy our commendations."* Regarding the skill of the inhabitants in mechanical pursuits our tourist speaks more favourably. "Part of their manufacture," he remarks, "is knitting of bonnets, and spinning [weaving] of Scottish cloth, which turns to very good account. Then, for their temper of metals, they are without compeer— Scotland has not better; and as they are artizans in dirks, so are they artists in fuddling, as if there were some rule in drinking, so that, to me, it represents as if art and ale were inseparable companions. Moreover, their wives are sociable comers [kimmers], too, yet not to compare with those of Dumblain, who pawn their petticotes to pay their reckoning. Here is a jolly crew of ale-men, but very few anglers, crowded

* It is curious that neither the Church nor the Dean Castle are noticed by our author. The former, he, perhaps, considered too humble an edifice for particular description; and the latter, being somewhat distant from the town, might escape his observation.

together in the small compass of a little corporation, curiously compacted."

From these scanty quotations a faint idea may be formed of the appearance of the town two hundred years ago. The mean condition in which Franck represents it is not to be wondered at; for it was then but a mere village, with no Magistracy or Town Council,* with little commerce, and, consequently, with few of the comforts and conveniences of life. It appears from his statement that the men of Kilmarnock were peculiarly skilled in the art of cutlery; and this is somewhat corroborated by another old book,† in which the town is noticed as "famous for all kinds of cutler's ware." We have found no other evidence, however, of such a trade having been ever carried on in the town to any very great extent; and we have seen only one instance of the word *cutler* being mentioned in the early Records of the Burgh. The minute in which it occurs is rather curious: "13th July, 1686.—The quhilk day James Thomson, ane of the dragoons of horse, Adam Black's companie, was decerned to pay to John Tod, *cutler* in Kilmarnock, the sum of 3s. 4d. Scots, and the said John Tod to give up to James Thomson his wyffis body cott, quhilk was pandit for threepence, and paid to the said James." That the inhabitants were "artists in fuddling," as Franck expresses it, we can more readily believe, for the Council, in by-gone times, were often under the necessity of making enactments for the suppression of drunkenness. In 1695, for example, it was enacted that "no ale be sold by vintners after ten o'clock on Saturday nights;" and, in 1702, a proclamation was issued, "strictly requiring all vintners, taverners, and

---

* The first magistrates were appointed in 1695; and for upwards of a hundred years prior to that time, the Burgh was governed by a baron-bailie, nominated by the Boyd family. There is still a baron-bailie appointed by the superior, and in virtue of his office he has a seat at the Board of Commissioners of Police.

† *A Journey through Scotland;* London, 1723.

other retaillers of Liquors, to shutt their doors nightly at the tolling of the bells at ten hours throw the week, and at the tolling of the nine hours bell at the Saturday's and Sabbath's night, and to allow none to drink in their houses after the s^d times, under the penalty of six shillings Scots, for each person, to be payed by the master or mistresse of the house." In the same proclamation all persons were also prohibited from "walking upon the streets unnecessarily, and from bringing in water, or carraying of burdens upon the Lord's Day." The following extract from the Minutes of the Kirk Session shows that special efforts were also made by that body to abate the social irregularities noted by Franck:

"SESSION, *Debr* 12*th*, 1689.—The qlk day the Sess. appoints the Elders in their respective quarters to go through and search the several Ale-houses and other suspect places therein each Saturdays night, immediatelie after nine a clock, and that they take exact notice of such as they find drinking there, after the sd hour, or any way deboshing, and make delation thereof to the Sess. from time to time.

"It is also appointed, That the Elders, who collect the charitie at the Kirk doors, do, immediatelie after the publick worship is begun, go through the town, and search for such as absent themselves from the publick ordinances, or are drinking, or otherwyse profaneing the Lords day: And that in the afternoon, after the publick worship is over and ended, they take notice of such as, by straying up and down the town or through the fields, or by idle discourse in companys together, or by drinking and otherwise, do profane the Sabbath; and that they make delation thereof accordinglie."

The principal architectural erections in the town and its immediate neighbourhood, at the beginning of the seventeenth century, were the Bridge, the Church, and the Castle; at least no other is mentioned by Pont.

The Bridge to which he alludes was no doubt situated on the same site which the Old Bridge, leading from Cheapside to Sandbed Street, now occupies, and was probably the one spoken of by the "piscatorian" traveller, Franck, as "unworthy commendations." According to the Town's Books it underwent some alteration in 1753, in order that it might be made "more safe for all sorts of traffic;" and, about 1762, it was rebuilt in consequence of having been much injured by floods. The present structure, we believe, is the one then erected.

Of the Church no trace now remains save the steeple, which still stands attached to the present Parish Church.* About thirty years ago the date, 1410, was inscribed on it—a date which some old people had recollected seeing on the lintel of one of the doors. That it belongs to that, if not an earlier period, its venerable appearance would seem to testify. In 1770 it was considerably repaired, as is shown by the following notice in the Town Treasurer's Books: "1770, Nov. 22.—N.B. This Day, the Roof of the Parish Steeple was Finished by John Reid, Plumer In Ayr. He agreed to take down the Old roof, & find a new One Compleat, for £52 Sterling. The Heritors to pay the One Half, and the Town Council the Other." It was also furnished, in August, 1853, with a finely-toned new bell, weighing twelve hundredweight, which cost about £100 sterling. The old bell, which weighed nearly four hundredweight, bore this inscription: "BLESSED IS THE PEOPLE THAT KNOW THE IOYFVLL SOVND, PS. 89, 15, NVM. 10, 10. ALBERT DANIEL, CELI ME FECERVNT, KILLMARNOCK, AN. DOM., 1697."† It may be added, that there is a tradition that the lower part of the steeple was used as a prison in the time of the Covenanters, and that some of them were therein incarcerated.

The Castle spoken of by Pont still exists, though in ruins, and is now known by the name of the Dean. It is, perhaps, the oldest building in the locality, and was long the stronghold of the ancient barons of Kilmarnock, whose names are closely interwoven with the early annals of the Burgh. We shall, therefore, give a brief description of it before entering more fully into other historical details.

---

* "When the old Church was taken down [in 1802], and the west side of the steeple laid bare, there were brought to view three niches in the wall, some five or six feet above the floor, and perhaps some six or seven feet in height, before which the altar stood, and the priest officiated in Popish times. These niches were arched at the top of a gothic shape."—*Letter of W. Gregory, Virginia.*

† The old bell was purchased for a church in Stewarton, and still does good service in that ancient village.

CHAPTER II.

See where the Dean her ruined fabric rears!
A mournful scene her naked wall appears;
The clasping ivy shades her tottering towers,
Where night-owls form their melancholy bowers.
Prone from the top, huge ruined fragments fall;
The howling wind sounds dreary in the hall;
No more the voice of mirth is heard to sound,
But melancholy silence reigns around.
                                GAVIN TURNBULL.

DEAN CASTLE, long the residence of the Boyd family, stands at the distance of nearly a mile from Kilmarnock, in a northeast direction. Its situation, though not the most romantic, can scarcely fail to delight the admirer of the gentle as well as the magnificent in nature. On the right and on the left the ground rises in pleasing elevations, and hence, probably, the Castle derived its name, as the word Dean, according to Dr Jamieson, signifies a small valley or hollow where the ground slopes on both sides. Close by the Castle the scene is enlivened by two little mossy streams, locally called the Borland and the Craufurdland, which there meet and mingle with each other, forming what is termed Kilmarnock Water.*

* In an old rhyme, given by Paterson in his *History of Ayrshire*, the Kilmarnock Water is called the *Carth:*

"The Water of Carth rins by the Dean
That ance was Lord Boyd's lodgin'—
The Lord wi' the loupen han'
Wha lost his title and his lan'."

We have seen no other instance, however, of the stream being so named at a former period. The old topographer, Pont, who wrote about 1609, calls it "the river Marnock;" and in Franck's *Northern Memoirs*, written in 1658, it is denominated "the river Marr." (See Chapter I.)

The view in the neighbourhood, too, is considerably beautified by several steep woody braes. From one of these, near Assloss, the Castle presents a majestic and stern appearance. Though grey and rent with years, it looks as if conscious of its strength, and as if frowning defiance down the valley that stretches before it. From the same eminences we have a glimpse of the town, with its towers and spires, which give to it an air of importance; and the eye, ranging still farther, rests delighted on the beautiful green hills of Craigie, and the more romantic heights of Dundonald. In early times, according to oral tradition, a dense wood, which stretched itself behind and on each side of the Castle, concealed it in a great measure from the scrutinizing eye of the invader, and made it almost inaccessible to strangers, save by the principal approach, which was from the south-west, in which direction were situated the huts or hovels of the vassals of the manor. In those days, therefore, this old baronial stronghold was not only picturesque and secluded, but was secure in a great degree from the attacks of neighbouring chiefs, or of the more ruthless hordes who sought to reduce the country to a state of thraldom; for the alarm could readily be given by the vassals from the glen, or by the warder, whose eye from the watch-tower could distinctly descry every movement of advancing foemen.

The Dean consists of two separate towers of unequal height, and appears to have been surrounded by a wall or rampart, part of which still stands. The period at which either of the towers was erected is unknown, but both bear the marks of considerable antiquity. Grose* supposes the higher one to have been built about the beginning of the fifteenth century. In the wall of a lower edifice, and looking into the court, is a stone, on which the family arms are sculptured, and beneath

---

* Grose visited the Castle, we believe, about 1789, and made a drawing of it for his *Antiquities of Scotland.*

which the words "*James Boyd and Catherine Craik*" were lately legible; and these being the names of the eighth Lord Boyd and his Lady, it has sometimes been conjectured that the whole of the lower mansion was erected in their time, namely, about the middle of the seventeenth century; for the estate devolved on the eighth Lord Boyd in 1640, and his death took place about the year 1654. This conjecture, however, appears to be incorrect; for Pont, in his *Cunningham Topographized*, which was written, as we have said, about 1609, speaks of both towers as then existing. That portion of the building, therefore, on which the arms are sculptured, must have been only an addition made by the eighth Lord Boyd. It also appears, from the same authority, that both towers are of greater antiquity than was supposed by Grose. Pont's words are: "Killmernock Castell. It is a staitly faire ancient bulding, arrysing in two grate heigh towers, and bulte arround courtewayes, vith fyve* low buldings; it is veill planted, and almost environed with gardens, orchards, and a parke; it belonged first to ye Locartts, lords thereof, then to the Lord Soulis, and now the cheiffe duelling almost for 300 zeirs of ye Lords Boyde." It may also be mentioned that on another part of the lower building the remains of two figures, a male and female, are or lately were discernible; but no inscription describing them, or leading to a knowledge of the date of their erection, can be traced.

As a place of strength, as well as a spacious manor-house, the Dean appears to have been superior to many of the strongholds of our Scottish barons of the olden time. The walls of

---

* There is great reason to suspect that the word *fire* here has been erroneously transcribed from the original MS. for *fine*; and that the allusion is simply to the cheerful and elegant range of building fronting the south, the walls of which still remain pretty entire. To the east and north, the enclosing rampart walls still stand to their full height, whilst the great tower, or donjon-keep, occupies almost entirely the western angle of the square; so that no possible site would appear within for any further structures of the least consequence whatever.—*Note supplied by the Editor of Pont's Cunningham.*

the higher tower are about nine or ten feet thick; the lower storey consists of several dark vaulted rooms; and on the second flat is a large hall thirty-eight feet in length, twenty-two in breadth, and twenty-six in height. It has a finely arched stone ceiling, and is furnished with stone seats, which jut out round the lower part of the walls, and which, in all likelihood, were cushioned or covered with some kind of cloth when the Castle was inhabited. From this apartment a short passage leads to the trap-door of the dungeon or prison, which is immediately beneath, in the centre of the wall, at the north corner of the tower. It measures fifteen feet by five, and must have been a dreary place for the poor wight whose misfortune it was to be incarcerated within it; for it had no aperture by which light or air could be admitted, save a little oblong opening about three or four inches wide; and even the little light that could thus enter had to struggle down, in a slanting direction, through the wall, which is about ten feet thick, ere it could soothe the prisoner with its cheering influence. The dungeon has now a door broken into it from the outside, and is, or lately was, used as a milk-house. Adjoining is another gloomy apartment, which, it is probable, was also a place of confinement. On the third flat there have been, apparently, two chambers. These are now roofless and otherwise much dilapidated. One of them, with a large window looking to the north, is said to have been the chapel. In the walls of these rooms are two curious little recesses. One of them, with two narrow loop-holes looking in different directions, was, perhaps, used as a watch-house in times of emergency. It has a small stone seat and a fire-place, but is so contracted in its dimensions that a person can scarcely stand upright within it. The other recess was probably a place for a bed, as there were sometimes such conveniences in the walls of ancient Scottish castles. The upper or attic storey has also contained two or more rooms; and, crowning the eastern corner, there seems to have been another watch-house, which must have commanded an extensive view of the adjacent country. On the top of the walls, a walk or passage, about four feet in breadth, leads round the tower. It was faced by a plain battlement or parapet, considerable portions of which yet remain, and in which, here and there, are little openings. A narrow spiral stair led to the various storeys; and the main entrance was by an arched doorway, which is still entire, at the north-east corner of the building.

In the lower tower, which was surmounted by an erection in the form of a belfry,* there have been at least four apartments above the ground floor; but, except some small patches of plaster still seen on the walls, nothing remains to give an accurate idea of their original appearance. The most commodious part of the building is that occupying the space betwixt the two towers, and fronting the south. It seems to have been the principal dwelling-place connected with the small tower, and has been lighted by spacious windows, which give to it, even in its ruins, all the attributes of some ancient seat of royalty, rather than of the abode of a Scottish lord in the days of feudalism.

It is not unlikely—though history is silent on the subject—that the Dean was sometimes beleaguered in the olden time, when chief contended with chief, through a love of gain, a love of revenge, or a love of glory. That such was the case is asserted, at least, by tradition, which affirms that it was once or twice besieged, and that every attempt to reduce it was altogether fruitless. The Castle, however, is not without its historical associations. Mary, the sister of King James Third, and wife of Thomas Boyd, Earl of Arran, was kept for some time within its walls "as in a free prison."† It is also noted

* This erection appears in a picture of the Castle engraved by an ingenious townsman, named Michael Reid, about the beginning of the present century. In the same print the roof is seen on the higher tower.
† See Chapter IV.

for having been used as a garrison by Captain Inglis and his soldiers in the dark days of the Persecution.

According to Pont the grounds around the Castle, as far back as the year 1609, were well planted and adorned with "gardens and orchards." The exact situation which these occupied, it would now be difficult to ascertain. Within the remembrance of persons lately living, an old pear tree grew on the beautiful green mound situated in what was formerly called Paddock Park; and it is not improbable that one or other of the gardens or orchards lay in that direction. At an early period one of the little streams that form the Kilmarnock Water flowed, it is alleged, between the mound and the smaller tower, and joined the other rivulet on the south side of the eminence. The scene, in a pictorial point of view, would then be truly interesting; for the two Castles, towering proudly amid their woody enclosures, with the braes rising gently on either side, and the water gliding peacefully in the foreground, must have formed a picture at once pleasing and imposing.

In 1735 the Dean was partly destroyed by fire. The lower Castle was the principal scene of its ravages, marks of which we lately traced on some of the wood connected with the mason-work. The fire was occasioned by some flax being accidentally ignited while in the process of being cleaned or spun by one of the maid-servants. The Earl of Kilmarnock (the unfortunate last Earl) was then on the Continent, and when on his way back to Scotland, had his attention directed to a newspaper, in which was an account of the destruction, by fire, of a Scottish mansion called the Dean, the particular locality of which was not given. Fearing that it was his own Castle, he hastened home, and found it reduced to a state of ruin. It may be mentioned that the eminent scholar, James Moor, LL.D., author of a well-known Greek Grammar, and sometime Professor of Greek in the University of Glasgow, was, at the time of the burning, tutor in the family of the Earl of Kilmarnock, and lost by the fire a "considerable stock of books, which he had collected for his own use."* The Dean was never afterwards put into a habitable condition, in consequence, perhaps, of the vast expense which its restoration would have required. But though nearly a hundred and thirty years have passed away since it suffered by the conflagration, it still presents, as we have said, a bold, stately aspect; and, though now roofless and desolate, its great strength may yet enable it to stand many centuries, an object of interest to the admirer of the picturesque, the historical inquirer, and the lover of hoar antiquity.

We may here add, that after the burning of Dean Castle the Boyd family resided in Kilmarnock House, which is situated between St Marnock Street and Nelson Street. This old mansion was, apparently, built at different times. The original part of it is supposed to have been erected about the end of the seventeenth century. The western portion was in the course of being finished when the last Earl of Kilmarnock took part in the Rebellion of 1745-6, and, in consequence of his connection with that unfortunate affair, the progress of the work, it is said, was suddenly stopped. That such was the case would appear from the fact, that when ingress was made into the large hall (which had been shut up for a considerable number of years after the above date), there were found within it the window frames, as if new from the tools of the joiner, together with a tradesman's apron and some shavings of wood.

The stately old trees with which the policies of Kilmarnock

---

* Moor, while travelling with the Earl, also collected a number of curious coins, which, no doubt, formed part of his valuable cabinet of medals purchased by the University of Glasgow.—*See notice of Moor in Chronicles of St Mungo, also Memoir of Dr Jamieson prefixed to his Dictionary.*

C

House were adorned, previous to the formation of St Marnock Street, gave to it a fine aspect of baronial dignity. One of these trees—a majestic beech—grew, till lately, immediately at the back of the mansion;* and a few others, which formed part of a woody avenue long known by the name of the Lady's Walk,† still remain along the line of Dundonald Road. This walk, at a comparatively recent date, was a sweet rural retreat, and must have been still more so at an earlier period, when the Kilmarnock Water flowed, as it did, in a westerly course, below Waterside, laving the grassy edge of the ridge forming the walk, and giving to the whole scene an air of freshness and beauty. But such are the changes which time and the spirit of commercial enterprise have made, that only a faint idea can now be formed respecting the appearance which Kilmarnock House and its environs exhibited, even forty years ago. Instead of the lordly dwelling rising in stately grandeur above the few humble, straw-roofed cottages, which were then in its vicinity, it is now itself thrown into the shade, by large modern structures erected near it; and its quaint old rooms, once the abode of the titled and the great, are now used for purposes connected with the Parochial Board—part of them being occupied as offices by the Inspector of Poor, and part of them as the Ragged School.

* The old beech tree alluded to was cut down on the 3rd May, 1859, in consequence of being much decayed. It measured upwards of ten feet in circumference.
† So called, it is said, from being a favourite walk of the last Countess of Kilmarnock in her hours of sorrow after her unfortunate husband's execution.

CHAPTER III.

Knights that wight and worthie were.
BARBOUR.

ACCORDING to the ordinary genealogical authorities, the progenitor of the noble family of the Boyds, to whom the Dean Castle and the Barony of Kilmarnock for a long period belonged, was "Simon, brother of Walter, the first High Steward of Scotland." His son Robert, it is said, was remarkable for his fair complexion; and hence he obtained the name of Boyt or Boyd, from the word *Boidh*, in the Celtic language, signifying *fair* or *yellow*.* Nothing of any moment, so far as we know, is recorded of him. His son, Robert Boyd, or Sir Robert Boyd, as he is sometimes called, was a person of singular bravery, and at the battle of Largs, in 1263,

---

* Mr Fullarton, in his introductory observations to Pont, expresses a doubt regarding the origin commonly given of the Kilmarnock family, and quotes the following statement from Mylne's manuscript collections in the *Advocate's Library*: "As to the origin of the sirname [of Boyd] I can make no conjecture. I have seen a late author who makes them originally a son of the noble family of Stewart. But that which proves this entirely fabulous is a contract, yet extant, betwixt Bryce de Eglingstoun, on the ane part, and the village of Irvine, in the year of our Lord 1205, to which *Dominus Robertus de Boyd, miles,* is witness; and [this] is some time before they alege Boyd's ancestour came of the family of Stewart." Mr Fullarton, after supporting at some length the same view of the subject, observes: "The first at all reliable intimation we have of the true ancestors of the Boyd family is as vassals of the De Morvilles in the regality of Largs; and there can hardly be a doubt that their progenitor had accompanied the first De Morville hither, and obtained a grant of lands from him. In whatever way the family name of Boyd may have arisen, in all probability they imported it with them from the country of their more ancient origin."

where Haco or Acho, King of Norway,* with a numerous army, was put to flight, he nobly distinguished himself, and was rewarded by Alexander the Third with "grants of several lands in Cunningham." Tradition maintains that Sir Robert, with the aid of the party he commanded at that engagement, threw into confusion, and finally defeated a strong detachment of Norwegians at a place called Goldberry Hill. The words *Gold Berry*, which sometimes appear on the lower scroll of prints of the Kilmarnock coat of arms, were probably adopted in commemoration of this feat of Sir Robert.† He died about the year 1270.

About twenty-six years after this date, when Edward the First of England took possession of several of our Scottish castles, and made the people all but bend to his decrees, Sir Robert Boyd, son of the foregoing, like other nobles of our country, was compelled to swear fealty to the usurper. But, throwing off the yoke of bondage and degradation which had been imposed upon him, Boyd, in the following year, 1297, joined the small but intrepid army of Sir William Wallace; and, by deeds of daring under the banner of genuine liberty which was hoisted by that hero, showed that he possessed a spirit imbued with patriotic ardour, which quailed not at the dangers of war when the dearest interests of Scotland were at stake. Blind Harry, who doubtless was accurate in many of his statements, speaks of Robert Boyd as a man "who scorned the English yoke," and who displayed uncommon bravery in the field. His name is honourably mentioned in

---

* "Acho king of Norroway landit at air wt 160 schipps and twentie thousand men of warre, and ye caus of his cum'ing was becaus macbethe had promissit to his predecessores some yles, qlk. yi had not gottine, viz. Boote, arrane wt ye tuo Cumbrais, having tane Arrane and Boote he come to the lairges in Cunynghame, qr Alexr foirfather to the first Stewart yt was king, discomfeit ym & sleu 16000 of his men. He [Acho] died throw sorrow. yr war slaine of ye Scotts, 5000."—*Hist. of Scotland, MS. quoted in notes to the Historie of Rowallane.*

† See Appendix.

the bard's account of Wallace's encounter with the English in the neighbourhood of Loudoun Hill, where the latter were completely routed when on their way to Ayr with stores for the garrison:

> "Some English yet, altho' their chief was slain,
> Them still abode, as men of meikle main;
> Where Wallace was, their deed was little ken'd,
> Tho' they did all themselves for to defend,
> For he behav'd himself so worthily
> With *Robert Boyd*, and all their chivalry,
> That not a Southeron ere even-tide
> Might any longer in that stour abide;
> But thought their part was plainly for to flee,
> Which even as many did as could win free."

Boyd also acted a noble part at the taking of the Castle of Ayr from the English. The historical minstrel, when describing that affair, calls him a prudent, wise soldier, and tells us that he

> "Won the port, and entered with all his men."

He likewise accompanied Wallace into England, where, with "the Earl Malcolm," he commanded the west gate at the siege of the city of York; and it appears from the authority just quoted, that he afterwards supported the Hero of Scotland in other engagements.

The next of the Boyds, namely, the third Sir Robert Boyd, inherited the noble virtues of his father in no ordinary degree. He was among the very first of the Scottish noblemen who rallied around the standard of Bruce; and, with the exception of that monarch's immediate relatives, he was perhaps the only person of distinction in Ayrshire who espoused his interest, when he first offered defiance to the King of England. He continued, too, a faithful supporter of the same cause till the independence of Scotland was established by the decisive and ever-memorable battle of Bannockburn, at which he acted as one of the principal leaders. Harvey, when describing, in his *Life of Bruce*, the positions which were assigned on that occasion to the various chiefs, thus makes allusion to Sir Robert:

> "Rang'd on the right the Southron legions stood,
> And on their front the fiery Edward* rode;
> With him *experienced Boyd* divides the sway,
> Sent by the King to guide him thro' the day."

For the important services rendered by Boyd to his country, he was rewarded by Bruce with gifts of the lands of Kilmarnock, Bondington, and Hertschaw, which had been forfeited by John Baliol, and which gifts were granted by Charters dated 1308 and 1316. According to Wood, he had also conferred upon him "the lands of Kilbryd and Ardnel,† which were Godfrey de Ross's, son of the deceased Reginald de Ross; all the land which was William de Mora's, in the tenements of Dalry; with seven acres of land, which were Robert de Ross's, in the tenement of Ardnel—all erected into an entire and free Barony, to be held of the King." Sir Robert, at his death, left three sons—Thomas, Allan, and James. The first of these succeeded to the estate; but nothing of any importance respecting him is recorded, save that he accompanied David the Second to the battle of Durham, and

---

* Edward Bruce, brother of the King.

† The lands of Ardnlell or Portincross, situated in the parish of West Kilbride, were conferred on Sir Robert Royd about 1308, and afterwards became the patrimony of a younger son of the family, with whose descendants, the Boyds of Portincross, they remained till 1737. The Castle of Portincross is thus noticed by Mr Fullarton in the *New Statistical Account:* "It stands on a ledge of rock projecting into the sea under the bold promontory to which it gives name, a singularly wild and romantic situation. Several royal charters of the two first Stewart Kings bear to have received the sign-manual at 'Arnele,' which unquestionably refers to this fortlet, and which has led to a notion, that Portincross had been at that period a royal residence of the Kings of Scotland. But there seems no evidence whatever to conclude it ever was such in the proper sense of the term. The probability is, that these sovereigns, in passing to and from Dundonald in Kyle, and Rothesay in Bute, had been in use to cross the channel at this point, and may occasionally, as circumstances or inclination suggested, have prolonged their stay a little at this convenient station. Contemplating the narrow walls of this sea-beat tower, it is certainly difficult to conceive that it should ever have afforded accommodation to the prestige of a royal court; yet when we reflect on the circumscribed nature of even Dundonald itself, the favourite residence of these same sovereigns, the contrast by no means appears so very extraordinary."

was there made prisoner along with that monarch. The second son, who is said to have been "valiant in war," was killed at the siege of Perth in the year 1339. This Sir Thomas left three sons—Thomas, his successor, William of Badenheath, and Robert of Portincross.

The next of the Boyds was Sir Thomas Boyd, who was designated *Dominus de Kilmarnock*. A feud, the nature of which is not explained by the writers we have consulted, appears to have arisen between him and one Neilson of Dalrymple; and, like many of the disputes among the turbulent chiefs of that period, it led to serious consequences; for the latter, we are told, was cruelly slain by the hand of the former, who afterwards obtained, in 1409, a remission for the deed, from Robert, Duke of Albany.

He was succeeded by his son, Sir Thomas Boyd, Lord of Kilmarnock, a man of distinguished abilities. He performed a principal part among the contending nobles in the reign of James the First. That monarch, as the historical reader is aware, had been kept for nineteen years a prisoner in England before his accession to the throne in 1424; and it was at length agreed that a ransom of four hundred thousand merks should be paid for his liberty; but the Scots, it would appear, could advance only part of the sum, and several noblemen, among whom was Sir Thomas Boyd, were given as hostages for the remainder. Some of our historians, when speaking of this time, mention that Thomas Boyd of Kilmarnock (whom we take to be Sir Thomas) was afterwards accused, along with others, of having wasted "the crown rents" during the Regency of the Duke of Albany, for which he was put into confinement at Dalkeith; but he soon obtained his liberty by the nobility interceding in his behalf, and by him making compensation for the offence by the payment of certain fines into the royal exchequer. He died in 1432, and, as mentioned in Chapter I, had a monument erected to his memory, and that of his spouse, Johanna Montgomery, in the old Church of Kilmarnock. Sir Thomas had two sons, one of whom, named William, was for some time Abbot of Kilwinning. The other, named Thomas, succeeded to the estate and title at the death of his father. He is recorded in history chiefly on account of having slain Sir Allan Stewart of Darnley, between Linlithgow and Falkirk, and of having been himself killed through revenge in July, 1439, by Alexander, a brother of Allan, at Craignaucht Hill, in the parish of Dunlop. Both of these feuds, or contests, are thus quaintly related by the old chronicler, Lindsay of Pitscottie: "In this meane tyme, quhill the countrie was walterrand to and fro in this maner, thair was nothing but murther, thift, and slauchter in the south and wast of Scotland, for Sir Thomas Boyd slew Sir Allane Stewart of Gartullie, knycht, at Pawmatt Horne,* thrie myllies from the Falkirk, for old feid that was betuixt thame, the third yeir after the death of King James the First. Quhilk death was soone revenged thairefter; for Alexander Stewart, to revenge his brotheris slauchter, manfullie sett vpoun Sir Thomas Boyd in plaine batle, quhair the said Sir Thomas was cruellie slaine with manie valient men on overic syd. It was foughtin that day so manfullie, that both the pairties wold vtter† and leive otheris sundrie tymes, and recounter againe at the sound of the trumpett, quhill at the last, the victorie inclyned to Sir Alexander Stewart, as said is."

This deadly contest, it would appear, had not the effect of calming the deeply-rooted animosity that existed between the two factions, for another of the Stewarts was afterwards slain in revenge by the Boyds, near the town of Dumbarton;‡ but such bloody deeds were not of rare occurrence at that time among our Scottish barons. Sir Thomas Boyd left two sons, Robert and Alexander.

* Polmais Thorn, according to other writers.
† Vtter, to go out of the lists.—*Jamieson.* Uter, to go outward.—*Ruddiman.*
‡ See Buchanan's *History of Scotland*, and also Lindsay's *Cronicles of Scotland*.

CHAPTER IV.

> With that there came an arrow keen
> Out of a trusty bow,
> Which struck Lord *Soulis* to the heart
> A deep and deadly blow.
> ADAPTED FROM THE BALLAD OF *Chevy-Chase*.

NOT long after this period, namely in 1444, a Lord Soulis, an English nobleman, was killed, it is said, in Kilmarnock, by one of the Boyds. Of the circumstances that led to this occurrence we find not the slightest trace in published records; but that such a deed was actually perpetrated would appear by the monument erected to his memory. It is probable that he was a descendant of the Lord Soulis to whom, according to Pont, the Dean Castle at one time belonged. The monument stands near the entrance to the High Church, at the head of Soulis Street, on the spot, it is believed, where he fell. Prior to 1825 it was a slender stone pillar, eight or nine feet high, but of very rude appearance, being entirely without architectural finish or ornament, except a small cross which was fixed upon its top. At that date it was tottering with age; and some of the more respectable inhabitants of the street in which it stood collected among themselves a sum of money for rebuilding it in a style more in harmony with modern taste. In the wall that encloses the burying-ground of the church a niche was formed, fronting the street, and a fluted pillar, surmounted by an urn or vase, placed within it. Over the whole is a handsome pediment, on which are the following words:

> "To the memory of Lord Soulis, A.D., 1444.
> Erected by Subscription, A.D., 1825.
> 'The days of old to mind I call.'"

The old monument, or Soulis Cross, as it was called, appears to have existed as far back as 1609, when Pont wrote his work on Cunningham. When speaking of Dean Castle, he observes: "Near to it is ther a stone crosse called to this day Soulis Crosse, quher they affirme ye Lord Soulis wes killed." Mr Fullarton, in his notes on the above work, says, "there is no probability that it is of so recent an age as the year 1444. If the de Soulises ever possessed the barony of Kilmarnock, we may far more safely assign to the Cross an existence coeval with the times of their possession." Chalmers also had doubts regarding the time to which the death of Soulis is attributed, and states that there was no Lord Soulis in Scotland, "either as a friend or an enemy," at the period referred to. Tradition, however, has its tales of Lord Soulis, one of which may be narrated.

In other years, as we have said, Dean Castle was almost embosomed in woods, and no road led to it except the principal one from the south-west, and a private path that lay along the stream in the direction of Fenwick. One of the vassals, who had strolled one afternoon into this walk, heard, or thought he heard, the voices of strangers among the trees; and, fearing that foemen were skulking in the locality, he ascended a small height and immediately discovered a party, who turned out to be Southrons, stationed upon an eminence at a short distance towards the west. The spot of ground here meant is that on which the Powder Magazine now stands; and, if we may believe tradition, it was the site of a Roman encampment in ancient times.* It commands an extensive view of the surrounding country, and was therefore well adapted for a military station in the days of feudal war-

---

* Until within the last thirty or forty years there was a well near this spot, long known by the name of the "Roman Well," which strengthens the supposition that the Romans at one period visited this locality. At the same place various urns were discovered during the latter half of last century.

fare. In breathless anxiety the vassal hastened to the Castle, and apprised the inmates of the discovery he had made. In a moment all was bustle and activity among the Boyds. The tenants of the manor, and several other adherents of the ancient house of Dean, among whom was the Laird of Craufurdland, were soon made aware of the circumstance; and, before the shades of evening had darkened the landscape, they were all marshalled on the green plain in front of the tower, from which, headed by the Boyd, they marched towards the encampment. On coming near the spot, a breathless silence reigned among the Southrons, as if they were refreshing themselves with sleep before attacking the fortress, which, in all likelihood, they meant to do during the night or early in the morning. "Shall we give them battle?" whispered one of the friends of the Boyd. "We shall," said he; "for I have always thought it best to remove evil ere it assumes a formidable shape: let us disperse them." At these words the followers of the Boyd rushed upon the English, who, notwithstanding this unexpected attack, displayed no symptoms of fear. With a ferocity common only in the days of feudalism, man met man; and each and all seemed to act as if more willing to die in the strife than to have their names associated with cowardice. In the midst of the conflict was one of the Southrons, whose stately appearance and signal prowess bespoke him the leader of their party. His form caught the eye of the Boyd, and in a moment they were in close combat, but were soon separated by the confusion of the others. At length, after a desperate struggle, in which several fell on both sides, the English, in spite of their commander, who urged them to keep their position, fled from the field, and concealed themselves in the fastnesses of the woods. From some of the vanquished, whose wounds rendered them unable to fly, it was learned that the name of their leader was Lord Soulis; but their object in coming to the locality they did not disclose.

The darkness of night was now gathering fast, and the heroes of the Dean returned in triumph to the castle, bearing along with them swords and other instruments of war, which had been left on the field by the Southrons.* During the night, watches were set around the castle, and as soon as the first ray of morning broke through the eastern clouds, the warder was at his station on the summit of the tower. In a short time he descried one or two of the fugitives lurking about the bottom of the glen. This intelligence was soon communicated to the Boyd, who immediately armed himself with his cross-bow, and, followed by only one or two attendants, left the castle in quest of the English lord. At a little distance below the beautiful green mound at the south side of the castle, he crossed the stream, and hurried, with the firm tread of a warrior, along its bank, in a southern direction, till he reached the field now known by the name of Clerk's Holm. On a brae, at the other side of the water, he espied the object of his search. With deadly aim he drew his cross-bow, and its arrow instantly pierced the heart of the ill-fated Soulis. On the night of that day a sumptuous feast was spread in the hall of the Dean—the wine cup was freely circulated—the festal song fell upon the ear of lady and of lord—and the arched chambers ceased not to echo the sounds of merriment till the beams of the morning had tinged with golden hues the turrets of the tower.

* Sometime during the year 1845, Mr Clark, farmer of Knockinlaw, when cutting a drain near the spot where this encounter is said to have happened, found, at a considerable depth beneath the surface, a sword of rather ancient appearance; but whether it was one of those used in the skirmish we have described is matter for conjecture. From Mure's *Historie of Rowallane*, we learn that one of the Boyds, at a later period, offered battle, near the same place, to the Earl of Glencairn. The paragraph in which the circumstance is stated is curious: "My lord of Glencairne proponing ane Richt to the Baronrie of Kilmarnock, procleamit ane court to be holdin at the Knockanlaw, quhair the said Rot Boyd Guidmane of Kilmarnock, & Mongow muir of Rowallane, wt the assistance of thair freindis, keipit the said day & place of court, offirit Battel to the said Earle of Glencairne, and stayit him from his pretendit court hoilding."

To return to the history of the Boyds. Sir Thomas, who was slain by Stewart of Darnley, left, as we have said, two sons, namely, Robert, his heir, and Sir Alexander, a man, as Drummond says, "singular for his education abroad and demeanour at home," to whom was intrusted the young prince, afterwards James the Third, "to be bred in knightly prowess."

Robert, the heir of Sir Thomas, was a man more eminently distinguished than any of his predecessors. In 1459 he was made Lord of Parliament by James the Second. He afterwards filled the office of Lord Justiciary of Scotland, and was also, in 1464 and 1465, ambassador to England. But the elevated position he had attained drew down upon him the envy of other nobles. He was accused, along with his brother Alexander, of having carried the young King James the Third from Linlithgow to Edinburgh, there to "enter upon the regal government" while he was yet in his minority. For the investigation of this matter a Parliament was called in 1466; but the Boyds, even by the King himself, were declared to have been only companions in that journey, and therefore innocent of all crime. A decree to this effect was registered among the Acts of Parliament.* In the same month Robert Lord Boyd was constituted regent, and intrusted with the defence of the king and the charge of his brothers and sisters, besides the command of all the fortresses and places of

* "The King of his own accord declared in Parliament that what Lord Boyd had done, was not of himself, but at the King's own desire, and what he esteemed good service, and more worthy of reward than censure, which he offered to confirm by a decree of the states, which was immediately made and registered on the 18th of October, 1468, and an extract made out, and confirmed by letters patent under the Great Seal. It is not clear upon what account this pardon did not operate au absolvitor to the Boyds; whether it was owing to their being refused an extract, or the privilege of the record on the trial, and so could not plead it before the Parliament, or that it was pleaded and judged ineffectual. Buchanan insinuates the last, and imputes it to an evasive distinction suggested by priestcraft, Buch. hist. lib. 12-29."—*Staggering State of the Scots Statesmen, by Sir John Scot of Scotstarvet.*

importance in the country. Boyd was now at the summit of distinction; and, "dazzled," as Drummond says, "with the golden sun of honour, to lay more sure the foundation of his greatness, he joineth in marriage Thomas, his eldest son, a youth of extraordinary endowments both of mind and body, with Margaret,* the king's eldest sister, not long before designed by her mother to have been given in marriage to Edward, Prince of Wales." By this union Thomas obtained considerable wealth, and was created Earl of Arran. He was also honoured by being sent to Denmark, with a magnificent retinue, to bring home Margaret, the daughter of Christiern the First, who, in accordance with a previous treaty between that monarch and the Court of Scotland, was to be given in marriage to the young king. But earthly possessions and honours, however extensive and dazzling, are not always the source of solid happiness: it proved so in the case of the Boyds. The rude nobility of those days grumbled at the advancement they had made, and studied to overthrow them; and even the common people testified their dislike to the state of affairs by frequent repinings. In a short time the affections of the king also were weaned from the Boyds by the insinuations of their enemies. At length a Parliament was called, and Robert Lord Boyd, and his brother Sir Alexander, were summoned to answer such charges as might be brought against them. According to the historian of Hawthornden, whom we have already quoted, Lord Boyd appeared on the day appointed for his trial, with a considerable number of his friends and vassals, in arms, for the purpose of overawing the nobles of the Court; but finding, by private intelligence, that they were bent upon his ruin, he fled into England. His brother, Sir Alexander, "arrested by sickness," and trusting in his innocence, appeared before the Parliament. The removing

---

* She is called Mary by other writers.

of the king from Linlithgow to Edinburgh (the principal crime with which they were charged) was declared to be treason; and in defiance of the Act of Parliament, passed in 1466, in favour of the Boyds, they were all found guilty, condemned to be executed, and had their lands forfeited. Alexander suffered accordingly on the Castle Hill of Edinburgh in 1469; and Thomas, Earl of Arran, and his father, were declared rebels, notwithstanding the former being absent on his mission to Denmark.* Lord Boyd, on hearing of the dismal fate of his house, died of grief soon after at Alnwick.†

The King still continued to cherish feelings of dislike towards the Earl of Arran, who, it would seem, knew nothing of these transactions till he arrived in Leith Roads with the royal bride. He was then apprised of the state of matters by his Countess, who had contrived, by disguising herself, to get on board before he landed; and accompanied by her, he immediately returned to Denmark, to avoid the impending danger. The king, however, pretended friendship to his sister, the Earl's wife, and, by flattering letters which he caused to be sent to her, encouraged her to return to Scotland. His solicitations at length she obeyed, in the hope of obtaining the pardon and favour of her royal brother for her husband, to whom she was tenderly attached; but, instead of meeting with a kindly welcome, she, as stated in Chapter II, was kept in

---

* Some of our modern historians state that the trial of the Boyds and the execution of Sir Alexander took place *after* the arrival of the Earl of Arran with the Danish fleet. In our account of the matter we have been guided by Drummond, Buchanan, and other old writers.

† A daughter of this nobleman—the Lady Elizabeth Boyd—was married to Archibald, fifth Earl of Angus, and was the mother of the old Scottish poet, Gavin, or Gawin Douglas, who was sometime Bishop of Dunkeld, and author of *King Hart*, *The Palice of Honour*, &c., as well as a metrical translation of Virgil's *Æneid*, remarkable as "the first version of a Latin classic into any British tongue." He was born at Brechin about 1474, and died of the plague at London in 1522. "He was an honour," says an eminent critic, "alike to the Episcopal bench and the Muse of Scotland."

confinement in the Dean Castle during the life of her husband;*
and her marriage, for reasons which history does not very
satisfactorily explain, was declared null and void. Her husband died at Antwerp, where a tomb, bearing "an honourable
inscription," was built to his memory by Charles Duke of
Burgundy. Soon after his death she married (by compulsion,
it is said) the Lord Hamilton, to whom the earldom of Arran
was then given.

Several years after the death of the Earl of Arran the
Lordship of Boyd, together with the lands of Kilmarnock and
others in the county of Ayr, were restored to his only son,
James; but a more gloomy fate than even that of his father
awaited him, for he was slain in 1484, while yet a young man,
in some petty feud, by Hugh Montgomery of Eglinton, and
his extensive possessions returned to the crown. The estate
was afterwards given to Alexander, son of the Lord Boyd who
died at Alnwick. All that we learn of this individual is, that
he was a great "favourite with King James the Fourth,
who, in 1505, constituted him Baillie and Chamberlain of
Kilmarnock." His eldest son, Robert, had the estate and
honours of Lord Boyd restored to him in 1536, by James
the Fifth. From the statements of different writers he seems
to have been a man of strong resolution and undaunted courage.
In the battle of "Glasgow Field," as some old writers term it,
fought about 1543, on a piece of ground now the site of the
Infantry Barracks, between the Earl of Lennox and the
Regent Hamilton, during the minority of Mary, he acted so
brave a part as to turn the tide of conflict in favour of
Hamilton. "In the heat of the battle," says the author of
the *Annals of Glasgow*, "while victory was doubtful, Robert

---

* Drummond says: "Instead of having access to her brother (the king) she was kept at Kilmarnock, the chief House of the Boyds, as in a free prison;" and in Grose's *Antiquities of Scotland*, it is stated that she was confined in Dean Castle till the death of the Earl.

Boyd, of the Kilmarnock family, arrived with a small party of horse, and having valiantly thrust himself into the midst of the combat, decided the fate of the day. . . . In this engagement there were about three hundred slain on both sides. The Regent immediately entered the city, and, being exasperated against the citizens, gave it up to his soldiers to plunder, which they did so completely, that, having carried away or destroyed every thing moveable, they pulled down the very doors and windows of the houses."

For thus perilling his life in behalf of the Regent, Boyd was immediately afterwards rewarded with additional honours, and was served heir to James Boyd, son of the Earl of Arran, in 1544.* Besides a son, he had a daughter who married one of the Montgomeries of Lainshaw; but this connection seems not to have engendered feelings of friendship between the two families, for we find that Robert, Master of Boyd, with Mowat of Busbie,† and others, assassinated Sir Niel Montgomery of Lainshaw, at Irvine, in 1547, through revenge for the death of his cousin, James Boyd, who, as we have stated,

---

* In the Appendix to the *Historie and Descent of the House of Rowallane*, it is stated, that "Robert Boyd, Guidmane of Kilmarnock, and Mungow Muir of Rowallane, entirit in the field of Glasgow, the said Mungow being lairglie bettir accumpanied then the foirsaid Robert; they behavit themselfe so vallantlie in that facht, that the Duik Hammiltone, quho reckonit both his lyfe & honor to be preservit be thair handis, maid the said Robert Boyd, Guidmane of Kilmarnock, Lord Boyd, lyk also as he Reverdit the said Mungow Muir wt dyvers fair Giftis."

† Busbie Castle, once the property and residence of the Mowats, stands on the banks of the Carmel Water, at a short distance below the town of Kilmaurs, and about two miles west from Kilmarnock. It consists of a single but rather massive tower, now roofless and otherwise in ruins. Robertson says: "The style of the building seems to belong to the middle of the fourteenth century, having both gunports and arrow slits in the walls as means of defence. The antique decorations of the *twisted cable* in the architraves indicate the same era." "Frequent notice of the Mowats of Busbie," says Mr Fullarton, "occurs in the public records, but for several centuries of the latter part of their history they do not appear to have occupied any very conspicuous place. Their career as lairds of Busbie would seem to have terminated in the early part of the seventeenth century." One of the Mowats—the Rev. Matthew Mowat, whom we believe to have been of this family—was minister of Kilmarnock at a period prior to the Revolution.

was killed by Hugh Montgomery in 1484. According to Robertson's *Description of Cunninghame*, this feud was the cause of much blood being afterwards shed throughout the district; and we are told by the historian of the Rowallan family, that the Master of Boyd, for some time after the slaughter of Sir Niel, durst not appear openly within the country "for feir of pairty," or, in other language, from dread of the Montgomeries and their adherents. A mutual agreement, we believe, was at last made between the two families.

Lord Boyd is said to have died in 1550, and at his death his son, Robert, became fourth Lord Boyd. History characterizes him as a man of integrity, and steady in his adherence to the unfortunate Mary, Queen of Scots, in whose interest, with a considerable body of men under his command, he fought at the battle of Langside, in 1568; and he was one of the nobles, it is recorded, who formed a guard around the Queen's person during the conflict. In the following year Lord Boyd, with the Bishop of Ross, had a commission, under the hand and signet of the Queen, to treat with Queen Elizabeth regarding "her rebellious subjects in Scotland."* But, for espousing the cause of Mary, he "fell," says the *Rowallan Memorandum*, "in the disfavour of the Regent Moray, and was commandit be the authority to passe affe the country, with both his sons," who had also, according to Chalmers, been engaged in the same combat. He afterwards obtained the favour of James the Sixth, and was one of the commissioners appointed in 1578 and 1586 to form a treaty with England. He died at the advanced age of seventy-two, in the year 1589. An epitaph to his memory may still be seen on a stone in the interior of the Low Church,

---

* This and another document, also under the hand and signet of Mary, entitled "A Mandate for prosecuting a Divorce against the Earl of Bothwell," were at one time among the Boyd Papers at Kilmarnock, but are now deposited in the Register House, Edinburgh. They were both dated at Wingfield, the one in May and the other in June, 1569.

Kilmarnock. The stone, which was part of the old church, was preserved by being put into the wall of the present building at its erection in the year 1802. The epitaph is as follows :

> "1389.
>
> "Heir lyis yt godlie, noble wyis lord Boyd
> Quha kirk & king & commin weil decoir'd
> Quhilke war (quhill they yis jowell all injoyd)
> Defendit, counsaild, governd, be that lord.
> His ancient hous (oft parreld) he restoird.
> Twyis sax & saxtie zeirs he leivd and syne
> By death (ye thrid of Januare) devoird
> In anno thryis fyve hundreth auchtye nyne."*

It would appear that by this time the town of Kilmarnock had become a place of some importance, for it was now erected into a Burgh of Barony on the 12th January, 1591, by a charter† granted in favour of Thomas, the fifth Lord Boyd,‡ which was ratified in Parliament on the 5th June, 1592.

Regarding the particular occupations of the inhabitants at the close of the sixteenth century we have but little information.

---

* Said to have been composed by Alexander Montgomery, author of *The Cherrie and the Slae*, *The Mindes Melodie*, &c. Montgomery was one of our best early Scottish poets. The place and date of his birth are uncertain; but it is generally believed that he was born at Hazlehead Castle in the parish of Beith, about the year 1546.

† An abridged translation of this Charter is given in the Appendix.

‡ This individual, who appears to have been much subject to bodily disease, was favoured by James the Sixth with a "pass" empowering him to go to foreign countries for the sake of his health. It begins thus: "We, understanding that our cousing, Thomas, Master of Boyd, is vext with ane vehement dolour in his heid, and other diseases in his body, as he cannot find sufficient ease and remeid within our realme, bot is in mynd to seik the same in forein countries, quhair the samyn maist convenientlie may be had, thairfor [we] be the tenor heerof gevis and grantis licence to the said Thomas, Maister of Boyd, to depart and pas furth of our realme, to the partis of France, Flanderis, Wall of the Spa, and otheris partis, quhair he pleases, thair to remain for seiking for cure and remedy of his saidis diseasis, for the space of thre zeiris after the date hereof." The concluding passage is as follows: "Providing always that our said cousing do not attempt nathing in prejudice of us, our realme and religioun, publiclie preachit and professit within our realme, or otherwais this our licence to be null and of none availl, force, nor effect. Gevin vnder our signet and subscrivit with our hand, at our castell of Striviling, the xiiij day of Julij, and of our reigne the twelfth zeir—1.5.7.9.   JAMES R."

It is probable, however, that several of the more primitive arts were carried on to some extent. In the Town's Books there is reference to "hose or stockings" being made in 1603; and bonnet-making, which is supposed to have originated here, was doubtless, at this time, one of the principal trades. About the year 1646 it was in a flourishing condition, and fears seem to have been entertained by the followers of the craft that it was then passing too rapidly into other hands. In glancing over the charter of this venerable corporation, we find that a court was "holden at Kirkdyke, the twenty ane day of December Sixteen hundred and fourty seven years, by ane Noble Lord, James Lord Boyd, John Cunninghame of Redlaw and John Mowat his Lordship's baillies," and that about thirty* bonnet-manufacturers "compeared" and complained of various abuses having crept into the craft, such as "feeing" each others' servants, and servants leaving their masters' work to do their own.† At this court it was ordained that "no

* In 1746 there were forty-four masters or manufacturers in the trade.
† In an old Minute Book belonging to the corporation of bonnet-makers we find some curious enactments regarding their servants. For example, at a "Court of the Trade holden in the Meal Mercat, 25th day of Aug., 1722, in presence of Adam Boyd and Robert Paterson, Baillies," it was enacted, "that no child or servant shall have liberty to leave their master's house in the morning with his work before family worship be performed, . . . under a penalty of Six Shilling Scots," which the master was to pay if he did not exact it from the servant. On the other hand, the master was bound not to "intertain," as the minute expresses it, "any child or servant with work" in the morning before the same religious duty was discharged. It was also enacted, that, "to prevent cabbawlling in the fields or elsewhere by the servants, there shall not be found above three together in one place, either to work or to play lawfully, without special leave asked and had from their masters at any time, under a penalty of Six Shilling Scots, to be detained of the first end of their week's wages: but if allowed by their masters" they were to be "exempted from the same fyne." Another act was, that if any servant was absent all night from his master's house "without ane Lawful Errand," and failed to state in what house he had been entertained, he was liable also to pay a fine of Six Shilling Scots, or to be imprisoned for twenty-four hours, on a complaint being made by the masters to the magistrates.

The following enactment respecting the funerals of the masters and their spouses seems a little curious, and may also be quoted: "Debr 27, 1744—The said day the Trade take to their consideration a fault much neglected in not going to the funerals of the masters and their spouses for the time by gane, and therefor after mature servant or other person presume to take up work at their own hand until first he be thought worthy by the Craft and have given in his *sey* [trial-piece] to them."*

James, the eighth Lord Boyd, who granted the above-mentioned charter, was, to use the language of a genealogist of the family, "a man of great worth and honour, and steady in his support of the unfortunate Charles, for which the Usurper [Cromwell] fined him £1500." As we formerly stated, it was during the life of this lord that that part of Dean Castle, on which the Kilmarnock Arms are sculptured, was erected. He was succeeded by his son William, who is mentioned as being "a man of wit and learning," and "much attached to royalty, for which King Charles the Second created him Earl of Kilmarnock, 7th August, 1661."

deliberation, hereby statutes and enacts that they shal punctuly attend every master and their spouses when asked by the Trades' Officer, under the penalty of Four Shilin Scots when warned, and this they allow to be payed upon ornnarly poynding, or produce a lawfull excuse who cannot attend, which is to be performed when any of the family shal hapin to decease; also, when any other corporation in the Brugh shal desire the favour of our corporation to attend them."

We may add that a laudable partiality was shown to those who had engaged in matrimonial life; for it was enacted in 1709, that a freeman's son, when entering the trade, was "to pay four pounds Scots *if unmaried*, but *if maried*" only "fourtie Shilling."

* In the Weavers' Charter, dated 1684, it is also stated that "none of the prentices or journeymen shall set up trade untill he be found ane sufficient worker."

CHAPTER V.

> Yes! though the sceptic's tongue deride
> Those martyrs who for conscience died;
> Though modish history blight their fame,
> And sneering courtiers hoot the name
> Of men who dared alone be free
> Amidst a nation's slavery:
> Yet long for them the poet's lyre
> Shall wake its notes of heavenly fire;
> Their names shall nerve the patriot's hand,
> Upraised to save a sinking land;
> And piety shall learn to burn
> With holier transports o'er their urn.
>
> HOGG.

ABOUT this period, as the reader is aware, the sword of persecution was unsheathed in many districts of Scotland, and the adherents of the Covenant were reduced to the necessity of seeking a hiding-place in the secluded glen or the less frequented moorland. The people in our own locality, and in the neighbouring parish of Fenwick, for their attachment to the truth, had much to suffer from the hatred and cruelty of their oppressors.

At the end of the year 1666 the heads of John Ross and John Shields, who were executed at Edinburgh, were set up at Kilmarnock. The former of these martyrs belonged to Mauchline, and the latter was a tenant of Sir George Maxwell of Nether Pollock. They were accused and found guilty of carrying arms, and of being in Kilmarnock for the purpose of bringing intelligence of the movements of the king's soldiers to the adherents of the Covenant. In the Low Church burying-ground is a stone to their memory, on which is this inscription:

"Here lie the Heads of John Ross and John Shields, who suffered at Edinburgh, Dec. 27th, 1666, and had their Heads set up in Kilmarnock.

"Our persecutors mad with wrath and ire
In Edinburgh members some do lye, some here;
Yet instantly united they shall be,
And witness 'gainst this nation's perjury."

In 1667, immediately after the defeat of the Covenanters at Pentland, General Dalziel, with his soldiery, was stationed in Kilmarnock, which for some time was his head-quarters in Ayrshire; and perhaps there is not a more appalling page in the history of the period than that in which are recorded the barbarous atrocities he committed here and in the neighbourhood. With the power of a despot he exacted money to the amount of fifty thousand merks from the inhabitants; but mere lucre did not satiate his fiendish propensities. Human life also was immolated at the shrine of his cruelty; and persons of various ranks were dragged before him and put to the torture. In the old prison-house of the town, which stood at a little distance west from the Cross, was a loathsome dungeon, called the "Thieves' Hole." A considerable number were driven like dogs into this unwholesome den, "where," to use the language of Wodrow, "they could not move themselves night or day, but were obliged constantly to stand upright." Here the poor sufferers endured for a while the most acute misery. Disease at length made its appearance among them, and one of the number was pining under its withering influence. His friends earnestly implored the commander for his liberty, which was granted on the condition that, dead or alive, his body should be returned. Shortly after his release from jail death put an end to all his sorrows; but his relatives were compelled to carry his corpse back to the door of the prison, where it lay exposed to the public gaze till Dalziel was pleased to give liberty for its interment.*

But deeds of still deeper dye were enacted by Dalziel in this quarter. An individual named Finlay, belonging to another parish, was ordered to be brought into his presence, and because he could not give certain information which the General wanted, he was condemned to be shot without even the form of a trial! In vain did the poor man plead for a few more hours of life to prepare for eternity. "I will teach him to obey without scruple," said Dalziel to his lieutenant; "go and despatch him!" This dread command, which appalled even the hardened soldiers, was instantly obeyed, and the unfortunate Finlay in a few minutes breathed his last. His body, after being stripped of its clothing, was left naked upon the ground.

Whether the Earl of Kilmarnock took any active part against the sufferers, the authorities we have consulted do not inform us;† but the Dean Castle was now used, not as a shelter for the houseless wanderers, who sought to worship God according to the dictates of their own consciences, but as a stronghold for their merciless enemies. At the time Dalziel occupied the town, a party of his soldiers was stationed in this fortress, and many were the severities which the people in the neighbourhood suffered from their doings. An instance of their cruelty may be given. When traversing the fields one day in quest of the sufferers, they observed an individual hurrying from them at a distance; and, suspecting that he

---

* The house in which the General lodged, and from the windows of which he used to give orders to his soldiers, was long after looked upon with dread, and pointed out by the inhabitants as the house of the bloody Dalziel. It stood upon the south bank of the water at the end of the Old Bridge, immediately behind what is now called Victoria Place.

† Lady Boyd, second wife of Robert, sixth Lord Boyd, was distinguished for her great sympathy with the persecuted Presbyterians. Her son, Lord Boyd, also warmly embraced the sentiments of the Covenanters, and subscribed the National Covenant on the 1st March, 1638, in the Greyfriars' Church, Edinburgh.—*See Anderson's Ladies of the Covenant.*

was flying through a consciousness of guilt, they pursued him like demons bent on some infernal enterprise. The man, however, kept in advance of them, and at length reaching a house, he passed through it by a passage that led to the back premises; and, with great presence of mind, concealed himself in a pool of water, where he stood with only his head above the surface. In the course of a few minutes the soldiers were in the house, expecting their prey; but no person, save the mistress of the cottage, could be found. They threatened her with instant death if she did not produce the object of their search. She acknowledged that a man had run through the house, but who he was or where he had gone she knew not. Maddened by disappointment, they seized her and led her captive to Kilmarnock, where, notwithstanding her declarations of innocence, she was condemned to be immured in a dark subterraneous apartment in Dean Castle. This harsh sentence, we need scarcely say, was promptly executed; and tradition affirms that the poor creature was never released, but left to perish in that dreary abode, among filth and vermin.*

In 1678, which was called by the country people "the year of the Highland Host," the town of Kilmarnock was again severely oppressed by the rigours of the military. One individual, named William Taylor, a merchant, had a whole company of soldiers quartered upon him for a night; and Mr James Aird of Milton had twenty-four for three weeks. Another person named Dickie was compelled to furnish meat, drink, and quarters to nine Highlanders for six weeks; and such was their heartless ingratitude, that when they left the house they carried with them "a hose full of silver money," besides other goods.† But the loss of property was not all

---

* See Wodrow's *Church History*, vol. ii.
† About the year 1786 some workmen, who were employed in taking down an old house at the corner of Green Street, found beneath the floor of one of the lower rooms

that Mr Dickie was forced to endure. These merciless marauders so maltreated his person that two of his ribs were broken. His wife, too, who was pregnant at the time, was pierced in the side with a dirk by one of the ruffians, and so injured by the wound and the terror it occasioned that she soon after died. The loss which Mr Dickie sustained in property was upwards of a thousand merks. Several of the inhabitants suffered similar losses at this awful period. The plunder obtained from individuals, however, great as it was, seems not to have satisfied the greed of the Highlanders, for they concerted measures to ransack and pillage the whole of the town. It was on a Sabbath that they resolved to put their plans into execution, and they had actually begun to rifle some of the houses when Mr Wedderburn, then minister of the place, endeavoured-to convince them of the heinousness of the crimes they were committing; but this good man, instead of being listened to with reverence and respect,

---

an earthen vessel containing a considerable quantity of money, which was supposed to have been hidden in the days of the Persecution. Some of the coins were of a very ancient date, but the greater part belonged to the time of Charles the Second. This valuable treasure was claimed by the proprietor of the house, who, in the course of time, sold it to the curious; and many conjectures were formed regarding the cause that led to its concealment. As most of the coins, however, were of the reign of Charles the Second, the general opinion was that they had been deposited there in the time of the Covenanters, when property as well as life was insecure, and when many were obliged to fly from their homes to avoid the cruel proscriptions of their sanguinary oppressors. The circumstance of the money being left there for so long a period may be accounted for on the supposition that the original owner, like many individuals of the time, met with a sudden death by the hand of tyranny, or was forced to fly to a distant land, whence he never returned.

In June, 1863, another quantity of ancient coins was found at the taking down of an old house near the foot of Fore Street; and a conjecture similar to the above may be formed regarding the cause of their concealment. They were all silver, and amounted in number to several hundreds. The most of them were about the size of our present crown pieces. Some bore the date 1553, and others belonged to the reigns of Charles the First and Charles the Second. The greater proportion of them were foreign pieces, and were comparatively beautiful specimens of ancient coinage. They were discovered in a leathern bag at the top of the wall immediately below the thatch, and were divided among the workmen employed in demolishing the building. The house, which was of two storeys, had been at one time an inn, and had a little court in front.

received a blow on the breast with the butt-end of a musket, which laid the foundation of the disease of which he died.* By the intercession of persons of influence, and by money which was given to the officers, the town was at length saved from the ravages of the soldiers.†

Next year, 1679, six individuals, natives of the parish of Kilmarnock, were sentenced to transportation to the plantations of America for being engaged in the rising at Bothwell. Their names were Thomas Finlay, John Cuthbertson, William Brown, Patrick Watt, Robert Anderson, and James Anderson. The number banished on that occasion amounted in all to two hundred and fifty-seven; and awful were the miseries they were compelled to suffer, not only during their confinement in the Greyfriars' Churchyard, Edinburgh, where about

---

* Mr Alexander Wedderburn was one of the indulged ministers of the period, and was much esteemed for his worth, piety, and learning. After his death a number of his sermons were collected and published in two volumes. He had been for some time minister at Forgan, in Fife, previous to coming to Kilmarnock. He died in 1678.

† A list of the losses occasioned in the different parishes of Ayrshire this year by the rapacity of the soldiers and of the Highland Host was drawn up by the noblemen and gentlemen of the county. From that account, which Wodrow has preserved, the following extract regarding the parishes of Fenwick and Kilmarnock is taken; and, though it is Scots money that is therein meant, yet, when we take into consideration the limited wealth of the people at this period, the amount of loss appears very great: "Rowallan's lands, for quarters, 1471*l.* 6*s.* Dry quarters, 589*l.* 6*s.* Plunder, 1071*l.* 16*s.*—Crawfordland, of quarters, 460*l.* Dry quarters to Captain Lumsden, 300*l.* Plundered, 368*l.* 11*s.*—Raith lands, quarters, 364*l.* 6*s.* Dry quarters and plunder, 596*l.*—Skimeland, quarters and plunder, 298*l.*—Glebeland, dry quarters, 52*l.* Plunder, 32*l.* Communion table-cloths and baptism-cloths, 30*l.*—Fenwick town, quarters, 58*l.* Dry quarters and brandy, 78*l.* Plunder, 68*l.*—Pockelly lands, quarters, dry quarters, and plunder, 1260*l.* 17*s.*—Hairshaw, quarters, 135*l.* Dry quarters, 101*l.* Plunder, 284*l.* 13*s.* 4*d.*—Hietrie, quarters, 156*l.* Dry quarters, 40*l.* Plunder, 22*l.*—Miltoun, quarters, 66*l.* 18*s.* Extraordinary drink, 16*l.* Dry quarters, 9*l.* Plunder, 13*l.* 14*s.*—Templetonburn, quarters, 15*l.* Dry quarters, 5*l.* Plunder, 6*l.*—Lawhill, quarters, 3*l.* 10*s.* Dry quarters, 18*s.*—Asloss, quarters, 70*l.* 10*s.* Dry quarters, 8*l.*—Silverwood, quarters, 25*l.* 16*s.* Plunder, 5*l.* 10*s.*—Town of Kilmarnock and lands belonging to my lord within the parish, quarters, dry quarters, and plunder, 5918*l.*—Glebeland of Kilmarnock, quarters, dry quarters, and plunder, 76*l.* 14*s.*—Grange lands, quarters, dry quarters, and plunder, 169*l.* 15*s.* 4*d.*—Camskeigh, quarters and baggage horses, 120*l.* Dry quarters, 64*l.* —In all, 14,431*l.* 0*s.* 8*d.*"

twelve hundred were kept prisoners, but also after their embarkation. Their daily allowance of food in the Greyfriars was limited in the extreme, being only four ounces of coarse bread to each man. Their bed was the cold ground on which they had stood or sat during the day; and any little necessaries, such as clothes, shoes, or money, that were given them by humane friends, were frequently stolen during the night by the unfeeling soldiery. Those who were exiled were doomed to endure many hardships still more severe and appalling. The captain, and even the sailors of the ship that bore them away, treated them with great harshness; and the ship itself, which sailed from Leith on the 27th November, encountered severe storms, and was driven into a violent sea, near the Orkney Isles, on the 10th of December. The prisoners, perceiving the impending danger, entreated the captain to set them ashore rather than let them perish; but he was deaf to their supplications, and caused them to be locked under hatches. The vessel at last was split upon a rock, and about two hundred of the hapless exiles were utterly lost amid the tempestuous billows. The rest, among whom was Patrick Watt, mentioned above, were saved by clinging to the floating timbers.

In the cemetery of the Low Church a plain but neatly executed stone, bearing the following inscription, has been erected to the memory of such of the sufferers as belonged to this parish:

"Sacred to the memory of Thomas Finlay, John Cuthbertson, William Brown, Robert and James Anderson (natives of this parish), who were taken prisoners at Bothwell, June 22nd, 1679, sentenced to transportation for life, and drowned on their passage near the Orkney Isles. Also, John Finlay, who suffered Martyrdom, 15th December, 1682, in the Grass-Market, Edinburgh.

"Peace to the Church! her peace no friends invade,
Peace to each noble Martyr's honoured shade;
They, with undaunted courage, truth, and zeal,
Contended for the Church and Country's weal;
We share the fruits, we drop the grateful tear,
And peaceful Altars o'er their ashes rear."

About 1680, so high ran the tide of persecution against those who were guided by conscience in matters of religion, that the curate of the parish—a Mr Carnegie—one Sabbath, at the close of his afternoon sermon, commanded the doors of the church to be locked, and then called over the names of all the heads of families in the parish, in order to ascertain who were attending conventicles or other places of worship. Those who were absent were immediately marked out for prosecution, and many of them were heavily fined. One of the victims was Mr James Aird of Milton, already mentioned, who was not only subjected to the payment of fines, but compelled to endure other evils alike unjust and oppressive. He was taken before the Justiciary and charged with being an actor at the battle of Bothwell Bridge; and though not the slightest proof could be adduced against him, yet he was so persecuted afterwards by parties of soldiers being sent in search of him, that for forty-two nights he was forced to seek a shelter in the fields and the woods, and ultimately to fly from his home and his family for a number of years.

In 1682, an individual named James Robertson, from Stonehouse, who was in the habit of travelling the country as a pedler, happened to come to Kilmarnock; and, on learning that an acquaintance of his was imprisoned here, he sought and obtained liberty to see him; but before he had been long in his presence he was seized by the minions of the law and dragged into another apartment, where he was confined without any particular charge being brought against him. His *pack*, containing perhaps all his wealth, was taken from him and never restored. During his imprisonment he was brought for examination before Major White, who treated him so cruelly that he "pulled him by the nose, and wrung it about till it gushed out in blood."* On one occasion when

* Wodrow.

this man was worshipping God in company with his fellow-prisoners, the captain of the guard rushed upon him, tore the Bible from his hand, and swore he would throw it in the fire if he again attempted to engage in such work! Soon after this time Robertson was escorted to Edinburgh by a military guard, whose treatment of him by the way was inhuman and disgraceful in the extreme. In Edinburgh he underwent a kind of trial; and, on declaring that it was lawful for men to rise in defence of the gospel and their own lives, he was sentenced to be executed. Wodrow says: "The great matter they took his life for, though they could have no probation for it, was a surmise that James Robertson was the person who affixed a protestation against the *test* on the church door of Stonehouse." John Finlay of Muirside, in this parish (the individual, we believe, whom Robertson visited in the jail of Kilmarnock), was executed along with him in the Grassmarket, Edinburgh, December 15, 1682. In their dying testimonies allusion is made to the cruelties inflicted upon them in Kilmarnock. Finlay thus expresses himself: " I give my testimony against John Boyd, called bailie of Kilmarnock, for his bloody courses in many things, and especially in his uplifting the cess and bloody fines, and in oppressing the poor in their consciences, and laying on of dragoons upon them most cruelly, which he did upon me four times; I wish God may forgive him for what he has done in that matter."*

Next year, 1683, Major White was fully empowered to fine and imprison such persons as were inimical to the Episcopal Church, or were supposed to give countenance to the rebels, as the Covenanters were termed by the law. Many, therefore, were summoned before him for the most trifling offences, or rather for no offences at all, and were made the victims of his severe tyranny. One of the sufferers

* *Cloud of Witnesses.*

was Mr Jasper Tough, surgeon; he was charged with nonconformity, and on acknowledging that he had not been in the church of the incumbent, Mr Pollock, for a certain time, was fined in the sum of nineteen pounds sterling; and on refusing to sign the bond of regularity he was, with several others, ordered to prison, where he lay for fifteen days. At length he obtained his liberty by paying twenty-seven rix-dollars. "But, within a little," says Wodrow, "Mr Tough was again attacked by Mr Arthur Hamilton for not hearing Mr Pollock, and paid to him five dollars, and half a dollar to the fiscal of the court; and in harvest this year, because he deserted another court then held for pressing regularity, no sooner did he appear again about his business, but he was imprisoned till he gave bond and caution, under five hundred merks penalty, to compear when called; and he had a dollar to give the clerk for writing it, and fourteen shillings Scots to the keeper of the prison, for about six hours' imprisonment. . . . Sometime after this, Lieutenant-Colonel Buchan held a court at Kilmarnock, and Mr Tough not being personally apprehended when cited, did not appear, but was forced to abscond, and to leave his house and shop to the care of his apprentice for six weeks. In absence he was fined in fifty pounds for non-compearance, and in a vast sum for absence every Lord's-day since Mr Pollock's coming to Kilmarnock." An inventory was likewise taken of all Mr Tough's household furniture, and every thing that was in his shop; and even his servant was cast into prison. About six months after, Mr Tough was again subjected to the rigours of military despotism. He was seized, put into confinement, and, although great interest was made for his liberation, he obtained it only by taking the test, and by paying another fine for non-compearance and nonconformity. Mr Tough's professional duties, at the period spoken of, could not well be dispensed with, in consequence of few medical practitioners being then in the town; for this reason his numerous friends and wellwishers used all their influence to procure his freedom. But what rendered him so obnoxious to the Colonel was the sympathy shown by him to the parties who suffered, particularly his dressing the wounds of such as were injured in encountering the soldiers.

In the spring of the same year, John Nisbet, younger, as he was called, to distinguish him from John Nisbet of Hardhill, was tried at Kilmarnock, for having been engaged in the battle of Bothwell Bridge. Of his early life or family connections history furnishes us with few particulars. He was a native, we believe, of the parish of Loudoun, and a man of great worth and sterling piety. It does not appear that any witnesses were examined at his trial; and the principal charges brought against him were his being at the rising at Bothwell, and owning its lawfulness—his refusing to tell what he knew regarding the place of concealment of John Nisbet of Hardhill—his acknowledging Jesus Christ to be the only Head of the Church, and Mr Donald Cargill, Mr John Kid, and Mr Richard Cameron to be faithful ministers of the gospel. Kilmarnock, though familiar with the barbarities of the persecutors, had as yet beheld no martyr executed within its boundaries; and it was therefore resolved, by the enemies of the Covenant, that Mr Nisbet should be hanged at the Cross, in order that the inhabitants and those in the neighbourhood might be awed into submission by the dreadful spectacle. No symptoms of fear were observable in his demeanour at the place of execution. He ascended the ladder with the greatest composure—prayed for some time—sung part of the 16th Psalm—and read the 8th chapter of the Epistle to the Romans. He prayed again, delivered his Bible to his uncle, and spoke for some time to the multitude, which, tradition says, was so great, that many, in order to hear and see him, had placed themselves on the roofs of the houses. Every step of the ladder, he said, he reckoned a step nearer heaven; but when he came to expatiate on his previous sufferings and his trial, a tumult was raised by the soldiers; on observing which he drew the napkin over his face, and was launched into eternity, when earnestly commending his soul to the care of his heavenly Father. The spot where the gallows stood is still marked by the initials of his name, formed with white stones, at the south corner of the Cross; and in the Low Church burying-ground is a stone to his memory, on which is this inscription:

"Here lies John Nisbet, who was taken by Major Balfour's Party, and suffered at Kilmarnock, 14th April, 1683, for adhering to the Word of God and our Covenants. Rev. xii. & 11.

"Come, reader, see, here pleasant Nisbet lies,
His blood doth pierce the high and lofty skies;
Kilmarnock did his latter hour perceive
And Christ his soul to heaven did receive.
Yet bloody Torrence did his body raise
And buried it into another place;
Saying, ' *Shall rebels lye in graves with me!*
We'll bury him where evil doers be.' "

CHAPTER VI.

> ———— In solitudes like these
> Thy persecuted children, Scotia, foiled
> A tyrant's and a bigot's bloody laws.
>
> GRAHAME.

ABOUT the same period Dean Castle was again the quarters of a party of soldiers, commanded by a Captain Inglis.* Day after day, and night after night, they searched the adjacent country with a wolfish eagerness for the Covenanters; and often, when disappointed of their prey, they gratified their revenge by destroying the property of the fugitives, or by

* The following letter, copied from the original, addressed to the "Laird of Rowallan," was written, we believe, by Captain Inglis, or Inglish, as the name was sometimes spelled, and may be given as illustrating in some degree the hostile feeling that existed between the soldiers and the people at the period under notice. Captain John Inglis is also mentioned in a "Commission for Ayrshire, July 28, 1683."

"KILMARNOCK, JANRY. 24TH, [16] 82.

"MUCH HONOURED,—I stayed longer than I intended at Aire, and came but home yesternight, when I found your Letter complaining off my soulders' miscarige. I have made inquiry anent the affair, but cannot find out the person or persons; so that if you think fitting, let the persons who are wronged come in here themselves with the soulders' names who have done it, and they shall have satisfaction; for it is hard to give justice without both parties being heard, farr less when I neither know the one or other parties; but one thing I hear for certaine, that all countriemen hereabout will not sell corn or strawe for ready monie, but shuts up their doors upon sight of the Soulders coming; and so long that the King keepes up soulders they must be maintained for their own monie; and when you examine farder in this affair, you will find something of truth in this which has been the cause of your complaining; and I heare they are so wickedly inclined that they will not take monie for their straw and corn; but, Sir, to prevent farder trouble, I have brought an Letter from the Earle off Drumfries, and sent it this day to the Earle of Lothian, for ane meetting to be kept att Machlen on Wednesday next be ten hours, where both their Lordships will be with others; and it is my advice that yourself be there also, with any whom you think fitt to advertise. I intend, God willing, to sende the half of my troops to Machlen on Moonday's morning, to give ease to this place and about it. The Sherrefs-depute will be at Machlen also with other gentlemen about Coomlock; so craving pardon for this trouble, I remain, Sir, your most humble Servant, "JO. INGLISH."

driving their wives and children from their homes, to pine or perish among the beasts of the field.

One of the persons who then sought a hiding-place among the uplands of Fenwick was the venerated Captain John Paton of Meadowhead; and though the parish of Kilmarnock can neither claim him as a resident, nor be honoured as the place of his nativity, still it may not be out of keeping with our humble design to give a brief outline of the sufferings he experienced at the hands of the military then stationed in this locality. A high reward had been offered for the captain's head; he durst not even enter his own dwelling; for the soldiers, like bloodhounds, were prowling around it. But though denounced as a rebel by the law, and deprived of the sweet endearments of his own family, yet, throughout the wide expanse of that bleak moor, there was scarcely a cottage the inmates of which were not willing to shelter him under its roof. One of these, namely, Lochgoin, was chosen by the captain as his safest and most retired retreat.* There, in the seclusion and solitude of the place, he hoped to remain for a short time unmolested, till his health, which had become impaired, would be somewhat restored. It was on a Sabbath morning that he, along with a few friends warmly attached to the Covenant, went for refuge to that hallowed abode.

* Lochgoin is situated on the estate of Rowallan, in the upper part of the parish of Fenwick. In the house are still preserved some interesting relics of the Covenanting times. Among these are Captain Paton's Bible, which he handed from the scaffold to his wife a few minutes before his execution; a sword with which he fought at Pentland, &c.; the drum and drumsticks used by his followers; and a flag which the men of Fenwick carried at the battle of Bothwell Bridge. There are also in the house a number of curious coins, which were found in an old dyke by which the garden was enclosed, and where they were no doubt secreted in the days of the Persecution. The farm is at present rented by a grandson of the author of the well-known *Scots Worthies;* and a lineal descendant of the family who occupied it in the days of the Persecution. The Rev. R. Simpson, in his *Gleanings among the Mountains* says: " The family of Lochgoin has subsisted on the spot for about seven hundred years, and came originally as refugees from some of the Waldensian or Piedmontese valleys, in the times of some of the early continental persecutions. No fewer than nine-and-twenty persons of the name of John Howie, or Hoy, have occupied the place in their successive generations."

"You are welcome to the shelter of our lowly dwelling," said old Mr Howie, the occupant, as they entered; "but, from a fearful dream I have had during the night, I much fear that our home will be the scene of bloodshed before many suns go down." "We will rely upon God as we have hitherto done," said Paton; "and if we *must* meet death, I trust we will do it manfully, and be prepared to enter that world which the righteous only shall inherit, and in which the sword of the tyrant shall never be unsheathed."

That day was spent by the little party at Lochgoin in preaching and in prayer; and nothing occurred to disturb the sacred solemnity of the scene till late in the afternoon, when intelligence was brought by a shepherd from a neighbouring *sheilin*, that a troop of soldiers from Dean Castle was coming up the moor. Watches were immediately placed on some of the eminences; but a storm was gathering in the sky, which considerably darkened the prospect towards the west, and the troopers could not be discovered. Night came on, but sleep closed not an eye within the house, though some of the inmates were much exhausted by previous hardships. In the twilight of the morning one of the sufferers, who had been some time out as a watch, returned with the agreeable tidings that no trooper appeared in view. The captain, on hearing this, retired to rest; and the Howies repaired to the outhouses to look after the cattle. But danger was at hand. A sergeant, named Rae, and five soldiers, a detachment from a stronger body, suddenly made their appearance, as if they had sprung from some secret retreat. With an air of insolence, the sergeant, who was in advance of the rest, approached the door, exclaiming, with a fiendish delight, "Ye dogs, we shall have you now." Isobel Howie, the mistress of the house, perceiving only Rae, but dreading that more of the soldiers were near, called upon Paton and his associates, who were in another apartment, to fly for their lives; at the same time, with a courage altogether masculine, and which does honour to her memory, she seized the sergeant by the collar, forced him from the door, and gave him such a blow as made him fall on the ground, where he lay for a few minutes gnashing his teeth with anger and cursing in a fearful manner.

While Rae was in this awkward, unsoldier-like position, the captain and his friends effected their escape; but before they had gone many paces from the house, a host of military was at their heels, declaring with demoniacal fury, that they would make food of them for the fowls of heaven. The sergeant, too, was instantly in pursuit; and, as if anxious to wipe off the stain that had been cast upon him by the heroine of Lochgoin, he presented his musket and discharged its contents among the fugitives, but, as Providence had willed it, without doing the smallest injury. One of Paton's party, named Kirkland, fired upon Rae in return; the latter had so narrow an escape, that the knot of hair upon his head was carried off by the shot of his opponent. A general firing now commenced; but none of the balls took effect, save one from the gun of Kirkland, which went through the thigh of a sergeant, who staggered and fell upon the heath. This event seems to have checked the ferocity of the soldiers, and Paton and his companions got considerably ahead of them. After enduring many hardships they found another hiding-place somewhere in the moors of Mearns or Eaglesham. Next day the ruthless soldiery returned to Lochgoin, and, actuated by feelings of revenge, or by a love of gain, plundered the house of all that was valuable.

Another incident in Captain Paton's life may be narrated. Many a day and many a night, as we have said, he was forced to forego the soothing endearments of his own hearth; and to him, whose bosom glowed with the tenderest feelings, what could be more painful? Reader! if you be possessed of parental affection—if your heart delight in the innocent prattle

of your little nurslings, when they are running about you in all
the sprightliness of rosy health—what would be your feelings
if compelled to be far from home when some fell disease had
confined them to their couch? To be denied the bliss of a last
farewell word or look—to be exiled from their presence when,
perhaps, they were breathing your name for the last time—
when the lips you had often kissed in parental joy were
growing pale with the hues of approaching death—what, we
ask, would then be your condition? Would it not be one of
intense misery? Would not your heart be swollen almost to
bursting with the tide of agony? Such then were the circumstances in which this revered martyr was placed. His child
was sinking rapidly to the grave; and he who would have
grasped its thin, pale hand with all the love of a tender
parent—who would have feelingly wiped the cold sweat of
death from its pallid brow—and who would have stood by its
side breathing, in deepest sincerity, a prayer for its temporal
or eternal welfare, dared not approach the house where it lay,
except at the peril of his own life. At length the sufferings
of the little one were terminated by death, and he resolved, at
whatever hazard, to perform towards it the last sad duties of
a father, by accompanying its remains to the mansions of the
dead. But even that mournful pleasure was denied him; for
intelligence of his intention was instantly communicated to the
soldiers at Kilmarnock, and his presence at the funeral urged
as affording a fit opportunity for his immediate apprehension.
And who, gentle reader, do you conceive was the informant?
Probably you will say he must have been the meanest of
mankind—some poor wretch in the lowest grade of society,
whose narrow circumstances had rendered him vicious, and
forced him, for paltry lucre's sake, to assume the degraded
character of a spy. If so, you are mistaken. He was a
person moving in a respectable sphere of life; one whose duty
it was, and whose profession especially bound him, to comfort

the afflicted—to inculcate peace and goodwill amongst men—to promulgate the humanizing, or, to speak more correctly, the Divine doctrines of Christianity. Start not when we disclose the fact—the individual referred to was a preacher of the gospel of peace, and the *reverend* incumbent of the parish!

When the hour of the funeral arrived, the captain, as chief mourner, was at the head of the small and sorrowing band that conducted the remains of his child to the grave; but, before reaching the place of interment, his friends, afraid of his apprehension, persuaded him to return, which he did with a melancholy heart, and again sought a refuge among his native wilds. Not long after this, however, he was apprehended by a party of soldiers at Floack, in the parish of Mearns; led captive to Kilmarnock, thence to Ayr, and afterwards to Edinburgh, where he was executed on the 9th of May, 1684.* In the churchyard of Fenwick a fine monument, the workmanship of Mr John Bowie, sculptor, Kilmarnock, has lately been erected to his memory. It bears the following inscription, copied from an old stone that formerly stood against the wall of the church:

"Sacred to the memory of Captain John Paton, late in Meadowhead, of this parish, who suffered Martyrdom in the Grass-Market, Edinburgh, May 9th, 1684. He was an honour to his country; on the Continent, at Pentland, Drumclog, and Bothwell, his heroic conduct truly evinced the gallant officer, brave soldier, and true patriot. In social and domestic life he was an ornament, a pious Christian, and a faithful witness for truth in opposition to the encroachments of tyrannical and despotic power in Church and State. The mortal remains of Captain Paton sleep amid the dust of kindred Martyrs, in the Greyfriars' Churchyard, Edinburgh.

"Near this is the burying-place of his family and descendants.

"Who Antichrist do thus oppose,
And for truth's cause their lives lay down,
Will get the victory o'er their foes,
And gain life's everlasting crown."

* According to various accounts Captain Paton displayed uncommon prowess and bravery as a soldier. Even General Dalziel, who goaded on his troops against the Covenanters, esteemed him for his heroism; and, on meeting him, when he was led prisoner to Kilmarnock, he embraced him, and said he would use his influence with the King in procuring him a pardon, which he succeeded in obtaining. Unfortunately, however, for Paton, the order came *after* his execution, and had been detained, it is said, by Bishop Paterson.—*See New Statistical Account.*

Notwithstanding the devastation that had been made and the blood that had been spilt in the parish of Kilmarnock, the emissaries of cruelty still continued their demoniacal work. In the beginning of May, 1685, a small band of Covenanters, consisting of twelve men, met one night for religious purposes in the house of James Paton, farmer of Little Blackwood, on the estate of Grougar. The place was lone and secluded, and they had assembled there in the hope that they would be undisturbed by any intruder; but when sitting by the hearth, in the interval of devotion, a noise was heard without, and fearing the enemy was near, they all hurried to another apartment. One of them, named James White, availed himself of the only gun in the house; and just as he was crossing the passage a party of soldiers, commanded by Patrick Inglis, forced open the doors. In the way of defence White at this moment made use of his musket; but the powder only flashed in the pan, and the light it emitted discovered his person to the soldiers, who shot him dead on the spot. Nine of the sufferers were in the *spence* endeavouring to make their escape, which two of them effected by forcing their way through the thatch. The other seven were arrested. John Gemmell and James Paton had fled for safety to the byre, and on their way thither were attacked by one of the party, who drew his bayonet to stab them. Gemmell wrested it from his grasp, thrust it into his body, and, hastening out by the door, knocked down a guard who was stationed outside, and made his escape amid the darkness of the night. The soldier thus stabbed by his own weapon was lifted by his companions and thrown, while yet streaming with blood, into the bed among Mr Paton's children. The other sufferers were still in the spence along with Mrs Paton, who had a babe at her breast. Calling Inglis by name, she pled with him for the sake of God to give them quarter, which he consented to do in consequence of knowing her some years before at her father's house of

Darwhilling, where he had been some time stationed; but this indulgence was granted on the condition that the sufferers should approach him one by one on their bare knees. The first that ventured into his presence was an aged man, named Findlay, who was instantly bound like a felon; and, in despite of quarter being given, one of the soldiers barbarously plunged his bayonet so deep into his thigh that its point came out behind; and all the consolation the unfortunate man received was hearing a volley of curses poured forth by Inglis upon the inhuman perpetrator of the act. The rest of the prisoners came from the spence in the same way, and also were bound. The whole of the premises were then narrowly searched. James Paton being found in the byre, was fettered like the others. A scene of plunder now ensued; and, after pillaging the house of every thing valuable, they seized the cows and horses and recklessly drove them over the body of White, which still lay in the passage. But their cruelty seems to have had no bounds; for with an axe they cut the head from the dead man, and used it next day as a football in their sports at Newmilns, to which place they conveyed the prisoners and the booty they had obtained.* When proceeding on their journey, the old man who was wounded signified his unfitness to walk; but Inglis, regardless of his sufferings,

---

* An epitaph, commemorative of White, and somewhat descriptive of the cruelty of his persecutors, is inscribed on a tombstone in the churchyard of Fenwick. Sir Walter Scott introduces it into one of the notes to *Old Mortality;* and, though not remarkable for his sympathy towards the Covenanters, he hesitates not to mention Inglis by the name of "monster"—a name that few, we believe, will consider altogether misapplied. The inscription on the tombstone is as follows:

"Here lies the body of James White, who was shot to death at Little Blackwood, by Peter Inglis and his party, 1685.

"This martyr was by Peter Inglis shot,
By birth a tiger rather than a Scot;
Who, that his monstrous extract might be seen,
Cut off his head, then kick'd it o'er the green;
Thus was the head which was to wear the crown,
A football made by a profane dragoon."

H

ordered him to be shot as soon as he appeared to retard their progress. At length they reached Newmilns, where they were imprisoned.

Next day Captain Inglis (father of Patrick Inglis), who kept a garrison there, commanded the whole of the sufferers to be shot, and they were brought forth immediately for that purpose. But a friend of the captain, who happened to be present, advised him against such rash procedure, as he might be called to account for such a deed if a change took place in the government of the country. At this suggestion the captain paused in his work of blood. He sent his son, however, to the Council at Edinburgh for an express order to shoot them, and they were again imprisoned. In the mean time their friends had concerted plans for their liberation; and, as if directed by an all-wise Providence, they assembled on the night previous to that which they had appointed for the rescue; and it was fortunate they did so; for Patrick Inglis had then returned from Edinburgh, and was lying in the vicinity with the order in his possession for their execution on the following day. With cool, yet dauntless hearts their friends attacked the garrison,* killed two of the soldiers,† broke up the doors and liberated the prisoners, with whom they marched triumphantly out of town. Next day the captain caused the whole of the place to be searched for the actors, and learning that they had fled to the country, he despatched his men in pursuit of them. They found not a single person, however, who had been engaged in the affair; but on the same day another and a darker deed of infamy characterized their proceedings; for, actuated by feelings of disappointment and revenge, they shot, it is said, two innocent men when returning from their bloody raid.‡

* A strong, square building, which yet stands in the village, and is known by the name of the Ducat Tower.
† One of the assailants, named John Law, was also killed.
‡ See Appendix to *Cloud of Witnesses*, Glasgow Edition, 1836.

In concluding these short sketches of the sufferings of the Covenanters in Kilmarnock and its neighbourhood, we congratulate the reader on the peaceful nature of the times in which we live, compared with those above referred to, when the arbitrary laws of the country retarded the exercise of conscientious principles, and wickedly interfered between man and his Maker in things pertaining to religious worship. The sword has happily been laid aside—man is no longer obliged to fly to the lonely cave or the tangled wood in order to worship unmolested the God of his fathers. All parties of professing Christians, to use the simple but beautiful language of Scripture, can now "sit under their own vine and fig tree, and none make them afraid;" and we trust that the progress of MIND, which has accomplished these happy changes, will be onward and onward, till tyranny and oppression be heard of only in the history of the past.

CHAPTER VII.

Such were the heroes of the ancient world;
. . . .
Prone to encounter peril, and to lift
Against each strong antagonist the spear.

HOME.

IN 1672 a second charter, conferring further rights and privileges on the town, was granted by Charles the Second in favour of William, the first Earl of Kilmarnock, who died in 1692. His eldest son, who succeeded to the estate and title of his father, died also towards the close of the same year. He left two sons, the elder of whom became the third Earl of Kilmarnock, and was served heir to his father in 1699. In the following year this nobleman gave a grant to the town of the whole common good, comprehending (to use the words of the disposition) "the common greens of the said town, shops under the tolbooth yr'of, the weights pocks and measures, the troan* and weights yr'of, and the customs of the faires and weekly mercats, and all other customes belonging to the s^d burgh and barony." The magistrates were then appointed by the lord of the manor from a list presented to him annually. In the grant above alluded to the manner in which they were to be elected, in the absence

---

* Within the last seventy or eighty years the "troan," or weigh-house, stood at the Cross. It was a wooden erection, consisting merely of a roof supported by three or four pillars.

of the superior, is thus specified: "And in caice it shall happen us our airs or successors fors^{ds} not to be living within the fors^{ds} bounds the time of the offering the for^{ds} leitts, then and in that caice, the s^{ds} bayllies and counsell for the time, making up and offering the fors^{ds} leitts to us and our fors^{ds} at our manor-place of Dean in p'nce of ane nottar and witnesses as effeirs, shall be also valide, effectuall, and sufficient to them to elect and choose bayllies in manner fors^{d,} as if we, our airs or successors were personally p'nt."*

Another clause, showing the powers bestowed on the magistrates, may be quoted: "The said^{s} bayllies to hold and affix Courts within the bounds of the s^{d} toun, and to decide, determine, and cognosce in all actions and causes, both civill and criminall that shall happen to be raised and pursued before them, and to give furth and pronounce de'cts and sentences thereintill, and the same to due and lawfull execution cause be put, and to uplift and receave the fynes, awards, and amerciaments of Court, and to apply the samen to the use, utilittie, and profett of the s^{d} toun and communitie. . . . With power likewise to the s^{ds} mag'rats and toun-counsell pr'nt and to come, to make and create burgesses of the s^{d} burgh of Kilmarnock, secluding and debarring all others from any merchandising, trade, or mechanisme, except them that shall receave burgess tickets from them for that effect."

By virtue of this grant and the formerly mentioned charters, the town held its municipal constitution up till the passing of the Burgh Reform Bill.

Of the trades which were carried on in Kilmarnock when these privileges were granted we have no distinct idea; all that we know is, that the principal were weaving, bonnet-making and stocking-making. The civil discords and persecutions that immediately preceded this period, had, no doubt,

* An election of this kind took place in 1723, when Mungo Moor, Adam Boyd and others from the Council went to the Castle with the Leit.

their influence in impeding the progress of commerce; yet the spirit of industry appears to have been active among the inhabitants; for we find from public documents that the trade of the place was then considered to be more extensive than that of any other town in the county.

The Earl of Kilmarnock was much attached to the interest of the House of Hanover. When George the First was proclaimed here, in August, 1714, the Earl appeared with the bailies and other gentlemen on the stairhead of the Old Council-house, where the ceremony was performed with great solemnity. The "stairhead," say the Burgh Records, was "covered with carpet" for the occasion; the "haill inhabitants" attended at the Cross, in which a large bonfire was kindled; the bells rung merrily; and the evening was spent by all parties in a loyal and joyful manner.

In 1715, when the Earl of Mar gathered the clans of the north, amounting to twelve thousand men, in order to aid the old Pretender "through slaughter to a throne," the Earl still further evinced his fidelity and zeal to his sovereign, by serving in the royal army with a considerable body of men, who were raised through his influence in Kilmarnock and its neighbourhood. These men, according to Rae's *History of the Rebellion*, were well disciplined, and presented a handsome appearance when the general muster of the fencibles of Cunningham took place at Irvine, in August, 1715. "It is not to be forgot," says Rae, "that the Earl of Kilmarnock appeared here at the head of above five hundred of his own men, well appointed, and expert in the exercise of their arms; and that which added very much unto it, was the early blossoms of the loyal principle and education of my Lord Boyd, who, though but eleven years of age, appeared in arms with the Earl, his father, and gracefully behaved himself to the admiration of all the beholders."

In the following month, while the rebels were gathering

at Perth, expresses were issued throughout the west of Scotland, stating that his Grace the Duke of Argyle thought it necessary that "all well-affected gentlemen" should collect their forces and assemble them at Glasgow. Great numbers immediately buckled on their armour and marched to that city; and, according to Rae, the men of Kilmarnock were among the very first who entered it. He says: "On Sabbath, the 18th of September, two gentlemen from Glasgow came there [to Kilmarnock], representing the danger the city was in by the number and nearness of the enemy, who were reported to be marching straight thither in order to surprise it, while it wanted sufficient defence through the absence of their own men, who, at the desire of the Duke of Argyle, were marching to Stirling. This sudden and surprising alarm so animated the people [of Kilmarnock], that on Monday, September 19, they universally assembled in arms by the sunrising, and, in presence of the Earl of Kilmarnock, offered cheerfully to march forthwith to Glasgow. And accordingly 220 men, who were best prepared, marched with the greatest alacrity (even those who contributed for the subsisting of others, not exempting themselves), and having come to Glasgow that day, to the great satisfaction of the inhabitants, were received and entertained with all the marks of friendship and gratitude. Next day the Earl came in himself with 120 men, whose presence very much added to the general satisfaction and courage of the city. And so they were the first of all the western parts that came to the assistance of Glasgow excepting Paisley, who, lying only about six miles off, were in about two hours before them. Next day they entered upon duty, keeping watch and ward night and day, till Saturday the first of October."

The opposition thus shown to the Stuarts by the men of Kilmarnock and others in Ayrshire is pointedly alluded to in one of our old Jacobite lyrics:

"The auld Stuarts back again,
The auld Stuarts back again;
Let howlet whigs do what they can,
The Stuarts will be back again.
Wha cares for a' their creeshy duds,
And a' Kilmarnock sowen suds?
We'll wauk their hydes and fyle their fuds,
And bring the Stuarts back again.

"There's Ayr and Irvine, wi' the rest,
And a' the cronies in the west,
Lord! sic a scaw'd and scabbit nest,
How they'll set up their crack again!
But wad they come or dare they come,
Afore the bagpipe and the drum,
We'll either gar them a' sing dumb,
Or 'Auld Stuarts back again.' "

At that time the daring Rob Roy, and the reckless clan of the Macgregors, were robbing and plundering in the Highlands; and, in compliance with a letter from the Duke of Argyle, the Earl of Kilmarnock marched thither with the volunteers of the west to curb the lawless doings of the insolent freebooters. The house of Gartartan, in Perthshire, was assigned as a garrison to the men of Kilmarnock, who, with those of Ayr, Kilwinning, and Stevenston, displayed considerable courage; for, according to the historian just quoted, they were the first that set out on the march from Glasgow, though the enemy, it was reported, had come within a few miles of the city. After continuing on duty at Gartartan from the 3rd of October till the 13th of the same month, our volunteers were relieved by a party of the Stirlingshire militia, and returned to Glasgow, where they were "honourably dismissed" on the 21st of November.

The Earl of Kilmarnock died in 1717.

The history of William, the fourth Earl of Kilmarnock, is fraught with a more melancholy interest than that of any of the former noblemen of this illustrious family. In the prosperity of the town and its manufactures he always displayed a deep interest; was frequently present at the meetings of council, and was much esteemed by the inhabitants. "He discovered," says a memoir of him published at London in 1746, "an early genius not unworthy the dignity of his birth; but his father's death leaving him too soon at liberty to be his own master, and the indulgence that is generally given to young noblemen, added to the natural sprightliness of his temper, soon gave him an aversion to a rigorous study of letters, though he had made some progress in classical learning, and had acquired some tolerable notion of philosophy and mathematics; but there was too much of the volatile in his disposition to continue long at exercises that required application; he was more happy in acquiring those which are called genteel accomplishments, such as riding, fencing, dancing, and some music; in all of which he excelled, and was justly esteemed by men of taste a polite gentleman."

We are told by the same biographer that when the Earl succeeded to the estate "it was pretty much alienated," and that his "income was infinitely short of what the generosity, or rather the profuseness of his temper would prompt him to spend." He married Lady Anne Livingstone, daughter and heiress of James, Earl of Linlithgow and Callander, who had been attainted for joining in the Rebellion of 1715. She was also presumptive heiress of the earldom of Errol, and, it is said, highly accomplished and beautiful. By her he had three sons, of whom some particulars are afterwards given. His lordship was the last of the Boyds who resided in the ancient Castle of Dean, for, as already stated, it was rendered uninhabitable by fire in 1735.

Nine or ten years after this date, Prince Charles, the Pretender, as is well known, planted his standard in Scotland, and succeeded in gaining the attachment and support of many of the nobles and gentlemen of influence. The Earl of Kilmarnock, too, became one of his adherents, but whether through a love to the cause of the Stuarts is uncertain. We know that previous to this time his public conduct betrayed no want of fidelity to the crown, but rather the reverse; as an instance of which it may be mentioned, that in 1727, when George the First died, the Earl sent an express from London —where he then was—to the authorities of Kilmarnock, acquainting them with the event, and calling upon them to have "the trainbands in readiness for proclaiming the Prince of Wales."* Smollett says, "he engaged in the Rebellion partly through the desperate situation of his fortune, and partly through resentment to the government on being deprived of a pension which he had for some time enjoyed."† Other accounts say that he was induced to join Prince Charles by the entreaties of his Countess, who was a Catholic, and consequently inimical to the House of Hanover; and some writers state that she was so charmed with the fine military appearance of Charles when he entered Edinburgh, "and the affability with which he treated her and all the ladies," that she became friendly to his cause, and prevailed upon the Earl to espouse it;‡ but of this we shall afterwards have occasion to speak. The zeal of this unfortunate nobleman in the cause of the young Chevalier was evinced soon after the breaking out of the Rebellion; for we find that the Prince, after marshalling the clans of the north, and when on his march to Edinburgh, lodged with his lordship one night in Callander House, while his army lay among the fields in the vicinity. Here he was welcomed with smiles of kindness, hospitably entertained, and assured of the utmost support by the Earl.

A tradition is still current in Kilmarnock, that, about the

* According to the Burgh Records the express from Edinburgh cost £6 Scots.
† It appears from the *Letters* of the Honourable Horace Walpole, that the pension had been obtained through the influence of his father (Sir Robert Walpole), and stopped by Lord Wilmington.
‡ See *Life of the Earl:* London, 1746.

same time, his lordship came to the town with the view of inducing the inhabitants to join the ranks of the Pretender; but our weavers, says the tradition, preferred their looms to the war-field; our worthy bonnet-makers declared their determination to wield the *shears* in the manufacture of their bonnets rather than the *sword* in the destruction of their fellow-creatures; and one or two individuals, more daring than the rest, exclaimed that they would more willingly lift up arms against his lordship's own person, than engage in so foolish and unnatural a rebellion. This story, so far as it bespeaks the sentiments of the inhabitants of Kilmarnock at that period, may be true, for they were then busily engaged in cultivating the more profitable arts of peace; and the remembrance of the many wrongs they had suffered at a former time by the hand of persecution, under the reign of the Stuarts, would, doubtless, make them indignant at every effort that was made to inflame them against the government; but if we may believe the Earl's own words in his petition to the King and to his Royal Highness the Prince of Wales, he made no attempt in this neighbourhood to raise men for the service of the Pretender. He says, "that he influenced neither tenant nor follower of his to assist or abet the Rebellion; but, on the contrary, that, between the time of the battle of Preston and his unhappy junction with the rebels, he went to the town of Kilmarnock, influenced the inhabitants as far as he could, and by their means likewise influenced their neighbouring boroughs to rise in arms for his Majesty's service, which had so good an effect that two hundred men of Kilmarnock appeared very soon in arms, and remained all the winter at Glasgow, or other places as they were ordered." A similar statement was made by his lordship at his trial before the House of Lords.

After the retreat of Prince Charles from England, his soldiers, it would appear, were greatly deficient in clothing and other necessaries. When in Glasgow he commanded the authorities to supply them with shirts, bonnets, waistcoats, shoes and stockings;* and many of the Highlanders, it is said, appropriated to themselves whatever they could find that answered their purpose; nor was it uncommon for bands of them to traverse the country for miles round in search of plunder. We mention these things in order to introduce a traditionary anecdote, illustrative of the state of public feeling in Kilmarnock at that memorable period. A party of the marauders had come so far west as the town of Stewarton; and, in consequence of their arrival there, a report was instantly circulated that a considerable body of the insurgents were on their march from Glasgow to the west, for the purpose of ransacking Kilmarnock. This rumour created an unusual sensation in Auld Killie. The town-drummer speedily patrolled the streets, and gave warning of the approaching danger; at the same time he announced that a public meeting would be held at the Netherton, for the purpose of devising measures for the protection of life and property. A large number of the inhabitants were soon on the ground, armed with old swords, muskets, and other weapons. After two or three thrilling speeches had been delivered, respecting the cruelty and thievish propensities of the Highlanders, it was agreed that the assembly should march in a body to meet the invaders, and give them battle before they reached the outskirts of the town. It was also resolved that the wives, during the absence of their husbands, should contrive means for securing everything that the mountaineers were likely to covet, such as pewter-plate and wearing apparel, which they immediately did, by sinking the former in the open wells at the backs of their houses, and by concealing the latter about the hedges in

---

* "Soon after their arrival at Glasgow, the rebels made a demand upon that city of 12,000 shirts, 6000 bonnets, 6000 pair of shoes, 6000 pair of stockings, and 6000 waistcoats, amounting to near £10,000 sterling in value."—*Scots Magazine for January*, 1746.

the vicinity. In the meantime the Kilmarnock heroes, with flying colours, passed through the centre of the town, up Soulis Street and Townhead, thence to the highway leading to Glasgow; but, on coming to Craigspout,* they learned from some travellers that the report which had caused so much alarm was all a hoax!—that no soldiers were on the road—that the Pretender and his army had left Glasgow, and were supposed to be on their way to Stirling. Our worthy volunteers then returned to the town, and, on arriving at the Cross, discharged their muskets into the air, gave three hearty cheers for King George, and, *unskaithed* by dirk or broadsword, repaired to their respective dwellings.

The majority of the inhabitants, therefore, were opposed to the House of Stuart; and we have heard of only one man whose principles inclined to the side of the Jacobites; but he evidently wanted the chivalrous spirit with which the true followers of "bonnie Prince Charlie" were actuated. This individual was commonly called *Auld Soulis*, from the circumstance of residing in the house† next to Lord Soulis's monument. A day or two before the battle of Falkirk he left Kilmarnock, and went to that town to gratify his curiosity, as he said, by seeing Prince Charles and his army. When he arrived in Falkirk, he was immediately accosted by some of the Highlanders, who asked, with an air of authority, whence he had come. He answered that he had come from Ayrshire, was friendly to the Prince, and was an acquaintance of the Earl of Kilmarnock, to whom he had brought a letter. "Join our party then, an' pe tam to you," said one of the Highlanders, "an' no pe stanin' there like some stupid deevil, or py Cot her nainsel's durk shall mak you do your duty." Auld Soulis, on hearing such vehement language, began to wish he

---

* A little waterfall about two and a half miles from Kilmarnock.
† The site which this house occupied is now part of the High Church burial-ground.

were again in Kilmarnock; but, anxious to see the battle, which was expected every hour to commence, he contrived to linger about the place till it was over; and besides seeing the hostile encounter, he had the satisfaction of beholding the young Pretender conducted by torchlight to his lodgings in Falkirk. Next day Auld Soulis was seized by the insurgents, and commanded to follow them in their march towards Stirling, and to lead a horse on which were placed two wounded men. Afraid to act contrary to orders, he took the horse and men under his charge, and proceeded slowly behind the army; but, on coming to a turn of the road, where an eminence concealed him from view, he left the two invalids to their fate, and hurried homeward, carrying along with him a loaf he had got for their use. He had not gone far, however, when he was met by several hungry Highlanders, who plundered him not only of the loaf, but even of the shoes that were on his feet.* We may add that Auld Soulis, in the course of two or three days, was again in Kilmarnock, amusing his friends with an account of his wonderful adventures at Falkirk.

* This part of the story of Auld Soulis harmonizes with accounts published at the time. In the *Scots Magazine* for January, 1746, it is stated that "the rebels were in great distress for want of provisions. The twenty-five soldiers who escaped out of the church of Falkirk reported that it was with the greatest difficulty they could get any provisions whilst they were in custody—the greater part of what had been ordered for their use having been forced from them by those who were their guards."

CHAPTER VIII.

Shades of the mighty and the brave,
Who, faithful to your Stuart, fell;
No trophies mark your common grave,
No dirges to your memory swell;
But generous hearts will weep your fate,
When far has rolled the tide of time;
And bards unborn shall renovate
Your fading fame, in loftiest rhyme.
GRIEVE.

To return to the Earl of Kilmarnock. He was appointed colonel of the hussars, and in that capacity accompanied the insurgents into England.* At the battle of Falkirk he was a principal actor; and on the day following he brought a party of his men into the town to guard some prisoners, a list of whom he presented to the Prince at his lodgings.

An anecdote in connection with the battle of Falkirk is told of the Earl's lady. She was then residing at Callander House, in the vicinity; and, in order to divert the attention of Lieutenant-General Hawley, the commander of the King's troops, from the movements of the Prince, she insidiously invited him to breakfast. This well-laid scheme was in some degree successful; for Hawley was so fascinated by the elegant appearance and engaging demeanour of the Countess, that he passed several hours in her company, during which time Charles found ample opportunity for choosing, as he did, a favourable position for his army. In short, the general had so far forgot his duty, that he had ultimately to be apprised

---

* The author of the memoir from which we have already quoted, says he "was received by the young Chevalier with great marks of esteem and distinction, was made Colonel of the Guards, and promoted to the degree of a General."

of the situation of the enemy by a messenger, who was
despatched to him for that purpose; and such, it is said, was
his confusion of mind when leaving the mansion, that he left
his hat behind him, and, *Gilpin-like*, hurried bareheaded to the
camp.* The battle of Falkirk, in which the young adventurer
was victorious, was fought on the afternoon of the 17th of
January, 1746.

In the course of a few days Prince Charles and his followers
marched to Stirling, and, after a fruitless attempt to besiege
the Castle, retreated to the north. By this time the Duke of
Cumberland had arrived in Scotland with additional forces for
the suppression of the Rebellion, and the day was rapidly
approaching when the golden hopes of the Prince and his
adherents were destined to perish. The Duke lost no time in
following them to the Highlands; and on the 16th of April
the two armies met on Drummossie Moor, near Culloden
House, at a short distance from Inverness. It is not our
province, perhaps, to describe the sanguinary conflict that
ensued; still, as it proved disastrous not only to the cause of
the Prince, but to the Earl of Kilmarnock, a succinct account
of it may be appropriately given in these pages. It is said
that the Earl, who commanded the foot-guards at this engagement, on beholding the cool, determined appearance of the
formidable ranks of Cumberland, felt an inward conviction
that the Prince's army would be involved in defeat and ruin.
But, notwithstanding the powerful aspect of their opponents,
the adherents of Charles, though greatly inferior in numbers,
attacked them like men resolved to conquer or perish. In the
words of the Jacobite ballad,

> "There was no lack of bravery there,
> No spare of blood or breath;
> For, one to two, their foes they dared
> For freedom or for death."

The following powerful description of the last charge of the

* See Chambers's *Rebellion*.

Highlanders we quote from Chambers's interesting *History of the Rebellion*: " Notwithstanding that the three files of the front line of the English poured forth their incessant fire of musketry—notwithstanding that the cannon, now loaded with grapeshot, swept the field as with a hail-storm—notwithstanding the flank fire of Wolfe's regiment—onward, onward went the headlong Highlanders, flinging themselves into, rather than rushing upon, the lines of the enemy, which, indeed, they did not see for smoke till involved among their weapons. . . . It was a moment of dreadful, agonizing suspense, but only a moment; for the whirlwind does not reap the forest with greater rapidity than the Highlanders cleared the line. They swept through and over that frail barrier almost as easily and instantaneously as the bounding cavalcade brushes through the morning labours of the gossamer which stretch across its path; not, however, with the same unconsciousness of the event. Almost every man in their front rank, chief and gentleman, fell before the deadly weapons which they had braved; and, although the enemy gave way, it was not till every bayonet was bent and bloody with the strife.

"When the first line had been completely swept aside, the assailants continued their impetuous advance till they came near the second, when, being almost annihilated by a profuse and well-directed fire, the shattered remains of what had been but an hour before a numerous and confident force, at last submitted to destiny by giving way and flying. Still a few rushed on, resolved rather to die than thus forfeit their well-acquired and dearly estimated honour. They rushed on, but not a man ever came in contact with the enemy. The last survivor perished as he reached the points of the bayonets."

According to various historians, the havoc which was made among the poor Highlanders, at the close of the battle, was dreadful in the extreme. In some places of the field their bodies lay in layers three or four deep; and many of the survivors were treated with the greatest inhumanity by the reckless soldiers of the Duke.* Many of the vanquished, who escaped death on the field of battle, were taken prisoners, among whom was the Earl of Kilmarnock, who, according to the *Culloden Papers*, had received a wound in the engagement. In the confusion of the flight, or by the wind—for the weather was tempestuous—his hat had fallen from his head, and he was escorted bareheaded along the lines of the royal army. His eldest son, who was an ensign in the King's service at the same combat, with feelings of pity and affection beheld him in that condition; and, at the risk of incurring the displeasure of his fellow-officers, he flew from the ranks, and, with his own hat, covered the head of his unfortunate father from the storm. Many eyes, it is said, were suffused with tears on witnessing this noble act of filial regard on the part of the youthful lord.†

The Earl of Kilmarnock, with other prisoners of distinction, was carried to London and imprisoned in the Tower.‡ A bill

---

* In a letter by one of the victors, published in the *Scots Magazine* for April, 1746, this sentence occurs: "The moor was covered with blood; and our men, by killing the enemy, dabbling their feet in the blood, and splashing it about one another, looked like so many butchers!"

† See Chambers's *Rebellion*. Another anecdote, also honourable to the memory of this young nobleman, may be related. Nineteen Highland officers, who had been severely wounded in the conflict, were afterwards found sheltered in the vicinity of Culloden House, and led forth to be shot. One of them, named Fraser, though he received a ball, did not expire. The butt of a musket was then applied to his head in order to despatch him, and he was left for dead on the ground. Soon after, Lord Boyd happened to pass the spot where he lay, and, moved with compassion for the unhappy man, who still showed symptoms of life, got him "conveyed to a secure place, where he recovered in the course of three months."—*See Griffin's Jacobite Minstrelsy.*

‡ The news of the defeat of Prince Charles and his followers, at Culloden, was received, it would appear, with much satisfaction in Kilmarnock. In the Town Treasurer's Book is the following entry: "Acct of Entertainment at Rejoicing on the victory at Colodin fight, to Will. Walker, May, 1746, £17 Scots." About the same time, the Duke of Cumberland's birth-day was celebrated here, and £7 10s. Scots expended by the bailies and councillors on the occasion.

of indictment having been found against him, he was brought to trial along with the Earl of Cromarty and Lord Balmerino, on Monday, the 28th of July, 1746, in Westminster-hall, which had been fitted up with great magnificence for the occasion. Unusual pomp was also displayed in the assembling of the Judges, the Lord High Steward, and the Peers, of whom a hundred and thirty-six were present. The "Rebel Lords," as they were called in the newspapers and magazines of the time, were brought from the Tower in coaches, alongside of which a strong military force marched as a guard. In the coaches with the prisoners were the Deputy-Governor of the Tower, Captain Marshall, and Mr Fowler (the gentleman-jailer), with the axe, which was covered, along with him. The court being assembled, and the sergeant-at-arms having made proclamation for the bodies of the prisoners, they were led to the bar accompanied by the gentleman-jailer, who carried the axe with its edge turned from them. The indictment of the Earl of Kilmarnock was then read, to which he pleaded guilty, and recommended himself to the mercy of the King. The other two lords being also found guilty, the court adjourned till the 30th, when sentence would be pronounced; and the prisoners, "with the edge of the axe turned towards them," were conducted back to the Tower.

On the day appointed the court again met, and the Lord High Steward* put the following question to each of the prisoners: "Have you anything to offer why judgment of death should not pass against you?" The Earl of Kilmarnock acknowledged the heinousness of the crime with which he

* "The Chancellor [Hardwicke] was Lord High Steward; but though a most comely personage with a fine voice, his behaviour was mean, curiously searching for occasion to bow to the minister [Mr Pelham], that is no peer, and consequently applying to the other ministers, in a manner, for their orders; and not even ready at the ceremonial. To the prisoners he was peevish; and instead of keeping up to the humane dignity of the law of England, whose character it is to point out favour to the criminal, he crossed them, and almost scolded at any offer they made towards defence."—*Walpole's Letters to Sir Horace Mann.*

was charged, confessed his guilt, and threw himself upon the sympathy and compassion of the court, whom he implored to intercede with his Majesty in his behalf. He alluded to the unsullied character of his ancestors; to the services rendered by his father in the support of the House of Hanover, and in the promotion of revolution principles; and to his own adherence and fidelity to those principles up till the moment at which he had been seduced to join in the Rebellion. He also alluded to the services of his eldest son in the cause of his Majesty; to the hatred of Popery and arbitrary power which he had instilled into his mind; "and is it possible," he asked, "that my endeavours in his education would have been successful, if I had not myself been sincere in those principles, and an enemy to those measures which have involved me and my family in ruin? Had my mind at that time been tainted with disloyalty and disaffection, I could not have dissembled so closely with my own family, but some tincture would have devolved to my children." He then pleaded that he had bought no arms, nor had raised a single man for the cause of the Pretender; that, when engaged with the rebels, he had not unfrequently made himself useful to his Majesty's subjects, by assisting such persons as were sick or wounded among the prisoners they had taken; that he separated from his corps at the battle of Culloden, and surrendered himself when he might have made his escape;* "but, my lords," he concluded, "if all I have offered is not a sufficient motive to your lordships to induce you to employ your interest with his Majesty in my behalf, I shall lay down my life with the utmost resignation, and my last moments shall be employed in fervent prayers for the preservation of

* His lordship afterwards acknowledged—and earnestly desired it might be published to the world—that this declaration was false; that he had no intention of *surrendering*; and that the party of the King's troops, towards whom he advanced, he had mistaken for *Fitz-James's horse*, with whom he intended to make his escape. —*See Foster's Account.*

the illustrious House of Hanover, and the peace and prosperity of Great Britain."

Notwithstanding these seemingly sincere sentiments of contrition for his errors, the Earl of Kilmarnock unfortunately found no favour from the court. At the close of the trial the Lord High Steward made a speech to the prisoners, and concluded by pronouncing sentence in the following words: "The judgment of the law is, and this high court doth award, that you, William Earl of Kilmarnock, George Earl of Cromarty, and Arthur Lord Balmerino, and every of you, return to the prison of the Tower from whence you came; from thence you must be drawn to the place of execution; when you come there, you must be hanged by the neck, but not till you are dead, for you must be cut down alive; then your bowels must be taken out, and burnt before your faces; then your heads must be severed from your bodies; and your bodies must be divided each into four quarters, and these must be at the King's disposal. And God Almighty be merciful to your souls."*

Petitions containing statements similar to those embodied in his speech at the trial were afterwards presented by the Earl of Kilmarnock to the King, the Prince of Wales, and the Duke of Cumberland. A petition was also sent to government in his behalf by the Town Council of Kilmarnock. His old family teacher, too, Professor Moor (mentioned in Chapter II), travelled all the way to London to intercede for him with persons of distinction; and it is said that his unhappy lady hastened thither for the same purpose; but none of these efforts had the effect of producing any mitigation of his sentence.† It is generally thought, however, that his life

---

* In cases of high treason this awful sentence is usually pronounced, but the most ignominious parts of it are generally remitted to persons of high rank.

† James, the sixth Duke of Hamilton, also exerted himself to procure a pardon for the Earl. Walpole says: "Duke Hamilton, who has never been at Court,

would have been spared had not the Duke of Cumberland believed that he had sanctioned an order which was issued by the leaders of the insurgents, and signed "George Murray," to give no quarter to the King's troops. That the Earl had no hand in that matter, he emphatically declared in his petition to the Duke, and also to his fellow-sufferer, Lord Balmerino, at their last interview, in presence of the Rev. Mr Foster and others, on the day of his execution.

The appearance of the Earl at his trial is thus described by the Honourable Horace Walpole, who was present: "Lord Kilmarnock is tall and slender, with an extreme fine person; his behaviour a most just mixture between dignity and submission; if in anything to be reprehended, a little affected, and his hair too exactly dressed for a man in his situation; but when I say this it is not to find fault with him, but to show how little fault there was to be found." The same authority states that "Lord Kilmarnock, with the greatest nobleness of soul, desired to have Lord Cromarty preferred to himself for pardon, if there could be but one saved."

<small>designs to kiss the King's hand, and ask Lord Kilmarnock's life. The King is much inclined to some mercy; but the Duke [of Cumberland], who has not so much of Cæsar after a victory as in gaining it, is for the utmost severity. It was lately proposed in the city to present him with the freedom of some company; one of the aldermen said aloud, 'Then let it be of the *Butchers!*'"</small>

CHAPTER IX.

Pitied by gentle hearts, Kilmarnock died.
JOHNSON.

He died, as erring man should die,
Without display—without parade.
BYRON.

THE Earl of Kilmarnock was attended from the 7th August till within a few minutes of his execution, by Mr James Foster, an eminent dissenting clergyman, who published an interesting account of his behaviour after his sentence. From that work, which is before us, this unfortunate nobleman appears to have been of a mild and benevolent disposition, and altogether guileless and ingenuous in his confessions. He assured Mr Foster "that, in the hours of his confinement and solitude, he had felt the crime of rebellion lie as a severe and heavy load upon his soul; and particularly upon these two accounts, which were peculiar aggravations of his guilt, that he had been a rebel against his conscience and inward principles, and in violation of his oath, solemnly and often repeated." When asked by Mr Foster what could be his *motive* for engaging in the Rebellion against his conscience, he said, " that the true root of all was his careless and dissolute life, by which he had reduced himself to great and perplexing difficulties ;* that the exigency

* Walpole, alluding, in one of his letters, to the Earl's straitened circumstances, says: "I don't know whether I told you that the man at the Tennis Court protests that he has known him [Lord Kilmarnock] dine with the man that sells pamphlets at Storey's Gate; 'and,' says he, 'he would often have been glad if I would have taken him home to dinner.' He was certainly so poor, that in one of his wife's intercepted letters she tells him she has plagued their steward for a fortnight for money, and can get but three shillings." This is surely exaggeration. According to accounts published at the time, the Earl gave a purse containing five guineas to his executioner.

of his affairs was in particular very pressing at the time of the Rebellion; and that, besides the general hope he had of mending his fortune by the success of it, he was also tempted by another prospect of retrieving his circumstances, if he followed the Pretender's standard." On Mr Foster telling him "that by joining the rebels he had not only attacked the personal rights of the King and his illustrious house, but endeavoured to destroy the national happiness, and frustrate the hopes of posterity; that he had been instrumental in diffusing consternation and terror through the land, obstructing commerce, giving a shock to the public credit, in the spoliation and ruin of his country; and ought to consider himself as an accessory to innumerable *private* oppressions and murders: His lordship added, with a sensible concern, *Yea, and murders of the innocent too!*" When talking of Prince Charles and the Popish religion, he said "that he himself was never, in the utmost heat of his rebellion, a well-wisher to tyrannical power and Popery, which *last* he could never embrace, without entirely renouncing his understanding as a man." On the subject of death he spoke calmly and rationally, like one who had been weaned from the world by the soothing influence of true religion; and when he did allude to the scenes of gaiety and pleasure in which he had mingled, it was apparently with no desire to taste again their deluding joys, but to point out the rock on which he had been wrecked and ruined. When told that the warrant for his execution had come, and that the day fixed was the 18th, he evinced almost no perturbation of mind; but seemed more concerned for the consequences of death than for the thing itself, of which, he said, "he had no great reason to be terrified; for that the stroke appeared to be scarce so much as the pain of drawing a tooth, or the first shock of the cold-bath upon a weak and fearful temper."

A minute detail of all the solemn and appalling circumstances that would attend his execution was given him by

General Williamson, to which he listened without betraying any inward emotion. Among other things, he was informed that the coffin would be in a mourning hearse, close to the scaffold, so that when the head was struck off, it would be ready to receive it; to which his lordship said, that he thought it would be better for the coffin to be placed upon the scaffold, for, by that means, the body would be sooner removed out of sight. He was also told that the executioner was not only expert, but a very good sort of man. "General," exclaimed the Earl, "this is one of the worst circumstances you could have mentioned; for I cannot thoroughly like, for such work, your good sort of men: one of that character, I apprehend, must be tender-hearted and compassionate, and a rougher and less sensible temper might, perhaps, be fitter to be employed." He then desired "that four persons might be appointed to receive the head in a red cloth when it was severed from the body, so that it might not, as he had been informed was the case in some former executions, roll about the scaffold and be thereby mangled and disfigured; adding, that though this was, in comparison, but a small circumstance, he was not willing that his body should appear with any unnecessary indecency after the just sentence of the law was satisfied." Mr Foster, with the view of strengthening his mind for the awful scene that awaited him, advised him "to think frequently on the outward *apparatus* and *formalities* that would attend his death;" and this he appears to have done; for, on the morning of his execution, he agreed with the reverend gentleman, "that they were not so terrible in themselves, as the dying after a dispiriting and lingering distemper, in a silent, melancholy, darkened room, with languid and exhausted spirits, and his friends standing round him with lively marks of sorrow and anguish in their countenances, expecting and deploring his fate."

"I now come," says Mr Foster, "to the conclusion of this

dismal scene—his behaviour on the day of his execution. I attended him in the morning about eight o'clock, and found him in a most calm and happy temper, without any disturbance or confusion of mind, and with apparent marks of ease and serenity in his aspect. . . . I had observed to him, that to affect to brave death, when he justly suffered for his crimes, could have no show of true decorum in it—and that, to manifest no concern at all, where the consequence was so awful and the stake infinite, was in some degree unbecoming even in the best of men—that not to fear at all where there was any great reason to fear, was altogether as absurd as to be extremely dejected and pusillanimous where there was ground of hope—and that true penitence was always humble and cautious, and not bold and arrogant. He assented to all this, and told me further, that for a man who had led a dissolute life, and yet believed the consequences of death, to put on such an air of daringness and absolute intrepidity, must argue him either to be very stupid or very impious. . . . He continued all the morning of his execution in the same uniform temper, unruffled, and without any sudden vicissitudes and starts of passion. This remarkably appeared, when soon after I had, at his own desire, made a short prayer with him, General Williamson came to inform him that the sheriffs waited for the prisoners. At receiving this awful summons to go to death he was not in the least startled, but said calmly and gracefully, '*General, I am ready; I'll follow you.*' At the foot of the first stairs he met and embraced Balmerino, who said to him, 'My lord, I am heartily sorry to have your company in this expedition.' From thence he walked, with the usual formalities, to the Tower-gate, and (after being delivered into the custody of the sheriffs), to the house* provided on Tower-hill, with a serenity, mildness, and dignity, that greatly surprised and affected the spectators."

* This house was about thirty yards from the scaffold.

After passing a short time in conversation with Balmerino, and in prayer with Mr Foster and others, "Lord Kilmarnock took his last farewell of the gentlemen who attended him in a very affectionate manner, and went out of the room, preceded by the sheriffs and accompanied by his friends. And I am informed," continues Mr Foster, "of the following particular by Mr Home, that as he was stepping into the scaffold, notwithstanding the great pains he had taken to familiarize the outward apparatus of death to his mind, nature still recurred upon him; so that being struck with such a variety of dreadful objects at once—the multitude, the block, his coffin, the executioner, the instrument of death—he turned about and said, 'Home, *this is terrible.*' This expression, so suitable to the awful occasion, must, to all who know the human heart, appear to be nothing else than the language of nature, and was far from being a mark of unmanly fear; being pronounced with a steady countenance and firmness of voice, indications of a mind unbroken and not disconcerted. His whole behaviour was so humble and resigned, that not only his friends, but every spectator was deeply moved; even the executioner burst into tears, and was obliged to use artificial spirits to support and strengthen him. After having talked with his lordship a considerable time, to support him in his penitence and resignation, I embraced, and left him in the same calm disposition, having quitted the scaffold some minutes before his execution."

What remains to be told of this mournful scene we will give in the words of Mr Jameson, another Presbyterian minister, who attended him till his last moment: "My lord's hair having been dressed in a bag, it took some time to undo it, and put it up in his cap. The tucking his shirt under the waistcoat, that it might not obstruct the blow, was the occasion of some further small delay. But as soon as these preliminaries were adjusted, his lordship gave the executioner notice what should be the signal, took out a paper containing the heads of his devotion, went forward to his last stage, and decently knelt down at the block. Whether it was to support himself, or as a more convenient posture for devotion, he happened to lay his hands with his head upon the block, which the executioner observing, prayed his lordship to let his hands fall down, lest they should be mangled or break the blow. Then he was told that the neck of his waistcoat was in the way, upon which he rose up, and with the help of one of his friends—Mr Walkinshaw of Scotston—had it taken off. This done, and the neck made bare to the shoulder, he again knelt down as before. And what sufficiently shows that he enjoyed full presence of mind to the last, Mr Home's servant, who held the cloth to receive the head, heard him direct the executioner that in two minutes he would give the signal. That dreadful interval, to his friends, who were then upon the rack, appeared much longer, but those who measured found it just about two minutes. This time he spent in most fervent devotion, as appeared by the motion of his hands, and now and then of his head; having then fixed his neck on the block, he gave the signal, his body remained without the least motion, except what was given it by the stroke of death, which he received full, and was thereby happily eased at once of all his pain."* His

* "From a rare contemporary print of the execution of Lord Kilmarnock, it appears that the scaffold was very small, and that there were not above six or seven persons upon it at the time his lordship submitted to the block. The block—which is still preserved and shown in the Tower—is a piece of wood considerably higher than may be generally supposed; the culprit only requiring to kneel and bend a little forward, in order to bring his neck a little over it. The cloth, which originally covered the surrounding rails, is turned up in such a manner as to give the spectators below an uninterrupted view of the scene. The culprit appears kneeling at the block, without his coat and waistcoat, and the frill of his shirt hanging down. The figures upon the scaffold, all, except one of fearfully important character, are dressed in full dark suits of the fashion of King George the Second's reign, and most of them have white handkerchiefs at their eyes, and express, by their attitudes, a violent degree of grief."—*History of the Rebellion, by R. Chambers.*

In a print of the execution in our possession, which was published according to

lordship's remains were, according to his own request, interred in the evening, close to the Marquis of Tullibardine's, in the church of St Peter. On the coffin were these words: "GULIELMUS COMES DE KILMARNOCK, DECOLLATUS 18° AUGUSTI 1746, ÆTAT. SUÆ 42."

Mr Walkinshaw of Scotston, as he is called in the above paragraph, was Colonel John Walkinshaw Craufurd of Craufurdland, in this parish. He was on terms of the closest intimacy with the Earl, and, besides holding the cloth to receive his head, he performed the last melancholy duty of a friend by getting him interred.* For this service, which

Act of Parliament in 1747, nine or ten persons in all appear upon the scaffold. The crowd of spectators is immense. Many are seen on stands apparently erected for the purpose; others are perched at the windows, and on the roofs of the various buildings connected with, and in the immediate neighbourhood of, the Tower, and some are observed clinging to the masts of ships in the river. A strong body of military, including both horse and foot, are thrown, as described in the *Scots Magazine* of the time, "into the form of a battledore, the round part enclosing the scaffold, and the handle, formed by two lines, extending to the Tower-gate."

In another curious old print, in the possession of a townsman, which shows the execution itself more prominently, about seventeen individuals are seen on the scaffold. The culprit is kneeling at the block, and the executioner, who is dressed in white, is standing beside him, in a bending position, with the axe uplifted ready to strike. The coffin is lying on the scaffold; the mourning hearse is waiting near ready to receive it; and, as in the other picture, a great many spectators appear on the tops of the houses in the neighbourhood, while a dense multitude fills up the foreground.

* A local anecdote is told of these two gentlemen and David Rankine, the rhyming blacksmith of Kilmarnock, as he was sometimes called. The colonel and his lordship were walking one day near Dean Castle, when they espied Rankine coming towards them carrying a bundle of straw. Wishing to draw from him some witty saying (for he was ever ready with his answers), they cried *boo* as he approached. The blacksmith looked at them for a moment, and then, apparently without the smallest effort, breathed forth the following satirical doggerel:

"There goes Craufurdland and Lord Boyd,
Of grace and manners they are void;
For, like the *Bill* among the kye,
They *boo* at folk as they gang bye."

He then threw the straw towards them, exclaiming, "Hae, beasts! there's a buttle o' strae to ye!" His lordship and the colonel were so well pleased with the extemporaneous effusion, that they instantly gave a piece of money to the author, who, after thanking them for their kindness, trudged on his way, inwardly congratulating himself on his good fortune.

was purely that of friendship, he was put to the bottom of the army list. He afterwards rose to the rank of major, and latterly to that of lieutenant-colonel. He died in 1793, aged seventy-two.

Soon after the Earl's death, his eldest son, Lord Boyd, who was then residing in Kilmarnock, where the family was much respected,* transmitted the following letter to the Colonel, at Scarborough, thanking him in feeling terms for his attention to his unfortunate father. The original MS. is in the possession of W. H. Craufurd, Esq. of Craufurdland:

"MY DEAR JOHN,—I had yours last post, and I don't know in what words to express how much I am obliged to you for doing the last duties to my unfortunate father; you knew him perfectly well, that he was the best of friends, the most affectionate husband, and the tenderest parent. Poor Lady Kilmarnock bears her loss much better than I could have imagined; but it was entirely owing to her being prepared several days before she got the melancholy accounts of it. I shall be here for some time, as I have a good deal of business to do in this country; so I shall be extremely glad to see you as soon as possible. I am, my dear John, your sincere friend and obedient humble servant,

"BOYD.

"KILMARNOCK [HOUSE], AUGUST 27, 1746."

According to a declaration made by the Earl, during his confinement, to his solicitor, Mr Ross, and to the Reverend and Honourable Mr Home, Lady Kilmarnock had no hand in exciting him to join in the Rebellion, but on the contrary had endeavoured to dissuade him from taking such a course. After his death she brooded in deepest melancholy over his fate. In a secluded avenue, called "The Lady's Walk," which we have already noticed, and part of which yet remains in the vicinity of Kilmarnock House, she was wont to wander alone, with downcast looks, and pour forth the sorrows of her heart. She died of grief at Kilmarnock, 16th September, 1747.

* As somewhat illustrative of this respect, the following traditionary anecdote may be related: A *flying stationer* came to the burgh, and began to hawk a paper containing an account of the Earl's execution; but the inhabitants, notwithstanding their disapproval of the part which he had taken in the Rebellion, felt indignant at hearing his name bawled aloud through the streets in connection with a subject so ignominious, and, rising in a mass, they mobbed the poor hawker to such a degree, that, for the preservation of his life, he was forced to hasten out of the burgh.

The following extract from her ladyship's "Testament Dative" shows her pecuniary circumstances at the time of her death. "It is to be remarked, however," as observed by Paterson, from whom we quote it, "that inventories of this kind were usually made up upon the lowest calculation, in order to avoid legacy-duty:"

"INVENTORY.

"There pertained and belonged to the said deceased Anna Countess of Kilmarnock, the time of her death foresaid, the particular goods and gear following, valued at the particular prices aftermentioned, viz. In the first, four cows, valued at one hundred and eighteen pounds Scots. Item, an hay-stack, at fifty-four pound Scots. Item, a little corn-stack, at twenty-four pound ten shilling Scots. Item, the whole furniture, utensils and domicils in and about the defunct's house at Kilmarnock, at two hundred and twenty-one pound Scots.

"Summa of the Inventory of the goods and gear is...........iv.c xviii.lb. x.s. Scots.

"In the next place, there was indebted and owing to the said defunct the time of her death foresaid, the sum of five hundred and seventy-four pound Scots money, arrears of her fortune on the lands and barony of Kilmarnock, due and resting for the one-half of cropt mvijc and forty-seven years and precedings.

"Summa of the Inventory of the debts is............................v.c lxxiv.lb. Scots.

"Summa of the Inventory of the goods and debts is........ix.c lxxxxi.lb. x.s. „

"Confirmation granted hereon in *Co. forma* by William Weir, commissar-depute, and Alex. Stevenson, clerk of the commissariat of Glasgow, at Glasgow, the fifth day of March, mvijc and forty-eight years."

Lord Kilmarnock, while in prison, wrote a letter to his eldest son, and another to his factor, Boyd Paterson, Esq. The latter of these is in the possession of Mr Paterson's great-grandson, M. T. Paterson, Esq., who has kindly permitted us to copy it. In a striking manner it exhibits the sterling honesty of the writer; and, on that account, we insert it in our pages, convinced that it will be perused with considerable interest. It is as follows:

"SIR,—I have commended to your care the enclosed Packet to be delivered to my Wife, in the manner your good sense shall dictate to you will be least shocking to her. Let her be prepared for it as much by degrees and with great tenderness as the nature of the thing will admit of. The entire dependence I have all my life had the most just reason to have on your integrity and friendship to my Wife and Family, as well as to myself, makes me desire that the enclosed Papers may come to my wife through your hands, in confidence that you will take all pains to comfort her and relieve the grief I know she will be in, that you and her friends can. She is what I leave dearest behind me in the World, and the greatest service you can do to your dead Friend is to contribute as much as possible to her happiness in mind and in her affairs.

"You will peruse the State before you deliver it to her, and you will observe that there is a fund of hers I don't mention, that of 500 Scots a year as the Interest of my mother-in-law's Portion, in the Countess of Errol's hands, with I believe a considerable arrear upon it; which as I have ordered a copy of all these papers to that Countess, I did not care to put in. There is another thing, of a good deal of moment, which I mention only to you, because, if it could be taken away without noise it would be better; but if it is pushed, it will be necessary to defend it: that is a Bond which you know Mr Kerr, director to the Chancery, has of me for a considerable sum of money, with many years' Interest on it, which was almost all Play Debt. I don't think I ever had fifty pounds or the half of it, of Mr Kerr's money, and I'm sure I never had a hundred, which however I have put it to in the enclosed Declaration, that my mind may be entirely at ease. My intention, with respect to that sum, was to wait till I had some money, and then buy it off by a composition of three hundred pounds, and if that was not accepted of, to defend it; in which I neither saw, nor now see, anything unjust, and I now leave it on my successors to do what they find most prudent in it.

"Beside my personal Debts mentioned in general and particular in the State, there is one for which I am liable in justice, if it is not paid, owing to poor people who gave their Work for it by my orders. It was at Elgin in Murray, the Regiment I commanded wanted shoes. I commissioned something about seventy pair of shoes and brogues, which might come to about 3s. or three and sixpence each, one with another. The Magistrates divided them among the shoemakers of the Town and Country, and each shoemaker furnished his proportion. I drew on the Town, for the Price, out of the Composition laid on them, but I was told afterwards at Inverness that, it was believed, the Composition was otherwise applied, and the poor shoemakers not paid. As these poor People wrought by my orders, it will be a great ease to my heart to think they are not to lose by me, as too many have done in the course of that year, but had I lived I might have made some inquiry after: but now it is impossible, as their hardships in loss of horses and such things, which happened through my soldiers, are so interwoven with what was done by other people, that it would be very hard, if not impossible, to separate them. If you'll write to Mr Innes of Dalkinty at Elgin (with whom I was quartered when I lay there), he will send you an account of the shoes, and if they were paid to the shoemakers or no; and if they are not, I beg you'll get my Wife, or my Successors to pay them when they can. . . . .

"Accept of my sincere thanks for your friendship and good services to me. Continue them to my Wife and Children. My best wishes are to you and yours, and for the happiness and prosperity of the good Town of Kilmarnock; and I am, Sir, your humble Servant,

"Kilmarnock.

"Tower of London, Augt 16, 1746."

The letter to his son was written on the day previous to his execution. We cannot refrain from presenting it to our readers; for, besides giving us a glimpse of the *heart* and *mind* of the unfortunate nobleman, it inculcates instruction of the highest importance:

"TOWER, 17TH AUGUST, 1746.

"DEAR BOYD,—I must take this way to bid you farewell, and I pray God may for ever bless you and guide you in this world, and bring you to a happy immortality in the world to come. I must likewise give you my last advice. Seek God in your youth, and when you are old he will not depart from you. Be at pains to acquire good habits now, that they may grow up and become strong in you. Love mankind, and do justice to all men. Do good to as many as you can, and neither shut your ears nor your purse to those in distress whom it is in your power to relieve. Believe me, you will find more joy in one beneficent action, and in your cool mornings you will be more happy with the reflection of having made any one person so, who, without your assistance, would have been miserable, than in the enjoyment of all the pleasures of sense—which pall in the using—and of all the pomps and gaudy shows of the world. Live within your circumstances, by which means you will have it in your power to do good to others. . . . Prefer the public interests to your own, wherever they interfere. Love your family and your children, when you have any; but never let your regard for them drive you on the rock I split upon, when on that account I departed from my principles, and brought the guilt of rebellion on my head, for which I am now under the sentence justly due to my crime. Use all your interest to get your brother pardoned, and brought home as soon as possible, that his circumstances and bad influence of those he is among may not induce him to accept of foreign service, and lose him both to his country and his family. If money can be found to support him, I wish you would advise him to go to Geneva, where his principles of religion and liberty will be confirmed, and where he may stay till you see if a pardon can be procured him. As soon as Commodore Barnet comes home, inquire for your brother Billie, and take care of him on my account. I must again recommend your unhappy mother to you. Comfort her, and take all the care you can of your brothers; and may God, of his infinite mercy, preserve, guide, and conduct you and them through all the vicissitudes of this life, and after it, bring you to the habitations of the just, and make you happy in the enjoyment of Himself to all eternity."

Lord Boyd, to whom this letter was addressed, served in the Scots Fusileers at the battle of Culloden. By a trust deed, dated 1732, and confirmed by the House of Peers in 1752, he recovered the lands of Kilmarnock, which had been forfeited, and which he afterwards sold to the Earl of Glencairn.* On the death of his grand-aunt, the Countess

* The first of the Earls of Glencairn, whose surname was Cunninghame, had the title conferred on him in 1488. His grandfather, Sir William Cunninghame, founded, in 1403, the collegiate church of Kilmaurs, near which are the remains of a richly-sculptured cemetery, that belonged to the family. Their ancient residence stood at a little distance from Kilmaurs, on the farm of Jock's Thorn, on the left side of the road leading from Kilmarnock to Stewarton. The estate of Kilmarnock

of Errol in her own right, he succeeded to the title of Earl of Errol in 1758. His brother, Charles Boyd, for whose welfare his father's solicitude is evinced in the above epistle, was also engaged in the combat of Drummossie Moor, but on the side of the rebels. He fled to the Island of Arran, the ancient property of the Boyds, where he concealed himself for a year. He afterwards went to the continent, where he married a French lady, and resided for about twenty years; and a pardon by that time having been granted to all the rebels, he returned to Scotland. In 1773 the celebrated Dr Johnson and his friend Boswell, when on their tour to the Hebrides, spent some hours with him and his brother, the Earl of Errol, at his seat of Slains Castle, in Aberdeenshire. "The house," says Boswell, "is built quite upon the shore; the windows look upon the main ocean; and the King of Denmark is Lord Errol's nearest neighbour on the north-east." Here the great colossus of literature met with a kind reception—was shown some fine prints, a portrait of the Earl by Sir Joshua Reynolds, a large collection of books, and some natural curiosities in the vicinity, with which he was much pleased. In the conversation of Mr Charles Boyd, the fastidious Johnson thought "there was too much elaboration;" and, on being told that Lady

was purchased by William, thirteenth Earl of Glencairn. He died in 1775. His son James, the fourteenth Earl, was the kind and principal patron of the poet Burns. His death, which took place in 1791, was lamented by the bard in strains, the poetic beauty and melting pathos of which have rarely been equalled:

"The bridegroom may forget the bride
  Was made his wedded wife yestreen,
The monarch may forget the crown
  That on his head an hour has been,
The mother may forget the child
  That smiles sae sweetly on her knee;
But I'll remember thee, Glencairn,
  And a' that thou hast done for me!"

This accomplished nobleman, being unmarried, was succeeded by his only brother, John, the fifteenth Earl of Glencairn; he likewise had no issue, and at his death, in 1796, the title became dormant.

Errol used no force or fear in educating her children, he exclaimed, "She is wrong;" and strenuously argued that the "rod" was most effective in making a child do its duty.

The advice of their father—"do good to others"—appears to have been acted upon by the Earl and his brother. Boswell informs us that the latter, who had acquired a knowledge of physic by poring over some medical books which he had accidentally met with when in Arran, was often useful to the poor in cases of sickness and distress; and the same author relates an anecdote of the former, which places his character in an amiable and benevolent light. "Lord Errol, who has a very large family, resolved to have a surgeon of his own. With this view he educated one of his tenant's sons, who is now settled in a very neat house and farm just by, which we saw from the road. By the salary which the Earl allows him, and by the practice which he has had, he is in very easy circumstances. He had kept an exact account of all that had been laid out on his education; and he came to his lordship one day, and told him that he had arrived at a much higher situation than ever he expected; that he was now able to pay what he had advanced, and begged he would accept of it. The Earl was pleased with the generous gratitude and genteel offer of the man; but refused it."

There is a tradition that, some years after his father's death, this nobleman visited Kilmarnock, so long the property and residence of his illustrious ancestors. The Dean Castle, the scene, we believe, of his own boyhood, he hastened to survey. At the head of the town his eye caught a view of its venerable walls. He paused to gaze upon them for a moment—painful associations were awakened within him—the remembrance of his father's unhappy fate rushed upon his mind—he could go no farther; but, bursting into tears, turned hurriedly away from the scene. He died at Callander House in the year 1778. The gifted Dr Beattie, author of *The Minstrel*, thus speaks of him: "He exerted his influence as a man of rank and a magistrate, in doing good to all his neighbourhood; and it has often been mentioned to his honour, that no man ever administered an oath with a more pious and commanding solemnity than he. . . . His stature was six feet four inches, and his proportions most exact. His countenance and deportment exhibited such a mixture of the sublime and graceful, as I have never seen united in any other person. He often put me in mind of an ancient hero; and I remember Dr Johnson was positive that he resembled Homer's character of Sarpedon."*

Of the history or character of the other brother, mentioned in the father's letter, we know nothing, save that he was in the Royal Navy, and was promoted in 1761 to a company of the fourteenth foot.

The present Earl of Errol, it may be added, is the direct descendant of the Boyd family, in the male line. In the Peerage of the United Kingdom he is Baron Kilmarnock of Kilmarnock.

* It may be locally interesting to state, that the Earl was elected Master of the Kilmarnock St John's Lodge of Free Masons in 1761. The following letter, thanking the Brethren for the honour they had done him, was addressed to Bailie James Paterson, one of the members:

"DEAR SIR,—I had the pleasure of yours last Friday, informing me of my being elected Master of the Kilmarnock Lodge, which I accept of with great satisfaction, as I do every mark of regard from that good town; and I beg you will, in my name, return all my Brethren my most hearty thanks. I have a most sincere affection for you all; and I wish it was in my power to show my regard for you in more than words. The time may come when it will be so; and I assure you I will most eagerly embrace the opportunity. Until I have the pleasure of attending you myself, I appoint Mr Wm Paterson my deputy. With my hearty good wishes to you all, I ever am, to every one of you, a most sincere friend and obedient servant,

"ERROL.

"EDIN., JAN. 21ST, 1761."

We may here mention, that the Earl's father, Lord Kilmarnock, was one of the originators of the Lodge in 1734, and was its first Right Worshipful Master. As a Free Mason, indeed, he appears to have been somewhat popular; for he had the honour of holding the Chair of Mother Kilwinning in 1742, and also of being elected, in the same year, to the Mastership of the Grand Lodge of Scotland.

CHAPTER X.

Tak' grey hairs and wrinkles, and hirple wi' me,
And think on the seventeen hundred and fifty.

SIR ALEXANDER BOSWELL.

THE Cross of Kilmarnock was, in early times, the site of a corn-mill, which was driven by a lade or stream that flowed through the same spot. Shilling-hill, or Sheelin-hill, near the Railway Station, was, as the name implies, the eminence on which "the kernels of the grain," to use the words of Dr Jamieson, "were separated by the wind from the husks."* Regarding the exact time of the erection of the mill we have no information. It appears, however, by the following extract from the Town Treasurer's Book, to have been removed about the beginning of the eighteenth century: "1703— June 26—Paid to Ballyie Hunter for the street wher the *miln* stood—£21 9s. 4d. Scots." We may likewise state, that the name of the last occupant of the mill was Rankin, from whom are descended the Rankins of Wardneuk, in this parish, and also David Rankin, Esq., postmaster of Kilmarnock. The Newmill, at a short distance from the town, on the banks of the Irvine, was also occupied at one time by the same Rankins, and was built, we believe, in 1703,† as a substitute for the one at the Cross; hence it obtained the name of the New Mill.

* "By every corn-mill a knoll-top, on which the kernels were winnowed from the husks, was designed the *Sheeling-hill.*"—*Agr. Surv. Peeb.*
† The late Mr Gavin Walker, miller, discovered this date on one of the stones forming part of the building.

At the time when the noble family of the Boyds ceased to have connection with Kilmarnock, namely, about the middle of the eighteenth century, the town presented a mean and inelegant appearance. The streets were crooked and narrow; the houses were low and poorly lighted; and to many of them that were two storeys high were attached outside stairs, that not only confined the already limited thoroughfares, but gave to the houses themselves a rude and clumsy aspect. The principal streets at that time were those now called High Street, Soulis Street, Fore Street, Back Street,* Croft Street, Strand Street, and Sandbed Street, which, with some buildings at the Cross, Nethertonholm, and a few back tenements and lanes, formed the whole of the town. The Cross was at that time somewhat contracted in form compared with the spacious appearance it now exhibits. A row of houses extended from Cheapside, in nearly a direct line, towards Fore Street, leaving only a narrow opening, near the site of the Tontine Buildings, that led to Croft Street, or formed part of it. A range of similar houses stood on the ground now forming the mouth of King Street; and the only outlet, in that direction, was by a road or pathway that led down to the river, between those houses and the corner of Waterloo Street. Neither was there any outlet where Duke Street now is, save a narrow path called Nailer's Close. The contracted and irregular plan on which the streets were then formed has not unfrequently called forth modern censure. It is true, they were contrived without any attention to ornament; but they doubtless served the purposes of the period at which they were built; for the trade of the place was then comparatively inconsiderable; the intercourse with other communities was also little; even carts were not in use in this county till 1726, being first employed that year (according to Aiton, in his *General View of the*

---

* This street was at one time called Smiddieraw. It is so named in the charter of the ground of the High Church.

County of Ayr), in conveying materials for the building of the bridge over the Irvine, between Kilmarnock and Riccarton.* Neither had stage-coaches been then introduced; and our worthy ancestors, in all probability, at the formation of these streets, had no thought of such vehicles.† The shops of the more wealthy merchants were chiefly in Fore Street, Croft Street, Strand Street, and at the Cross, but were scarcely so attractive in their appearance as those of many of our less opulent merchants of the present day.

At a very early period Kilmarnock was noted not only for the manufacture of bonnets, but for its stockings and other woollen fabrics. According to Loch's *Essays on the Trades and Fisheries of Scotland*, the woollen manufacture was introduced, about the year 1728, by a Miss Maria Gardiner (half-aunt to the late Lord Kilmarnock), who, through a praiseworthy spirit of patriotism, and for the encouragement of useful arts, brought spinners and weavers of carpets from the town of Dalkeith, then distinguished for its woollen products. Under the encouraging auspices of this lady the woollen or carpet trade, which is now one of our chief sources of wealth, increased, comparatively speaking, to a considerable extent; and we feel somewhat surprised that her memory has not been preserved in the town by some public memorial. We also regret that it is not in our power to give a more extended notice of her. Even the place of her nativity and the time of her death are unknown to us. It appears, however, from

---

* Since the above was written, we observe, from the Town Records, that carts were used here as early as 1718. Mr Aiton, therefore, must either have been misinformed on this subject, or mistaken regarding the date.

† "In April, 1749, the first stage-coach began to run between Edinburgh and Glasgow twice a week; but this project was soon relinquished for want of employment."—*Chalmers's Caledonia.*

Even the advantages of the mail-coach were not enjoyed by the inhabitants of Kilmarnock till 1787, when, in consequence of a memorial from the Council to the Postmaster-General, the "Camperdown," as it was called, began to pass through the town on its way from Carlisle to Glasgow.

Loch's work, that she lived to an advanced age; for she was alive when it was written, namely, in 1777 or 1778, about fifty years after she had introduced the woollen manufacture.

The spirit of commercial industry, however, to which the town is indebted for its present importance, began to display itself more prominently after 1743. In this year a society was formed for establishing a woollen manufactory—the one, we believe, which is now carried on so extensively in Green Street, by Gregory, Thomsons and Company. A petition, requesting ground and liberty to raise stones from the Town's Quarries, for the purposes contemplated, was presented by the projectors to the Town Council, and met with generous encouragement. Ground was allowed them at the Greenhead for a trifling annual feu-duty, and the use of the quarries was also granted. In 1746 they likewise obtained from the Council a piece of ground whereon to build a Wauk-mill, together with liberty to erect a dam near "the foot of the Path leading to the Meal Mercat." The undertaking appears to have been in every way successful. In 1749 the Earl of Glencairn and his eldest son, "William Lord Kilmares," as he is styled in the agreement, were admitted partners in the firm. In 1765 Richard Oswald, Esq. of Auchincruive, was also enrolled as a proprietor; and among the other shareholders was the Rev. John Cunningham of Monkton. At this time the company's stock in trade amounted to six thousand one hundred and fifty pounds.

Towards the close of last century carpet-weaving was also carried on, though on a small scale, in East Netherton Street. Burns alludes to it in the *Ordination*, when he says to the Rev. Mr Robertson:

> "Or, nae reflection on your lair,
> Ye may commence a shaver,
> Or to the *Netherton* repair,
> And turn a carpet-weaver,
> Aff hand this day."

About the same period there was also in the town a considerable traffic in nightcaps, which were principally exported to Holland and worn by the Dutch seamen. In 1777, according to Loch, there were two hundred and forty looms employed in the weaving of silk, which had been introduced seven years before that date.* There were likewise sixty-six looms employed in the weaving of carpets, forty in the weaving of linen, thirty in the weaving of blankets, thirty in the weaving of serges and shalloons, twenty in the weaving of duffles, and six frames for the making of stockings. The blankets were made by Robert Thomson and Company from the wool of our own country, and, except in the quality of the material, were equal, it is said, to those manufactured in England. There were likewise two tanyards in the town, and the shoe trade was carried on somewhat extensively. The goods for export were shipped from Irvine to Greenock, and from that place to foreign countries. The principal manufacturers or merchants were James Wilson and Son,† and Messrs Parker, Hunter and Smith. The number of adults at that time, 1777, in the parish, amounted to 4500.

Of what are called public buildings, there were none save the Old Town-house, already mentioned, the Meal Market, and the Low and High Churches. The first of these buildings, as formerly stated, was situated west from the Cross, nearly opposite the present Crown Hotel. It was a gloomy-looking structure, two storeys high, with a small "Bell-house," and

* In a petition from the magistrates, in 1776, to the Lords of Council and Session, anent the feuing of part of the Town Green (see Appendix) mention is made of the silk manufactory being then in a flourishing condition.

† "The Woollen Factory in Kilmarnock is now carried on under the firm of Wilson, Gregory and Co., who manufacture the following articles, viz.: Blankets of all sizes, in the English and Scotch manner, Dutch and Canada Blankets, Plush, Damask, and all kinds of Scotch Carpets, Narrow Tweeled Cloths of different colours, Horse and Collar Cloths fit for saddlers."—*Glasgow Mercury*, 24*th December*, 1778.

shops on the ground floor, facing the street.* The bell that belonged to it is still used in the present Council-house, and bears this inscription: "This bell was gifted by the Earl of Kilmarnock to the town of Kilmarnock for their Council-house. A.M., Edin. 1711." Down a lane at the west end of the building was the Thieves' Hole, formerly mentioned; and above were two dungeon-like apartments, called the Tolbooth, at the stairhead of which hung the *juggs* or iron collar, in which petty delinquents were doomed to stand for a given time, exposed to the gaze of the multitude. The part of the upper flat nearest the Cross formed the Hall or Court-house,† the entrance to which was by a broad outside stair faced with a parapet. From the head of this stair the whole of the market-place was seen; and here, on public occasions, such as Kings' birthdays, the Bailies and Councillors, accompanied sometimes by the lord of the manor, would assemble to drink his Majesty's health, and give other loyal and patriotic toasts.‡ The Old Tolbooth was taken down about the beginning of the present century.

* As affording some idea of the rents realized about 1720 for these places of traffic, it may be stated that the "little shop under the Council-house stair," as the Records express it, was let that year to William Aitkene, cooper, for £8 Scots.

† A curious and elaborately carved mantelpiece, which belonged to the Old Court-house, has been preserved by being built into one of the rooms of the present Council Chambers.

‡ One of these rejoicings, which took place when George the Third was proclaimed King, is thus recorded in the Town's Books:

"31st Oct., 1760.—The said day the Council received the news of our late Sovereign King George's death, do order that his Royal Highness the Prince of Wales, his Grandson, be immediately proclaimed King under the name of King George the Third, with the usual solemnitys, and the Proclamation being drawn up and read, is approven of and signed by the Council. . . . At 4 afternoon, the above Proclamation was made accordingly, and read by Wm Paterson, Clerk, to Bailie Muir, who proclaimed it; the whole Council, ministers, and principal inhabitants of both town and neighbourhood present; and afterwards the loyal healths drunk under a discharge of three several fires from Captain Hugh Maclean's company of the Argyleshire fencible men standing in arms with their officers at the Cross. Thereafter the whole company and officers went to the Council-house, where the healths were repeated, and the night concluded with other demonstrations of joy."

The Meal Market, situated in High Street, was built in 1705, and rebuilt in 1840. Its appearance is of the plainest order. As its name indicates, it was originally appropriated for the sale of meal, and for many years was the only place in the town where the public could be supplied with that useful commodity.* Our farmers were then more homely-looking individuals than at present; they came personally to the market, where they stood on certain days of the week, cheerfully disposing of their farm produce, and showing little partiality to the difference of their customers; nor did they consider it below their dignity to retail the smallest quantity to the poorest of the poor. According to Sinclair's *Statistical Account*, published towards the close of the eighteenth century, the grain then sold here was "always a penny or three half-pence a peck cheaper than in the Glasgow or Paisley markets."

The Low or Parish Church, to which we have alluded, was taken down in 1801. Of it and the present Low Church we shall have occasion to speak afterwards. It may not be inappropriate, however, to mention here, that the Church of Kilmarnock belonged, in the olden time, as stated in Chapter I, to the Monastery of Kilwinning. "The monks," says Chalmers, "enjoyed the tithes and the other revenues, and found a curate to serve the cure. As the parish was formerly large, and a great part of it fertile, the produce of the tithes was considerable. At the Reformation the monks enjoyed, as an income from the tithes of Kilmarnock, 347 bolls, 2 firlots, and 1 peck of meal; 21 bolls, 2 firlots, and 1 peck of bere; and £33 6s. 8d. in money, being the rent of a part of the tithes, which were leased for payment of that sum yearly. The lands, which belonged to the Church of Kilmarnock, passed into lay hands after the Reformation. In 1619 Archbishop Spottiswoode, who was commendator of Kilwinning, transferred the patronage of the Church, with

* In 1757 the Council enacted that all meal be vended in the Meal Market.

the tithes of Kilmarnock, to Robert Lord Boyd, who was proprietor of the lordship of Kilmarnock; and he obtained a charter from the king of this property, in August, 1619. The patronage continued, at the end of the seventeenth century, in this family. . . . In the eighteenth century, the patronage passed from the Earl of Kilmarnock to the Earl of Glencairn, from whom it was purchased, about the year 1790, by Miss Scott, afterwards Duchess of Portland."* At present the patronage belongs to the Duke of Portland.

The following document, originally written in Latin, and translated some years ago for one of our local prints, we insert as illustrative of the ecclesiastical privileges enjoyed by the parishioners of Kilmarnock in Popish times:

"In the name of God, amen. Be it evidently known to all men by this present public instrument, that in the year of the incarnation of the Lord 1547, on the 17th, 18th, 19th, and 20th days of the month of November the sixth of the Indiction, and of the Pontificate of the Most Holy Apostolic Father and our Lord Paul III, by Divine providence Pope, the thirteenth year—In presence of us notaries public and witnesses subscribed, compeared personally the parishioners of the parish Kirk of Kilmarnock to whom the election of the parish priest thereof is known of full right to belong *(quibus electio clerici parochialis ejusdem pleno jure dignoscitur pertinere)*, namely, Allan Cunynghame, James Cunynghame, senior, John Kirkland, George Tailzeour—[Here follow the names of the other parishioners, amounting to about three hundred in number†]—neither actuated by force or fear, fallen into error, or circumvented by guile, but at their own simple, pure, free, and spontaneous good will, from their own certain knowledge gave and preferred, and every one of said parishioners for himself separately and successively gave and conferred, as by the tenor of the present public instrument they give and confer, and every ope for himself gives and profers their voices of election, and their votes for the office of Clerk (or Priest) of the said parish Kirk of Kilmarnock (now vacant by the death and departure of umquhile Thomas Boyd of Lyne, last Parish Clerk and possessor of the said Kirk), to a worthy and distinguished young man, Alexander Boyd, son of a renowned man, Robert Boyd, master of Boyd, of Kilmarnock, and they elected and nominated as by the tenor of the present public instrument, they elect and choose the said Alexander Boyd as a proper person in and to the office of Parish Clerk of Kilmarnock; and they publicly inducted and admitted as by the tenor of the present public instrument, they induct and admit the said Alexander, personally present, to the real, actual and corporal possession of the said office of Clerk of Kilmarnock, by delivery to him of the Bell, Cup, and Sprinklers of Holy Water,

---

* In 1795, when Miss Scott "came of age," the event was celebrated in the town by a public rejoicing.

† See page 5.

and the keys of the doors of the said Kirk of Kilmarnock, with the accustomed solemnities and ceremonies as use is: on the said Alexander, or his doer, procurator, or substitute, undertaking and performing the duties and services belonging to said office during the whole time of his life, with all and sundry its rights, revenues, feus, teinds, endowments and profits whatsoever to be enjoyed, used, and possessed, without any impediment, obstacle, or contradiction whatever. Upon all and sundry of which, as in the premises, the said Master of Boyd, in the name and on the part of his foresaid son, asked of us notaries public subscribing an instrument, or instruments to be constructed. These things were done within the foresaid parish of Kilmarnock, and parish Kirk thereof, on the days, in the year, month, Indiction, and Pontificate, as above, in presence of Robert Boyd, son of Patrick Boyd of Hungryhill; John Boyd of Nairstoun; James Cunynghame of Clonbeith; James Wyllie; and Robert Colvile; with several other witnesses called and required to the premises.

"Subscribed by George Boyd and John Parker, notaries, with the usual docquets."

About the year 1731 the Low Church was found to be insufficient for the accommodation of the increasing population, and to supply the deficiency, the High Church, which is situated at the head of Soulis Street, was then erected. The Magistrates and Town Council, with whom the scheme of building it originated, and to whom and whose successors in office a charter of the ground was granted, advanced £30 sterling towards the undertaking. Subscriptions were also raised among the operatives of the town attached to the Established Church, who held shares in the property according to the sums of money they had subscribed. The funds were likewise increased by the generosity of the Earl of Kilmarnock and Mr Orr of Grougar, whose united subscriptions amounted to 1000 merks. The Earl still further encouraged the undertaking by freeing the contributors of the feu-duty formerly charged for the ground they had purchased; in other words, only one penny Scots was to be given for it yearly, and as the charter states, was to be paid "on the ground of the said Lands at the feast of Whitsunday in name of Blanch Farm, if asked." According to the same document, "the two collegiate ministers" of the parish were to "take separate charges or preach by turns in the said new kirk;" and the

Magistrates and Council were bound "to grant, subscrive, and deliver sufficient rights to all persons within the Town and paroch of Kilmarnock claiming a property in the said new kirk as contributors thereto, ane suitable proportion effeiring and corresponding to the sums respectively advanced or to be advanced by them, with the necesar Burdens of upholding the Kirk Roof and Fabric thereof, steeple and Kirkyeard dyke." The cost of the building was about £850 sterling, and this, we believe, was independent of the expense of the steeple, which was not erected till 1740. We may add that in 1763 "the Council denuded themselves of the chapel to the managers, which was done by a bond."

Externally the High Church can boast of little architectural ornament, save the steeple, which is about eighty feet in height. Its interior, however, which is nearly square, has a more handsome appearance, being beautified by a tastefully ornamented ceiling, and by two rows of massive pillars, by which the roof is supported. Attached to the church is a neat and extensive burial-ground, in which are some fine tombstones; but none of them, we believe, mark the resting-place of any very remarkable character, except it be that of the late Rev. James Robertson, of Clerk's Lane Chapel, who was much famed for his wit and theological attainments. Of this individual a brief sketch will be given in a subsequent chapter. For many years the High Church had only one principal approach, which was from Soulis Street; but some time ago another was made from Portland Street, that has not only rendered the church more convenient to the public, but has given a more modern look to the edifice itself.

In 1811 this church, which had formerly been a chapel of case, was, by the Court of Teinds, made a distinct parish church, and had a separate district assigned to it, under the name of the High Kirk Parish. It affords accommodation for nine hundred and fifty-two sitters.

Till the year 1764 the High Church, or Chapel, as it was then called, was supplied, as already shown, by the ministers of the Parish Church, who preached alternately; but, in the above year, the proprietors engaged a pastor of their own—the Rev. Mr Oliphant, who figures in Burns's poem of the *Ordination*. This individual was afterwards minister of Dumbarton, where he died in the spring of 1818, in the eighty-fourth year of his age and fifty-fourth of his ministry. Some years before his death he had the misfortune to lose his sight; but, notwithstanding that calamity, he still continued to discharge his duties as a preacher. He was author of a *Sacramental Catechism*, first published in 1779.

Mr Oliphant's successor in the High Church was the Rev. John Russell, who was ordained in May, 1774. His name is also associated with the writings of Burns. He is one of the *dramatis personæ* in the *Kirk's Alarm*, the *Holy Fair*, &c. The lines beginning,

> "His piercing words, like Highland swords,
> Divide the joints and marrow,"

are truly characteristic of him as a preacher, for he was more ready to thunder forth the terrors of the law than to woo the wicked from the error of their ways, by setting before them the Saviour's love, so fully and freely manifested in the soothing and soul-captivating strains of the gospel. His appearance, too, completely harmonized with his severity of manner; for he was uncouth and robust in person, remarkably dark-complexioned, and stern and gloomy in countenance. On Sabbaths, during the intervals of Divine service, he would frequently go through the streets, and even to the outskirts of the town, with a large walking-stick in his hand, watching for disorderly boys and other stragglers; and such as he discovered, he would visit on the following morning, and severely rebuke for their ungodliness. In short, he was such a terror to the inhabitants, especially on the Sabbath, that the moment the sound of his ponderous staff was heard upon the streets, the doors that chanced to be opened were instantly closed, and every countenance assumed an air of the deepest sanctity. In theological knowledge few of his contemporaries were more deeply versed; and, in religious controversy, he was not easily driven from his position. Even Burns, beneath whose strokes of satire the clergy of Ayrshire were wont to lie prostrate, was on one occasion defeated, it is said, by his determined mode of arguing. They had met accidentally in a barber's shop in Fore Street, and whether Mr Russell knew the poet and meant to chastise him for his reputed heresy, we know not; but they soon became engaged in a warm discussion respecting some particular point of faith; and, according to our informant, who was present, the poet, with all his ingenuity and argumentative powers, was so baffled by his opponent that he became silent, and left the shop in a hurried manner.

Mr Russell, we believe, was among the first, if not the first, to propose the establishment of a Sabbath School in Kilmarnock; at least, so far back as 1798 he laid a plan before the Town Council for the management of such an institution, and a committee was appointed to carry the scheme into execution. He was a native of Moray, and, before coming to Kilmarnock, was parish schoolmaster in Cromarty. The late celebrated Hugh Miller, in his *Scenes and Legends of the North of Scotland*, gives a somewhat lengthened account of him in connection with that locality. A brief extract may be made: "He was, I believe, a good, conscientious man, but unfortunate in a temper at once violent and harsh, and in sometimes mistaking its dictates for those of duty. At any rate, whatever the nature of the mistake, never was there a schoolmaster more thoroughly feared and detested by his pupils; and with dread and hatred did many of them continue to regard him long after they had become men and women.

His memory was a dark morning cloud resting on their saddened boyhood, that cast its shadows into after life. I have heard of a lady who was so overcome by sudden terror on unexpectedly seeing him, many years after she had quitted school, in one of the pulpits of the south, that she fainted away in the pew; and another of his scholars, named M'Glashan—a robust daring young man of six feet—who, when returning to Cromarty from some of the colonies, solaced himself by the way with thoughts of the hearty drubbing with which he was to clear off all his old scores with the dominie. Ere his return, however, Mr Russell had quitted the parish; nor, even if it had chanced otherwise, might the young fellow have gained much in an encounter with one of the boldest and most powerful men in the country. . . . He was, with all his defects, an honest, pious man; and had he lived in the days of Renwick or Cargill, or a century earlier, in the days of Knox or Wishart, he might have been a useful one. But he was unlucky in the age in which he lived, in his temper, and in coming in contact with as hard-headed people as himself."

Mr Russell, about the year 1800, removed to Stirling. He lived to an advanced age, and till his latest days was remarkable for the same solemnity and sternness of character for which he had been noted in Kilmarnock.

Mr Russell's successors in the High Church were—
Mr Wright, ordained July 12, 1800;
Mr Dickson, ordained March 10, 1802;
Mr Hamilton, ordained April 11, 1804;
Mr Main, ordained August 8, 1839; and
Mr Aitken, the present minister, ordained 1843.

CHAPTER XI.

A merry place, 'tis said, in days of yore.
WORDSWORTH.

OF the habits and pastimes of the people of Kilmarnock during the eighteenth century little is recorded. In those days the fairs were the chief sources of amusement. The town was then, as it still is, the most flourishing one in Ayrshire; and, consequently, it was resorted to on these occasions by many odd characters, who came to offer their wares for sale, or to procure, by less honourable means, one or two days' livelihood. Tinkers, ballad-singers, wheel-of-fortune men offering to make all rich in a *jiffie*, slight-of-hand blackguards swallowing burning flax or knives and forks to gull the lieges, and a host of other worthies, too numerous to detail, thronged the market-place and other nooks of the burgh; and sometimes a scene of riot would ensue in consequence of a collision of these adventurers with the town's people, or from the freaks of John Barleycorn, which frequently ended in the effusion of blood. The magistrates had then no police force at their command; but a guard of tradesmen belonging to the town was usually formed to preserve order and tranquillity; and some of our old men yet recount, with much glee, the difficulties they encountered in keeping the *land-loupers* and other *clamjamphrie* that attended the fairs from getting the ascendency. The guard, or "Fair-keepers," as they were termed, were supplied with ale, &c., at the expense of the town. Even the wandering pipers who came to the fair were sometimes paid from the town's funds for their services; and every encouragement was given to harmless mirth and innocent amusement.*

Kings' birthdays, too, which were then commemorated with great spirit, afforded the inhabitants another opportunity of suspending labour and meeting in the alehouses. The civic authorities assembled at mid-day in all due form in the Court-house, and pledged his Majesty's health in flowing bumpers, while the crowd on the outside responded to the toast by repeated huzzas. The juvenile portion of the community amused themselves in the evening by kindling bonfires on the streets with coals supplied by the town, and sometimes with casks, crates, &c., the property of private individuals, stolen by the boys for the purpose of prolonging their noisy and enthusiastic manifestations of loyalty.† A few individuals, styled *Blacknebs*, who looked upon all these proceedings as utterly childish, took no part whatever in the general rejoicings, but treated the affair with contempt. One of them, we

---

* "1737.—For Highland pipers at the July fair, £0 12s. Scots."—*Town Treasurer's Book.*

† A few extracts from the Burgh Records relative to these rejoicings may be amusing:

"1713, Feb. 6.—Payt for six load of Coals for a bondfire, £1 16s. Scots."

"Feb. 12.—For ale for the Queen's birthnight, £1 Scots. Ribbon for cockade to the Drummer's Bonnet, 4s. Scots."

"March 4.—Paid at the Bailie's order to James Boyd for ale drunk at the Cross on Queen's birthnight, £1 4s. Scots."

"1719.—Paid to Bailie Moris for wine on King George's birthday, £9 18s. Scots."

"1737.—For raisings and almonds at King's birthday, £1 7s. Scots. For ringing the bell, nuts, gunpowder, &c., £3 19s. Scots. For 2 blew Bonnets to John Lawry & Stenson at the King's birthday, 12s. Scots."

"1740.—Given Robert Cumming for necessarys to repairing his Drum, being broke at King's birthday, £3 12s. Scots."

"1770.—By Wm Wilson, 15 Bottles Port, at King's birthday, at 18s. sterling per Dozen, £1 2s. 6d. By Alexr Mitchel, 6 pints Rum made into punch, King's birthday, £1 16s. sterling."

"1789.—To Nathan Hodge for attending King's birthday, 5s. sterling." This individual was a barber, and attended, we believe, to make and serve out the punch to the Bailies and Councillors.

"1821, April 26.—Entertainments—paid women for carrying water to make Toddy, 2s."

have heard, in the *way of derision*, had on one occasion the head of a dead horse, adorned with nettles, hemlock, and so forth, placed in his window, in opposition to those in which were displayed the fairest of flowers.

The day also of Riding the Marches, as it was called, was one of some amusement. Its purpose may be gathered from the following minute of Council, dated 1710: "The said day it is inacted, statute and ordained by the Bailies and Council convened, that upon the last Munday of May instant, and that upon the first Munday of May yearly in all tyme hereafter, there shall be chosen by the bailies for the tyme, Twelve young men, who with such a number of the burliemen* in town, or the most old men as the bailies also shall condescend upon, shall visit and take inspection of the Marches in and about the whole lands to the town pertaining and belonging, and that what marches are wanting be set up and keeped in memory from tyme to tyme." We have been told by old people that such of the inhabitants as wished to witness the "inspection," generally formed into procession and proceeded to the various landmarks, accompanied by the magistrates and the town-drummer. The old men pointed out the marches; and as they did so it was usual to give some of the boys who were present a hearty drubbing, so that they might remember in after life the identical situation of the said marches.† Such a custom was not without its use, as those knowing the landmarks thoroughly were sometimes required to settle disputes between

---

* "Laws of Burlaw are maid and determined be consent of neichtbors, elected and chosen be common consent, in the courts called the Byrlaw courts, in the quhilk cognition is taken of complaints betwixt nichtbour and nichtbour. The quhilk men sa chosen as judges and arbitrators to the effect foresaid, are commonly called Byrlaw-men."—*Skene.*

† A Mr James Reid, who died in 1822, at the advanced age of eighty-two, was present at one or two of these "inspections," and his account of the affair was similar to that we have given. Mr Reid was an innkeeper, and was the first in the town, we are informed, who kept gigs on hire. He was admitted a Burgess of the Burgh in 1770, and it was probably about this time that he introduced these useful vehicles.

proprietors. For example, in 1757, a dispute arose respecting "a barricade or fence," as the minutes term it, "on the side of the Town's ground opposite Pipe's Brae,"* and various individuals who were supposed to know the marches were appointed by the Council to inspect the place along with the proprietor of the brae, and to settle the dispute by that inspection.

Processions of the Trades also were common in past times, and afforded occasional relaxation from labour, as well as some amusement. The most imposing of these displays was that of St Crispin's Society. A King, who was chosen from their own number, and who was usually an individual of a somewhat dignified deportment, walked majestically in front, arrayed in regal robes, with a dazzling crown on his head, and several smart little pages bearing up his train. Though holding the lofty position only for the moment, he was always an object of great attraction, and was sure to be honoured with the name of *king* during the remainder of his life. A Lord Mayor, an Alderman, an Indian King, and a Champion encased in a coat of mail, were also distinguished personages in the parade. This custom of the shoemakers began, we believe, about 1773; at least the robes and other articles used in their processions were purchased in that year, and, according to an old minute book, cost £23 14s. 5d.†

* Pipe's Brae was adjoining to the ground now known by the name of the Town Holm, and was then rented by, or belonged to, Mr Paterson, town-clerk.

† The last parade of the shoemakers was in celebration of the marriage of His Royal Highness the Prince of Wales, 10th March, 1863. On that auspicious occasion the other trades of the town also processed, together with the Magistrates and Councillors, Justices of the Peace, Commissioners of Police, the Volunteers, the Masonic Lodges, the Odd-fellows, the Post-office officials, &c. In the afternoon the Provost and Magistrates and other influential gentlemen dined in honour of the occasion in the George Inn; and a dinner was served gratuitously to about two hundred old men in the Market of the Corn Exchange. Tea was also given to about six hundred poor people, chiefly females, in St Marnock's Church. In the evening a grand ball took place in the George Inn Hall, a large bonfire blazed at the Cross, and the Council Chambers, some of the churches and other public buildings, as well as many private establishments, were brilliantly illuminated.

But one of the most important days of amusement was Fastern's E'en,* the celebration of which was discontinued by the Magistrates and Council about 1831, after having been observed annually for five centuries.† The manner in which the day was spent we will briefly describe. In the forenoon the fire-engines of the town were brought to the Cross, filled with water, and the management of the pipes intrusted to some expert individual, who all of a sudden began to pour the cooling liquid in all directions; and the Cross being by this time thronged with the inhabitants and people from the country, a scene of disorder and confusion ensued, to the infinite delight of those who had the good luck to escape with a dry skin. Ramsay—a native poet—describes the scene with much truth:

> "Out-owre the heighest house's tap,
>   He sent the torrent scrievin';
> The curious crowd aye nearer crap,
>   To see sic feats achievin':
> But scarcely had they thicken'd weel,
>   And got in trim for smilin',
> When round the pipe gaed like an eel,
>   And made a pretty skailin'
>   'Mang them that day."

This part of the day's sports continued for about an hour. Preparations were then made for a foot race. The officers or beadles of the town, accompanied by a drummer and a fifer, marched through the principal streets bearing a halberd, from the top of which were suspended a cloth pouch, a pair of leather breeches, a pair of shoes, and a broad blue bonnet. These represented the particular trades of the town, and were (or their value in money) to be awarded as prizes to the

---

* Shrove Tuesday; or, as Dr Jamieson explains it, "the evening preceding the first day of the Fast of Lent."
† *New Statistical Account.*

respective winners. The pouch represented the tailors, the breeches the glovers,* the shoes the shoemakers, and the bonnet the bonnet-makers. This, though an annual affair, always attracted universal attention. After going their rounds the officers halted at the Town-house, where the Bailies and Councillors formed into procession in front of the crowd, and all marched off at the sound of the drum and the fife to the race-ground, which was usually the Ward's Park, in the vicinity of Kilmarnock House. In a local poem, the odd characters that joined in the procession about the beginning of the present century, are thus alluded to:

> "And queer auld chaps I trew were there,
> Pye Robin, wi' his lang tied hair,
> Snap Tam, Bird Will, and twa three mair
>   O' sic degree,
> A' marching out wi' proud-like air
>   The sports to see."

Two or three races were run; and, as the competitors were generally from the moorland districts and swift of foot, remarkable feats of running were often displayed. These pastimes, though not the most rational that might have been devised, may have had their advantages; but some of the day's proceedings were marked by acts of cruelty, revolting to reason, religion, and humanity. We allude to the fiendish and disgraceful practice of cock-fighting. Two or three dozens of individuals, having the external form of human beings, but devoid of the finer feelings, engaged in that work in different parts of the town; nor was the practice confined to young men alone; the aged also mingled with the others in the arena of cruelty, and eyed the contest with as much interest as if the

---

* There were a considerable number of glovers at one time in the town. In 1729 we find them complaining to the Council of certain persons in the trade selling "leather breeches without being stamped;" and the Council, with the Earl of Kilmarnock, accordingly pass an act for their protection.

fate of nations had been about to be decided by the feathered combatants. The youths attending school, too, had their cock-fights on Fastern's E'en; and in some instances the schoolmaster, forgetting his position in society and duty to the rising generation, encouraged the barbarous practice by presiding over the scene of action; and every biped that was killed he greedily claimed as a sort of reward for the service he had rendered.*

Another custom that prevailed here to a great extent, during the last century, but which is now almost abolished, was that of *first-footing* on the morning of New-year's day. As soon as the town clock had numbered twelve, hundreds of persons of both sexes sallied forth from their domiciles to greet their friends and acquaintances, and treat them with intoxicating liquors. The town immediately assumed the appearance of some vast rendezvous of bacchanalians, rather than the peaceful abode of beings gifted with reason. That the practice originated in a desire to strengthen the ties of friendship and sociality is probable; but it often led to consequences painful to contemplate, and engendered feelings the very reverse of those it was intended to cherish. Swearing, quarrelling, and fighting, were its frequent attendants; and in our own time, namely, on New-year's day morning, Old Style, 1815, a circumstance occurred by which human life was sacrificed. The victim was a miner, named James Muir. He had been holding the New-year, and got into a scuffle with some intoxicated individuals in Soulis Street, and was killed on the spot. John Craig, a soldier on furlough at

---

* It appears from the Town's Records that Fastern's E'en did not always pass away without some disturbance of the public peace. In 1755, for example, a tumult arose, when the Magistrates were "insulted," and the "dykes of the Town Green demolished." The Council afterwards agreed to raise a prosecution "before the Sheriff of Ayr against Mathew Fairservice, John and William Muir, and John Thomson, glovers, who were represented to have been chiefly concerned in the riot, &c."

the time, was tried for the offence at the Ayr Circuit Court, in April of the same year; but though the strictest investigation was made into the matter, no proof could be adduced of his guilt, and he was dismissed from the bar.

In justice, however, to our ancestors, we may state that many of them hailed the dawning of a new year in a way altogether apart from irrationality and drunkenness. The father, who, like John Anderson, had seen his "bairns' bairns," would invite them all to breakfast, place the "weel-hain'd kebbuck," or, perhaps, a haggis, "warm, reekin', rich," with abundance of cakes, before them; and, after asking a blessing from the Giver of all good, would bid them partake heartily, and be happy. In the evening they would again assemble, and spend a few hours in social conversation over some simple beverage.

One or two other customs, which were then common, may be noticed. In consequence of a want of proper conveyances, many of the inhabitants, who had occasion to go from home, performed the journey on foot. This primitive mode of travelling rendered it necessary that the day, to use an old phrase, *should be taken by the end;* and, that none might be disappointed in their projects of business or pleasure, a warning drum was beat through the town every morning (Sabbath excepted) as early as four o'clock. The drummer had no regular pay; but, on New-year's day, he called upon the more respectable people, and took whatever sum they were pleased to give for his services. To those who rewarded him handsomely he would afterwards show his gratitude by giving an extra beat or two at their doors, when going on his solitary rounds. At an earlier period, the same work was performed by a piper, who, like the drummer, paraded the streets at an early hour, blowing his pipes with "micht and main," and sending the bold melody into every nook and corner of the town.

It was also customary, about a century ago, for the women of Kilmarnock to attend funerals, especially those of their relatives or immediate neighbours. An old man, who distinctly recollected the custom, informed us, that the dress they wore varied according to their rank in society. Those of the poorer classes were generally attired in blue mantles or cloaks, and the more opulent ladies had garments of the same form, fringed with fur, but of a red or scarlet colour. About the same period, when a death occurred in the town, the public were made aware of the circumstance in the following manner: A hand-bell, called *the skellat-bell*, and by some, *the passing-bell*, from being used when the spirit of an inhabitant had passed from time into eternity, was rung through the streets by an individual, who, as he went along, announced, with a solemn air, that such a person (mentioning his or her name) had departed this life. He also named the day and hour when the remains of the deceased would be interred, and invited all to attend them to their last resting-place. The bell alluded to is still preserved in the Town Buildings, and bears the inscription, "Kilmarnock, 1639."*

A writer of the olden time, when speaking of this district, says, "it abounds in strong and valiant men;" and several remarkable instances of longevity among the inhabitants of Kilmarnock during the last century are on record, one of which is that of a porter, named John Craig, who was able to carry parcels at the advanced age of 105. Another is that of an individual who, according to the Kirk Session Records,

---

* It appears also from numerous entries, such as the following, in the early Session Records, that the church-bell was often rung at funerals in the olden time:

"1714.—For Thomas Smith's wife's burial-bell, £3 Scots."
"1714.—From Robert Miller, his burial-bell, £3 Scots."
"1718.—Received a crown for John Andrew's dead-bell, £3 Scots."
"1721.—Received for ye Ringing of ye bell at Mrs Mowat's funeral, £3 Scots."
"1723.—Received from Mathew Dickie for ringing ye big bell at ye funerals of John & Andrew Boydes in Northcraig, £6 Scots."

had reached the wonderful age of 118 years.* Perhaps it was mainly to out-door recreations and athletic sports and games, which were then common, that the men of Cunningham were indebted for that robustness of constitution alluded to. In the more genial months of the year, bowl-playing,† throwing the stone, wrestling, &c., were the principal pastimes;‡ and, in the winter season, "when Boreas blew his blasts sae bauld," the game of curling, which prevailed here as far back as the year 1644, was a favourite amusement. The curlers of one quarter of the town would frequently challenge, as they still do, those of another, and persons of all ranks, young and old, would join in the *bonspeil*:

> "Youth, em'lous, tried what sleight could do,
> While age told deeds that sleight had done;
> And laurels bound the victor's brow
> Dearer than warrior ever won."

The scenes of their contests were usually the mill-dams in

---

* "1716, Septemr 18.—To ane old man ane 118 years age, on precept, 12s. Scots."—*Kirk Treasurer's Book.*

† In a minute of Council, dated 5th March, 1764, mention is made of "a Shooting Prize of £5" having been placed, about the year 1740, in the hands of a Mr Paterson, "towards erecting a bowling-green, and purchasing bowls, as being thought a more agreeable diversion than shooting."

‡ We have never heard any of our aged townsmen talk of the May-pole; or of the rural festival of the "First of May" being observed in the district. The following entry, however, in the Town Treasurer's Book, for 1780, would imply that it was celebrated about that period: "Paid Robert Fraser, *for dressing a May-pole*, 2s. 6d. sterling."

The May-poles, or "Simmer Trees," as they were called, were prohibited by Act of Parliament, in the reign of Queen Mary. "And gif onie women," says the Act, "or uthers about simmer-trees sing and makis perturbation to the Queenis Lieges in the passage throw Burrowes and uther Landward Tounes: The women perturbatoures for skafrie of money or utherwise, sall be taken, handled, and put upon the Cuck-stules of everie Burgh or Towne." After the restoration of Charles the Second, this apparently harmless festival was again revived; and it is still customary, we believe, for the youths of several places in Scotland to "go a Maying" on the first day of May, when, to use the beautiful words of Milton,

> "—— The bright morning-star, day's harbinger,
> Comes dancing from the east, and leads with her
> The flowery May, who from her green lap throws
> The yellow cowslip, and the pale primrose."

the vicinity, where, with the best of feeling, they strove with each other for the palm of victory; and, when their "roaring play," as Burns terms it, was over, it was not uncommon for them to meet together by some "canty ingle," where they would regale themselves with "pap-in,"* or home-brewed ale, the favourite beverage of the time, and spend the evening in mirth and harmony.

The Cross, too, strange as it may appear, was sometimes converted into a curling pond. The late Robert Montgomery, Esq. of Bogston, who was the eldest son of Bailie John Wilson, merchant, Kilmarnock, and who adopted the name of Montgomery on inheriting the above-mentioned estate, told our informant, the late James Dobie, Esq. of Crummock, Beith, that his father (Bailie Wilson) curled, in 1740, at the Cross of Kilmarnock, for twenty-three successive days, excepting Sundays. The water was raised from a well—probably the present Cross Well—and was dammed up for the purpose. The winter of 1740 was very severe, and long talked of as the hard winter.

At the present time, Kilmarnock contains many *keen* and *scientific* curlers; and, judging from the minute book of one of the oldest clubs, they have often won laurels in their contests with the players of other towns.

Besides the facility afforded by our streams for the practice of the game, there are two excellent lochs in the district—one at New Farm, rented by the various clubs, and one at Craufurdland Castle, to which the proprietor of that ancient mansion makes all welcome.

In a small work, published in Kilmarnock in 1828, entitled, *A Descriptive and Historical Sketch of Curling*, the following history of the game in Scotland is given, which we quote, not only for its general interest, but for the slight allusion

---

* A mixture of small beer and whisky.

which is made therein to the practice of the game at an early
period in the parish of Kilmarnock: "The earliest notice of
curling," says that account, "which has been discovered, is in
Cambden's *Britannia,* published in 1607. In it Copinsha,
one of the Orkney Islands, is mentioned as famous for
'excellent stones for the game called curling.' This proves
that it was then in considerable repute, when stones were
sought at so great a distance from any place where the game
could be practised. Before the middle of the seventeenth
century, curling was generally practised on Sunday (Baillie's
Letters), that sacred day, even some time after the Reformation
from Popery, being allotted for amusements of all kinds. In
1684 the game is noticed in Fountainhall's *Decisions;* and,
in 1792, Pennant, in his *Tour,* describes it at length.
Pennycuick, who flourished in the seventeenth century, calls
it 'a manly Scottish exercise;' and celebrates it as calculated

'To clear the brain, stir up the native heat,
And give a gallant appetite for meat.'

The other Scottish poets who have described or alluded to it
are, Allan Ramsay, in the beginning of the last century;
Græme, who died at Lanark in 1785; Burns; Davidson of
Kirkcudbright; and Grahame, the author of the *Sabbath.*
In such high repute was the game about the beginning of last
century, that the magistrates of Edinburgh marched in a body
to the North Loch, to spend the day in curling. In going
out and returning, they were preceded by a band of music
playing appropriate airs. . . . The upper and middle
wards of Lanarkshire, certain parts of Peebles, Edinburgh,
Perth, Dumfries, and Ayr shires, are distinguished for their
attachment to the game. It has long been practised in the
parish of Kilmarnock. As a proof of this, we find it stated in
the *Life* of the celebrated William Guthrie, who, in the year

1644, was ordained minister of Fenwick (then called New Kilmarnock, and separated in 1642 from the parish of Kilmarnock), that he was fond of 'the innocent recreations which *then prevailed,* among which was playing on the ice.' "*

A curling stone, said to have been used by Mr Guthrie, is still preserved at Craufurdland Castle. Compared with those of the present day it is truly antique in appearance.

A neatly executed monument, bearing the following inscription, was recently erected to the memory of Mr Guthrie in the churchyard of Fenwick:

"In memory of the Rev. William Guthrie, first minister of this parish, and author of the *Christian's Great Interest.* Born, 1620; ordained, 1644. Ejected by Prelatic persecution, 1664: worn out by labours and sufferings, he died, 1665, and was interred in the Church of Brechin. His active and self-denied ministry, through the Divine blessing, produced a deep and lasting impression. This stone is erected, 1854, as a token of gratitude, by the Christian public."

* Other games, such as shovel-board, seem to have been practised in the olden time in Kilmarnock, and to have drawn forth the censure of the ecclesiastical authorities. For example, we find the following regarding it in the Session Records: "March 23, 1693.—This day report was given in to the Sess. of some intimly and unseasonable gamin at shufle-board, which the Session resented, and appointed it to be discharged."

CHAPTER XII.

*Swith to the Laigh Kirk ane and a',
And there tak' up your stations.*
            BURNS.

THE people of Kilmarnock have long been noted as a religious and church-going people; and though some of their pastimes in former years, as we have shown, were at variance with the humanizing spirit of Christianity, yet they were ever regular in their attendance at the church; and the Sabbath, externally at least, was kept so strictly sacred, that the town on that day had all the appearance of a place deserted by its inhabitants. If it happened that a few stragglers were on the streets, and if the minister had chanced to make his appearance, such was the respect he commanded, or awe he inspired, that they instantly hastened to their respective dwellings. But, though thus respecting the clergy, and the religious usages of the land, there were times when acrimonious feelings would arise in the community on subjects connected with the church. Patronage, about which there have been so many dissensions in our own day, was then looked upon as an evil of no small magnitude; and an instance is on record of the peace of the town being disturbed by the bitter animosity and opposition of its enemies. We allude to the riotous conduct of the people at the admission of the Rev. William Lindsay to the Low Church, in the year 1764. Burns, in his poem of the *Ordination*, makes allusion to this affair in the well-known lines,

"Curst Common Sense, that imp o' hell,
Cam' in wi' Maggie Lauder;"

and though no poet abounds more in expressions at once clear and intelligible, yet, to many of the readers of the gifted ploughman, these lines are invested with some obscurity. A glance at the case, however, to which he refers, will somewhat elucidate their meaning.

In consequence of the death of the Rev. Robert Hall, in June, 1762, the second charge in the Low Church became vacant. Whether the affections of the parishioners were fixed upon some favourite preacher, whom they wished as his successor, we are not aware; but the Earl of Glencairn, who was then patron, had resolved, it would appear, to exercise his own judgment in the matter; and the Rev. Mr Lindsay, who was then minister of Cumbray, in Buteshire, was appointed by the earl to fill the vacancy. In the estimation of the people he held not a very elevated place as a preacher; but his religious opinions were liberal, and he espoused what were then denominated the *common sense* principles. It is also said that the wife of Mr Lindsay, whose maiden name was Margaret Lauder, had been sometime housekeeper or governess in the Glencairn family, and that, in consequence of her friendship or influence with the earl, she obtained the situation for her husband—hence the lines of Burns, above quoted.*

By the following extracts from the minute books of the Kirk Session of Kilmarnock, it appears that great opposition was manifested, on the part of that body, to Mr Lindsay's settlement:

"Septr 23, 1762.—The Session appointed a Committee, consisting of Mr Leslie [the minister of the first charge], Mr Boyd, Mr Hunter, William Muir, and Bailie Wilson, to meet with a Committee of the Town Council to consider of and draw up a Petition to the Earl of Glencairn, to grant us a hearing of some young men to supply the second minister's charge in this place."

* Chambers, in his recent edition of the *Life and Works of Burns*, says: "There was a popular notion that Mr Lindsay had been indebted for his presentation to his wife, Margaret Lauder, who was believed, but I am assured erroneously, to have been housekeeper to Lord Glencairn."

"Nov. 24, 1762.—The Modr acquainted the Session that the Earl of Glencairn has given a Presentation to Mr Wm Lindsay, minister of the gospel in Cumbray, to fill the vacant charge of second minister in this place, and that Mr Lindsay has accepted of the same, and that it is given in to the Modr of the Presby, under form of Instrument, to be laid before the Presby at next meeting."

"Dec. 23, 1762.—This day the Session taking under their serious consideration the Presentation given by the Right Honble the Earl of Glencairn to Mr Wm Lindsay, minr at Cumbray, to fill the vacant collegiate charge of second minister in this place, and Mr Lindsay's acceptance of the same in a way quite unprecedented in this place, unanimously declared their disapprobation both of the manner of the Presentation and acceptance; and that they could not concur with said Presentation at present; and appoint a Committee of their number to meet and draw up reasons in form to be laid before the Session at next meeting, why they cannot concur with said Presentation."

On the 6th day of January, 1763, this Committee brought up a paper, specifying the reasons for refusing to concur with the presentation. This document was adopted by the Session, who instructed this Committee to lay it before the next meeting of Presbytery, and to do all in their power to prevent the settlement. The Presbytery, though evidently favourable to the objectors, gave no legal effect to this paper, but appointed the moderation of the call to take place on the 3rd day of February. On that day a Committee of Presbytery met at Kilmarnock, and the call was signed by "Charles Dalrymple of Orangefield for the Earl of Glencairn, William Paterson, Writer in Kilmarnock, for himself and for John Crawford of Crawfordland, John Orr of Barrowfield, William Park of Langlands, Robert Ainslie for Rowallan, and by other *Heritors*." None of the Session signed the call; only three *Heads of Families* signed the concurrence; and the elders, twenty in number, presented another remonstrance against the proceedings. The Presbytery delayed their judgment till the middle of March, when, without a vote, they resolved that they could not sustain the call. Against this sentence the Doers for Lord Glencairn protested and appealed to the Synod, whereupon, in the words of the Session Minutes:

"April 7th, 1763.—This day the Session appointed a Committee of their number, consisting of Bailie James Wilson, Doctor Hunter, John Gemmell, and Hugh Muir, to attend the next Synod at Air in the affair of Mr Wm Lindsay."

R

The Synod confirmed the sentence of the Presbytery, and the Doers for the Patron appealed to the General Assembly. So determined was the spirit of the Session, that they despatched a special envoy, William Muir, to Edinburgh, to do every thing necessary to get the previous sentences affirmed.

During the dependence of the case before the General Assembly, attempts at a compromise were made. The Earl offered that, if the Session and people would agree to accept Mr Auld of Mauchline as their minister, he would give him the presentation. This offer reached Kilmarnock from Edinburgh on Thursday, the 26th day of May, 1763; a Session was immediately summoned; the elders canvassed that night the whole town and parish; they met by eight o'clock next morning; it was reported that the parishioners were unanimous in favour of Mr Auld; delegates from the Kirk Session and Town Council, accompanied by the first minister, hurried to Mauchline, to urge Mr Auld to accept immediately; but he was inexorable. On the return of the delegates in the evening the Session again met, and despatched an answer to Edinburgh, reporting their want of success with Mr Auld, but proposing to Lord Glencairn the names of three other clergymen, any one of whom they bound themselves to accept.

The Assembly, however, took its own way in the matter. Without a vote, it reversed the sentences of the Presbytery and Synod, sustained the presentation, and ordered the Presbytery to proceed without delay to adjudicate on the question of Mr Lindsay's translation.

To extract again from the Session Records:

"June 30th, 1763.—Reported that the Presby has appointed at their last meeting the parish of Cumbray to be called before them to answer the reasons of transportation given in by the Doers of Ld Glencairn."

"Aug. 11, 1763.—Reported by the Modr that the Presbytery at their last meeting having under their consideration the affair of Mr Lindsay, had refused to transport him from the parish of Cumbray, and that the Doer for the Earl of Glencairn had appealed the affair to the next Synod to meet at Glasgow, Oct. next."

"Oct. 20.—The Committee appointed to wait on the Synod to oppose the settlement of Mr Wm Lindsay to be minister in this place reported that, having fulfilled the appointment, the Synod had referred the affair to the next General Assembly."

"May 28, 1764.—Reported that the Assembly had ordered the Presby of Irvine to ordain [admit] Mr William Lindsay to be minister of the gospell of Kilmarnock, before the 17th July next."

Thursday, the 12th of July, was the day fixed for the admission.

From the following minute of the Town Council, it appears that that body also, as might be inferred from the above extracts, was opposed to Mr Lindsay's settlement:

"22 Nov., 1762.—The Council having before them a letter from the Earl of Glencairn, patron of the parish, acquainting them of his lordship having presented Mr Lindsay, minr of Cumbray, to the vacant charge of the Collegiate Church of Kilmarnock, and desiring them to signify their approbation of said Presentation; and having considered the said letter, unanimously disapprove of said Presentation, the Presentee being in their opinion unqualified for such a charge."

From the *Caledonian Mercury*, of May 28, 1764, we are enabled to show more fully how the case terminated. That paper says:

"This day the Committee (appointed to draw up an answer to his Majesty's letter, the Assembly then sitting) proceeded to the consideration of the cause anent the settlement of the Collegiate Church of Kilmarnock, when, after a long hearing, the Assembly reversed the sentence of the Presbytery of Irvine, sustained the reason for the transportation of Mr Lindsay from Cumbray to the parish of Kilmarnock, appointed the Presbytery to admit Mr Lindsay minister of Kilmarnock betwixt and the 17th of July next, and ordained them to report to the Commission their having done so; and the Assembly likewise empowered the Commission finally to determine any question that should come before them by complaint, reference or appeal relative to this cause."

As to some extent explaining, if not palliating, the disturbance that ensued, it may be mentioned that Mr Leslie, the first minister, had died not ten days before the final decision of the Assembly. The town was in a state of ecclesiastical anarchy; there was no minister at all; the elders could not exercise their functions; and, as it happened, there was not even a session-clerk. The Town Council were virulent and practical in their opposition to Lindsay: it was during the discussions on his presentation, in 1763, that they altered the constitution of their own "Chapel," the present High Church, so as to preclude the possibility of his being in any way connected with it; and only a fortnight before the final decision of the Assembly the new "managers" of the chapel had appointed a minister of their own, the Rev. James Oliphant.

As soon as it was generally known that Mr Lindsay was to be admitted their pastor, a portentous murmur of discontent was heard among the inhabitants in every street and nook of the town; and, as the time of the settlement drew near, their dissatisfaction waxed louder and louder. Every sort of missile they secretly collected as ammunition with which to assail their opponents. At length the much-talked-of day arrived; and, according to all accounts, a scene of disorder and tumult ensued such as never before was witnessed in Kilmarnock. Labour seemed altogether suspended; numerous parties assembled on the streets, and, ere the hour of induction had come, surrounded the church, determined to oppose the proceedings. A mere outline of the affray is all we are enabled to give. The mob, who had placed themselves in a convenient position for attack, no sooner observed the patron and the clergymen approaching than they assailed them with a storm of execrations, and pelted them to such a degree with mud, dead cats, and other filthy substances, that it was with the greatest difficulty they gained the interior of the church. Here a scene of confusion and uproar took place, which even Hogarth, so noted for his faithful delineations of the ludicrous, would, we believe, have failed to depict. Several volleys of the missiles we have spoken of were discharged at the devoted heads of those friendly to Mr Lindsay's appointment. All, indeed, was riot, noise, and disorder. The precentor, William Steven, had his wig torn from his head. The wig of one of the magistrates, too, was tossed into the air, amid the cheers of the mob; the Earl of Glencairn was struck on the cheek with a dead cat; and one of the clergymen, belonging to the neighbouring village of Fenwick, convinced of the truth of the old saying, that "*ae pair o' heels is worth twa pair o' hands*," mounted his horse and fled from the scene in the utmost consternation.*

The *Caledonian Mercury*, for July 21, 1764, thus alludes to the tumult:

> "By a letter from Kilmarnock we learn, that on Thursday se'nnight, the day appointed by the General Assembly for the transportation of the Rev. Mr Lindsay from the Cumbrays to Kilmarnock, the patron, with a number of gentlemen and ministers, went to the church, in order to proceed in the settlement; but divine service was not well begun, when a mob of disorderly persons broke into the church, throwing dirt and stones, and making such noise, that Mr Brown, the minister who officiated, could not proceed, on which the patron, with the gentlemen and ministers, retired to a house in the neighbourhood; 'tis said Mr Lindsay is to be ordained in the Presbytery house in Irvine."

In a *Scoffing Ballad*, as Burns terms it, which was written at the time, we have a more minute account of the matter. The verses have been kindly handed to us by a gentleman in town, who took them down from the rehearsal of his father who was an eye-witness of the uproar. Considered as poetry,

---

* The following humorous anecdote regarding the flight of the Fenwick clergyman is related by Chambers, in his edition of *Burns:* "The minister of Fenwick fled in trepidation, and mounting his horse, proceeded to ride home, with the fearful scene still occupying his excited imagination. It happened that an English commercial traveller was at the same time leaving the town on his way to Glasgow. He asked the road, which was then somewhat difficult to find, and very bad when it was found. 'Keep after that man for the first four miles, and you cannot go wrong,' said the people. The minister, finding a horseman following him very hard, thought it was an outraged Calvinist. He clapped the spurs to his beast, and flew faster than before. The Englishman, fearful to lose his way, put his horse to speed too, and then the affair became a John Gilpin scamper, only with two actors instead of one. At last the poor minister turned down a lane to one of his farmers, on whom he called in desperation to bring out his people and save his life. The Englishman, following close up, rode into the farmyard at the same moment, when, instead of a deadly combat on theological grounds, there took place only an explanation. The whole party enjoyed the joke so much, that the farmer insisted on keeping the stranger as his guest for the night, with the minister to help away the toddy."

the ballad is mere doggerel; but it may be looked upon as a true and graphic description of the tumult, and on that account we present it to our readers without further apology :

"VERSES, WRITTEN IN 1764,

"ON THE VIOLENT INDUCTION OF THE REV. MR LINDSAY.

"Puir John Macrone* has ta'en the road,
And sair he did his auld beast goad
To bring in time his noble load.†
  Good people, hear my ditty.

"And Orangefield,‡ Dalrymple called,
Frae Finlayson,§ or some sic fauld,
To quell the mob, now grown so bauld.
  Good people, hear my ditty.

"But some folk had it in their head
His Lordship wad mak' nae sic speed
If Maggie Lauder‖ had been dead.
  Good people, hear my ditty.

"This as it may, I canna tell,
Glencairn he kens it best himsel',
His reason thus the kirk to fill.
  Good people, hear my ditty.

"Now thro' the windows stanes did reel,
And Hacket** said it was the de'il,
Syne wi' his brethren took fareweel.
  Good people, hear my ditty.

"While Brown†† was praying, I suppose,
A stane cam' whirring near his nose,
Says he, "Our wark we now maun close."
  Good people, hear my ditty.

 * Valet to the Earl of Glencairn. † The Earl of Glencairn.
‡ Hew Dalrymple of Orangefield. He was then a military officer, and probably was called to act as such for the suppression of the disturbance.
 § The Earl of Glencairn's residence. ‖ Mrs Lindsay.
** The Rev. Mr Halket of Fenwick, who went home on horseback at full speed. He died April, 1779, in the thirty-eighth year of his ministry.
 †† The Rev. Mr Brown of Kilbirnie.

"Puir Taylor Steen,* precentor there,
They rave his wig aff ilka hair,
And left the body's noddle bare.
   Good people, hear my ditty.

"And Bailie Baps† he gat a shog,
Outowre the head, wi' Lambert's‡ dog,
That laid him senseless as a log.
   Good people, hear my ditty.

"Though meek and gentle Lindsay§ was,
And had at heart the guid auld cause,
Yet nocht could mak' the rabble pause.
   Good people, hear my ditty.

"Their fury raise to sic a height,
That here he durst not pass the night,
But aff to Irvine took his flight.
   Good people, hear my ditty.

"Pursued 'mang hisses, yells, and groans,
And mony a shower o' dirt and stones,
Their wicked rage he sair bemoans.
   Good people, hear my ditty.

"And there he fixed his dwellin'-place,
Till ance their madness and disgrace
Wad yield to better sense and grace.
   Good people, hear my ditty.

"At e'en, Lang Tam,‖ that howkes the stanes,
Gaed to the Inn to pike the banes,
And to *gie in* the leaders' names.
   Good people, hear my ditty."

Such is the metrical account of the riot. It was written, we are informed, by an eccentric son of St Crispin, named

---

* William Steven, formerly mentioned. He felt so indignant at the insult, that he never again acted as precentor in the parish church, but became a staunch dissenter.
† Mr William Paterson, baker. ‡ Lambert, gardener to Mr Paterson, town-clerk.
     § Rev. Mr Lindsay.
‖ This individual was tacksman of a quarry in the neighbourhood. He was afterwards a schoolmaster, and much noted for his servility to those above him in station.

Hunter. He was the author of many satirical rhymes, fragments of which are still remembered; and some of them, it is affirmed, were so severe as to effect a change in the conduct of those against whom they were directed. One of his productions, entitled, the *Yill-wife's Lamentation*, was the means of frustrating a scheme which the brewster wives had formed for raising the price of ale. Hunter was a native of Kilmarnock. He served as a soldier in the American war, for which he received a pension of sixpence a day. We have yet a faint recollection of the appearance he had a year or two previous to his death. He was rather below the ordinary size, wore tied hair, was dark complexioned, and, to use a homely phrase, *very spare made*. Indeed, he was latterly so reduced in body, that he himself waggishly remarked one day to a neighbour, that his friends would be able to carry him to the grave in a *pocket-napkin!* He died at a very advanced age, about the year 1822.

To return to the subject of the riot. The magistrates issued a proclamation by tuck of drum, offering a reward of £10 sterling for the guilty persons. "Lang Tam," as he is styled in the ballad, appears to have given information respecting a goodly number of them; at all events, ten of the ringleaders were seized, imprisoned, and afterwards tried at the Autumn Court at Ayr. To quote again from the *Caledonian Mercury* of 1764:

"Alexander Thomson, William Wylie, James Crawford, John Hill, Adam White, David Dunlop, William Nemmo, William Davies or Davidson, Hugh Thomson, *alias* Bulloch, with Robert Creelman, tradesmen and journeymen in Kilmarnock, were indicted for raising a tumult at and in the church of Kilmarnock at the settlement of Mr Lindsay as minister of that parish in July last. The last seven were acquitted by the jury, and the first three found guilty, and sentenced to be imprisoned for a month, and whipt through the streets of Air, and to find caution for keeping the peace and a good behaviour for a twelvemonth."

The Rev. Mr Lindsay died in 1774, and was succeeded by Mr Mutrie, whom also Burns has noticed in the *Ordination*.

Soon after Mr Mutrie's death, which occurred in June,

1785, the late Rev. James Mackinlay, D.D., whose ordination formed the subject of Burns's poem just alluded to, became minister of the second charge of Kilmarnock. He was a native of Douglas in Lanarkshire, and was born in 1756. He was licensed on the 3rd July, 1782, and delivered his first sermon at Riccarton. Through the influence of Sir W. Cunningham of Auchenskeith, in whose family he had been for some time tutor, he obtained the presentation to the Low Church from the Earl of Glencairn in 1785. On the Rev. Mr Grant being translated to Edinburgh in 1808, his Grace the Duke of Portland, in compliance with a petition from the inhabitants of Kilmarnock, appointed Mr Mackinlay to the first charge. He died suddenly, on the 10th February, 1841. A volume of his sermons was lately published, with a memoir by his son, the Rev. James Mackinlay of Glasgow, and a portrait of the author from a painting by our talented townsman, William Tannock, Esq.

As a preacher few divines have been more generally admired and esteemed. The sweetness and compass of his voice imparted a charm to all his sentiments; and the energy and warmth of his manner marked him as one peculiarly fitted for his sacred calling.

The Rev. John Robertson—another of the clerical gentlemen on whom the bard of Ayrshire vented his satire—was for several years the colleague of Dr Mackinlay. He was ordained on the 25th April, 1765, and died June 5th, 1798.

When the Reformation was effected, in 1560, it was naturally impracticable, at first, to appoint properly qualified ministers for all the churches or parishes of the land. It was found necessary to associate three, four, or more contiguous parishes under the charge of one minister, who alone was legally authorized to administer the sacraments and to solemnize marriages, while in each parish a "reader" or "exhorter" was appointed to conduct public worship and communicate religious instruction. This arrangement, under various modifications, subsisted till after the beginning of the seventeenth century; and from the *Book of Assignations of Stipends*, we learn that the parishes of "Lowdoun" and "Ricartoun" were thus associated with "Kilmarnok." The district, which now forms the parish of Fenwick, was also included in this combined parish. In the year 1574, the minister of the conjoined parishes was "Maister Robert Wilkie,"* James Hall was "reidare" at Lowdoun, and that office was vacant in the two other parishes. The annual stipend of the minister was fixed at £133 6s. 8d. Scots, "with the Kirkland of Kilmarnok," estimated at £4 Scots, while that of the reader was £20 Scots.†

We have found it impossible to draw up a complete list of the ministers of Kilmarnock during the troublous period, extending from the Reformation to the final establishment of Presbyterianism in 1689. In the beginning of the seventeenth century, Hew Fullarton held the office, and was succeeded by Michael Wallace, who was minister till 1640. From that date till about 1670 the chief minister was Matthew Mowat, a man of some mark among the Presbyterian party of the period. He seems to have enjoyed and exerted great influence, secular as well as ecclesiastical, in the town of Kilmarnock.

* From the *Diary* of James Melvill, and Calderwood's *History of the Church of Scotland*, in which Wilkie is frequently mentioned, it appears that he had a not unimportant share in the labour of establishing the Protestant faith and worship in Scotland. In the Acts of the Secret Council (1587, &c.) directed against "Jesuits, seminarie Priests, and excommunicat Persons," he is named as one of the Pastors before whom "all and sundrie Earls, Lords, Barons, Freeholders, Gentlemen, Inhabitants of our Burrowes, and other our Lieges whatsoever," were to "conveen" and sign the statutory confession of their faith. In the Act of the Convention of the Kirk held at Edinburgh, in November, 1592, he is mentioned as one of the ministers specially instructed to watch and report the practices "of all Papists, Jesuistes, and reseatters of them within thair bounds, and all uther weightie enormities that sall fall out and com to thair knawlage."

† The minister's stipend would thus be £11 8s. 10¾d., that of the reader £1 13s. 4d. English.

Along with several other clergymen of the district (the most conspicuous of whom were Nevay of Newmilns, Wyllie of Mauchline, and the well-known Guthrie of Fenwick), he took part in the great celebration of the Lord's Supper on Mauchline Muir, in June, 1648, when the Covenanters, on the last day of the solemnity, were attacked, and a number of them slain, by a body of troops under the orders of the Earl of Callander and the Earl of Middleton.

The first meeting of the Kirk Session of Fenwick was "holden," as the minute expresses it, "be Mr Matthew Mowat, minister at the Old Kirk of Killmarnok, upone the twentie-sevene day of June, the year of God, 1644." In the same minute the church of Fenwick is called "the New Kirk of Killmarnok." Mr William Guthrie, the first minister of Fenwick, had not then been appointed. His ordination took place on the 7th November of the same year.

It is not distinctly known under what arrangements the Church of Kilmarnock became a collegiate charge; but it is ascertained that, for some time previous to 1648, Mr Mowat had the assistance of a "helper;" and that in that year, or about four years after the disjunction of the new parish of Fenwick, Mr James Rowat was appointed "conjunct" or "colleague" minister with Mr Mowat. We do not hear of any other second minister till the appointment of Mr Wright in 1700, when unusual exertions were made by the Heritors, the Kirk Session, and the Town Council, to secure a stipend for the second charge.

Mr Mowat died before the last and severest heat of the Persecution set in; but Mr Rowat continued to minister at Kilmarnock till the period of the Indulgence. He survived the Revolution, and died in 1692.*

---

* According to the following list of charitable bequests, Mr Rowat left 100 merks to the poor of the parish. The list was copied from two old boards, which were

We have already had occasion to mention Mr Alexander Wedderburn,* who was minister at Kilmarnock for some time previous to the Revolution. He was one of five ministers deposed, in April, 1665, by the (then Episcopal) Presbytery of Saint Andrews, for alleged contumacy and rebellion, at the instance of the well-known primate, Archbishop Sharp. He accepted the Indulgence, and appears to have been a man of moderate views and estimable character. After his death in December, 1678, the indulged ministers of the district in turns officiated in Kilmarnock for some years. For six years previous to 1688 the ecclesiastical history of the parish is almost a blank, for we know nothing more than that the name of the Episcopalian curate was Robert Bell;† and that, as there is reason to believe, the Presbyterians continued to worship privately in a "Meeting-house" in the town, under the pastorate of Mr James Osburn, who was the first minister after the Revolution.

discovered in 1851 at the repairing of a house (formerly the sexton's), opposite the west corner of the Low Churchyard. The boards, it is believed, hung in the interior of the old church, which was taken down in 1802:

"William Taylor, merchant, died April, 1675, left 100 merks."
"James Rowat, minister, who died Feb., 1692, left 100 merks."
"John Harper, merchant, died Sept., 1716, left 500 merks."
"James Hutchison, malster, died October 20th [year obliterated], left 100 merks."
"Mathew Miller of Glenlee, who died January, 1722, left 200 merks."
"Jasper Tough, surgeon, died January, 1731, left 100 merks."
"John Adam, merchant, Glasgow, who died 1734, left 100 merks."
"[Two obliterated] one, 1742, left 400 merks."
"Janet Livingston, spouse to Robert Montgomerie, who died 1743, left 200 merks."
"Margaret Cunninghame, relict of Adam Galt, wright, Riccarton, who died 1746, left 100 merks."
"William Derby, who died March, 1756, left 100 merks."
"John Murchland, merchant, Kilmarnock, who died May 5th, 1759, left to the poor £100 sterling."

* Sir William Mure of Rowallan, who suffered imprisonment with his father during the troubles of the Church of Scotland, had a son baptized by Mr Wedderburn. The baptism is thus recorded in the old Session Book of Fenwick: "May 24, 1676—William, son to Sir William Mure and Dame Mary Scot of Rowallan, was baptized by Mr Alexr Wedderburn, minr of Kilmarnock."

† For a further notice of Mr Bell, see Appendix.

LIST OF THE MINISTERS OF THE LOW CHURCH SINCE THE REVOLUTION.

(The italic *o* indicates ordained; *a*, admitted; and *t*, translated.)

NAMES.	SECOND CHARGE.	FIRST CHARGE.	DIED OR REMOVED.
JAMES OSBURN,		*o* Aug. 9, 1688,	*t* To Aberdeen, July, 1696.
FRANCIS FINLAYSON,		*o* May 11, 1699,	Died Feby 6, 1710.
WILLIAM WRIGHT,*	*o* Sep. 26, 1700,	*a* May 3, 1711,	Died July 4, 1724.
GEORGE PEDEN,	*o* May 3, 1711,		Died Dec. 23, 1721.
PATRICK PAISLEY,	*o* May 6, 1724,	*a* In 1725,	Died Dec. 11, 1736
LAURENCE HILL,	*o* May 6, 1725,	*a* In 1739,	*t* To Glasgow, March 8, 1750.
ROBERT HALL,	*o* April 11, 1739,		Died June 5, 1762.
JAMES LESLIE,		*o* Jan. 17, 1751,	Died May 19, 1764.
WILLIAM LINDSAY,	*a* In 1764,		Died April 30, 1774.
JOHN ROBERTSON, A.M.,		*o* April 25, 1765,	Died June 5, 1798.
JOHN MUTRIE,	*o* March 8, 1775,		Died June 2, 1785.
JAMES MACKINLAY, D.D.,	*o* April 6, 1786,	*a* Feb. 12, 1809,	Died Feby 10, 1841.
DAVID RITCHIE, D.D.,		*a* Feb. 27, 1800,	*t* To Edinburgh, July 2, 1801.
ANDREW GRANT, D.D.,		*a* May 6, 1802,	*t* To Edinburgh, Oct. 13, 1808.
JOHN M'LEOD, D.D.,	*a* Nov. 23, 1809,		*t* To Dundonald, Feby 15, 1816.
ROBERT STIRLING, D.D.,	*o* Sep. 19, 1816,		*t* To Galston, Feb. 12, 1824.
GEORGE SMITH, D.D.,	*o* Sep. 16, 1824,		*t* To Penpont, May 9, 1833.
DAVID STRONG,	*o* Aug. 29, 1833,	*a* Sept. 2, 1841,	*t* To Dailly, Septr 21, 1843.
JAMES B. HAMILTON,		*a* Nov. 9, 1843.	
DANIEL V. THOMSON,	*o* Nov. 9, 1843.		

* In Wodrow's *Analecta*, printed for the Maitland Club in 1843, Mr Wright's death is thus noticed: "July, 1724.—In the beginning of this moneth this Church, and particularly thir bounds, susteans a great loss by the death of Mr William Wright, minister at Kilmarnock, pretty suddainly. He had preached on the Monday at Dreghorn, and dyed on the Saturday morning. He was a man of great integrity and considerable learning; an excellent preacher; of strong passions, but of great piety and painfulness. He printed his *Heptarchus* at the Union, and a paper against Calder, and some things upon the Overtures where he acted and spoke, as informed from his acquaintances at Glasgow."

CHAPTER XIII.

The schoolmaster does not do all; but he lays the foundation of all that is angelic amongst men.

JOHN KENNEDY.

RESPECTING the schools and schoolmasters of Kilmarnock, in early times, we have comparatively little information. In the Boyd charter-chest is a paper purporting to be a grant by James Lord Boyd, "for keeping ane schoole within the parocheine of the Old Kirk of Kilmarnock, and for provisioune of ane constant rent and stipend for holding ane schoolemaister in the said parocheine of the Old Kirk of Kilmarnock, quho may also serve as musician in the said Old Kirk in all tyme coming." Unfortunately the document has no date attached to it; but the grant is supposed to have been made by the eighth Lord Boyd previously to the year 1654. The words "Old Kirk of Kilmarnock" were no doubt used to distinguish it from the "New Kirk of Kilmarnock"—a name given, as we have shown in the preceding Chapter, to the church of Fenwick when the two parishes were disjoined in 1642. That the community enjoyed the advantages of a parish school, at least from that time, is well ascertained. In 1633 Parliament passed an Act to establish a school in every parish of Scotland, "upon a sum to be stented upon every plough or husband land according to the worth;" and in 1696 another Act rendered this assessment imperative.

The first teacher of whom we have mention is "Johne Andersoune, scholemaster of Kilmarnock," who died in 1629.

"Thomas Mure, Doctor* of the School," is appointed precentor, December 2, 1647. After his time mention is made of James Alexander, David Airth, and James Osburne, as having been successively schoolmasters of Kilmarnock, but the dates of their appointment cannot be ascertained. There is reason to believe that the last-mentioned of these is the same person who was afterwards minister of the parish. It may be worth noticing that in 1677, some time after his demission, he estimates the balance of school salary due to him as "six pound starling money," by far the first mention, we believe, of sterling money in any of our local records. From a minute of Session dated December 14, 1676, it appears that "the quarter payments for the schoolers" were "23s. 4d. for Latine, and 16s. 8d. for the Scots," or English, as it would now be called.

On the 10th May, 1677, Mr Robert Young was appointed "maister of the grammar-school;" he was to have a stipend of eight score merks, and the fees above-mentioned. The school had been vacant for a considerable period, and now there was every disposition to foster it, as is evident from the following curious extract:

"May 24, 1677.—The Session desires the Magistrats to take a course for payment of deficient quarter payments.

"Also, this day the Session appoynts that the elders in their respective quarters shall bring in a list of the boyes fit for the school, that their parents may put them to school.

"Also, the Session will pay the quarter payments of the poor whom they list to be put to school.

"Also, the Session appoynts that non be put to inferior schools who are fitt for the publick school."

The next schoolmaster was a Matthew Cunningham, who seems to have taught under Episcopalian auspices—at least

* "DOCTOR—The title anciently given to the masters of the High School of Edinburgh. The rectorship of the High School was once reckoned a more honourable station than that of Professor of Humanity in the University."—*Jamieson's Scottish Dictionary.*

the Presbyterian Kirk Session, after the Revolution, had considerable difficulty in getting the parochial registers out of his hands.

The funds available for the payment of the schoolmaster seem to have suffered before, or at, the Revolution; for several times we find intimation that "the Doctor of the School is not sufficientlie provided;" and the Kirk Session had to make advances for the support of the institution "till they should be riplie advised about a settled sallarie." The Act of Parliament of 1696 would partly remove this difficulty.

The first settled teacher after the Revolution was Mr John Sprott,* appointed in 1690. He does not seem to have been well supported, for he was very speedily followed by James Menteith, who also withdrew after about a year's service. His successor, Robert Murdoch, remained for five years. By this time the Act of 1696 was in force, and from the time of the appointment of his successor, Mr John Thomson, previously schoolmaster of Prestonpans, the institution seems to have continued to flourish. All along the schoolmaster was also session-clerk, and, as such, keeper of the parochial registers.

The next in order of the parish schoolmasters was Robert Montgomerie, appointed in 1704. He was suspended from the office in 1709, but reponed in 1716; and during the interval the duties were performed by John Adam and Thomas Breakanridge. Montgomerie finally retired in 1736, and was succeeded by James Smith.

During the incumbency of Montgomerie the parish school of Kilmarnock was made a collegiate charge. One of the

---

* "1693.—To John Sprott, Doctor in the grammar-school, for his Sallarie from Lambua, 1693, to Martimas, 1693, £5 Scots."—*Kirk Treasurer's Book.*

We cannot learn from the Records in what part of the town the school-house was then situated; but it appears from the first of the following brief extracts to have been a very humble erection: "1693.—To a man for turffs to cover the School, 6s. Scots." "Jan. 29, 1694.—To James Cathcart for 13 foot of glass to the School windows, £3 18s. Scots."—This would be sixpence a foot, English money.

masters superintended the parochial or grammar-school, as it was termed, and was restricted to the teaching of Latin, Greek, &c. The other had the management of the burgh school, in which English and the more common branches were taught.* The former teacher was supported by the landward heritors, and the latter from the town's funds.

In reference to the origin of the burgh school, an extract or two may be given from the records of the Kirk Session:

"23rd March, 1727.—The Session of Kilmarnock being met and constituted—the Rev. Mr Paisley, moderator—

"*Inter alia*—The Session agree to give forty pounds Scots per annum for encouragement of an English school, but only during pleasure, the Town Council granting twenty pounds Scots for the said end."

"17th November, 1728.—The Session being met and constituted—

"Sederunt—The Rev. Mr Paisley, moderator, with Mr Hill and the elders.

"*Inter alia*—The Session finding that the Presbytery will not sustain their grant of forty pounds yearly for encouraging an English school, unanimously agree to stop further payment of the said grant."

The following, relative to the same matter, is from the books of the Town Council:

"27th March, 1727.—The said day Langlands having reported from the Kirk Session, that they were willing to give the encouragement of forty pounds Scots yearly of sallary, to ane English schoolmaster, during pleasure, upon the Town Council assisting to augment that sallary, which, with the great occasion for a well-qualified schoolmaster being considered by the Town Council, they agree to give twenty pounds Scots yearly for the encouragement of such a schoolmaster yearly, during pleasure, they being always satisfied with the person, and recommends to Langlands, Baillie Dickie, Alex. Brown with Baillie Moor, to treat with the Kirk Session, anent a fit and proper person, and report."

Such, apparently, was the origin of the burgh school of Kilmarnock, which was merged in the Academy in 1807. From 1736 till 1748 the salary was forty pounds Scots, or £3 6s. 8d. sterling yearly; and from the latter date it varied till 1803, when Mr Andrew Henderson, the incumbent at that time, got it increased to £15, in consideration that the parochial schoolmasters had got an augmentation of their

* See Report of a Committee of the Directors of the Kilmarnock Academy, published in 1852.

T

salaries. From 1745 till 1782 the English schoolmasters were Mr Eddie, Mr William Dun, Mr Adie, and Mr William Henderson. The latter died in the beginning of the last-mentioned year. Regarding their efficiency or success as teachers we have no account.

We find James Smith, the parish schoolmaster, mentioned in the Council Books, in 1748, as complaining of his colleague, Mr Dun, the English schoolmaster, "assuming to teach Latin, and thereby encroaching on Mr Smith's privileges."* Of the state of the parish school under his mastership we know nothing. Through the medium, however, of a small work, entitled, *Genuine Memoirs of the Life of John Graham, A.M.*, who was grammar-school teacher here from the year 1763 till 1779, we learn that the parish school at that period was one of considerable repute. The sons of gentlemen of the first rank, and even boarders from families of distinction in America, attended it; and, on account of Mr Graham's brilliant talents and engaging manner, they profited much under his care. Along with the mastership of the school, Mr Graham held the situations of precentor and custodier of the parish records; and during the sixteen years he resided here he maintained a high character as an instructor of youth.

Happy, perhaps, had it been for Graham had he remained in the quiet locality of Kilmarnock, where he enjoyed all the necessaries, and even many of the elegancies of life; but ambition, which has led many eminent men into the vortex of ruin, lured him from the path of virtue; and vice, which

---

* Some time after this period, namely, in 1766, the interests of the English teacher also were considered to be injured by other English schools being opened in the town. The matter is thus noticed in the minutes of Council: "The which day the Council considering the state of the English school, and that several strangers have of late set up English schools to the prejudice of the public teacher, the Council do therefore appoint the Rev. John Robison, Mr James Oliphant, with Bailie John Wilson, Bailie Hugh Parker, and Doctor Alexander Tough, to examine said schools, and to report to the Council how far the said teachers are qualified, that if they are not, proper methods may be taken to suppress them."

never fails to inflict condign punishment upon its votaries, hurried him on to a melancholy end.

The particulars of his history are worthy of record. He was the son of a respectable farmer in Perthshire, and was born in the year 1734. In his early years he made great proficiency in the Latin and Greek languages, and soon became so thoroughly versed in the ancient classics as to be able to explain many doubtful passages. When about the age of eighteen he entered the University of Glasgow, where he distinguished himself during the first year as a student of philology. The second and third years he spent in the study of logic and moral philosophy under Dr Adam Smith, the celebrated author of the *Wealth of Nations*. But Mr Graham, who was destined for the ministry, had the misfortune about this time to lose his father by death; and that event so narrowed his pecuniary circumstances, that he was compelled to leave the university before taking his degree. In the intervals of leisure from his regular studies he had acquired a considerable knowledge of the polite arts, especially of music; and being thus highly accomplished, and having an ingenuous turn of mind, his society was much courted by his fellow-students, who mourned over the blank which his absence had occasioned among them.

"In 1756," says the writer of his memoirs, "when he was only twenty-two years of age, he was obliged to accept the place of private tutor to the son of a gentleman in the south of Scotland, where he spent three years, and then accompanied his pupil to the University of Glasgow. When he arrived the second time at that famed seminary, his uncommon abilities began to display themselves in the most shining manner; and the learned Mr Moor, then professor of Greek, employed him during his leisure hours as an assistant. Patient and indefatigable in the discharge of his duty, he continued at the university till his pupil had completed his studies, and along with him he took the degree of *Master of Arts*. For his integrity in this service he received a considerable gratuity, and was recommended to another family of rank as a tutor to their son in the University of Edinburgh."

In 1763 a teacher was wanted for the grammar-school of Kilmarnock. Mr Graham, who possessed all the necessary qualifications, was elected to the office, and the school immediately became one of the most efficient in Ayrshire.

Being now comfortably situated, Mr Graham married the daughter of a farmer near Douglas, in Lanarkshire, whose amiable disposition tended in some measure to increase the number of his boarders. For several years after this period the stream of his life, if we may so speak, experienced not the slightest agitation, and unclouded happiness presided over his domestic circle. His varied scholastic attainments, too, procured him many acquaintances, who proffered him their friendship.

But, unfortunately for Graham, an intimacy which he formed in 1779 with an individual of the name of H———r, proved the source of his ruin. This person is called by Mr Graham's biographer "a miscreant fellow, an adventurer and shárper, who, under the pretence of being a man of fortune, cheated many industrious men of their all; and would have been punished for a cheat," continues the same authority, "had he not made his escape to London." From that city he transmitted several letters to Graham, picturing in flattering colours the advantages he would obtain by leaving Kilmarnock, and opening a boarding-school in the vicinity of the great metropolis of England. Fired with the idea of becoming great and opulent, Mr Graham hastily formed the resolution of removing to London. He never dreamed that the extravagant representations which his correspondent had made tended only to deceive; nor did he take into account the many obstacles which a stranger, particularly one advanced in years and without influential patrons, was likely to meet in a strange locality, ere he could establish himself as a teacher of a genteel seminary. Unhappily, too, for Graham, his connection with H——r had lessened to such a degree the number of his particular friends, that no one thought of offering him advice on the subject. He had also incurred the displeasure of many of the inhabitants by claiming, in virtue of his office, certain dues or emoluments, to which they thought he was not entitled.

Mr Graham's household furniture was so extensive and his books so numerous that a whole week was spent in disposing of them by auction; and the sum derived from the sale was very considerable. With his wife, eight children, and a servant-maid, he then set out for London, in a "hired coach," which in those days must have been very expensive for a journey of four hundred miles. After being a month or two in London, he opened a school at Pancras Wells, trusting to his own abilities for success; but he soon discovered that his means were inadequate to establish himself in that manner which was necessary to command attention and respect. However, like Geordie Chalmers, he determined to "set a stout heart to a stey brae;" and with his own scanty means and sums of money which he succeeded in borrowing, he furnished his house in as splendid a style as possible; but when applications were made for the payment of the debts, he had nothing to give save his furniture, part of which he gave to some of his creditors as security. In short, before he had been many months at Pancras, his circumstances became so desperate "that he formed the fatal resolution of committing a forgery upon the Bank of England."

"Ruminating one day," says his biographer, "upon his distressed situation, he went into a house in the Rules of the Fleet Prison, where, happening to enter into conversation with an engraver, he employed him to engrave a ten pound bank-note. The engraver was a prisoner in the Fleet, and, as it is well known that most of these gentry, to use their own expression, *know how to err on the safe side*, he took what money he could obtain from Graham; and, as soon as the plate was finished, in order to save his own neck, gave information to a city magistrate, upon which Graham was apprehended, and brought to trial at the Old Bailey, in October, 1781; but, as none of the notes had been issued, he escaped with his life, and was sentenced to six months' imprisonment."

The punishment which he thus received seems not to have acted as a warning to him; for, as soon as the term of his confinement had expired, he again began to forge upon the bank, and in a way somewhat ingenious and novel. From bank-notes of fifteen pounds he erased the letters *e e n* out of the word *fifteen*, and by means of a type cut for the purpose, artfully introduced a *y* in their stead, thus making the notes appear as of *fifty* pounds value. These were generally passed by Mrs Graham, who, the better to avoid suspicion, "travelled in her post-chaise," and was arrayed in a style of elegance equal to that of a lady of fashion. In this unlawful mode of living they were for some time very successful. At length the fraud was detected at the bank. Suspicion fell upon the guilty parties; and they were apprehended at an inn in Southampton, by a Mr Wright of Tothill-Fields Bridewell. Wright had followed Graham thither from Winchester, where he had been on a visit to Tyrie, who was shortly afterwards executed at Portsmouth for high treason.*

At their trial Mr Graham and his wife upbraided or blamed each other; but they were both found guilty and sentenced to be executed. Mrs Graham was recommended to mercy; but the hapless schoolmaster, whose talents might have procured him honour and respect, had they been properly directed, suffered at Tyburn, October 15, 1782.

* Graham, when visiting Tyrie, gave him half a guinea, wherewith to purchase implements to break out of prison.—*See Scots Magazine.*

The history of Graham is not without instruction. The writer of his life truly remarks, that "neither natural abilities nor a liberal education are sufficient to screen men from the power of temptation, unless the love of virtue and the fear of God regulate their conduct. . . . Too eager a desire to procure wealth often defeats its own intention. Riches are generally acquired in a slow, prudent manner; but when men seek for affluence all at once, they frequently bring shame and ruin on themselves and their families."

Mr Graham was succeeded in the parish school of Kilmarnock by Mr John Duncan, afterwards minister of the gospel at Ardrossan. He is the first of the parish schoolmasters officially designated "Rector of the grammar-school."

The next of our parish schoolmasters was Mr Shepherd, appointed in 1789, who, we understand, was obliged to resign his situation in consequence of his delicate state of health. He was succeeded, in 1797, by Mr William Thomson, afterwards rector of the present Academy, whose talents and success as a public instructor are so well known as to preclude any comment on our part. It is a fact worthy of record, that no other teacher in Ayrshire, and, we may venture to affirm, no other in Scotland, sent to the university so many well-qualified youths, who, in after life, occupied honourable and lucrative situations in the senate, the army, the pulpit, and at the bar.

Of the burgh schoolmasters we have little account till the beginning of the present century, when we find Mr Andrew Henderson—a teacher of considerable celebrity—the burgh schoolmaster. He had a large establishment for boarders, which was numerously attended, and most efficiently conducted. He died in 1805, and was succeeded by Mr Morton, who, in 1807, was translated to Dunbar, and who was succeeded by Mr William Henderson, youngest son of Mr Henderson, above-mentioned.

At this time, 1807, the present building was erected, and

designated the Academy.* One-half of the expenses was defrayed by the landward heritors; and the other half was made up from the town's funds and private subscriptions. The foundation stone was laid with much solemnity on the 25th June of that year. The Magistrates and Councillors, the Ministers and Teachers, together with several Masonic Lodges, and a great concourse of spectators, were present, as appears from the following copy of a document which, we believe, was deposited in the foundation of the building:

F. D. O. M.
Magistratibus Concilioque Municipali Cellamarnensi
Et Agrorum Possessoribus ejusdem Parochiæ
Ad Juventutem bonis in Literis instituendam
Academiam ædificandam curare inter sese statutis,
Hujusce Ædificii Fundamenta, in hunc usum dicati,
POSUIT
GULIELMUS PARKER, Armiger de Assloss, et Municipii Magistratus senior,
VII. Kal. Julii, Anno Christi nati M.DCCC.VII.
Artis vero Architectonicæ VM.DCCC.VII.
Serenissimo Principe Georgio Tertio annum XLVII. Regni agente;
Præsentibus ROBERTO BORLAND, Armigero, Magistratu juniore,
Aliisque ex Concilio Municipali,—MINISTRIS Verbi Dei,
PRÆCEPTORIBUS eorumque Discipulis,
Opificum MAGISTRIS,—ARCHITECTO,—et Operis REDEMPTORIBUS;
Adstantibus Magistris Fratribusque Sodalitatis Architectorum
Ædium Sti Joannis, Sti Marnoci, Sti Andreæ;
Et magna stipante frequentia spectantium, cunctisque plaudentibus;
Civibus armatis circumstantibus:
QUOD FELIX FAUSTUMQUE SIT, FAXIT
DEUS OPT. MAX.

Mr William Thomson, then parish schoolmaster, was, like his predecessors, restricted to the teaching of the classics, and was made rector of the Academy; Mr Henderson was elected teacher of English; and Mr William Jamieson teacher of the commercial department. Mr Thomson held his office, discharging the duties thereof, as we formerly said, with great

---

* Before the erection of the present Academy, the parish school was that house at the corner of Green Street, next the Corn Exchange Buildings. It was built, we believe, about 1752, and was then only one storey in height.

skill and efficiency, till 1830, when he died, and was succeeded by Mr Alexander Harkness as classical master.

Mr Henderson resigned his situation in 1813, established a school in King Street, and became the most popular teacher in the West of Scotland. When the population of the town and parish was little more than 12,000, he had upwards of seven hundred pupils. He was an excellent disciplinarian, and a most efficient and indefatigable teacher. In the early part of his career, for five days in the week, he taught most assiduously from six o'clock in the morning till late in the evening; and Saturday, during the shooting season, was generally devoted to field-sports, of which he was passionately fond.

In 1828 Mr Jamieson resigned his situation, and afterwards embarked for Australia, but died on the voyage. He was succeeded by the aforesaid Mr William Henderson, who, in 1843, retired, and was succeeded by Thomas Lee, F.R.A.S., the present master of the commercial and mathematical department.

In 1813, on Mr Henderson's first leaving the Academy, he was succeeded by the Rev. William Thomson, afterwards minister of Old Monkland. He resigned his situation in 1820, and was succeeded by Mr Andrew Weir. Mr Weir was a painstaking and successful teacher. He wrote a series of English school-books, which have been pronounced, by competent judges, excellent works. During the latter years of his incumbency some disputes arose between him and the Directors; and in 1847 he removed to Glasgow, where he died in September, 1852. He was succeeded by Mr Paul R. Forrester, who was appointed master of St Andrew's Sessional School, Glasgow, in 1852. He died in March, 1854. His successor in the Kilmarnock Academy was Mr John Graham, who removed to Stirling in 1860, and was succeeded by Mr William C. Logan, the present English teacher.

In 1830 the Directors appointed a fourth teacher, Mr James

Connell, a native of Kilmarnock, who, by much perseverance and mental application, had attained considerable celebrity as a student of mathematics and geography. But this arrangement was merely ephemeral. Either the inhabitants would not or could not support such a teacher. He accepted the situation of commercial teacher in Irvine Academy, was afterwards translated, in 1834, to a similar situation in the High School of Glasgow, and while there had the degree of LL.D. conferred on him. He died in the spring of 1846.

"Dr Connell," as one of his biographers has said, "was no ordinary man; endowed by nature with talents of a superior order, he had cultivated them by the most careful and unremitting study. . . . There was scarcely a branch of knowledge with which he was not somewhat conversant. But natural history, especially in the marvels of insect variety and transformation, was his delight; and while he was extensively read in the works, and familiar with the researches, of all the great naturalists of modern times, his ever active mind led him to make observations for himself, the fruits of which appeared in an interesting and yearly increasing collection of natural curiosities, made both here and on the Continent."

Mr Harkness, the parochial schoolmaster already mentioned, who bore a high character as a teacher and classical scholar, died 17th June, 1851. He was succeeded by Alexander Smith, A.M., who was appointed to the office in April, 1852.

In connection with the parish there are two other schools, usually called "Side Schools"—one on the estate of Rowallan, and one in the barony of Grougar. The former is conducted by Mr William Brown, and the latter by Mr John Watson.

In the town there is a considerable number of private or adventure schools, the principal of which are the New Academy, conducted by Mr William Gunnyon; West Langland Street Academy, conducted by Mr James Rose; Clark Street Academy, conducted by Mr James Stevenson; East

George Street Academy, conducted by Mr Daniel Wyllie; and Allanhill School, conducted by the Misses Grant. In the first of these, the classics and the modern languages are taught along with the more ordinary branches; and in the last, the pupils are instructed in German, French, music, &c.

There are also two schools in connection with the Free High Church. In one of them—the Townhead District School, opened in 1853, and conducted by Mr Donald Ferguson—the ordinary branches are taught as in promiscuous schools. In the other, which is composed of young girls, and under the superintendence of Miss Templeton, the branches are knitting, sewing, reading, and writing.

The educational institutions established by societies and through the influence of benevolent individuals are—East Shaw Street School, the Free School, the School of Industry, the Nelson Street School of Industry, the Nelson Street Elementary School, and the Holm Mission School.

East Shaw Street School was instituted in 1798 by the feuars resident in the district, and is under the management of a committee chosen annually from their number. It is conducted by Mr William Fraser; and the branches taught are reading, writing, grammar, arithmetic, and book-keeping.

The Free School, Dundonald Road, which is taught by Mr John Cameron, was instituted in 1817, and is supported entirely by voluntary contributions. It is under the management of twenty-four directors chosen from the subscribers; and its object is " to teach the elementary branches of education to those children only whose parents are unable to pay for their instruction at other schools."

The Female School of Industry was founded in 1830, and is taught by Miss Roxburgh. It is supported partly by the fees and work of the scholars, and partly by the benevolence of a society of ladies, under whose auspices it is conducted. A handsome and commodious school-house, with suitable play-ground attached, was erected for this institution in West Netherton Street in 1859, when there was added a department for instruction in reading, writing, and arithmetic, which is under the superintendence of Miss Miller.

The Nelson Street Female School of Industry, and the Nelson Street Elementary School, were instituted by, and at the expense of, Mr John Stewart, clothier. The Female School, which is conducted by Miss White, was commenced in 1845, and was projected for the purpose of teaching the children of the poor some useful branch of industry, and also of supplying them at the same time with moral and religious instruction. The branch of art taught is Ayrshire needlework. The pupils pay one penny a week, and receive the entire proceeds of their labour. The object of the Elementary School, which was opened in 1851, and is taught by Mr Dods, is to supply cheap education to the children of such poor parents as have large families, and who may be averse to have them educated at institutions purely gratuitous. Reading, writing, arithmetic, grammar, and geography are taught. For the first branch one penny a week is charged, and for all the branches, twopence.

The Holm Mission School was instituted through the exertions of the Rev. James Banks. It was opened in 1858, and is conducted by Mr James Cree. Reading, writing, grammar, arithmetic, and geography are taught. For reading the pupils pay one penny a week, and for all the branches, three half-pence.

Besides these institutions there are three schools under the auspices of the Parochial Board. In the first, which is conducted by Mr Thomas Cuthbertson, reading, writing, and arithmetic are taught. In the second, which is composed of young girls, and managed by Miss Weir, the branches are reading, sewing, and knitting; and in the third, which is also composed of girls, and superintended by Miss Glover, the branch taught is Ayrshire needlework.

CHAPTER XIV.

> For years among his people he had toiled,
> Holding the gospel message forth with zeal.
> No laggard watchman he—no careless guardian
> Lethargic at his post—no miser churl,
> Who, knowing truth, would dole it out to others
> In scanty morsels, cold, insipid, dead;
> Starving the hungry, lulling those that sleep,
> Improving none! His heart was in the work;
> He loved the labour, and thought nothing hard
> If souls could but be won.
>
> W. H. MADDEN.

IN 1765 the town was somewhat improved by the Earl of Glencairn, who caused a new line of street (now called Glencairn Street and Titchfield Street) to be opened up between Kilmarnock and Riccarton. Like the other old thoroughfares of the burgh, the road leading to that village was crooked and narrow; but the one which was formed under the auspices of the earl has the very opposite qualities, being broad and straight. It is about half a mile in length; and though many of the houses are of an humble kind, it appears even at the present day one of the most respectable streets of the town. The feu-duty charged by the earl was moderate; and the feuars were enabled to add to their houses pretty extensive gardens, the advantages of which require no comment.

In 1772 the first of our Dissenting churches was built. We refer to the Secession Meeting-house, or Wellington Street United Presbyterian Church, as it was latterly called, which stood at Gallows-knowe,* and which was taken down in 1861. Like other public buildings of the period of its erection its style was plain and homely. In 1859 the congregation, in order to have a more centrical place of worship, erected a commodious and elegant edifice in Portland Road, which bears the name of Portland Road United Presbyterian Church. The foundation stone was laid on the 7th March of the same year. The building is in the Byzantine style, from a design by Peddie and Kinnear, architects, Edinburgh. It cost about £1900, and accommodates eight hundred and fifty sitters. The first minister of this church was the esteemed and pious Mr Robert Jaffray, author of an *Essay on the Reasons of Secession from the National Church of Scotland*. Mr Jaffray died in 1814, having faithfully discharged the duties of his office for thirty-nine years.

Not long after his decease the congregation met for the purpose of nominating his successor. A Mr Young and a Mr Tindal were proposed, when a considerable majority voted for the former. The decision of the meeting having been communicated to Mr Young, he signified his willingness to accede to their wishes by accepting the pastoral charge. But the Presbytery, notwithstanding their sustaining the call, opposed, for reasons unknown to us, the desire of the majority and of their candidate.

The friends of Mr Young, disappointed with the decision of the Presbytery, threw up their connection altogether with the Secession body, and applied for preaching to the Old Light Burgher denomination, which movement ended in the ordination of Mr Peter Campbell as pastor of the church at Gallowsknowe, in connection with the party last named. The friends

---

* So called in consequence of being the place of execution in the days of feudalism. The Boyd family had at one time the right of "pit and gallows"—a privilege, says Dr Jamieson, "conferred on a baron, according to our old laws, of having on his ground a *pit* for drowning women, and *gallows* for hanging men convicted of theft."

of Mr Tindal, on the other hand, adhered firmly to the Secession, and hired as a place of worship that house which is now occupied as a school-room in East George Street. By the arrangements of the Presbytery they were regularly supplied with sermon for four years, during which period their numbers considerably increased. A disagreeable lawsuit, respecting the property at Gallows-knowe, had just been brought, by mutual consent, to an amicable adjustment. The Old Light party built a more commodious house in Wellington Street, now known as the Free Henderson Church; on their removal to which the New Light party once more had access to their former premises, and soon after gave a unanimous call to the Rev. George Lawson of Bolton, whose settlement took place in October, 1818. Mr Lawson, who laboured successfully amongst them for nineteen years, was then translated to Selkirk, and was succeeded by the Rev. James Lindsay, who demitted his charge in August, 1854. The present minister is the Rev. Alexander Hamilton, A.M., ordained March, 1855.

In 1775 the Clerk's Lane Church, or Antiburgher Meeting-house, as it was then called, was erected. About thirty years after, the congregation had so increased that it was found inadequate for their accommodation: it was, therefore, rebuilt on a larger scale in 1807. It now contains nearly one thousand sittings. In an architectural point of view it is a very plain structure. Its original occupants were a branch of the Rev. Mr Smeaton's congregation at Kilmaurs, which was formed in 1740, and the first of the sect established in Ayrshire.

Connected with Clerk's Lane Church there have been several ministers, whose talents were of no common order, and whose fame has extended far beyond the bounds of the locality. The first and most remarkable of these was the Rev. James Robertson, alluded to in a previous Chapter. He was the son of a farmer at or near Whitburn, in Linlithgowshire, and was born about the year 1749. By diligent and unwearied application to study, he made, while a youth, rapid progress in the path of learning, and soon became master of six different languages. His ordination took place on the 9th September, 1777. The salary which Mr Robertson at first received was only forty or fifty pounds a year, and it never afterwards rose above eighty; but notwithstanding this very moderate income, his frugal mode of life enabled him not only to live comfortably, but also to maintain a respectable position in society. Of him it may be truly said, as of Goldsmith's village pastor,

> "A man he was to all the country dear,
> And passing rich with forty pounds a year."

His desire for information led him to purchase a great number of books, many of which, being in folio and quarto, must have been very expensive. They amounted to four thousand volumes, and at his death were bought by the Secession Church, and formed the foundation of that superb collection of theological works in Glasgow called the Robertsonian Library. His manner of preaching was peculiar to himself. His discourses, though couched in the plainest language, and abounding in homely similes, seldom failed to impress his hearers with a just sense of what was duty. He was not one of those "things," as Cowper calls them,

> "—————— That mount the rostrum with a skip
> And then skip down again; pronounce a text;
> Cry—hem; and reading what they never wrote,
> Just fifteen minutes, huddle up their work,
> And, with a well-bred whisper, close the scene."

On the contrary, he threw his whole soul into his subject; or, in other words, he was devout, solemn, and earnest. Sometimes, it is true, he was too censorious; but his strokes of satire, though frequently personal, were always put forth with a view to make an indelible impression on the hearts of his hearers; and, with all his severity and familiarity of expression, no minister, perhaps, was ever more beloved by any congregation. Though deeply versed in scholastic lore, he laid no stress on the elegancies of composition, but preferred the substance to the shadow; and that every one might clearly understand him, he studied to be plain and pointed, rather than showy and attractive. An instance or two may be given of the peculiar manner in which he sometimes contrived to rivet his meaning on the minds of his audience.

When preaching one day in the open air on the atonement of Christ, he observed, at one side of the tent, an individual who had lately failed in business, and had paid his creditors with two shillings and sixpence a pound. At the other side he saw another person who had also become bankrupt, and had offered a composition of five shillings. With a stern countenance he looked towards the one and exclaimed, "It wasna half-a-crown in the pound that Christ paid;" then turning round in the direction of the other, "nor five shillings in the pound; but the *whole* pound; as every man wishing to obtain an honest name *should* do."

At the time that Napoleon Bonaparte, with the French army, was spreading terror and devastation over the Continent, and threatening to invade our own country, Mr Robertson happened to preach a sermon before the Associate Synod in Glasgow. He had heard it remarked by some, that the immoral French would never be permitted by Providence to gain the superiority over this "more righteous" kingdom. "Granting," said he, in his discourse, "that we are a' as guid as thae sort o' folk think, Providence is not always nice in the choice of instruments for punishing the wickedness of men. Tak' an example frae amang yoursels: your magistrates dinna ask certificates o' character for their public executioner; they generally select sic clamjamphrie as hae rubbit shouthers wi' the gallows themsels."

With the exception of the late Dr Mackinlay, Mr Robertson was the most popular preacher in Kilmarnock; and when the former happened to be from home, a great many of his hearers generally attended the church of the latter, and sometimes came in for a share of his sarcasm. One Sabbath, when their own favourite preacher was absent, they made a rush into Mr Robertson's chapel just as he had concluded the prayer. The rustling which their entrance occasioned attracted his attention; and, in his usual laconic manner, he said, "Sit roun', sit roun', my frien's, and gie the fleein' army room; for their wee bit idol, ye ken, is no at hame the day."

Mr Robertson, like the Master whom he served, often drew his similes from passing events. At this time the subject of *faith* and *good works*, considered apart from each other, was a fertile theme of controversy. One day, when preaching in a tent at Kilwinning, directly opposite the island of Arran, he said emphatically, and pointing across the Frith of Clyde, "Ye talk of your good works, as if, forsooth, ye had ony claim to God's free grace by your ain merit! I tell you, my frien's, it's a delusion, a diabolical delusion; ye may as weel attempt to sail owre to Arran there on a hen's feather as to get into the kingdom o' heaven by your good works alone. But, my frien's," he continued, "dinna misunderstand me, or draw the rash inference that we undervalue good works; this is by no means the case—everything's bonnie in its ain place; water, for instance, is good for mony a purpose, although ye're a' aware we canna theek kirks wi't!"

On another occasion, after having spoken somewhat freely of the corruption and profligacy of the English Church, he told his hearers that he had been sometimes blamed for so doing, and had been met by the argument that many men of real talent and sterling piety were to be found in the sister establishment. This, he said, though true, was no argument at all; Prelacy was still Prelacy; and as for the worthies spoken of, they were like the bees in Samson's lion, no very nice about their quarters.

Like John Knox, Mr Robertson feared not the face of man; and being shrewd and sensible at all times himself, he could not tolerate nonsense from others, but was sure to show his aversion to it in some shape or other. In the Synod of his church he was on one occasion a party in a discussion. His opponent was weak in argument, but made up the deficiency by noise and vapouring. Mr Robertson burst out into immoderate fits of laughter, for which the Moderator called him to order. "I will not be restrained, sir," answered Mr Robertson; "for I will laugh at nonsense wherever I hear it, for evermore, amen."

In his general conversation also he was pointed. On one occasion a very young minister preached in his church. At the close of the service Mr Robertson asked one of his elders what he thought of the sermon. "In my opinion, sir," said the elder, "there was owre muckle scripture in't." "That was the very best o't, man," returned Mr Robertson; "for sermons without scripture, like brose without lumps, are aye unco fusionless."

These sayings, though but a sample of the many that might be given of this eccentric clergyman, afford perhaps a clearer insight into his character than could be obtained by the most elaborate biography.

Mr Robertson was author of a pamphlet, the object of which was to expose the errors and heresies that were supposed to be contained in a work entitled, *A Practical Essay on the Death of Jesus Christ*, published about the year 1786, by Dr M'Gill of Ayr. This heretical publication, as many reckoned it, created considerable discussion in Ayrshire, and gave rise to Burns's *Kirk's Alarm*, which was written as a satire on the doctor's opponents.

Mr Robertson died on the 3rd of November, 1811, and

was interred, as we formerly said, in the cemetery of the High Church, where a handsome tombstone was erected to his memory, at the expense of his congregation.

Mr Robertson was succeeded by the Rev. John (afterwards Dr) Ritchie. He took a deep interest in the temporal and spiritual welfare of the people under his charge, and of the inhabitants in general; and, like his predecessor, displayed an earnestness and energy in his pulpit orations that strongly evinced his sincerity and zeal as a preacher of the gospel. He was also a zealous advocate for the principles of the Secession. In 1825 he was translated to Potterrow Church, Edinburgh,* and his place in Kilmarnock was filled by the Rev. David Wilson, formerly minister in Balbiggie. Mr Wilson had faithfully discharged his official duties for a series of years, when some misunderstanding arose between him and his congregation; the consequence was, that disagreeable feelings were engendered, which marred, in some measure, his ministerial usefulness, and finally ended in his demitting his charge in 1839.

In the following year the congregation made choice of Mr James Morison (now Professor Morison, D.D., of Glasgow) as their pastor; but about the time of his settlement a pamphlet which he had published on the question, *What must I do to be saved?* created dissatisfaction regarding his theological views among a few of the members of the church, and also among his brethren in the ministry. Some of the doctrines, too, which he preached from the pulpit, were considered to be at variance with the Secession standards. At length, in March, 1841, the matter was brought before the Presbytery in Clerk's Lane Chapel. Considerable excitement prevailed during the trial. Mr Morison advocated his cause in an earnest and eloquent manner, and carried along with him

* Dr Ritchie died at Edinburgh in May, 1861, aged about eighty years. He was a native of Ayr.

the feelings and sympathies of a considerable portion of the auditory. The meeting took place at an early hour of the day, and the deepest interest seemed to be taken by all parties in the proceedings of the Court, which continued its sittings till midnight. An hour or two before the business was closed, the pressure and agitation so much increased, that some of the pews were fairly broken down. The Court wound up the affair by passing a deed of suspension against Mr Morison, who, in his turn, lodged a protest, and appealed to the meeting of Synod. The Supreme Court, after hearing the parties, sustained the decision of the Presbytery, and ultimately decided that Mr Morison be no longer considered either a minister or a member of the Secession Church.

Those of the congregation (about forty in number) who differed from Mr Morison, or, in other words, who adhered to the Secession standards, immediately withdrew, and were for a time supplied with sermon in the hall of the George Inn. They afterwards erected an exceedingly chaste and elegant church in Princes Street, which is now in connection with the United Presbyterian body. In 1842 their present minister, the Rev. David T. Jamieson, was admitted. Under his efficient ministrations, the congregation, which then consisted of about a hundred and twelve persons, has been steadily increasing in prosperity and numbers.

The other party, namely, Mr Morison's adherents, continued to worship in Clerk's Lane Chapel, which, according to arrangements made with those who withdrew, became their property. In 1843, along with other churches holding the same views, they adopted the name of "The Evangelical Union," which now comprises a considerable number of congregations. In 1851 Mr Morison accepted a call from the Evangelical Church, Glasgow, now assembling in a new chapel in North Dundas Street. We may mention that, in 1843, a Theological Academy was instituted at Kilmarnock, in connection with the Union, and is now carried on in the Hall of Dr Morison's Church, Glasgow.

Mr Morison's successor in Clerk's Lane Church was the Rev. Davidson Black. He was appointed in the beginning of 1854; and after discharging the duties of pastor for two years, he removed to Dundee. He was succeeded by the Rev. William Bathgate, author of the *Characteristics of a Superior Popular Literature*, and other works. Mr Bathgate was inducted in August, 1857.

About two years after Mr Bathgate's settlement his congregation erected a new church in Winton Place, Dundonald Road, partly that they might have greater accommodation, and partly that they might be in a more healthy locality. It was opened for public worship in November, 1860, and is a very beautiful building in the Early English Gothic style, from designs by James Ingram, Esq., architect, Kilmarnock. It is seated for about nine hundred persons, and cost upwards of £2600. A number of those who worshipped in Clerk's Lane Chapel remained there and formed a new congregation. By an amicable arrangement with the other party, they acquired the property, including the church and manse, at a cost of £300. They have given a call to Mr Robert Hislop, student of the Evangelical Union Academy, to become their pastor. He has accepted the same, and will be ordained about October of the present year, 1864.

CHAPTER XV.

The Pen and the Press, blest alliance! combined
To soften the heart and enlighten the mind;
For *that* to the treasures of knowledge gave birth,
And *this* sent them forth to the ends of the earth;
Their battles for truth were triumphant indeed,
And the rod of the tyrant was snapped like a reed;
They were made to exalt us—to teach us—to bless—
Those invincible brothers, the Pen and the Press!
                                        PRINCE.

THE next subject that presents itself in chronological order is the press; and it appears from a little work published at Ayr, in 1832, under the title of *Ayrshire*, that the honour of introducing the art of printing into Kilmarnock belongs to a Mr M'Arthur. The press which he established here was, according to the same authority, the first in Ayrshire. He was succeeded about the year 1780 by Mr John Wilson, the printer of the first edition of the poems of Burns; and though few works of celebrity appear to have been issued from the establishment during the first six or seven years of its existence, yet the circumstance of a printing-office being then required, shows distinctly the progressive state of the inhabitants at the period spoken of. An edition of *Paradise Lost* was printed by Mr Wilson in 1785, and an edition of *Virgilii Bucolica, Georgica, et Æneis*, in 1789.

Mr Wilson was a native of Kilmarnock, and, at the time referred to, was the principal bookseller in the town. His shop was in one of the old buildings which stood where Portland Street now opens into the Cross; and his printing-office, in which the poems of Burns were first put into type, was in the attic storey of that land on the left of the Star Inn Close, as entered from Waterloo Street. The entrance to the office was by a short outside stair at the back of the building. The property then belonged to the late Mr James Robertson of Tankardha', whose sister, the late Mrs Buntine, used to tell our informant, that, when living in the Star Inn Close, she noticed frequently the visits of Burns to the printing premises when his work was in the press. Mr Wilson latterly removed to Ayr; but previously, in conjunction with a brother who was established in the stationery business in that town, he projected and commenced, in 1803, the *Ayr Advertiser*, the first newspaper published in the county. When in Kilmarnock, Mr Wilson was for some time a magistrate, and as such was much esteemed. He died at Ayr in May, 1821.

From the Kilmarnock press of Mr Wilson, as we have said, the incomparable poems of Robert Burns were first issued.* This was in July, 1786; and such is the distinction that genius confers on everything with which it is connected, that the name of Kilmarnock has obtained on that account an imperishable place in the literary annals of our country. Before that time Ayrshire had few genuine poetical productions. A proud day, therefore, it must have been for Kilmarnock, when it sent forth to the world the volumes of the bard of Mossgiel, which bore upon every page the genuine impress of "sovereign genius," and which were destined to inspire the hearts of his countrymen with a warmer love, a sweeter joy, and a purer patriotism, than they had hitherto felt. But the mere circumstance of the work being printed

* Burns, it would seem, did not entertain a very favourable opinion of his printer; at least if we may judge from the following epitaph, which it is said he composed as applicable to him, and which appeared in the Kilmarnock edition of the poems:

"HIC JACET WEE JOHNNIE.

"Whoe'er thou art, oh reader, know
That death has murder'd Johnnie;
And here his body lies fu' low—
For saul he ne'er had ony."

here is not all that the town has to be proud of regarding our great national poet. It has a higher and a nobler cause for exultation—*it cherished him in the days of his early adversity;* in other words, when the friends of Burns were few, and before his fame had widely spread, a party of Kilmarnock gentlemen cordially proffered him the hand of friendship. The individuals to whom we allude were Mr John Goldie, merchant; Major Parker of Assloss, banker; Mr Paterson of Braehead, town-clerk; Dr Hamilton, Kilmarnock House; Dr William Moore; Mr Thomas Samson, seed-merchant; Mr William Brown, manufacturer; and Mr Robert Muir, wine-merchant; to the last of whom several of the poet's letters were addressed, and who, besides taking seventy-two copies of the first edition of the poems, subscribed for forty of the second, published at Edinburgh. Mr Gilbert Burns, when speaking of the poet's early friends, in a letter to Dr Currie, thus expresses himself respecting Mr Muir: "Mr Robert Muir, merchant in Kilmarnock, was one of those early friends that Robert's poetry procured him, and one who was dear to his heart. This gentleman had no very great fortune, or long line of dignified ancestry; but what Robert says of Captain Matthew Henderson might be said of him with great propriety, that 'he held the patent of his honours immediately from Almighty God.' Nature had, indeed, marked him a gentleman in the most legible characters. He died, while yet a young man, soon after the publication of my brother's first Edinburgh edition."

Like Mr Muir, the rest of those early patrons of the bard were all men of high respectability. Mr Thomas Samson was greatly noted as a sportsman, and as such has been graphically portrayed by Burns, whose high opinion of his worth and integrity is evinced by the well-known epitaph:

"Tam Samson's weel-worn clay here lies,
  Ye canting zealots, spare him;
If honest worth in heaven rise,
  Ye'll mend or ye win near him."

At Mr Samson's residence of Rosebank, Braehead, Burns was always welcomed with the utmost cordiality. There he frequently dined in company with a few choice friends, who were drawn around him by his fascinating conversation. Among these may be mentioned John Laurie, Esq. of Isles, or Old Laird Laurie, as he was commonly called. The laird had been, for a considerable time, a quartermaster in the Sixth or Enniskillen Dragoons, and had consequently seen much of the world. He was, besides, well acquainted with books, fond of a social glass and a good joke, and his society, therefore, could not fail to be greatly relished by the poet. He died in 1814, in the seventieth year of his age. Another individual, who was seldom absent on these occasions, was Mr Charles Samson. He was a nephew of their worthy host, "Tam Samson," and was then a clerk with Mr Paterson of Braehead. For him and Mr W. Parker, already mentioned, Burns entertained the warmest respect; and, in his usual free manner, he speaks of them, in one of his letters to Mr Muir, as "men whose friendship he would be proud to claim both in this world and that which is to come."* Mr Parker is also favourably spoken of in the song beginning,

"Ye sons of old Killie, assembled by Willie,"

the last verse of which breathes a fine masonic feeling:

"Ye powers who preside o'er the wind and the tide,
  Who markèd each element's border;
Who formèd this frame with beneficent aim,
  Whose sovereign statute is order;
Within this dear mansion may wayward contention,
  Or witherèd envy ne'er enter;
May secrecy round be the mystical bound,
  And brotherly love be the centre."

The song was addressed to the brethren of St John's Lodge,

* The original manuscript of this letter is in the possession of David Rankin, Esq., postmaster, Kilmarnock.

No. 22, of which Mr Parker was then Right Worshipful Master, and of which Burns was an honorary member. Mr Samson, the hero of the well-known elegy, Mr Wilson, the printer of the first edition of Burns's works, and Gavin Turnbull, the poet, were also members; and the lodge-room, in which they spent their "cheerful, festive nights," was in Croft Street. The election of Burns as an honorary member is thus recorded in the minute book of the lodge:

"Oct. 26, 1786.—Present the Right Worshipful Master, Deputy Master, and several Brethren, when John Galt, farmer in Cressland, was, upon his petition, made an entered apprentice. At same time, ROBERT BURNS, poet from Mauchline, a member of St James's, Tarbolton, was made an honorary member of this Lodge.
(Signed) "WILL. PARKER."

Several of the alehouses which Burns frequented have been traced out and described with great minuteness. The house of Nanse Tinnock, in Mauchline, has been much talked of; and the Edinburgh taverns of Johnnie Dowie and Lucky Pringle, where he often met Nicol of the High School and others, have also been noticed by some of his biographers; but nothing has been said, so far as we are aware, respecting the house of Sandy Patrick, in which the poet was wont to spend many merry evenings in *Auld Killie*, with the hero of one of his happiest poems, namely, Tam Samson, and other boon companions. Sandy, who was married to a daughter of Mr Samson, brewed within his own premises the *cap ale*, which the old sportsman used to drink with Burns and other social *cronies* after a day's shooting. Sandy's Public, which consisted of two storeys, and which was famed

"Thro' a' the streets and neuks o' Killie"

for its superior drink, was situated at the foot of Back Street (at that time one of the principal thoroughfares of the town), and was called "The Bowling-green House," from being near the old Bowling-green, which lay immediately behind it, in the direction of the present George Inn. But, like Sandy himself, and the other jolly mortals who were accustomed to assemble within its walls, the house which the presence of genius had hallowed, and which would have been an object of interest to many at the present day, is now no more, having been taken down about the time that East George Street was formed. In our humble opinion, however, the name of Sandy Patrick is worthy of a place in the biographies of the poet, along with those of Nanse Tinnock, Lucky Pringle, and Johnnie Dowie.

Burns tells us, in a note to the elegy on Tam Samson, that this worthy sportsman, on one occasion, when going on a shooting excursion, "expressed a wish to die and be buried in the muirs," and that "on that hint he composed his elegy and epitaph." From a respectable source we have learned the following additional particulars regarding the origin of the poem. On the occasion referred to, Mr Samson was longer than usual in returning from his "fields." Burns was then in Kilmarnock; and being in company with Mr Charles Samson, the conversation turned upon the shooting season. "By-the-bye, Burns," said Charles, "have you heard any thing of my uncle to-day?" "Not a syllable," replied the bard; "but why that question?" "He has been longer than his wont in returning from his sports," answered Charles; "and his wish about dying among the muirs has, perhaps, been realized." "I recollect the words of the game old cock," said Burns; "but I trust it will turn out otherwise." The poet, however, became a little thoughtful; and, taking a piece of paper from his pocket, wrote the first draught of the elegy and epitaph. In the course of the evening Mr Samson returned, safe and sound. A meeting of his friends took place, and Burns, of course, was one of the party. To amuse them he read the elegy. "Na, na, Robin," cried the subject of the poem, "I'm no fond o' that mournfu' story; I wad rather ye wad tell the world that I'm hale an' hearty." Burns, to gratify his friend, retired for a short time to another apartment, and wrote the *per contra*, with which he immediately returned, and which he read to the company:

> " Go, Fame, and canter like a filly,
> Thro' a' the streets and neuks o' Killie;
> Tell every social, honest billie
>   To cease his grievin';
> For, yet unskaithed by Death's gleg gullie,
>   Tam Samson's livin'."

The rehearsal of the verse, we need scarcely say, restored the old sportsman to his wonted good humour.

Mr Samson died in December, 1795, at the age of seventy-two, and nearly ten years after the composition of his celebrated elegy. His grave, which is in the Low Church burying-ground, is marked by a handsome tombstone, on which the epitaph already quoted is engraved. It may be worth while to add, as a curious coincidence, that the remains of the Rev. Dr Mackinlay and the Rev. John Robertson, who are mentioned with Mr Samson in the first verse of the elegy, are buried so near to the "weel-worn clay" of the worthy sportsman, that they all occupy one spot in the churchyard, as they do one stanza in the poem—the dust of the two former being separated from that of the latter by only a few inches of ground.

John Goldie, who also has obtained enduring celebrity in the writings of Burns, was a man of more than ordinary mind. At his house the poet was a frequent visitor during the time that his manuscripts were in the hands of the printer; there he corrected his *proofs*, and first met several of those kind patrons whose names we have mentioned. Goldie was a native of the parish of Galston, and first settled in Kilmarnock as a cabinet-maker. He was afterwards a wine-merchant at the Cross. From his boyhood he was much given to study and reflection; and by close application to books, obtained a considerable knowledge of some of the more abstruse sciences. Turnbull thus alludes to him in one of his poems:

> "Wha will explain the circling year,
> And represent the rolling sphere,
> Or mak' the solar system clear
>   As ony bead?
> John Goudie could, what need ye speer?
>   But noo he's dead."

At an early period of his life Goldie was a staunch Antiburgher, and was so devoted to his church that he was in the habit of travelling every Sunday from his father's house on the banks of the Cessnock to the village of Kilmaurs, to hear the Rev. Mr Smeaton.* But about the year 1764, when the Rev. Mr Lindsay, of whom we have already spoken, was settled in the Low Church, the religious opinions of Goldie underwent a material change, occasioned, perhaps, by the acrimonious disputes which then prevailed in the district regarding the Calvinistic and Arminian creeds. Some years after this he took an active part in the arguments between the New and Old Light parties, and at last ventured before the world as an author. The first of his productions was printed at Glasgow in 1780, under the title of *Essays on various important Subjects, Moral and Divine, being an attempt to distinguish True from False Religion*. This work was designated by the people *Goudie's Bible*, and had the effect of rendering his name somewhat famous throughout the west of Scotland.†

---

* Many persons attended the same place of worship from more distant localities. M'Gavin, author of the *Protestant*, tells us, in his memoirs, that his father and mother went regularly "on one horse," from Auchinleck to Mr Smeaton's church at Kilmaurs, a distance of twenty miles, and returned the same day. "Mr Smeaton's congregation," says M'Gavin, "extended over a diameter of nearly a hundred miles. It was the mother church of the Antiburgher congregations in Greenock, Paisley, Ayr, Kilmarnock, Kilwinning, Beith, and Auchinleck."

† *Goudie's Bible* was not unfrequently the subject of satirical remark. An instance of this is given in the *Contemporaries of Burns:* "Happening to go into a bookseller's shop one day, in Ayr, he met a clergyman of his acquaintance at the door. 'What have *you* been doing here?' jocularly inquired Goldie. 'Just buying a few ballads,' retorted the minister, 'to make psalms to your bible.'"

The peculiar views which he therein inculcates respecting original sin, and his strictures on particular portions of Scripture, created considerable alarm among the more orthodox part of the community. A second edition of Goldie's work appeared in 1785, bearing the title of *Essays on various Subjects, Moral and Divine, in one volume, by John Goldie; to which is added, the Gospel recovered from a Captive State, in five volumes. By a Gentle Christian.* In reference to the impression which the *Essays* made upon the public mind, Burns addressed to the author the verses beginning thus:

> "O Goudie, terror o' the Whigs,
> Dread o' black coats and rev'rend wigs,
> Soor Bigotry, on her last legs,
>   Girnin', looks back,
> Wishin' the ten Egyptian plagues
>   Wad seize you quick."

Besides the *Essays*, Goldie was the author of a volume entitled, *Conclusive Evidences against Atheism*, which was printed at Kilmarnock in 1808. He had projected another publication also, to be called *A Revise, or a Reform of the present System of Astronomy;* but this work was never published.

As literary productions the writings of our author are rather defective; but in some instances they exhibit his reasoning faculties in a favourable light. They are now only to be found in the libraries of the curious. Though somewhat heterodox in his religious sentiments, as a man he bore an unblemished character, and lived on terms of intimacy with the most respectable inhabitants of the town. He was also honoured with the correspondence of several literary men of celebrity.

In the commercial prosperity of Kilmarnock, Goldie always displayed a warm interest, and at one time suggested the idea of forming a canal from the town to the harbour of Troon. He even carried the project so far as to survey the line; but the scheme, which might have been advantageous to both localities, was abandoned, probably in consequence of the vast expense it would have incurred.* He died in 1809, in the ninety-second year of his age.

Another of the individuals with whom Burns became acquainted about this time in Kilmarnock was Gavin Turnbull, the poet. According to Crichton's *Sketches of Alexander Wilson*, the American Ornithologist, Turnbull "was born in one of the border counties, washed by the Tweed." Be that as it may, it is certain that, at a very early period of his life, his parents settled with him in Kilmarnock. Here he received his education, and was bred to the trade of carpet-weaving. From his own writings, too, it is evident that in this locality his poetical genius first displayed itself. We view him, therefore, as one of our early local bards, and gladly assign him a place in our humble narrative.

Thomas Turnbull, the father of our author, followed the vocation of a dyer; and, though rather an eccentric character, had the good sense to bestow upon his son the rudiments of a classical education, which he no doubt intended to complete, so as to qualify him for some respectable profession. But a family misfortune is said to have blighted their hopes, and marred the prospects of the youthful scholar. As he advanced in years his pecuniary circumstances underwent no improvement, judging from the cheerless appearance which the interior of his dwelling presented. We had occasion some years ago to describe the domicile of the poet in the *Contemporaries of Burns*, and may here repeat the description. He resided alone in a small garret in Soulis Street. The bed on which he lay was entirely composed of straw, and had only an old patched coverlet, which he drew over him during the night. He had no chair or stool. A cold

---

* According to the Council Records, it was contemplated, about 1796, to apply to Parliament for an Act to make a canal from Riccarton to Troon. The idea was perhaps taken from Mr Goldie.

stone placed by the fire served as a substitute; and the sill of a small window at one end of the room was all he had for a table from which to take his food, or on which to write his verses. In short, the bed alluded to, an old tin kettle (his only cooking utensil), and one spoon, comprised the whole of his household property—the lid of the kettle on every occasion making up for the want of a bowl or plate!

Turnbull's works were printed in Glasgow in 1788, under the title of *Poetical Essays*. They were favourably noticed by Campbell in his *History of Poetry in Scotland;* but whether they received a similar welcome from the public is doubtful. Burns was then, as he still is, the chief of Scottish poets. His bold original lyre was just sounding through the land; and it may, therefore, be inferred that the tamer though harmonious strains of Turnbull would be heard with comparative indifference by the lovers of song, as we carelessly hear the voice of the linnet when the thrush pours his more animating music through the grove.

Turnbull's pieces are chiefly written in imitation of Gray and Shenstone; and they are not marked by originality of thought. About the time when his poems were published, he removed from Kilmarnock; and, according to Crichton's statement, he became "unsettled in his mode of life, entered on the stage, and married one of the actresses." While following this profession in Dumfries he was sometimes in company with Burns, who thought not meanly of his poetical talents. Burns was then (1793) engaged in furnishing songs for Thomson of Edinburgh; and, in one of his letters to that gentleman, he thus speaks of Turnbull's lyrics: "The following is by an *old acquaintance* of mine, and I think has merit. . . . Possibly, as he is an *old friend* of mine, I may be prejudiced in his favour, but I like some of his pieces very much."

In 1794 our author published a second work, entitled

Poems, by Gavin Turnbull, Comedian. Besides his acquaintance with Burns, he enjoyed the friendship of Alexander Wilson, author of *American Ornithology*, &c.; and, like that enterprising son of genius, he emigrated to America. Regarding his fate in that country we have no account.

Another individual belonging to Kilmarnock, who attracted the attention of Burns, and who is worthy of being remembered, was Jeanie Glover, author of the popular song of *O'er the muir amang the heather.* Respecting her history little is known. She was the writer, so far as we are aware, of only one single lyric; yet the peculiar sweetness and simplicity of the piece mark it as the offspring of a mind endowed by nature with a talent for song-writing—a talent with which few have been gifted, and which some of our greatest poets have failed in cultivating. Poesy is an impulse, not an art; and such, at all events, may be truly said of lyrical composition; for unless the hand that touches the harp be guided and directed by the influence of nature, the melody produced will be tame and uninspiring. We, therefore, look upon the individual who composes one exquisite song as a "poet of Nature's making," although little else of a literary cast should flow from the same mind. Such was Lowe, author of *Mary's Dream*, so replete with beauty and feeling; such was Laidlaw, author of *Lucy's Flittin'*, so full of truth and tenderness; such was Jane Elliot, author of the *Flowers of the Forest*, so sweet and affecting; such was Lady Anne Lindsay, author of *Auld Robin Gray*, so simple and pathetic; and such, we hesitate not to say, was Jeanie Glover, whose little ballad occupies a respectable place among our pastoral lyrics.

Jeanie was the daughter of a weaver, named James Glover, and was born at the Townhead, Kilmarnock, October 31, 1758. The education she received was in keeping with the humble circumstances of her parents, who instilled into her youthful mind the principles of morality and religion. Burns, in language somewhat uncharitable, first introduced her name to the world; and, from his account of her, it appears that she abandoned the course of virtue in which she had been trained, and ultimately became irregular in her habits.

About the year 1790 she became acquainted with a man of the name of Ritchie or Richard, who was travelling through the country as a sort of actor or showman. With this person she left Kilmarnock, and afterwards accompanied him in his wanderings. One of our aged townsmen, who has seen her in different localities, describes her as beautiful in person, and sprightly in disposition. She was likewise a superior singer; and, at the entertainments given by Ritchie to the public, she acted as principal vocalist, and frequently sung the piece that preserves her name.* Little more of her is known. After living in this manner for several years, she went to Ireland, and there pursued the same profession. The late Sergeant John Osborne saw and conversed with her in the town of Letterkenny in 1801. She then appeared in excellent health, and displayed all the vivacity and cheerfulness which characterized her in her earlier years; but it would seem that she died soon after this interview; for before Mr Osborne had been two months in the place he was informed of her death.

* The old Croft Street Lodge was the place where they used to give their entertainments in Kilmarnock. In the books of St John's Lodge, to whom the property belonged, we find this entry: "Sept, 1793.—By cash from Jean Glover's man, 7s."

CHAPTER XVI.

Look on the ghastly scene—
A scene of death, of sickness, and of wo.
REV. J. G. SMALL.

TOWARDS the close of the eighteenth century, Kilmarnock, in a commercial point of view, was one of the most flourishing towns in the west of Scotland. In addition to the trades we formerly enumerated, several others were by this time introduced, such as the weaving of muslin and the printing of calicoes. About the year 1791 the under-mentioned articles of manufacture were valued yearly as follows: Carpets, £21,400; shoes and boots, £21,216; skins tanned, £9000; sheep and lamb skins dressed, £6500; printed calicoes, £6500. Other fabrics also were produced, but of less value. The number of inhabitants at that time in town and parish was 6776. The aspect of the town itself, however, had as yet undergone no very great change; and it had all the zig-zag appearance that characterized it in former years. Indeed, so intricate and winding were its streets, and so squeezed together, as it were, that a stranger, when once within the town, was often at a loss to find his way out again. Such was the case on one occasion with a commercial traveller from England. He had come, of course, upon business; after settling which he mounted his horse and set out on his journey; but he soon became so bewildered with the various turns and bends of the streets, that before a few minutes had elapsed he was again at the Cross, declaring that he had never been in such a place before. "It is easily enough got into," he exclaimed;

"but the devil himself had surely a hand in its formation, for I can't for the life of me discover a way out of it." One of the inhabitants, who is still alive, voluntarily conducted him beyond the bounds of the town; for which service he received a thousand thanks from the stranger, who seemed as glad as if he had escaped from a place of confinement.

Kilmarnock has at different times been seriously injured by fire; and the contracted plan on which it was built would doubtless facilitate the progress of its ravages. On the 22nd May, 1668, the whole of the town, as stated by various authorities, was burned; and, according to the following extract from the minutes of the Synod of Fife, the number of families who suffered was one hundred and twenty; and from this number comprising "the whole town," as is stated, we may infer that the population, not including the parish, was then under six hundred:

"SYNOD OF FIFE, ST ANDREWS, 6 OCTOBER, 1669.

"CONTRIBUTIONS FOR TOUN OF KILMARNOCK.—The Lord Archbishop and Synod having a supplication presented to them from the inhabitants of the toun of Kilmarnock, that wheras upon the 22nd May, 1668, the whole toun was burnt into ashes by a violent fire that broke out accidentallie, and about 120 families wer cast out of all habitation and brought to povertie and beggarie; wherupon the petitioners, having presented ther deplorable condition to the Lords of his Majestie's Privie Council, had an act of the saids Lords in ther favours, recommending them to the Archbishop and Bishops for a charitable contribution towards ther relief. The Lord Archbishop and Synod, taking the petition to ther consideration, do appoint all ministers within this dioces to go about the said collection immediately after they have collected for Cupar."—[Cupar had suffered from a fire in April, and about twenty families were quite ruined by it.]

The occurrence is also alluded to by Chambers in his *Domestic Annals of Scotland*. His words may be quoted as further illustrative of the condition of the inhabitants at the time:

"1668, May 22nd.—The town of Kilmarnock was wholly destroyed by an accidental fire, 'wherethrough about sexscore families are set to the fields destitute both of goods and houses'—indeed, 'in a condition of starving.' Matters were the worse for them, by reason that they, 'being all poor tradesmen, and having no other means of livelihood but their daily employment,' had some time before been reduced to 'great misery and affliction,' in consequence of the quartering upon them of a great party of the King's forces, when these were sent to the west to prevent a rebellion."

In Lamont's *Diary* the same calamity is also noticed :

"1670, May 29.—Being the Sabath, the solemnitie of his Maj. K. Ch. the 2, his birthday and restitution to his 3 Kingdomes, was observed throwout the 3 nations, be sermon in most places to that purpose, shooting of cannon, ringing of bells and bonfyrs att night. That day Mr John Auchinleck, m. did preach at Largo ch.; his text was Ps. 116: 12, 13, 14, 'What shall I render to the Lord,' &c. The said day there was a collection through the ch. of Largo for the towne of Kilmarnock, who leatlie suffered some losse be fire, being appointed be the diocesian synod throwout the diosscie."

The school-house, too, which is said to have been situated in College Wynd, was burned at a later period;* and we may mention, that the burial-place or aisle of the parish church, belonging to the family of Rowallan, was then used as the place of instruction; but it was soon abandoned, in consequence of its dampness and impure air causing fever among the children.†

Another disastrous fire occurred in Netherton Holm (now Low Glencairn Street), on Saturday, the 26th April, 1800. It originated on the east side, in a malt-kiln that had been overheated; and, with amazing rapidity, it spread in all directions, kindling the houses on the other side, and covering the street with such masses of flame and smoke, that no person, save the most daring, could pass along it. Even the mail-coach was arrested on its way by the dense and appalling volumes of fire and vapour that choked up the thoroughfare. The weather had been dry for several weeks, and the houses, being thatched, were readily ignited; a strong east wind also was blowing when the accident occurred; and these circumstances so aided the destructive element in its impetuous career, that every effort on the part of the people to allay its

* See *note*, page 3.
† One of the sculptured figures that adorned this aisle may still be seen in the garden of James S. Gregory, Esq., Nelson Street. Other parts of the sepulchral ornaments are preserved, we believe, at Craufurdland Castle.

fury appeared impotent and unavailing. Happily, the event took place at mid-day, else the loss of life might have been very considerable. As it was, many were in the most imminent danger, owing to the instantaneous nature of the occurrence; and it was only in few instances that household furniture or domestic utensils could be saved. At length the roofs were cut from some of the houses which the fire had not yet reached, and by that means its progress was obstructed. But dreadful was the devastation it had wrought; above thirty-two houses, including the Holm School, were reduced to a mass of blackened ruins in the short space of an hour and a half; and seventy-six families, consisting of more than *three hundred persons*, chiefly dependent on daily labour for support, were rendered homeless and destitute.

Subscriptions for the relief of the sufferers were immediately opened among the inhabitants of the town and neighbourhood; and liberal contributions were obtained not only from many persons at home, but from gentlemen in foreign countries who were connected with the town by birth or otherwise.* It may also be remarked that since this event other two fires of a very extensive and destructive kind took place—one in the same

---

* The money collected amounted to £1639 13s. 2½d. The Marquis of Titchfield contributed £100; and £315 were obtained in London through the influence of the late Sir James Shaw, then Alderman Shaw. The bill for this sum was accompanied by the following letter from Sir James to the magistrates:

"LONDON, 8TH MAY, 1800.

"GENTLEMEN,—Your letter of the 29th ultimo I duly received, acquainting me with the dreadful fire in the Netherton on the Saturday preceding, which has burnt out seventy-six families, consisting of upwards of three hundred persons, and requesting my assistance for the relief of the unfortunate sufferers. You add that providentially no lives were lost. In this part of your information I exceedingly rejoice; for great as the pecuniary loss may be, the liberality of the public will soon make it up to the necessitous part of them. In aid of this fund the gentlemen here from Kilmarnock, and Lloyd's Coffee-house, have subscribed three hundred guineas, agreeably to the annexed list, for which sum you will receive herewith a bank post-bill. Mr Wilson will now take up the subscription a few days longer, and will write you his success. —I am, with great respect, gentlemen, your obedient servant,

"JAMES SHAW."

locality, and one in Back Causeway, in 1825, at which one man, two women, and a child fell a sacrifice to the flames.

The mention of fires recalls to our recollection a fearful explosion of gunpowder, attended with loss of life, which took place, in 1810, in an ironmonger's shop that stood where Duke Street now branches off from the Cross. The occurrence, which caused considerable alarm from its sudden and unusual nature, is thus recorded in our oldest county paper, the *Ayr Advertiser:*

"At eight o'clock on the morning of Saturday, February 3, 1810, a melancholy catastrophe took place in the town of Kilmarnock, by the accidental explosion of some gunpowder in the shop of Messrs Andrew and Stewart, in consequence of which the walls of the house were instantly thrown out to the street, and the roof precipitated to the ground. There dwelt at the moment, in different apartments of the house, ten persons, whose lives were providentially saved, excepting John Brown, a lad from the isle of Arran, who was employed in the shop. The magistrates, accompanied by Major Parker and the Local Militia, and other gentlemen of the town, used every exertion to quench the fire, to get the rubbish cleared away, and to prevent further fatal consequences. . . . It is impossible to say how the unfortunate accident happened—the young man who, it was understood, was the innocent cause of it having perished. He was seen a little after eight o'clock taking off the window shutters; and it is conjectured, that a spark from a candle, which he had got lighted for the purpose of kindling the fire, had communicated with a quantity of gunpowder. The explosion took place at a quarter past eight, dispersing pieces of the house and some of the shop goods to a considerable distance; but what is singular, instead of blowing the roof, and Mr M'Kean's family who lived above the shop, into atoms, the roof merely fell in. Nearly at this time Mr M'Kean came to the spot, and rushing into the ruins, tore away a quantity of rubbish, and got into the kitchen, where he found his wife's sister, his son and daughter, lying under a large beam of wood. They were extricated with trifling injury. He again entered the ruins in search of his wife and infant, where he continued till nearly suffocated; and when helped out and recovered, he found they had been both thrown from their bed into the street without receiving any material injury. The only other person hurt is Mr Hunter's servant-girl, who was going to the well when the accident occurred. The singular circumstance of the falling in of the roof, is accounted for from the weakness of the shop walls, and the door being open, which gave vent to the powder, and thus saved M'Kean's family."

On Sabbath, the 18th of October, 1801, an occurrence still more melancholy in its effects than those we have just noticed, and one which will long form a principal feature in the annals of Kilmarnock, took place in the old Low

Church. This building, which stood nearly on the site of the present Low Church, was erected when the population of the town and parish was very inconsiderable, and, at the time of the accident, was greatly deficient in point of accommodation. The plan on which it was constructed was far from being judicious. The passages were few in number and limited in breadth; the stairs leading to the galleries were within the church, and were steep and narrow. Their outlets, too, were by the same doors that led to the area; and much inconvenience was thereby occasioned, both at the entry and dismissal of the congregation. The poorer portion of the hearers usually sat on temporary seats in the passages, which added not a little to the general disorder. The substantiality of the building as a whole was likewise doubted by some individuals; and a prophecy had been long prevalent in the locality that it was destined to fall upon the congregation. This prediction, with the supposed insecurity of the house, tended, in no small degree, when it was crowded, to create alarm in such minds as were not fortified by reason and reflection.

On the day of the calamity, the Chapel, or High Church, as it is now called, and some of the churches in neighbouring parishes, were vacant; and many persons belonging to these flocked to the Low Church, attracted by the popularity of Dr Mackinlay, who was then in the zenith of his fame as a preacher. The house was, therefore, crowded to excess; but nothing occurred during the forenoon service to disturb the tranquillity of the audience; and when the bell announced the hour of meeting in the after part of the day, they again assembled, unconscious of any casualty being about to happen; but nothing is more uncertain than the term of human existence. As the poet beautifully says,

> "The spider's most attenuated thread
> Is cord, is cable, to man's hold of life."

The last sound of the bell had scarcely ceased to vibrate on the ear, and the minister was just about to enter the church, when a small piece of plaster fell from the ceiling, or when, as some said, a seat cracked in one of the galleries. A cry was instantly raised that the building was falling;* and the alarm, spreading with the rapidity of lightning, created a scene of confusion and death almost incredible, and such as no language can accurately delineate. A number who were seated in the lower part of the house immediately made their escape to the outside; those in the galleries were not so fortunate; they rushed to the staircases with the view of flying from the supposed danger; but in their wild precipitation they became so jammed together that one of the railings gave way, and many fell into the area, suffocating those on whom they descended, and dreadfully crushing and maiming each other. The doors at the foot of the stairs folded inward, and were unfortunately closed by the sudden rush that was made towards them; and all egress, at these places, being thereby prevented, despair was added to dread; the strong, unconscious of their own recklessness, trampled on the weak; body lay piled upon body; and the house resounded with the shriek of despondency, the wail of wo, and the moan of death.

Never, perhaps, was exhibited a more singular instance of the direful effects of fear and credulity. Some, believing that the prophecy was about to be fulfilled, and that the galleries

* According to the Session Records a similar panic arose in the parish church in 1735, but no mention is made of any person having been injured. We may give the words of the minute: "Sabbath, May 25, 1735.—Mr Paisley preached a little tyme on Colos. i. 14; and was obliged to stop and dismiss the people, by reason of ane uproar, occasioned by the danger of the falling of a part of the North Loft. Afternoon, Mr Hill preached in the church-yeard on 1 Cor. ii. 29."

We may also mention that about three years previous to the above date a shock of an earthquake was felt in the town, and is thus briefly recorded in the minutes of Session: "Sabbath, July 9, 1732.—This day a sensible shook of ane earthquake was felt here, and several other places, a little before two in the afternoon."

In connection with this, we may state, that on the 11th of the same month, a shock was felt at Glasgow, between two and three afternoon.—*See Dom. Ann. of Scot.*

were falling, threw themselves into the body of the church; some leapt from the windows into the graveyard; and others, conceiving that death was inevitable, stood riveted to the spot. Two or three individuals, whose minds were more collected, ascended the pulpit to exhort the congregation to order and quiet; but such was the bewildering feeling which the scene before them inspired, that, like the others, they soon became victims to the general terror, and hastily abandoned their position. So great, indeed, was the delusion, that many, after rushing to the street, durst not pause for a moment to look behind, lest they should be crushed to death by the walls, which their disordered senses led them to believe were falling to pieces; and it may be mentioned, as a striking instance of the force of imagination, that one individual declared to the minister, whom he met near the church, that the steeple itself was tumbling to the ground, though it was then, as it still is, entire and substantial. The reverend gentleman, struck with surprise at the tumultuous scene before him, and dreading that the consequences would prove fatal to many, clasped his hands in an attitude of devotion, and ejaculated with a pitying voice—"My people! oh, my people!"

In the meantime, intelligence of the catastrophe spread into every corner of the town. All were overwhelmed with consternation. For the preservation of order the Royal Kilmarnock Volunteers were summoned to the spot, already thronged by hundreds of the inhabitants inquiring anxiously for their friends, their relatives, or their neighbours. In consequence of the number who stood pressed together or lay prostrate on the stairs, many were still confined in the galleries; and it was suggested that their release might be effected from the windows by ladders, which were instantly procured; but so general was the panic that few could be found with sufficient resolution to place them against the walls. At length some individuals, actuated by feelings of humanity, ventured into the interior to alleviate, if possible, the agonies of the sufferers. The scene that presented itself to their view was peculiarly distressing. At the foot of each of the stairs a mass of persons of both sexes lay wedged together, maimed, dead, or dying. With considerable difficulty one layer of bodies was removed from above another, and the appalling announcement was ultimately made, that *twenty-nine* had breathed their last. Some of them were so disfigured that their friends could only recognise them by their apparel. The bodies of two of the females were shockingly injured, their breasts being deeply marked by the heavy shoes of an individual, whose " brutal hurry," during the calamity, is not yet forgotten.*

The bodies of the dead were carried into the burial-ground, and also such persons as were severely injured; and here another scene was exhibited, not less dismal than that which had been witnessed in the church. In one place might be seen some poor sufferers, writhing in convulsions; in another, individuals sunk in a state of utter insensibility. Some were weeping over the corpse of a beloved father or mother—some

* In an account of the accident, published at the time by the authority of the magistrates, the names of those who were killed are thus mentioned:

" KILMARNOCK PARISH.—Townhead quarter—William Muir, glover; and Jean Paterson, residenter.—Soulis Cross quarter—John Logan, shoemaker.—In Back quarter—Mary Reid, daughter of William Reid; and Thomas Abraham, an orphan. —In Mid quarter—James Gilchrist, shoemaker; and Janet Dickie, daughter of Joseph Dickie.—In Brewland quarter—Andrew Aitken, staymaker; and Margaret Wilson, daughter of David Wilson, shoemaker.—In Holmhead quarter—Widow Howat.—In Netherton Holm quarter—a daughter of Robert Kechan, weaver; Widow Mary Taylor; Janet, a daughter of Widow M'Intosh; and John Deal, weaver, from Ireland.—In Townend and Glebe quarters—Charles Wilson, a servant; William Smith, weaver; Margaret Stevenson, widow of James Smith, carter; William Tannahill, wright; William Baird, son of William Baird, weaver; and a daughter of James Wilson, plasterer.—In West quarter—George Guthry, son of Mr John Guthry, at Mount; and in Grougar quarter, —— Bell, in Oldwalls, son of Widow Bell.

" KILMAURS PARISH.—Mary, daughter of Walter Smith; Jean Stewart; Jean, daughter of the late William Anderson, in Corsehouse; James Fairlie, farmer; Janet, daughter of James Muir, in Holms; Janet, daughter of David Brown, collier; and a daughter of John Stevenson, in Hallbarns."

were mourning in all the bitterness of wo over the lifeless form of a son or daughter—others poured forth their sorrows by the remains of a brother or sister. In short, the corpse-strewed ground—the blood-stained garments of the victims—and the rueful countenances of the multitude—rendered the scene awfully impressive; and, as we have heard a spectator remark, gave to it the sad characteristics of a battle-field, covered with the wounded, the dying, and the dead.

It was also affecting to behold the removal of the bodies to the homes they had so lately left in all the cheerfulness of health. Some were attended by groups of sorrowing relatives and acquaintances; others, by only two or three mourners; and, in one instance, an individual was observed, unaccompanied, carrying the corpse of a brother, and weeping like a child as he went along. But the picture, sad as it is, assumes a more gloomy and touching appearance, when the distressful cases of individuals are considered. One man, when humanely endeavouring to rescue others from danger, was overwhelmed by the dreadful pressure, and smothered on the spot. A young lady, whose father had caught her in his arms, despairingly exclaimed, "We are gone!" and was instantly suffocated. Another female, when a young man was attempting to save her, cried in the same desponding tone, "You can do me no good!" and was immediately crushed to death; and so great was the breach made in one little circle of six acquaintances who had met together in the morning, that only two escaped with their lives. It is rather remarkable that no infant, though several were in the church, sustained the smallest injury; on the contrary, after the tumult had subsided, a little child, whose mother had left it in despair, or had been driven from it during the commotion, was found safely and calmly sleeping in one of the pews.

As formerly observed, an unusual sensation was created in the community; and the gloom of sorrow appeared to deepen as the evening approached, and as the names of the departed, most of whom were amiable persons, became generally known. Night came on—serene and beautifully arrayed by the beams of the silver moon; but no heart was at ease; and small parties might still be seen hurrying from street to street, to administer relief or consolation to the surviving sufferers. Here and there, groups of individuals, with countenances shaded by sadness, stood earnestly conversing together. In fine, death and distress were the all-engrossing themes; and the voice of mourning was heard, not only in the abodes of the widow and the orphan, but in the dwellings of many others, whose grief had been awakened by the heart-rending occurrence.

One of the injured (Mrs Milroy), who survived the disaster, died soon after; the others, amounting to about eighty, were, by proper care and medical assistance, somewhat restored; though many of them carried to the grave the marks or scars they had received on that melancholy occasion.

As was to be expected, the causes and consequences of the calamity gave rise to many vague and visionary stories; one of which was to the effect, that on that day several persons had seen a coach, decorated with all the sable emblems of mourning, and drawn by six horses, pass through the centre of the burying-ground, and that no less a personage than the devil was seated within it. An individual, on hearing the statement, is said to have remarked, that his Satanic Majesty was surely improving in his circumstances, when he could afford to ride about in his carriage and six! And we are in no way surprised at the observation of the wag; for such a story as the above was better fitted to excite contemptuous merriment than to produce serious reflection.*

* See *Narrative of the Accident* published at the time. As a further evidence of the superstitious notions which prevailed in the public mind, we may mention that, about the same period, suicides were sometimes denied a grave in the common burying-ground. For example, the remains of an old woman named Kerr, who

On the following day the magistrates, and other philanthropic gentlemen of the town, opened a subscription for the benefit of the more necessitous sufferers; and though the sums collected could not make up for the loss of near and dear relatives, still, to the widow and the fatherless, they were highly beneficial in mitigating their pecuniary sufferings, and in yielding comfort to their grief-torn hearts.

No sermon was afterwards preached in the same building; for, on being examined by competent judges, it was found, in some respects, deficient; and the heritors, anxious to remove every cause of alarm, agreed that it should be rebuilt on a larger and more commodious plan, which was accordingly done in 1802. The foundation stone was laid with masonic honours on the 20th April of that year.*

hanged herself in her own house at the foot of Croft Street, were thrown into an old coal-pit near Dean Castle. The body of another old woman, named Jenny Whitly, who hanged herself in Back Street, met with a fate still more revolting to humanity. It was taken by stealth from her own house, and cast into a pit in the vicinity of Riccarton. It was afterwards brought back to Kilmarnock, and boiled during the night at the Town Green, in a large pot which had been taken from the door of an ironmonger's shop. This was done, we believe, by some individuals who wanted her bones to form a skeleton.

* The old church appears to have been erected about 1750; for we find from the Town's Records that £14 8s. 8d., Scots, was paid that year as the town's proportion of stent for rebuilding it. Of the church that occupied the same site previous to 1750 we have no account, save an occasional incidental mention of it in the early Session Books, such as: "1712—Given to Robt Hunter for upholding ye roof of ye kirk, for his pension from Whits., 1711, to Whits., 1712, £6 13s. 4d. Scots." "1713— To James Cathcart, his yearly Salary for mending ye kirk windows from Whitsunday, 1712 to 1713, £3 6s. 8d. Scots." A few years ago, the Boyd Coat of Arms, carved in oak, that adorned the family-seat, or aisle, in this old edifice, was discovered, and is now in the possession of Spencer Boyd, Esq. of Penkill Castle, Girvan.

It may be mentioned that, when the ground was dug for the foundation of the present church, there were discovered, huddled together, in one or two places, about two cart-loads of human bones, the appearance and size of some of which attracted considerable attention. Mr Gregory of Virginia, speaking of them in a letter to his brother, says: "There was a thigh-bone among them, which, from its great size, was the subject of some speculation. I saw William Wallace of Hawket Park draw up his knee, and lay this bone on his thigh; and from its much greater length than his, it was supposed by the gentlemen present that it had belonged to a man at least a foot taller than Mr Wallace." Mr Wallace was about six feet in height.

CHAPTER XVII.

Hech! what a change ha'e we now in this town.
　　　　　　　　　　　SIR ALEXANDER BOSWELL.

By this time, 1802, the population of the town and parish had increased to 8079. The various trades also were on the increase; and a taste for public improvements began to manifest itself among the inhabitants. An Act of Parliament for improving the town was applied for and obtained; and soon afterwards "Auld Kilmarnock," as Burns styled it, assumed a somewhat new appearance. Many of the antique-looking tenements of the olden time, and some of the narrow lanes, rapidly disappeared. In 1804 the New Bridge, as it was long called, was built; in the same year, one of our principal thoroughfares, namely, King Street, was opened up. In 1805 the Council Chambers, or Town-house, was erected. It is situated, as the local reader is aware, on the arch of the bridge just mentioned; and though rather incommodious for the present business of the burgh, it bespeaks, in various respects, the good taste and liberal views of its projectors. The lock-up cells belonging to it are, perhaps, the most objectionable parts of the building, being low-roofed, almost without light or air; and such, in short, as would, in all likelihood, have called forth the disapprobation of the philanthropic Howard, had he, in Providence, been permitted to visit them.* Though used only as places of temporary confinement, these cells are not without their tales of wo and

---

* Several other cells were erected some years ago at the back of the building.

terror. In one of them, about forty years ago, an individual, who was charged with the crime of forgery, and who had been imprisoned here for a night previously to his removal to Ayr, committed suicide, and was found in the morning with his throat cut from ear to ear. The unhappy man, it was thought, had performed the foul deed to avoid the ignominy of being publicly executed.

In the hall or court-room is a fine full-length portrait of Sir James Shaw, the production of our gifted townsman, the late James Tannock, who presented it to the Magistrates and Town Council in 1817, as a mark of respect for his native place. In a local publication of that period, the painting is thus described: "Sir James is in a full-dress court suit, with the robes and insignia of Lord Mayor of London. He appears as if in the act of speaking in Guildhall, and holds the king's warrant of precedence (which regulated his place in the procession at Lord Nelson's funeral) in his right hand, which rests on the top of the table supporting the city mace and the sword of state. There is, properly speaking, no background, though a fine fluted column upon the right hand of the baronet, and the drapery of a curtain on his left, fill up the painting."

This portrait has been much admired by many lovers of the fine arts; and, as a likeness, it is famed for being exceedingly accurate; so truly, indeed, does it represent the baronet, that we have heard a gentleman, who has himself acquired considerable distinction as an artist, state, that, on one occasion, when Sir James (whom he had never seen before) was on a visit to Kilmarnock, he recognised him from a previous inspection of the portrait. Four other portraits adorn the hall: one of the late Sir John Dunlop, Baronet, first Member of Parliament for the Burghs; one of Benjamin R. Bell, Esq., first Sheriff-Substitute for Kilmarnock; one of the late Earl of Eglinton; and one of Robert Burns, which was placed there at his Centenary, January, 1859.* Those of Sir John Dunlop and Robert Burns were painted by Mr James Tannock, that of Mr Bell, by Mr William Tannock, and that of the Earl of Eglinton, by Sir John Watson Gordon, from a painting by John Graham Gilbert.

Soon after the opening up of King Street, Portland Street and Wellington Street also were formed; and so materially was the town improved and beautified by the formation of these streets, that it no longer presented the village-like aspect exhibited in former years, but seemed "transformed," as one of our topographical writers has remarked, "into a minor city." Previously to this date, the main road through Kilmarnock from Glasgow to Ayr was along the steep and narrow path called Dean Lane, thence along High Street, Soulis Street, and Fore Street, and, passing through the Cross, it awkwardly diverged into Waterloo Street, and then abruptly turned along the Old Bridge at the Flesh Market into Market Lane, &c. A more tortuous and inconvenient thoroughfare could scarcely be devised; and, in those days of stage-coaches and similar vehicles, the lives of the passengers, and even of the inhabitants dwelling along the route, must have been greatly endangered.†

* Burns's Centenary, which will long be memorable in the literary annals of our country, was celebrated with great enthusiasm in Kilmarnock. A procession of the Trades and Masonic Lodges took place during the day; many of the shops were closed; and in the evening no fewer than fifteen public meetings were held throughout the town. The principal assemblage was in the George Inn Hall. Archibald Finnie, Esq., Provost of Kilmarnock, acted as chairman, and the late R. P. Adam, Esq. of Tour, as croupier. The meeting was in every respect a decided success, which was owing in a great measure to the indefatigable exertions of the secretaries, James Wilson, Esq., banker, and David Rankin, Esq., post-master. Besides the president and vice-president, the principal speakers were John Thomson, surgeon, Alexander Smith, A.M., Academy, William Gunnyon, teacher, James Aitken, M.D., John Torrance, writer, Captain Picken, and John Sturrock, writer; all of whom, as well as the rest of the large assemblage, evinced a hearty appreciation of the manly worth and transcendent genius of him whose centenary they had met to celebrate.

† Several of the houses, as formerly stated, had outside stairs, which rendered the thoroughfares still more inconvenient; and the stage-coaches, when passing along, were so near to these structures, that on one occasion a bowl of porridge,

The advantage gained to the public by opening this new line of street, already named, must have been very considerable. The Cross—the most spacious, perhaps, in Scotland—became more open and elegant in consequence of the new streets branching from it; and many of the old houses being thrown into the shade by the more lofty modern buildings, the town, as a whole, presented an air of comfort and elegance to the eye of the stranger, and impressed him with a favourable opinion of the taste and industry of the inhabitants. Some of the minor streets, such as Dean Street, were also formed about the same period.

For some time after these improvements were effected, we find little worthy of notice in the history of Kilmarnock. The war which then raged between France and Britain afforded the inhabitants an opportunity of displaying their attachment to their king and country. Two regiments were formed— the Sharpshooters or Rifles, commanded by Captain James Thomson; and the Volunteers, commanded by Major Parker of Assloss; and so universally did the spirit of loyalty and the dread of French invasion prevail, that, till the overthrow of Napoleon at Waterloo, a warlike propensity appeared to actuate all classes of the community.

Speaking of Waterloo, we are reminded of the name of the late Sergeant Charles Ewart, of the Scots Greys, a native of Kilmarnock, who nobly distinguished himself in that memorable conflict, by seizing a French eagle, and bearing it in triumph from the field. The struggle which he had for the standard is thus described in a letter written by the gallant sergeant: "It was in the first charge I took the eagle from the enemy. He and I had a hard contest for it. He thrust for my groin. I parried it off, and cut him through the head;

---

which the better half of a worthy bonnet-maker had placed on the top of one of them to cool for the breakfast of the *bairns*, was lifted up by a passenger, and carried away, amid the laughter of his fellow-travellers.

after which I was attacked by one of their lancers, who threw his lance at me, but missed his mark, by my throwing it off with my sword to my right side; then I cut him from the chin upwards, which went through his teeth. Next, I was attacked by a foot-soldier, who, after firing at me, charged me with his bayonet; but he very soon lost the combat, for I parried it, and cut him down through the head; so that finished the contest for the eagle. After which I presumed to follow my comrades, eagle and all, but was stopped by the general saying to me, 'You, brave fellow, take that to the rear; you have done enough till you have got quit of it.' I retired to a height and stood there for upwards of an hour, which gave a general view of the field; but I cannot express the horrors I beheld. The bodies of my brave comrades, and horses innumerable, were lying so thick upon the field that it was scarcely possible to pass. I took the eagle into Brussels, amid the acclamations of thousands of spectators."

Sergeant Ewart was born at Waterside, Kilmarnock, and entered the Scots Greys in 1789. He was an excellent swordsman, and was master of fence in the Greys. For his heroic conduct at Waterloo he was promoted to the rank of an ensign in the 5th Royal Veterans. In 1816 a number of gentlemen in Edinburgh, among whom was Sir Walter Scott, invited him to a public dinner, at which his health was proposed, in eloquent and laudatory terms, by the gifted novelist. A similar entertainment was given him about the same time in Kilmarnock. He died at Davy Hulme, near Manchester, in the spring of 1846, aged seventy-eight.

To return to the matters of the burgh. In 1807 an unusual sensation was created among the inhabitants by the murder of two females, named Alexander and Peacock. Alexander was a small grocer, and occupied that corner shop in Waterloo Street next the Flesh Market Bridge. The back apartment, which she used as a dwelling-house, was the scene of the murder. When their dead bodies were discovered, Alexander was lying on the floor with a rope, with which she had been strangled, drawn tightly about her neck; and Peacock, who was reclining against a bed, had evidently been put to death by the same means; for around her neck also a napkin or handkerchief was firmly twisted. The following notice of the murder appeared at the time in the *Ayr Advertiser:*

"On Saturday morning, November 7, 1807, Jean Alexander, huxter, Kilmarnock, was found murdered in her back shop, along with another woman called Christian Peacock. They had been both strangled, the former with a cord, the latter with a handkerchief. It was known that Jean Alexander had about £70 in notes and cash, which, with three gold rings taken from her fingers, were all carried off. Two Irishmen, shoemakers, named William Burnside and Thomas Taggart, have been lodged in Kilmarnock jail on suspicion of the murder."

These individuals, we believe, had been in the habit of frequenting the house, and it was supposed had committed the inhuman act in order to obtain the money which Alexander had in her possession. Burnside's watch, too, had been pawned with Alexander; and this strengthened the suspicion which had been awakened against him. They were both tried for the crime at the Ayr Circuit Court on the 24th of September, 1808, and pleaded not guilty. A servant-girl swore she had seen the prisoners coming out of Alexander's shop on the morning of the murder. No proof, however, of their actual guilt could be adduced, and they were, therefore, acquitted on a verdict of *not proven.*

Another circumstance, not less appalling, and one which also produced a great amount of public sympathy, occurred early on the morning of Sabbath, December 25, 1808. We allude to the melancholy fate of James Millar, a young soldier of the 91st regiment, who was one of a party stationed here on recruiting service. He was a native of Perth, and had entered the army in 1804, when only fourteen years of age. Being fifer to the party, of good character, and rather prepossessing in appearance, he soon became well known in Kilmarnock, and was much respected by many of the inhabitants. The particulars of the case may be briefly told.

On the night when the unfortunate affair occurred he and two other individuals, one of whom was his comrade, named Robert Walker, had been spending a social hour in the house of Mr Thomas Bicket, spirit-dealer, Fore Street. Walker was the first to retire and go home to his lodgings. The two others remained in Mr Bicket's till midnight; they then left; and when entering the Cross on their way homeward, Millar's companion discovered and pointed out to him a person named William Rowan, a deserter from the 26th regiment. The fifer instantly seized the deserter, who at first made little resistance; he led him in the direction of Nailer's Close,* for the purpose of handing him over to the officer of the party, whose quarters were in Green Street. The other individual, notwithstanding the part he had acted, now went off, and Millar was left alone to struggle with his captive. But, alas! a lamentable fate was impending over him; for no sooner had they entered the close than the latter drew a knife from his pocket, and cruelly stabbed him in several places. The deserter now made his escape; and the poor fifer, without friend or assistant, was left faint and bleeding, and so injured by the weapon of the assassin, that his entrails protruded. With the utmost difficulty he crawled along the snow-clad ground to the officer's lodgings, where his wounds were carefully dressed, and every relief afforded him that medical skill and humanity could devise. During the day he was able to walk about his room, and slight hopes were entertained of his recovery; but in the evening it was found that mortification had begun in his bowels, and he died on the following morning. He was interred with military honours in the Low

* A little narrow close that led from the upper end of the Cross to Green Street, before Duke Street was formed. (See page 90.)

Church burying-ground; the light company of his regiment from Ayr, and some hundreds of our townsmen, accompanied his remains to the grave.

Rowan, who was a native of Ireland, was sought for in every direction; and a reward of twenty pounds sterling was offered for his apprehension; but, notwithstanding every exertion made to secure him, he contrived to conceal himself from the vigilance of the law. The bloody knife with which he perpetrated the deed was, it is said, afterwards found stuck into a tree near Kilmarnock House; but he himself was never again seen or heard of in this part of the country.*

A monument was erected over the grave of the young soldier by the regiment to which he belonged, at an expense of fifteen guineas, one-third of which was generously contributed by the recruiting officer. It was a plain, modest-looking structure, in form resembling a pyramid, with an inscription which simply told the story of his death. About the year 1847 it had become somewhat ruinous; and no funds being available for its reparation, it was removed altogether.

To resume the subject of the town and its trades: they continued gradually to increase; and by 1811 the population amounted to 10,148. In the course of other three years the Tontine buildings were erected, which added considerably to the beauty of the Cross.†

---

* A notice of the murder in the *Ayr Advertiser* of the time says: "Diligent search was soon made after the inhuman villain, and in all probability he would have been taken, had not one of his countrymen, whose house was first searched, made quick despatch by a bye-road to his lodgings, and warned him of his danger."

† The building of the Tontine was resolved upon at a meeting of influential gentlemen held on the 9th December, 1813, and in the course of the two following years it was erected. Previously to that time, there was no commodious or convenient public reading-room in the town. The only one, we believe, was a small apartment in King Street, connected with the Sun Inn, or Bryan's Inn, as it was called, from the name of the landlord, Mr John Bryan, whose tall, erect form, long powdered hair, and gentlemanly manner, must still be remembered by our aged townsmen.

CHAPTER XVIII.

O deem not, midst this worldly strife,
An idle art the Poet brings;
Let high Philosophy control,
And sages calm the stream of life;
'Tis he refines its fountain-springs,
The nobler passions of the soul.
                                CAMPBELL.

KILMARNOCK, though it could boast of a printing-press as far back as 1780, had no magazine or periodical of any description till 1817, when two works of that kind were started, namely, the *Ayrshire Miscellany, or Kilmarnock Literary Expositor*, and the *Coila Repository, or Kilmarnock Monthly Magazine*. These publications were commenced in the same month, August, 1817; but the latter, though containing much useful reading, lived only for a year. Another periodical, entitled the *Kilmarnock Mirror, or Literary Gleaner*, was soon afterwards published. Its pages were enriched with some clever essays and pleasing pieces of original poetry; but its existence, like that of the *Repository*, was somewhat ephemeral. The *Miscellany* appeared in weekly numbers, at twopence each, and was read in almost every town and village in the county. It existed till the beginning of May, 1822. During the time of its continuance periodical literature was scarcely accessible to the bulk of the people;* this little work, therefore, though humble in a literary point of view, must have exercised a salutary influence on the moral and intellectual

---

* The publication of the cheap periodicals of Chambers, Knight, and others, did not begin till 1832.

feelings of its readers. In its pages the young aspirants after literary fame found publicity for their effusions; and matters of local interest, such as markets, accidents, deaths, &c., being therein recorded, it served, in some measure, the purposes of a newspaper to the inhabitants generally.

The projector and editor of the *Miscellany* was James Thomson, mentioned in the preceding Chapter as captain of the Sharpshooters; and as he was the first who established a weekly intelligencer in the town, we deem it proper to register the particulars of his life. He was a native of Kilmarnock, and was born on the 9th May, 1775. His father, who was a tanner, and proprietor of the large tanwork at present in the possession of the Messrs Crooks, bestowed upon him a liberal education, with a view to fit him for the ministry. He afterwards became a licentiate of the Secession Church; but his parents now thought that the duties of the clerical profession might tend to injure his health (which, at the time, was unpromising); and through their persuasion he relinquished the design of preaching, and became a partner with his father in the business of tanning.

Thomson, as before said, was honoured, about the year 1804, with the command of the Kilmarnock Sharpshooters, and few men were more zealous in the cause for which that regiment was raised. But his patriotic enthusiasm involved him in pecuniary embarrassment, and called forth the censure of his more immediate friends. A brother, who was in business with him, withdrew from the firm; his father, too, and he differed; the company was dissolved; and the tanyard and stock were soon afterwards disposed of.

From his boyhood Thomson evinced a predilection for literature; and, with the intention of living by his pen, he now repaired to Edinburgh, where he found employment in writing for a work entitled the *Scottish Review*. Here he remained only a year, when his love of military glory again turned his attention to the army, and he succeeded in procuring a commission in the Argyleshire Militia. With that corps he served in Ireland; but he was ultimately obliged to resign his commission in consequence of declining health. He then returned to Kilmarnock. But the golden sun of prosperity, which, in early life, had here poured upon him its cheering beams, had now set, and he was left to struggle with the ills of adversity. Thomson, however, possessed a clear and reflecting mind, the further cultivation of which afforded him consolation amid all the trials and changes of life. From his boyish years he had been an occasional worshipper at the shrine of Apollo; and soon after his return he published a small collection of poetical pieces, which procured him the esteem of several philanthropic gentlemen. His next literary undertaking was the *Ayrshire Miscellany*, already alluded to. A considerable number of the pieces contained in it were from his own pen.* In 1824 he again published a poetical

---

* The following simple yet graphic account, by Thomson, of a remarkable funeral of a miser, which took place in the town in 1817, appeared in the first volume of the *Miscellany*, and may not inappropriately be transferred to our pages:

"In Glen Street [now East Shaw Street], Kilmarnock, on Friday, 17th July, 1817, died William Stevenson, aged eighty-seven years. He was originally from the parish of Dunlop, and bred a mason; but, during many of the latter years of his life he wandered about as a common beggar. Thirty years ago, he and his wife separated upon these strange conditions: that the first that proposed an agreement, should forfeit one hundred pounds. This singular pair never met again, and it is not now known whether the heroine yet lives.

"Stevenson was much afflicted, during the last two years of his life, with the stone. He often grievously reflected why Providence should keep him in such lingering torment. Nothing seemed to give him more concern than his inability to earn his bread; or that the money he had scraped together should be exhausted before he died. As his disease increased, he was fully aware of his approaching dissolution; and for this event he made the following extraordinary preparations:

"He sent for a baker, and ordered twelve dozen of burial cakes, and a great profusion of sugar biscuit; together with a corresponding quantity of wine and spirituous liquors. He told the baker, that if this quantity was not sufficient, he should provide more, as nothing but whole cakes were to be served about at his funeral. He next sent for the joiner, and ordered a coffin decently mounted, with particular instructions, that the wood should be quite dry, and the joints firm, and impervious to water. The grave-digger was next sent for, and asked if he thought

volume, bearing the title of the *Ayrshire Melodist, or Select Poetical Effusions*. He also contemplated publishing a paraphrastic version of the book of *Psalms;* and it is evident, from the merit of one or two pieces which he issued as specimens, that in his hand the sacred lyre was not degraded. For fifteen years previous to his death, he was subject to bodily affliction, and secluded from active life. He died July 23, 1832, in the fifty-seventh year of his age.

Contemporary with Thomson were John Burtt and John Kennedy; and the merits of their poetical and prose produc-

he could get a place to put him in after he was dead. He said, he daresay he might. The spot fixed upon was in the churchyard of Riccarton, a village about half a mile distant. He enjoined the sexton to be sure and make his grave roomy, and in a dry and comfortable corner; and he might rest assured that he would be well rewarded for his care and trouble. Having made these arrangements, he ordered the old woman that attended him to go to a certain nook, and bring out nine pounds, to be appropriated to defray funeral charges. He told her at the same time not to be grieved, for he had not forgotten her in his will. In a few hours afterwards, in the full exercise of his mental powers, but in the most excruciating agonies, he expired. A neighbour, and a man of business, were immediately sent for to examine and seal up his effects. The first thing they found was a bag, containing large silver pieces, such as crowns, half-crowns, and dollars, to a large amount. In a corner was secreted, amongst a vast quantity of musty rags, a great number of guineas and seven-shilling pieces. In his trunk was found a bond for £300, and other bonds and securities to a very considerable amount. In all, we have heard, the property amounted to £900. His will was got among some old papers; leaving to his housekeeper £20, and the rest of his property to be divided among his distant relations. As it required some time to give his relatives intimation of his death, and to make preparations for his funeral, he lay in state four days, during which period, the place where he was, resembled more an Irish wake than a deserted room, where the Scotch lock up their dead. The invitations to his funeral were most singular. Persons were not asked individually, but in whole families; so that, except by a few relatives dressed in black, his obsequies were attended by tradesmen in their working clothes, barefooted boys and girls, and an immense crowd of tattered beggars; to the aged among whom he left sixpence, and to the younger threepence. After the interment, this motley group retired to a large barn fitted up for the purpose, where a scene of waste, profusion, and inebriety was exhibited, almost without a parallel. Scarcely one of them that were there could stagger home without assistance; and some were obliged to remain all night stretched among the corn-sacks in a nook of the barn. . . . .

"After all this profusion, a few worthies who were neglected to be invited, threatened to raise the corpse, if they were not allowed to do honour to Stevenson's memory. And in order to prevent such a catastrophe, the place has continued a scene of dissipation ever since."

tions justly entitle them to a brief notice. Burtt was born at Knockmarloch, in the parish of Riccarton, about the year 1790. When five or six years old, his grandfather, to whose care he had been left when a mere child, settled with him in Kilmarnock. Here he received the rudiments of his education, and was taught the art of weaving. From his childish years he was characterized by a thirst for learning; and, though the sphere in which he was placed was not the most favourable for mental cultivation, yet, by diligent application to books, and by private study, he soon acquired a considerable understanding of the French and Latin languages, and no mean knowledge of miscellaneous literature. But while thus devoting himself to useful studies, and, in all probability, cherishing the hope of rising to some respectable position in society, his expectations were suddenly blighted; for, happening, in 1807, to visit the town of Greenock, he was there impressed for the service of the navy. No circumstance could have been more painful to his feelings; for he naturally recoiled from all that was cruel and oppressive; but to plead for his liberty was vain—the die was cast; and he was speedily immured in a ship of war, and subjected to all its rigorous discipline. At length, in 1812, he effected his escape, and returned to Kilmarnock. He again wrought at the loom, and spent, as before, his leisure hours in the attainment of knowledge. He afterwards opened a school, and was pretty successful as a teacher. In 1816 his little work, entitled *Horæ Poeticæ*, which consists of pieces of prose and poetry, was published. An exalted tone of morality, feeling, and intellect pervades its pages. The prose compositions, especially the *Sailor's Fate*, *Eliza's Tomb*, and the *Bible*, bear the impress of a truly-cultivated mind. Burtt was also the author of several lyrical productions, which appeared in the provincial magazines and newspapers of his time. One of these, entitled *O'er the mist-shrouded Cliffs*, has been sometimes mistaken for an effusion of Burns, and as such has been printed in different editions of that poet's works.

In the same year, 1816, Burtt removed to Paisley, and was led, by the impulse of his patriotic feelings, to exercise his talents for the advancement of the political movement of that period; but, finding that the Legislature was deaf to the voice of the people, and that his own liberty was at stake, he emigrated to America in the summer of 1817.

After being about two years in that country he published a little volume, entitled *Transient Murmurs of a Solitary Lyre: consisting of Poems and Songs in English and Scotch.* As in his former publication, his poetical pieces are illustrated by remarks in prose, which add considerably to the value of the work. Among the songs is the one alluded to as having been sometimes ascribed to Burns.

In the land of his adoption fortune has looked upon our author with a more friendly aspect. For some time he acted as a schoolmaster; and, to fit himself for the church, he studied at Princeton College, New Jersey; after which he was appointed pastor of a Presbyterian congregation at Salem. In the beginning of 1831 he removed to Philadelphia, where he was editor of a newspaper called the *Presbyterian.* Two years afterwards he went to Cincinnati, where also he was a minister, and the conductor of a paper called the *Standard;* and in August, 1835, he received a call to the chair of Ecclesiastical History in a Theological Seminary in that city. The latest intelligence we have of him is, that in 1857, he was pastor of a Presbyterian church at Blackwoodton, in the neighbourhood of Philadelphia.

John Kennedy, author of *Fancy's Tour with the Genius of Cruelty, and other Poems,* and of the more popular work entitled *Geordie Chalmers, or the Law in Glenbuckie,* was born in Kilmarnock in 1789. Like the subject of the preceding sketch, he was bred to the loom, and evinced at an early age a love of learning and a superiority of intellect. To be educated for one of the learned professions was his principal ambition; but a common education was all that his father, from his humble circumstances, was able to bestow upon him.

Disliking the loom, and probably feeling a desire to know more of the world, he enlisted in 1807 into the Royal Ayrshire Militia. To him, however, a soldier's life had few enjoyments; on the contrary, he looked upon it as a life of thraldom; at least we are led to that inference from the feelings of delight to which he gave utterance in one of his poems, composed on receiving his discharge at the general peace in 1815. He again settled in Kilmarnock, and assiduously employed his leisure time in the cultivation of his mind. With John Burtt he was on terms of friendship, and in 1816 became teacher of the school which that individual left when he went to Paisley.

About this time great commercial distress prevailed among the working classes in this district, and in other parts of the country. The necessity of Parliamentary reform was much discussed; and a meeting for considering the expediency of petitioning His Royal Highness the Prince Regent and the Houses of Parliament, for a redress of grievances, was held at Dean Park, on the 7th December, 1816. At that meeting Kennedy was a speaker. His theme was military flogging; and with great energy and animation, and in striking language, he depicted the miseries which the poor soldier endured by so degrading a system of punishment. From that time, as the reader is probably aware, the cry for Parliamentary reform continued to increase. Physical force was at length talked of as the only means whereby the desired object could be obtained; and, in 1819, Government, to quell the excitement, caused a few of the principal leaders to be seized and imprisoned. Kennedy, though he had been always an advocate for sound constitutional reform, and though he had taken almost no part in political matters subsequent to the Dean

Park meeting, was suspected as a chief actor in the movement. His house was searched by the magistrates for seditious or treasonable papers;* and he himself was apprehended and sent to Ayr for examination before the Sheriff. Nothing transpired, however, that could criminate him; and he was set at liberty, after giving bail for his future appearance.

About the middle of April, 1820, Kennedy was once more apprehended, along with others, and escorted by a party of cavalry to the county prison. He was again subjected to the strictest examination; but, as in the former instance, no charge that was brought against him could be proven, and he was set at liberty, after being nineteen days in confinement.

In the month of June of the same year, he obtained the situation of teacher at Chapel Green, near Kilsyth. Here the happiest portion of his life was spent; and here also the greater part of *Geordie Chalmers* was written. It was not the fortune of the author, however, to see it published; for while it was in the press his health began to decline; and we are told, in a short notice of him appended to the book, that "while the last sheet was in his hands for the purpose of correction, he was summoned to his great account," on the 4th October, 1833.

Besides *Geordie Chalmers*, Kennedy was the author of three poetical volumes. The best of his productions, however, is *Geordie Chalmers*, in which are graphically portrayed the trials and disappointments which Geordie—an obscure and unfortunate teacher—was doomed to experience in his professional career.†

* Among the papers found were two or three manuscript chapters of *Geordie Chalmers;* and the worthy bailies, suspecting they were seditious communications from some dangerous radical of that name, despatched them to Ayr for the inspection of the Sheriff; but of course it was discovered that *Geordie* was only an imaginary personage, and the papers were returned to the author.

† The particulars of the above sketches of Thomson, Burtt, and Kennedy, have been taken from memoirs formerly written by the author of the present work for the *Contemporaries of Burns.*

CHAPTER XIX.

*Freedom is not the thought of being free
From strangers who would yoke us with disgrace;
'Tis not the pride that we have bowed the knee
To no stern tyrant of a foreign race;
Such may exist, and Briton still may be
The slave of Briton, holding the vile place
Where independence cringes to command,
That makes the heart more servile than the hand.*

                                        BURRINGTON.

As we stated in last Chapter, great commercial distress prevailed among the working classes about the year 1816; and the partial manner in which the people were then represented in the Commons' House of Parliament, together with the extent of the national debt, and the annual taxation of the country, amounting to about seventy millions sterling, were reckoned by many as the chief sources of the evil. Kilmarnock at that time contained nearly 13,000 inhabitants; and among that vast number only *one* person, the late Major Parker of Assloss, had a vote for a member of Parliament. Of the necessity, therefore, of Parliamentary reform the majority of the people appeared to be convinced;* and, for the purpose of considering the propriety of petitioning his Royal

---

* At an earlier period, namely in 1792, a general desire seems to have prevailed in Kilmarnock for Parliamentary reform. In December of that year delegates from nine societies met in the Angel Inn, Mr Wylie in the chair, and resolved "that the thanks of the meeting be given to Mr Fox, Mr Erskine, Mr Sheridan, the Duke of Norfolk, the Marquis of Landsdown, Mr Grey, and others, for their steady adherence in Parliament to the cause of liberty." Resolutions were also passed, thanking other leading gentlemen "for the wise and temperate measures adopted by them for prosecuting a Parliamentary reform, and for their avowed principles for the peace and good order of society."

Highness the Prince Regent and the Legislature on the distress of the country, a public meeting of the burgesses and other inhabitants was held at Dean Park, on Saturday, the 7th December, 1816. The day was cold and stormy; but it cooled not the patriotic enthusiasm of the people; for, notwithstanding the showers of hail and snow with which they were assailed, a vast multitude, amounting to five or six thousand, assembled.

The business of the meeting was opened by Mr Alexander Maclaren, a talented tradesman, who, in a brief and energetic address, alluded to the sufferings of the country, and ascribed their existence to the narrow-minded policy of her rulers. Mr James Johnston was then called to the chair, and spoke in a similar strain, attributing the distress that prevailed to the want of a proper representation in Parliament. "This county," he said, "is supposed to contain nearly 170,000 inhabitants,* and of this number only 156 have any right to vote for a member to serve in Parliament; and even these do not vote freely; for it is notorious that two powerful individuals have ruled the elections in this county for the last forty years. Thus you see that in Ayrshire there is a population of 169,844 who have no right to vote, nor are any more represented in Parliament than the cattle on the hills."

The next speaker was Mr Archibald Craig, who dwelt principally on the ruinous consequences of war and the national debt; the magnitude of the latter he showed by one or two ingenious calculations.

At the close of Mr Craig's speech a series of resolutions, amounting to sixteen in number, and breathing the most liberal, or rather radical, sentiments, were read by Mr John Kennedy. An extract from one of these, showing the extent

---

* This statement appears to be incorrect; for we find, by consulting the *Enumeration of the Inhabitants of Scotland taken from the Government Abstracts*, that, in 1821, the total number of persons in the county was only 126,932.

of the elective franchise at that period, may be made: "The meeting cannot but pronounce the present representation of Scotland to be altogether unreasonable, unconstitutional, and unjust; considering that, of two millions of inhabitants, only 2700 have a right of voting for members of Parliament, the remaining 1,997,300, although tax-payers, directly or indirectly, having no more right of voting than if they were an importation of slaves from Africa."

After the resolutions were read, two other speeches were delivered, one of which was written by Mr John Burtt, author of *Horæ Poeticæ*, who was then residing in Paisley. The other was the composition of a Mr White, who also was absent. The address by Burtt, with the exception of one or two striking passages respecting war and the army, was confined to the miseries of his suffering countrymen; and, like his other writings, it was marked by vigorous conception, sincerity of feeling, and beauty of language. Mr White's speech, in its general tone and bearing, was, perhaps, more *radical* than the others. He contended that the people had no representatives—that the half of their scanty earnings was extorted from them in the shape of taxes—that the golden treasures of the nation had been drained by an offensive war—that nature had formed all men in the same mould, had gifted them with kindred minds—and that the *few* had no right to hold over the *many* an unlimited authority.

The proceedings were wound up by Mr John Kennedy, who, as before stated, expatiated with great energy on military flogging. He earnestly exhorted the meeting to be temperate and exemplary in their conduct—to make the page of history their evening hours' amusement—to think for themselves—to let their devotion at the shrine of liberty be next in ardour to their love of Deity. He concluded in the language of Burns: "May tyranny in the ruler, and licentiousness in the people, find in each of us an inexorable foe."

The speeches delivered on the occasion were afterwards printed in a small pamphlet, with the motto,

"Why should Rome fall a moment ere her time?"

The pamphlet, four hundred copies of which were thrown off, was sold by Mr Thomas Baird, merchant, who had been appointed by a committee to superintend the printing and publishing of it. Several of the expressions or statements it contained were considered to be highly inflammatory and seditious, particularly one in the opening address, by Mr Maclaren. It did not long escape the vigilance of the law; for, on the 26th of February, 1817, Mr Maclaren was apprehended and taken before the Sheriff-Substitute of the county for examination. Mr Baird also, who had published or sold the pamphlet, was apprehended and examined; and the result was, that they were indicted for sedition, and in the following month (March, 1817) brought to trial before the High Court of Justiciary, at Edinburgh. No trial of a similar kind had taken place in the country for several years; and considerable interest was, therefore, excited regarding it, especially in Kilmarnock and its neighbourhood, where Messrs Maclaren and Baird were well known and esteemed. Almost every witness examined spoke favourably of the general conduct of the panels. They had also the benefit of able counsel; but, after a protracted trial of two days, they were found guilty, the one of uttering, and the other of circulating or publishing, sedition. They were sentenced to be imprisoned for six months in the Canongate Tolbooth of Edinburgh; Mr Maclaren to find security to keep the peace for three years, under a penalty of forty pounds sterling, and Mr Baird, for the same period, under a penalty of two hundred.

Mr Maclaren, who was highly respected in his sphere of life, was a native of Perthshire, and had been resident in Kilmarnock eight years previous to his trial. His health, we believe, was so impaired by the imprisonment, that he did not survive many years. Mr Baird, too, was much and justly esteemed by his fellow-townsmen, and, at one period, was honoured with the command of the Rifle Volunteers. His health also was injured by the confinement. He died in December, 1826, aged forty-nine.

The objects sought by the Dean Park meeting, we need scarcely say, were not obtained. The radical principles, however, continued to spread among the working classes; but no other remarkable demonstration of their opinions took place till 1819. On Saturday, the 18th September of that year, a meeting of the friends of radical reform was held on a field at the back of Morton Place.* During the early part of the day immense numbers marched into the town in systematic order; and, by one o'clock, seven thousand, it was said, had assembled on the ground. Few flags were displayed; but the men of Galston and Newmilns indicated their love of country by carrying large Scotch thistles. Considerable talent was shown by the different speakers; and *universal suffrage* was advocated as the only sure means of reforming the House of Commons, and mitigating the distresses of the country. A feeling prevailed at the meeting, that it was vain to remonstrate with Parliament on the subject of their grievances; but it was agreed that a petition should be sent to the Prince Regent. For the preservation of the peace, a party of military was at the command of the magistrates; but the meeting dispersed in the most orderly manner; and the day passed away without the slightest symptom of disturbance.

On Saturday, the 20th November following, a "county meeting," as it was called, was held at the same place. By

---

* No other spot could be obtained; and the field alluded to was freely offered by the late David Mitchell, Esq., who then held it in tack. Mr Mitchell was an intelligent, public-spirited individual, and was always ready to aid in the cause of general progress. He died in 1835, aged about eighty years.

eleven o'clock, A.M., vast crowds had assembled. Those from the neighbouring towns marched into the field in military order, amid the stirring music of drums, clarionets, and bagpipes, and bearing flags with mottoes expressive of their principles. An old banner, which had stood the "battle and the breeze" on the famed field of Drumclog, waved among the others.

Mr Archibald Craig, formerly spoken of, was called to the chair; and, after being crowned with a cap of liberty, introduced the business of the meeting. Eight or nine other speakers followed, all of whose addresses were deeply imbued with the spirit of radicalism. As at the former meeting, it was agreed that an address be presented to the Prince Regent, urging the necessity of Parliamentary reform. The number present was estimated at from fourteen to sixteen thousand.

After this period the proceedings of the radicals assumed a more daring aspect. Their petitions to Parliament had proved ineffectual; and the delusive scheme of physical force was now talked of as the only means by which their purpose could be effected. At length the first day of April, 1820, was fixed upon as the time they should muster in arms against the government; and large placards,* announcing the same,

* From one of the placards, which is still in the possession of a townsman, a sentence or two may be given as illustrative of the spirit in which it was written: "Let us show to the world that we are not that lawless, sanguinary rabble which our oppressors would persuade the higher circles we are—but a brave and generous people, determined to be *free*. LIBERTY or DEATH is our *motto*; and we have sworn to return home in *triumph* or return no *more*. . . . Soldiers! shall you, countrymen, bound by the sacred obligation of an oath to defend your country and your king from enemies, whether foreign or domestic, plunge your bayonets into the bosoms of fathers and brothers, and at once sacrifice at the shrine of military despotism, to the unrelenting orders of a cruel faction, those feelings which you hold in common with the rest of mankind? . . . Forbid it Heaven! Come forward then at once and free your country and your king from the power of those that have held them too, *too* long in thraldom. . . . Britons! God, Justice, the wishes of all good men, are with us. Join together and make it one *cause*; and the nations of the earth shall hail the day when the standard of LIBERTY shall be raised on its native soil." The document is dated "Glasgow, 1st April, 1820," and signed, "By order of the Committee of Organization for forming a Provisional Government."

were posted throughout Kilmarnock and other towns in the west of Scotland. Considerable excitement prevailed respecting the matter. The more prudent radicals regarded it as the device of foolish, or designing men, who studied to endanger the cause of reform, by luring the unwary and the ignorant into the labyrinths of rebellion. Others, more sanguine in their expectations, believed that the hour of their political redemption was at hand, and secretly provided themselves with weapons for the coming struggle.

At last the day arrived for commencing hostilities; but no banner was hoisted; no sword was drawn; every one, indeed, seemed to expect that his neighbour would take the lead in the enterprise; and none having the hardihood to do so, the whole affair proved abortive. But though no public outbreak was the consequence, certain individuals were marked as leading characters; and for the purpose of securing and making an example of these, a considerable body of cavalry, and other soldiers were brought from Edinburgh to Kilmarnock. They arrived here before daybreak, on the morning of the 14th, with one piece of cannon, which they placed in the Cross. They then surrounded the town, patrolled the various streets, and kept the inhabitants within doors; while the magistrates, accompanied by a small party of military, proceeded to search for the ringleaders; but the more active of these had been forewarned of their danger, and eluded apprehension. Several individuals, however, were taken from their homes, sent to the county prison, and there kept for some time in close confinement; one of them in particular, Mr Archibald Craig, was detained for sixteen or seventeen weeks, though nothing criminal was found against him.*

For the purpose of keeping the peace, a regiment of

* Mr Craig, in the following year, emigrated to America, where he became a preacher of the gospel. He died at Mount Carmel, Indiana, North America, on the 29th June, 1844, in the fifty-third year of his age.

volunteers was formed about this time in Kilmarnock, and commanded by Major Parker of Assloss; but, happily for all parties, the tranquillity of the district was not disturbed, and the corps was soon afterwards disbanded.

The next political movement in which the people of Kilmarnock took part, was that which brought about the Reform Bill, in 1832. With an earnestness and enthusiasm worthy of the cause, they joined in the great national struggle; and though many of them thought that the *majority* should have been included in the elective franchise provided by the bill, yet they hailed the passing of it as the dawn of a happier era, and the bill itself as a measure that would ultimately bring peace and prosperity to the people at large.

So enthusiastic were the people at that time in the cause of liberty, that one of the petitions for reform was signed by three thousand persons in the short space of three days; and at one of the public meetings held on the lawn in front of Kilmarnock House, the number present was estimated at seventeen thousand. At the close of the meeting about seven thousand, of whom fifteen hundred were from other towns, formed into procession, and headed by Mr Paton, town-officer, on a gallant charger, marched through the principal streets. On that occasion there were displayed no fewer than one hundred and twenty flags with bold, patriotic mottoes. Two or three other large meetings were afterwards held; and when the Reform Bill became law, a general illumination took place in the town. Among the principal speakers at the public meetings of that period were Mr William Wallace, Mr John Morton, Mr Andrew Love, Mr Thomas Adam, Mr Hugh Craig, Mr John Torrance, Mr Hugh Gibb, Mr John Brown, Dr Thomson, and Mr Robert Roger.*

* Mr Roger, who was landlord of the Turf Inn [now the Crown], created unusual merriment at one of these meetings by some humorous remarks which he made on the bishops. As many of our readers are aware, he accompanied Green, the cele-

At a later period, the men of Kilmarnock—particularly the working classes—took an active part in the Chartist agitation; and, in conjunction with other towns in the county, sent the late Hugh Craig, Esq., as a representative to the National Convention.* The election took place at a public meeting, held at Kilmarnock on the 3rd November, 1838. The cause of the chartists, we may add, like that of the radicals, was injured by the extreme measures proposed by some of its adherents. The Convention, after sitting for three months in London, was removed to Birmingham; and becoming involved in some illegal disputes, it was soon afterwards dissolved, without effecting anything beneficial to the country at large.

It may be stated, that since the passing of the Reform Bill, Kilmarnock, in connection with Rutherglen, Renfrew, Port-Glasgow, and Dumbarton, has been represented in Parliament, successively, by five individuals, namely: Captain Dunlop, of Dunlop, elected in 1832; Dr John Bowring, elected in 1835; John C. Colquhoun, Esq. of Killermont, elected in 1837; Alexander Johnston, Esq., elected in 1841; the Honourable E. P. Bouverie, first elected in 1844; and reëlected at the general elections in 1847, 1852, 1857, and 1859.

brated aëronaut, in his ascent from the Cross of Kilmarnock in the summer of 1830. Thousands had assembled to witness the spectacle, and fears were expressed by many for the safety of the daring aërial voyagers. Mr Roger, however (who was dressed with light-coloured trousers and blue jacket, which he had got made for the occasion), took his seat in the car of the balloon without the least symptom of dread. The day was a fine one—almost without a cloud; and the balloon, which ascended beautifully amid the cheers of the spectators, glided away in a north-easterly direction, and ultimately alighted in perfect safety in a hay-field in the neighbourhood of Eaglesham. Mr Roger afterwards used to describe the strange appearance which the objects beneath him presented when the balloon was far above the earth. The Cross, in which were many ladies, arrayed in gay attire, appeared, he said, like a bed of flowers, the streams like silver threads, the hills like little mounds; and one of his own coaches, which he saw upon the Glasgow road, seemed dwindled down to the size of a child's toy. Besides ascending in the balloon, Mr Roger, on one occasion, went down to the bottom of the sea in a diving-bell, at the harbour of Portpatrick. He died at Greenock in 1837.

* Mr Craig died in April, 1858.

CHAPTER XX.

The plague went on—and oh! what dire distress,
And wo, and lamentation, and despair,
And clouded brows, and melancholy dark,
O'er all the village spread! and still anon
Deep wailings for the dead, and mingled groans,
Of agonized life expiring fast,
From many a dwelling came.
                                    MACQUEEN.

FOR some time after the political excitement of 1819 and 1820, nothing occurred in the affairs of Kilmarnock that calls, in a particular manner, for historical detail. According to the *Government Abstracts* of 1821, there were then in the town and parish 1320 houses; and the number of families occupying these was 2696, of whom 120 were employed in agriculture, and 2576 in the various manufactures and handicrafts. The number of uninhabited houses was five, and five were in the course of erection. The total number of inhabitants was 12,769. Trade was not in a very flourishing condition; but the spirit of public improvement was still actively progressing.

In 1822 a joint-stock company was formed for supplying the town with gas. The funds necessary for the undertaking were raised by the subscribers in shares of £10 each. The works, which are situated in Park Street, were erected in the following year; and various important additions have since been made to them.

About 1770 calico-printing was introduced at Greenholm, by Mr John Macfee; and in 1824 Mr William Hall began the printing of worsted shawls at the same place. This fabric had not been previously printed upon in Scotland, at least to any extent worthy of notice. This proved of great benefit to the town, as it gave employment not only to printers, but to a considerable number of handloom weavers. So great, indeed, at one time was the demand for this cloth, that 3000 looms were employed in the weaving of it in Kilmarnock and the villages in the neighbourhood. About the year 1845 or 1846 there were engaged in the various printfields upwards of 1000 persons, not including about 800 boys and girls. The money then paid for wages every four weeks amounted, on an average, to £3400, or £850 weekly. The trade is still extensively carried on, there being at present eight printworks in the town.

In the same year, 1824, a society was formed under the name of the Kilmarnock Building Company, the object of which was to erect houses, on a uniform plan, for the members. The number of shares was eighty-one. Each member was to pay £3 sterling of entry-money, and 10s. per month till the whole cost of the buildings should be defrayed. Soon after its institution the company began operations; house after house was erected, till, in the course of a few years, an entire new street—Robertson Place—was added to the town.

Passing from 1824 till 1832, during which time nothing important occurred, we come to the gloomy period of the cholera. In the spring of the last-mentioned year this awful disease, after devastating the inland provinces of Russia, and other continental countries, made its appearance on the shores of Britain. With frightful rapidity it spread from town to town; and so great were its ravages that, in some localities, a fifth of the inhabitants was swept away; nay, in one little village (Inver), in the north of Scotland, the half of the population was consigned to the dust by its deadly influence.

In July following it broke out in Kilmarnock. The first case known to the public occurred in the family of Mr Petrie, a carrier, residing in Low Church Lane, who, it was supposed, had brought the infection from Paisley. The next two cases were those of a female who frequented the house, and of the medical gentleman who happened to visit the family. These tended, in no small degree, to impress upon the public mind a belief in the contagious nature of this awful disease; and a painful sensation was thereby created throughout the community. Many, we are aware, talked of the pestilence with stoical indifference, and believed that it existed only in the imaginations of the timid; but it continued its silent and onward course—case after case, and death after death, followed in rapid succession, proclaiming the feebleness of man, and proving to a demonstration, that he, with all his knowledge and boasted ingenuity, however willing, was utterly unable to stop the progress of the desolating disease.

Many of the deaths were awfully sudden. Individuals, who were heard in the morning bewailing the loss of a friend or neighbour, might have been seen, before the dawn of another day, enwrapt in the robes of the dead. An instance of this is yet fresh in our memory. We had strolled to the outskirts of the town, where we happened to enter into conversation with a person engaged in rural labour. We talked of the dreadful ravages of the cholera. In feeling language he made several inquiries regarding it, and trusted its continuance would be but of short duration. On the following morning we had occasion to inquire for the same individual; but, alas! we received the sad intelligence that *he*, too, had fallen a victim to the malady, and was already prostrate in the grave.

To check, as far as possible, the virulence of the pestilence, a temporary hospital was erected by public subscription, at Ward's Park, for the accommodation of the poorer patients; and, we believe, it had in a great measure the effect contemplated. To describe the state of terror into which the public mind was thrown would be a difficult task. Some, to avoid the danger, held no intercourse with society at large. Others changed their place of residence; but even these were not secure; for instances occurred of individuals being seized with the distemper when in the act of removing, or immediately after they had removed to another locality. Compared, however, with some other towns in the west of Scotland, Kilmarnock suffered slightly. The greatest number of deaths in one day was fourteen; and from the breaking out of the pestilence in July, till its disappearance in the middle of October, the whole was about two hundred and fifty.

The bodies of the victims were interred in a piece of ground, obtained for the purpose, at the south corner of Ward's Park. This was done, we believe, partly because the common burying-ground of the town was then considered too small to meet the necessities of the case, and partly to prevent apprehended infection, as the graves in the new locality might remain in an undisturbed condition for a longer period.

It may be proper to notice the important fact, and a profitable lesson may be drawn from it, that many of the sufferers were persons of irregular and dissipated habits, such as were reduced to a state of extreme indigence by their own folly and want of circumspection. The temperate and the virtuous also, it must be confessed, fell before the scourge, but not in the same proportion. The constitutions of those broken down by debauchery were predisposed for its reception, and sunk beneath its resistless sway, as the shattered tenement falls into ruins beneath the power of the wintry tempest.

The medical gentlemen of the town, particularly Dr John Miller and Dr John Borland, were assiduous and active in their exertions to save their townsmen from the gulf that yawned around them. The former was officially employed, and received a weekly salary. The latter, though not so engaged, was of great use to the community. In the most praiseworthy manner he attended patient after patient, and often in quarters, too, where the circumstances of the sufferers held out no hope of the smallest remuneration. The services of both gentlemen were highly appreciated by the public at large; and each of them was afterwards presented with a handsome gold watch, as a token of gratitude for their indefatigable exertions at that melancholy period.

On the 15th January, 1849, the cholera again broke out in Kilmarnock, but, fortunately, with less virulence than in 1832. It continued till the 3rd April following; and the number of deaths was one hundred and thirty. An unoccupied printwork at the foot of Welbeck Street was fitted into a temporary hospital for the poorer patients; and the medical attendant was Dr John Borland, mentioned above. He was afterwards presented at a public meeting—over which Provost Cumming presided—with a purse containing sixty guineas, as a mark of the deep sense entertained of his services. We may also state that, in 1853, a Cholera Hospital was built at a short distance from the town on the banks of the Irvine, at an expense of upwards of £500. It has never been used, in consequence of the epidemic not prevailing to any great extent since its erection. The last appearance of the disease was in the beginning of 1854, when the number of deaths was thirty-four.

In January, 1831, the first Kilmarnock newspaper was started under the name of the *Kilmarnock Chronicle;* but, though advocating popular principles, and conducted with considerable ability, it met with but a slender share of public support; and, after struggling with various difficulties till January, 1832, it ceased to be published. It was again revived on the 3rd April following, by its former publisher and conductor, Mr James Paterson, a gentleman who has since written an interesting *History of the County of Ayr*, besides various other works. Mr Paterson, it may be mentioned, was the first to introduce an *iron* printing-press into Ayrshire, namely, a Columbian, which is still in Kilmarnock, in the establishment of Messrs Smith Brothers. The second attempt to establish the *Chronicle* was also unsuccessful, for it continued only till the winter following.

In February, 1833, another paper was started, and printed at the same press, entitled the *Ayrshire Reformer and Kilmarnock Gazette*. This print was edited by the late Dr John Taylor of Ayr, a man of acknowledged talent and extensive information; but, though the energies of his mind were earnestly devoted to its management, its existence, like that of its predecessor, was somewhat ephemeral.*

On the 7th February of the following year, 1834, the first number of the *Kilmarnock Journal* was issued. This paper, which was published during the greater part of its career by Messrs H. Crawford and Son, booksellers, was given up on the 8th May, 1857. It was started by a joint-stock company for the advocacy of Reform principles. It afterwards became moderately Conservative, and latterly espoused the Liberal interest. During the twenty-three years of its existence, it was generally under the management of talented editors. The first of these was John Donald Carrick, author of a *Life of Sir William Wallace*, and the original editor of the *Laird of Logan* and *Whistle Binkie;* in both of which works many clever pieces appeared from his own pen. The early parts of the latter publication, especially, are enriched by several of his poetical delineations of humble Scottish life—a

* Dr Taylor died at Larne, in the north of Ireland, on the 4th December, 1842. He twice contested the Ayr district of burghs on radical principles: once with T. F. Kennedy, Esq. of Dunure, and James Cruikshank, Esq. of Langley Park; and once with Lord James Stuart. On the former occasion he polled 164 votes, and on the latter, was defeated by a majority of 95.

Dr Taylor possessed a fine literary taste, and contributed many spirited articles to the local prints. A collection of his more serious poetical effusions has been printed for private circulation since his death. The volume, which is exceedingly elegant, is embellished with a faithful portrait of the author; a sketch of his birthplace, Newark Castle, near Ayr; and a view of Island Magee Church, where he was interred. A monument, consisting of a pedestal and statue, was erected to his memory in the Wallacetown New Cemetery, Ayr, in October, 1858.

species of composition in which he made no mean figure. He was a native of Glasgow, and died in August, 1835.

Mr Carrick's successors in the editorship of the *Journal* were Messrs John Leighton, John Beaton, William Wallace Fyfe, John Willox, Matthew Wilson, Alexander Campbell, J. C. Paterson, James Paterson—the publisher and editor of our first broadsheet—and W. C. Paterson, some of whom have also added in various ways to the literature of the country. In July, 1855, Mr J. C. Paterson became sole proprietor of the paper, which he greatly enlarged, and otherwise improved; but the encouragement extended towards it in its new form was not sufficiently remunerative, and it was therefore discontinued at the date mentioned above.

From the commencement of the *Journal*, till July, 1838, there was no other paper published in Kilmarnock. At that time the Liberals, or rather the Radicals of the town, anxious to have an organ of their own, began the *Ayrshire Examiner*. It was ably conducted by John R. Robertson, Esq.; but, like all the other prints that had been formerly issued in Kilmarnock in support of popular politics, it sickened for want of encouragement, and was given up in November, 1839.

The next paper started was the *Kilmarnock Herald*, published by the proprietor, the late Mr James Mathie, bookseller. It continued from the 20th September, 1844, till the 19th May, 1848. It was liberal in principle, and enjoyed a respectable share of public patronage. Two editors were successively engaged on it, namely, Mr Alexander Russell, now of the *Scotsman*, and the late Mr John Gibson, author of *Pictures in Print*.

In January, 1854, another Liberal organ was commenced by Mr James Millar, bookseller, under the title of the *Kilmarnock Chronicle;* and perhaps none of its predecessors displayed more ability in the discussion of political, social, or literary subjects. In June, 1855, it was changed from a large weekly to a small thrice-a-week paper; but on reaching the twenty-seventh number of the new series, it ceased to be published. The *Chronicle*, during the first three or four months of its career, was edited by Mr J. C. Paterson, formerly mentioned, and afterwards by the Rev. Peter Landreth.

At present there are two newspapers published in the town; the *Kilmarnock Weekly Post*, started by Mr James M'Kie, bookseller, in October, 1856, and the *Kilmarnock Standard*, started by Mr Thomas Stevenson, bookseller, in June, 1863.

When speaking of the press, we may mention, that, during the last thirty years, various efforts were made to establish a magazine or literary periodical in Kilmarnock. Every attempt, however, proved abortive, either from a want of genuine talent on the part of the contributors, or in consequence of the introduction of cheap weekly literature from other quarters. But in the publication of its annuals Kilmarnock has been more successful. The first of these was published in 1835 by Mr William Hutchison, bookseller. Besides some pleasing poetical contributions from Galt, Bowring, &c., it contained several spirited prose productions.

The next Kilmarnock annual was the *Ayrshire Wreath*, which was published by Mr James M'Kie, bookseller, and first issued in 1843. It appeared for three successive years,* and consisted of tales, sketches, and poetry, written by native authors, and a few others, on subjects chiefly connected with the county. The work, as a whole, was creditable to the contributors, and also to the editor—the late Robert Crawford, Esq., bookseller, Kilmarnock.

Mr Crawford, who was a man of refined taste and literary attainments, retired from business in 1845, and went to reside with a sister in Ireland, in the hope that his health, which was then declining, might be improved. Change of place, however,

---

* A fourth volume was published for 1855.

afforded him little or no benefit, and in June, 1846, he put himself under the treatment of the Hydropathic establishment at Rothesay, but apparently without obtaining any relief; for he died there on the 20th of the same month, at the early age of forty-six. Though a business man, in the strict sense of the term, Mr Crawford was much attached to literary pursuits; and, for a considerable period, he wrote the reviews of new publications in the *Kilmarnock Journal*. A sound judgment, a just appreciation of the truly beautiful in composition, and a simple yet elegant diction, characterized these notices. He also contributed numerous articles, in prose and poetry, to various periodicals, among which was the *Phrenological Journal*. From a conviction that intellectual studies were highly conducive to the growth and spread of morality, he was always ready to encourage the youthful literary aspirant, with whom he happened to be acquainted, by giving him his counsel, and by furnishing him with books of reference from his own private library, which was carefully selected, and comprised many valuable and curious works. In short, though earnestly devoted to business, he was a friend to mental as well as physical recreation, not only for their own sakes, but for the salutary influence which the alternate and moderate exercise of mind and body has upon both. For the same reasons he was a friend to the system of early shop-shutting, believing, in the words of Shakspeare,

> "Sweet recreation barr'd, what doth ensue
> But moody and dull melancholy;
> And, at his heels, a huge, infectious troop
> Of pale distemperatures, and foes of life?"

By Mr Crawford's will, of which we shall afterwards speak, the interest of a considerable sum of money will ultimately fall to the Kilmarnock Library; and this, of itself, is a decided evidence of the warm interest he manifested in the intellectual prosperity of his native town.

CHAPTER XXI.

Truth's beacon-lights, these sacred altars stand,
The watch-towers and the bulwarks of our land.
M. P. AIRD.

AMONG the dissenting places of worship that remain to be noticed, the most conspicuous in architectural beauty and importance is King Street United Presbyterian Church. It was built in 1832, from a design by Mr Robert Johnston, architect, and does great credit to his taste and talents. Its style is a combination of various orders of architecture, and has an imposing and beautiful effect. The interior is plain yet elegant, and is capable of containing an audience of nearly one thousand five hundred. This, we may remark, was the second dissenting church in Scotland on which a steeple was erected, and the first, we believe, from which issued the sounds of the Sabbath-bell. The expense of the spire was defrayed, in a great measure, by public subscription.* It is one hundred and twenty feet in height, and contains, with one exception, the largest bell in Kilmarnock; it is also furnished with an excellent clock, the dials of which can be seen from almost every part of the town.†

The history of this church may be briefly stated. Its original members seceded from the parish church of Riccarton, about the year 1799, in consequence of the patron refusing to

---

* The cost of the building, including the steeple, bell, and clock, was £3839 13s. 11d., of which £415 6s. 6d. was subscribed by the public.

† The clock was the workmanship of the old firm of Breckenridge and Son, Kilmarnock.

grant them the choice of a minister. Immediately afterwards they connected themselves with the Relief Presbytery of Glasgow; and, till better accommodation could be procured, they met for divine worship in a barn-yard in Riccarton. At length, in 1802, their first meeting-house was erected in that village.

About the same period their first minister—the Rev. Daniel Macnaught—was inducted. He was a man of considerable ability, and was much esteemed for his diligence and zeal as a pastor and preacher. He was translated to Biggar about the year 1808. The congregation then obtained, for a limited period, the ministerial services of the Rev. John Lawson, a man of rather an eccentric cast of mind, who, however, displayed an unwearied assiduity and pious care in the discharge of the important duties belonging to his sacred calling.

Their next minister was the Rev. James Kirkwood, who was appointed to the charge in 1811. His ability as a preacher, and the interest which he manifested, on all occasions, in the general welfare of his flock, induced many individuals to attach themselves to his church; and not a few of these were persons belonging to Kilmarnock. But, though gradually increasing, the congregation had yet to contend with pecuniary difficulties. Other causes, too, such as the great distance between the church and the residences of the members, considerably retarded its general prosperity. At length the congregation, with a view to remedy these evils, agreed to remove to Kilmarnock, where a more extended field presented itself for the encouragement of the principles they had espoused. In this laudable scheme they were cordially assisted by their minister, and by a number of respectable individuals of Kilmarnock, who subscribed largely for the erection of a new church in this quarter, which was built in 1814, on the site of their present building in King Street.

In 1818 Mr Kirkwood received a call from James's Place Church, Edinburgh, which he accepted. Soon after his removal the congregation elected the Rev. Mr Limont as their pastor. He was a man of genuine ability; but, when only about fourteen months in Kilmarnock, he also was translated to Edinburgh, where he died in the bloom of youth.

Mr Limont's successor in Kilmarnock was the Rev. Alexander Harvey—a man distinguished by great perseverance, ardour, and energy; and one whose time and talents were cheerfully employed for the advancement of the best interests of the party committed to his charge, and also for the improvement and prosperity of the entire community. After being about five years in this locality, he was appointed to a charge in Calton, Glasgow, where he died in 1844. The vacancy occasioned by his removal from Kilmarnock was filled by the Rev. William M'Dougall, who maintained, by his energetic talents, the high character which had been conferred on the church by his gifted predecessors.

In 1842 Mr M'Dougall was translated to Paisley, and was succeeded by the Rev. William Ramage. Mr Ramage, who was very popular as a preacher, received, in 1847, a call to Campbell Street Church, Glasgow, which he accepted. His successor—the Rev. John Symington, the present minister—was inducted on the 14th December, 1847.

The Reformed Presbyterian Meeting-house in Mill Lane, was opened in May, 1825, and since then has been much improved by various alterations. It contains about six hundred sittings. Prior to the date of its erection, the congregation, which was established in 1774, had their place of worship at the village of Crookedholm. Like King Street congregation, they came to Kilmarnock for the better accommodation of many of their adherents, and because there was here a wider field for making their principles more generally known.

Their first pastor, the Rev. William Steven, was ordained in October, 1777. Few ministers of his time possessed, it is said, a greater share of those qualities which constitute an influential and efficient preacher. Sound piety, acuteness of mind, and dignity of expression, marked his pulpit ministrations. He died in 1796, and was succeeded by the Rev. Adam Brown, who was ordained in June, 1802. It was during Mr Brown's ministry that the congregation removed from Crookedholm to Kilmarnock. As a man and as a minister he was amiable and unassuming; and though not gifted in a high degree with the attractive powers of oratory, he had many qualifications that endeared him to his hearers. His discourses were imbued with a spirit of genuine piety, which rendered them at all times deeply impressive, as well as profitable, and which, in his later years, strictly harmonized with his plain, patriarchal appearance.

Mr Brown died in 1838, in the sixty-fourth year of his age and thirty-sixth of his ministry. In the following year a volume of his discourses was published, with a well-written memoir by his successor, the late Rev. Peter Macindoe, D.D. —a gentleman from whose pen several important literary and religious productions have emanated; the chief of which is *A Treatise on the Application of Scriptural Principles to Civil Governments*—a work which is replete with liberal sentiments and sound argument.

Dr Macindoe was a native of Lanarkshire, and died at Troon, 2nd September, 1850, aged fifty-six years. He was succeeded by the Rev. George Lennie, who was ordained 1st July, 1852, and died 23rd September of the same year. The present minister is the Rev. Thomas Ramage, ordained 8th December, 1856.

The Independent Chapel, built in 1826, and since greatly altered and improved, is situated in Clark Street. It is a neat, plain building, and accommodates about six hundred sitters. The congregation was established in 1824, and soon after obtained the ministerial services of the Rev. John Campbell, now widely known as Dr Campbell of London, author of the *Martyr of Erromanga*, &c. Principally through his exertions the funds for erecting the chapel in Clark Street were collected; and while here he displayed an untiring energy and earnestness in the work of the ministry. He was translated to London in March, 1829, and was succeeded by the Rev. John Hill, who was appointed to the charge in July of the same year. In 1832 Mr Hill left Kilmarnock, and was afterwards settled at Gornal. His successor was the Rev. John Ward, who was admitted November, 1832. He was talented, devout, and energetic. He removed to Annan in 1837. The next minister of the Independent Church was the Rev. John Dickinson, appointed September, 1838. Besides being diligent in the discharge of his official duties, he was much attached to scientific studies, and not unfrequently delivered interesting public lectures on chemistry, &c. Mr Dickinson's stay in Kilmarnock, like that of his predecessors, was of short duration. He left in 1842, and was succeeded by the Rev. Robert Weir, who was admitted in the autumn of 1843. Mr Weir removed to Glasgow in 1848; and for some years after, the congregation had no settled pastor. In May, 1855, the Rev. John Campbell was ordained to the charge, which he was ultimately obliged to resign in consequence of declining health. He died in Glasgow in March, 1859, and was succeeded, in February, 1860, by the Rev. A. Henry Lowe, who removed in December, 1861, to Hazelgrove, Stockport. The present minister is the Rev. John C. Macintosh, ordained to the pastorate in St Andrews in 1854, and inducted here in September, 1862.

St Marnock's Church, in St Marnock Street, is an elegant edifice. Its front and tower are rich in Gothic ornament and architectural beauty. It was designed by Mr James Ingram, architect, and was built in 1836, at an expense of £5000. It contains one thousand seven hundred and thirty sittings. It was supplied by the ministers of the parish church till about the time of the Disruption, when it was closed; and after it had remained so for fifteen years, the company under whose auspices it had been erected, denuded themselves of their proprietorship in favour of the Presbytery; whereupon it was reopened, and a congregation formed, by the ministers of the parish church, who for some time officiated in it under the same arrangements as their predecessors. In January, 1859, a regular minister was appointed, namely, the Rev. Charles Stewart. Through his exertions, and those of the Rev. D. V. Thomson, the Rev. James Aitken, and some of the principal managers, funds were raised for endowing and erecting the church into a parochial charge, which was effected in 1862. W. C. S. Cunninghame, Esq. of Caprington, subscribed £100; and William Paterson, Esq. of Paterson, contributed the same sum. The fine large bell of the church had been given gratuitously by Mr Gillespie of London; and the tower clock (the workmanship of Messrs Breckenridge, Kilmarnock) was supplied through the liberality of Messrs Smith, of Windyedge. The Rev. Mr Stewart was translated to Strichen in September, 1862, and was succeeded by the Rev. John Thomson, the present minister, who was inducted in March, 1863.

St Andrew's Church, at the foot of East Netherton Street, in connection with the Establishment, was built in 1841, at a cost of £1700. It is surmounted by a neat belfry, and is otherwise pleasing in appearance. Soon after its completion, the Rev. Neil Brodie was ordained minister of this church, but left, with the greater part of the congregation, at the Disruption in 1843. From this date till 1848 it was but partially used as a place of worship. In the spring of the latter year its second minister, the Rev. Daniel Macfie, was appointed. He was only a short time, however, in connection with the congregation, having been translated, in 1850, to the second charge in the Canongate Church, Edinburgh. Towards the close of the same year his successor, the Rev. Thomas Martin, the present minister, was ordained.

Those who seceded with Mr Brodie erected, in 1844, the Free St Andrew's Church in Fowlds Street. It is a substantial and commodious building, containing nine hundred and thirty sittings, and cost about £1200. Mr Brodie, in the beginning of the same year, accepted a call from Shandon, and was succeeded by the Rev. William Young, the present minister, ordained June, 1844.

The Free High Church, in Portland Street, was built about the same time, at an expense of nearly £3000, and has since been improved in appearance by various alterations, at a cost of about £900. It contains one thousand two hundred and twenty-eight sittings, is adorned by a tower, and has a neat and decent appearance. Its first minister, the Rev. Thomas Main, was ordained minister of the High parish church in 1839, and also seceded from the Establishment in 1843. Mr Main, who was much esteemed by his congregation, was translated in October, 1857, to Free St Mary's Church, Edinburgh, to be colleague and successor to the Rev. Dr Henry Gray. He was succeeded by the Rev. Patrick W. Robertson, inducted 28th January, 1858.

Henderson Church, Wellington Street, was erected in 1818, at an expense of £1000; and since then £950 have been expended on it for various alterations and repairs. Its interior has been entirely remodelled, which has rendered it more beautiful; and its exterior also has been somewhat modernized and improved. It contains about six hundred and fifty sittings. The congregation, when established, belonged, as we formerly stated, to the Original Burgher Associate Synod. They were afterwards allied to the Church of Scotland, and are now in connection with the Free Church. As mentioned in Chapter XIV, their first minister was the Rev. Peter Campbell, ordained in 1815. He died in March, 1850, in the fifty-eighth year of his age, and was succeeded by the Rev. David Landsborough, the present pastor, who was ordained in July, 1851.

The Roman Catholic Chapel, which is dedicated to St Joseph, was opened for public worship by the Right Reverend Dr Murdoch in June, 1847. It stands on an elevation north of Portland Street, and commands a view of the entire town, and of a considerable part of the surrounding country. It is built in the modern style of Gothic architecture. Its exterior is bold and beautiful, to which its interior, though less ornamented, corresponds. As yet it has no gallery, save a small one for the choir, where a beautiful and well-toned organ is placed. The church is seated for seven hundred and twenty, and cost about £3000. The first minister of this church was the Rev. Thomas Wallace, who removed to Old Cumnock in 1853, and was succeeded by the present minister, the Rev. John Maclaughlan.*

Trinity Episcopal Church, situated at the corner of Dundonald Road and Portland Road, was erected in 1857 at an expense of about £1400. It was consecrated on the 11th August of that year by the Right Reverend Walter John Trower, D.D., Bishop of Glasgow and Galloway, and was first opened for public worship on the Sabbath following. It is built in the Early English or Pointed style, from plans by Mr James Wallace, builder, Kilmarnock, and consists of a nave with an organ-gallery, a chancel, and a vestry. The chancel, which is beautiful in appearance, is lighted by a large Gothic window of finely stained glass. The pulpit is composed of stone, and the inner roof of open, oak-varnished

* Mr Wallace died at Old Cumnock on the 10th April, 1861.

timber-work. The organ-gallery is richly carved, and bears the arms of the Bishop; P. Boyle, Esq.; Captain Montgomery; W. Lancaster, Esq.; and J. R. Craufurd, Esq. On the "Memorial Font" is this inscription: "To the Glory of God, and to the memory of the Rev. R. Wildbore, first minister of this congregation." Mr Wildbore died in May, 1852, and was succeeded in July following by the Rev. John T. Brien, who removed in August, 1855. The next minister was the Rev. Edward James Jonas, author of *Recollections of Syria and Palestine.* He was appointed in 1855. To his exertions the erection of the church may, in a great measure, be attributed. He removed to Coatbridge in 1861, and was succeeded in July of the same year by the Rev. Ernest Spooner, who resigned in September, 1862. The present minister is the Rev. W. W. Penney, M.A.; who was instituted in November, 1862.

The Original Seceders' Church in Fowlds Street was erected in 1857. It is a small plain building, and has a neat external as well as internal appearance. It affords accommodation for upwards of two hundred sitters, and cost about £500. Its first minister was the Rev. John Graham, ordained in 1836. He resigned, in consequence of bad health, in May, 1863. The church is at present without a regular pastor.

Besides these, and the churches formerly mentioned, there are several other religious societies in the town, who worship in halls and school-rooms.

CHAPTER XXII.

"The hand that wiped away the tears of want,
The heart that melted at another's wo,
Were his; and blessings followed him."

KILMARNOCK till of late could boast of no public monument that was worthy of the name. The one, however, now erected to the memory of the late Sir James Shaw, Bart, which was executed by the celebrated sculptor, the late James Fillans, Esq., is an object of special attraction.* It consists of a pedestal and statue, each about eight feet in height. The statue is cut out of one solid block of Ravaccione marble, weighing about twelve tons, and represents the venerable baronet in the dress costume of Lord Mayor of London, holding in his right hand the warrant of precedence. The site of the monument is in the Cross, where it has a noble effect, and is seen from the principal streets. The inauguration of the statue was celebrated on the 4th August, 1848, and was honoured by the attendance of various masonic lodges, the magistrates and council of the town, the committee of management, and several distinguished gentlemen. In a cavity of the basement, a box was deposited, containing the coins of Queen Victoria, a copy of the first edition of the present work, a copy of the *Kilmarnock Journal* of the 3rd August, 1848, and other documents. The Rev. D.V. Thomson offered up an impressive prayer; after which the stone was laid—George Johnston, Esq., Redburn, acting as Grand Master.

* Mr Fillans was a native of Lanarkshire, and died suddenly in September, 1852, at a comparatively early age, having been born in 1808. Among the last works which he modelled was a statue of "Grief, or Rachel weeping for her children," which he intended to be placed over his father's grave.

During the erection of the monument thousands of the inhabitants congregated at the Cross, anxious to see the completion of the work, and to be favoured with a view of the statue of their distinguished townsman. About three o'clock it was placed upon the pedestal, though still enclosed in the wooden case in which it had been brought from the studio of the sculptor, in London. About the same hour the "Brethren of the Mystic Tie" marshalled in the Town Green; and, after perambulating several of the principal streets, proceeded to the Cross, displaying, in the most picturesque manner, the insignia of their ancient Order, and accompanied with bands playing suitable and stirring airs. The bells of the various churches, too, sent forth a merry peal, which added to the general harmony; and the time-honoured banners of the town waved from the balcony of the Council Chambers. The number of spectators by this time had greatly increased; and, as the boards that enclosed the figure were being removed, the anxiety of all to behold it appeared to become more intense. At length, about four o'clock, the statue was unveiled, when a simultaneous and enthusiastic cheer from the crowd greeted the discovery of an achievement in art, the high merits of which it would be difficult to describe. The day was serene and beautiful; and, just as the figure was exposed to view, a gleam of sunshine burst upon it, displaying, in the most favourable manner, its varied artistic beauties, and giving to the entire scene a sublime and imposing appearance. The cheering had scarcely subsided when the Cavalry Band struck up the impressive air of *Old Hundred*, the solemn influence of which, to use the words of a literary friend, "finely soothed and subdued the enthusiasm of the assemblage, and imparted a reverential character to the interesting scene."

On the afternoon of the same day a considerable number of gentlemen, among whom were Sir John Shaw, Bart, and the eminent sculptor of the statue, James Fillans, Esq., dined, in honour of the occasion, in the hall of the George Hotel—C. D. Gairdner, Esq., presiding, and John Dickie, Esq., one of the magistrates, acting as croupier. The meeting was one of considerable interest, being attended by several literary gentlemen, among whom was the eldest son of our national poet, Robert Burns.

The statue, as already said, is composed of marble from Carrara; the pedestal is of the same material; and the base is of Aberdeen granite. The height of the whole structure is about seventeen feet. The statue is a noble work of art, worthy of the creative genius of the sculptor, Mr Fillans, and no less worthy of the venerable baronet whom it commemorates, and of whom, we believe, it is a faithful likeness. In symmetry of form it is truly admirable. The mild, benevolent features of Sir James are finely developed; and, as a whole, it is replete with that seeming animation and intellectual expression which mark the superior powers of the sculptor, and give to the object itself a high and permanent interest. As one of the London journalists remarked at the time of its erection: "It is a classic work, in which the ideal has imparted to the reality the grace and dignity befitting a civic magistrate, and an honest public servant. His robes of office hang as gracefully as the toga of the Roman; nor does the costume of modern times debar the artist from setting forth the manly developments of a Scot, who stood six feet three inches from his mother earth."

The situation in which the monument is placed is, in some respects, judiciously chosen. Proudly it stands in the midst of our spacious Cross, an ornament to the town, and an incentive to the youths, who daily behold it, to imitate the various virtues of him it represents—virtues which have hallowed his memory, and have procured for his name that honourable and enduring celebrity with which it is now invested.

Sir James Shaw, Bart, was the son of a highly respectable farmer, and was born at Mosshead, in the parish of Riccarton, in the year 1764. On the death of his father, which occurred about five years afterwards, his mother and family removed to Kilmarnock, where he was educated at the grammar-school, then taught by the accomplished, but unfortunate, John Graham, A.M., of whom a short memoir is given in a preceding Chapter.

At the age of seventeen the subject of our sketch went to America at the request of his brother David, who held an appointment in the *commissariat*, and by his interest was placed in the commercial house of Messrs George and Samuel Douglass of New York. After being with them on the most amicable terms for about three years, he returned to this country, and in a short time became a junior partner of the same company in London. From the great respectability of the firm, he soon became widely known among the more wealthy and influential circles, and gradually attained that estimable reputation, as a gentleman and a citizen, which led to his future success and elevation in society.

In 1805 he was elected Lord Mayor of London; and while holding that dignified and important office, he took a warm interest in everything connected with the welfare and honour of the city. The spirited manner in which he obtained the warrant of precedence, soon after his election, is worthy of particular notice. This is a privilege which, in virtue of his office, the mayor enjoys in taking the lead at all public processions in the city. However exalted in birth or station, none save the Sovereign has a right to precede him on these occasions. Whether his predecessors in office had ever availed themselves of this prerogative, or whether it had, in earlier times, been acted upon by them and fallen into disuse, is a point we are not qualified to decide. The latter, we think, is more probable; at all events, Sir James (then Mr) Shaw resolved to establish his claim, and make use of the privilege at the funeral of Lord Nelson, in January, 1806. He therefore waited on Lord Liverpool, then Prime Minister, to whom he introduced the subject. His lordship appeared unwilling to move in the matter, probably from being aware that the Prince of Wales and his six brothers were to attend the funeral (which was to take place on the following day), and would be at the head of the procession. Mr Shaw, with the honour of the city at heart, said, "Well, my lord, if you do not grant my request, I shall put another pair of horses to my carriage, which is at the door, and go forthwith to his Majesty at Windsor, from whom I have received much kindness, and *he*, I have no doubt, will not hesitate to favour my wishes." His lordship, who was taken by surprise at the firmness displayed by the mayor, replied, "Give me a little time and I will see what can be done." "There is not a moment to lose," rejoined the mayor; "there is to be a meeting of council early to-morrow morning; and I trust I shall then be able to state my success." "Then, give me *till to-morrow morning*, and I will see about it," returned his lordship. Here the conversation ended, and the mayor left. His object, however, was gained. The deed was forwarded in due time to the city on the following morning, to the great satisfaction of the corporation. At the funeral procession Mr Shaw took precedence of the Prince of Wales and his brothers, but courteously gave way to his Royal Highness on entering the Cathedral of St Paul's.

By integrity and diligence in the discharge of the important duties of mayor, Mr Shaw continued to rise in respectability and eminence. In 1809 his Majesty, George III, conferred on him the rank of baronet. During his mayoralty, he was also elected one of the members for the city of London, and occupied that honourable position in three successive Parliaments.

Sir James retired from Parliament in 1818, but continued to discharge the duties of alderman with great honour till 1831. At that period, upon the decease of Richard Clerk, Esq., he was elected to the honourable and lucrative office of chamberlain of the city of London, which situation he continued to hold till May, 1843, when he resigned it. His death, which was deeply lamented, took place on the 22nd of October of the same year, after a long illness, which he bore with the utmost resignation.

In person Sir James was tall and commanding, with none of the obesity usually imputed to a London alderman. He possessed great energy and muscular power; as an instance of which we may state, that, in 1816, when the mob surrounded and broke open the gates of the Royal Exchange, he seized one of the ringleaders, and retained him till he was perfectly secured. He also took a flag which was borne by one of the rioters on that occasion.

Few men have left behind them a more honourable name for integrity in public or private life. He was indefatigable in his exertions to serve, not only his youthful relatives, but many others who had little claim on his benevolence, as the numerous cadetships, as well as civil appointments, which he procured for them in India, will testify. Literary and artistic merit, especially that of individuals belonging to his native place, he always encouraged with his patronage. After the death of Burns he showed his deep appreciation of the genius and talents of the poet, by taking a leading part in London in raising the sum which was then collected for behoof of his widow, and by afterwards procuring respectable situations for his sons.* Kilmarnock, too, frequently experienced his

* "Mr Alderman Shaw, of London, an Ayrshire gentleman, some time after the death of our admired poet, patronised a subscription for the benefit of his widow and children. The sum so raised was vested in the three per cent. annuities, and amounted to £500 of that stock. Last week, the alderman being in company with Sir Francis Baring, the conversation turned on Burns and the circumstances of his

liberality. In times of commercial or other public distress, his princely donations were often the means of lessening the wants of many of the inhabitants, and, we may venture to say, of restoring, in many instances, the blessings of health to the humble invalid, who, without his bounty, might have pined in protracted debility, or drooped into an untimely grave, the victim of cheerless penury.

These philanthropic actions, we are proud to say, have not been forgotten in this locality, but, on the contrary, are still remembered with a grateful feeling. In 1845, in consideration of the many public and private deeds of benevolence conferred by Sir James on the town of Kilmarnock, the Magistrates and Council took the lead in opening a subscription for the purpose of erecting the monument to his memory, and, in the most handsome manner, subscribed £50 for that object. The scheme was highly appreciated by the friends and admirers of the baronet; and subscriptions, amounting to nearly £1000, were soon added to the sum subscribed by the council.

Sir James Shaw was succeeded in his title and fortune by his estimable nephew, John, now Sir John Shaw, son of John Macfee, Esq. of Greenholm, Kilmarnock, by the sister of the late baronet. He assumed the name of Shaw in 1813, in lieu of his patronymic, Macfee.

Sir John, from his generous public acts, appears to have inherited the philanthropic virtues for which his distinguished relative was so widely and justly esteemed.

family. The worthy baronet, who is a warm admirer of our poet, requested that he also might have the honour of being a contributor, and immediately put into his hands £100, which was also bought into the same stock, and the receipts sent to the magistrates; and with the £500 makes £676 19s. 10d. three per cents., standing in the name of the provost and bailies of the town of Ayr, for the benefit of the widow and children of Robert Burns."—*Newspaper paragraph*, 1804, *quoted by R. Chambers in his recent edition of Burns.*

According to another paragraph, also quoted by Chambers, Sir James was the means of raising £310 for the benefit of two illegitimate daughters of the poet, namely, Elizabeth Burns, the daughter of Elizabeth Paton, and Elizabeth Burns, the daughter of Anne Park.

CHAPTER XXIII.

Fair Science frowned not on his humble birth.
GRAY.

ONE of the objects of greatest interest in Kilmarnock is the Astronomical Observatory, at Morton Place. It was erected in 1818 by the late Thomas Morton, Esq., at an expense of about £1000, and is now the property of Thomas Lee, Esq., Fellow of the Royal Astronomical Society. Its height is seventy feet; and, being on an elevated situation, it commands an extensive and delightful view. In fine weather, when the atmosphere is unclouded, the Frith of Clyde, the romantic hills of Arran, Dundonald Castle, Brown Carrick hill, Cumnock hills, Cairnsmuir, Blacksidend, Loudoun Castle, and Fenwick moors, are distinctly seen from its summit.

But to the lover of the astronomical and optical sciences the Observatory has greater attractions. It is furnished with two excellent telescopes of different sizes. The large one, which is constructed on the Newtonian principle, is $9\frac{3}{8}$ inches in diameter. The other is of the Gregorian construction, and is seven inches in diameter. They are both the workmanship of Mr Morton, and are fine specimens of mechanism. The large one in particular, besides possessing great power, has many admirable conveniences. In the Observatory there is also a *camera obscura*, by which, in suitable weather, the visitor can behold, as in a series of enchanting pictures, the whole of the varied and beautiful scenery of the surrounding country.

That Mr Morton conferred a benefit on his fellow-townsmen by the erection of the Observatory, must be acknowledged by all. The tastes and studies which it tends to foster are truly ennobling—perhaps more so than any other in which the human mind can be engaged; for "the telescope," to use the eloquent words of Dr Chalmers, "enables us to see a system in every star, and suggests that, above and beyond all that is visible to man, there may lie fields of creation, which sweep immeasurably along, and carry the impress of the Almighty's hand to the remotest scenes of the universe."

Mr Morton, who obtained considerable celebrity as an ingenious mechanic, was not indebted either to birth or to opulence for his reputation or standing in society. He rose to distinction by diligent perseverance and by the earnest cultivation of the inventive faculties with which he was favoured by nature. A few biographical particulars regarding him may not be uninteresting. He was born at the village of Mauchline in 1783; but, when only three years of age, his father, who was a brickmaker, removed with him to Kilmarnock, where he afterwards resided, with the exception of a short portion of his boyish years, which he spent in the capacity of a herd with an uncle at Stair. While engaged in this humble calling he frequently amused himself with basketmaking—an art which affords considerable scope for the exercise of the constructive organs; and this circumstance, in all likelihood, first awakened the mechanical genius by which he was distinguished. At an early period of life his ingenuity was also displayed in constructing balloons, &c. When about the age of ten he returned from Stair to Kilmarnock; and after the lapse of other five years—the winters of which he spent at school,* and the summers at brickmaking with his father—he

* One of Mr Morton's teachers was a Mr Findlay, whose school was on Tankardha' Brae. He also attended, for a short time, another school, which was kept by a Mr George Campbell, in Low Church Lane. Mr Campbell, who was a native of Kilmarnock, had been originally bred to the trade of shoemaking, but latterly was a minister of the gospel at Stockbridge, where he died about 1818. He was author of a little volume of poems, printed at the Kilmarnock press by John Wilson in 1787, and also of a collection of sermons, printed at Edinburgh in 1816.

was apprenticed to Mr Bryce Blair, turner and wheel-wright, and thus entered on a line of business which must have been more congenial to one of his predilections.

In the course of three or four years after the term of his apprenticeship had expired, he commenced business on his own account; and about the same time, his talent for mechanics began to display itself more prominently. Before this period, indeed, he had evinced a strong propensity for mechanical pursuits. Every scientific instrument that came within his reach he eagerly and minutely examined; in short, so great, in early life, was the bias of his mind in this way, that, when wandering Italians came to Kilmarnock with telescopes, barometers, &c., for sale, he might have been seen following them in the streets, admiring their various articles, or endeavouring to obtain a knowledge of the principles on which they were made. At length Mr Morton attempted the construction of a telescope, and was successful in finishing it. But he did not rest satisfied with this achievement; for, observing that the telescopes then in use were somewhat defective, he soon applied his genius to remedy the deficiency, and ultimately succeeded in adding several conveniences to this useful instrument.

But Mr Morton's greatest work—at least the one that has been most conducive to the commercial prosperity of Kilmarnock—is the barrel or carpet machine, which is still in use, though now somewhat superseded by the Jacquard loom, which also he improved. The three-ply carpet machine also is, we believe, in some measure, the fruit of his invention; and, likewise, the Brussels carpet machine, which works five colours with four needles. In 1808 the Board of Trade, convinced that his talents were highly serviceable to the manufacturing interests of the country, bestowed upon him the sum of twenty pounds. Nor were his usefulness and ingenuity overlooked by his fellow-townsmen. In 1826 they invited him to a public dinner, and presented him with an elegant silver punch-bowl, richly carved, and bearing an inscription expressive of their gratitude for the benefits his genius had conferred on their manufactures. In 1835 he was elected an honorary member of the Royal Scottish Society of Arts. He died in March, 1862.

Among the more eminent individuals connected with Kilmarnock, we may also notice the Rev. Robert Findlay, D.D., Professor of Theology; F. G. P. Neison, F.L.S., author of *Contributions to Vital Statistics;* the late Thomas Y. M'Christie, who was Revising Barrister for the city of London; and the late Professor Johnston, author of the *Chemistry of Common Life,* &c.

The Rev. Robert Findlay, D.D., sometime Professor of Theology in the University of Glasgow, is mentioned in the *New Statistical Account* as one of the eminent characters connected with Kilmarnock, but no biographical details are given in that work regarding him. From other authorities we learn that he was born in Bank Street, or at the foot of Strand Street, in 1721. His father was William Findlay, merchant, son of John Findlay of Waxford, and his mother was Barbara Hodgeart, daughter of Robert Hodgeart, surgeon, Kilmarnock.* According to the *Scottish Nation,* Professor Findlay received his education at the University of Glasgow, went to Leyden, and, after returning, studied for the medical profession, but soon embraced that of the ministry. In 1744 he was appointed minister of Stewarton. In the following year he removed to Galston, which he also left and went to Paisley. He settled ultimately in Glasgow as minister of the

* A Robert Hodgeart, probably the same person, was one of the magistrates of Kilmarnock in 1707. In the Low Church burying-ground a flat grave-stone marks the spot where the Professor's parents and some of their children are interred. The inscription is somewhat obliterated, but the following is still legible: "Also is interred under this stone the body of Barbara Hodgeart, spouse to the said William Findlay, who was afterwards spouse to Alexander Cunninghame, merchant in Kilmarnock, who died a widow, 27th December, 1786, in the eighty-eighth year of her age."

North West Parish Church, and in 1782 was elected Professor of Theology. He is said to have been much distinguished as a pious divine, and as an accomplished scholar. He was the author of *A Vindication of the Sacred Books, and of Josephus against Voltaire*, the *Divine Inspiration of the Jewish Scriptures Asserted*, and *A Persuasive to the Enlargement of Psalmody*. He died in 1814.

Mr Neison, before leaving Kilmarnock to fill the situation of Actuary to the Medical Invalid and General Life Assurance Society, London, gave many indications of superiority of mind. In our literary institutions he occasionally delivered interesting lectures on mathematical subjects, and appeared, at all times, to take a lively interest in such schemes as were devised for the mental and moral advancement of the community.

Among the statistical writers of Britain Mr Neison occupies a prominent position. The first paper published by him was written at the request of the Council of the Statistical Society of London, and read before that body in January, 1844, in reply to a paper read at a previous meeting of the society, by the celebrated Edwin Chadwick, then secretary to the Poor Law Commissioners. Both papers excited considerable interest among the members of the society, and were afterwards printed in the seventh volume of the *London Statistical Journal*. Mr Neison's next work, *Contributions to Vital Statistics*, which was read in March, 1845, before the same society, and published in that year, was hailed by a considerable portion of the British press as a useful and valuable publication, and as one likely to effect very beneficial improvements in the laws and workings of Friendly Societies. These important *Contributions* were the result of four years' labour and research, and were made up from several thousand returns obtained, at great expense, from Friendly Societies throughout the kingdom. The Rev. N. M'Michael, Dunfermline, Professor of Divinity, a native of Kilmarnock, in his papers on *Benefit Societies*, in

HISTORY OF KILMARNOCK.   239

Hogg's Weekly Instructor, bestows a flattering encomium on Mr Neison's work. He says: "We consider this paper as the most valuable contribution to the laws of sickness and mortality which has hitherto appeared. It has placed the author at once in the foremost rank of statists, though he is but a young man." A third and greatly enlarged edition of the *Contributions to Vital Statistics* was published in 1857.

Mr Neison's next publication was a paper, entitled *Statistics of Crime in England and Wales, for the years* 1842, 1843, *and* 1844, which was read before the statistical section of the British Association, at Southampton, in September, 1846. This was followed by another contribution on the same subject, for the years 1834 and 1844, which was read before the same scientific body, at their meeting at Oxford, in June, 1847. These pamphlets have been pronounced valuable by many critics in this country, and on the Continent have received considerable attention. Like his larger work, they display great research and industry on the part of the author. Their tendency must be beneficial. They exhibit, as in a faithful picture, the actual state of the country in a moral point of view, and may be the means of impressing the public mind with the vast importance of the subject of which they treat, and thereby lead to the adoption of measures for the removal of the evils which they disclose. In *Hogg's Instructor* for October, 1847, an excellent popular abstract of these papers is given by the Rev. N. M'Michael, above mentioned.

In 1846 or 1847 the genius of Mr Neison was also brought to bear upon the statistics of India. In a pamphlet, entitled *Vital Statistics of the East India Company's Armies in India, European and Native*, by Lieutenant-Colonel W. H. Sykes, we observe that great obligations are expressed by that gentleman to Mr Neison, who "worked out," it would appear, the principal tables which it contains.

Mr Neison prepared for the Home Office the Act (9 and 10

Vic., chap. 27) for the regulation of Friendly Societies. It may be added that he has since published some interesting tables relative to the mortality of the British army.

Thomas Y. M'Christie, whose life affords a striking example of the progress that may be made in the "pursuit of knowledge under difficulties," was born at the Townhead, Kilmarnock, in 1797. Soon afterwards his father opened a little wayside inn at Beansburn, in the neighbourhood of the town. Its sign—the rising sun and compass—with the words,

> "The best ale under the sun,
> To fill a bottle I'm begun,"

must yet be distinctly remembered by many of our townsmen. When about six or seven years of age, Thomas was sent to the "Wife's School" in the Foregate, so called from being kept by a woman who belonged to Fenwick, and travelled from that place to Kilmarnock, every morning, to superintend her little charge. When attending this school he received an injury to one of his knees from a stone-ball while playing at *shinty;* and so severe was the accident, that it confined him to bed for three years. But gradually recovering, at least so far as to be able to walk on crutches, he was sent to a school kept by a Mr Thomson. He was afterwards placed in the English department of the Kilmarnock Academy, then presided over by the late Mr William Henderson; and so rapid was his progress there, that that able teacher soon appointed him to be his principal assistant. He was also a pupil of Mr Jamieson in the commercial department, and of Rector Thomson in the classical, in both of which he made considerable proficiency. When about fifteen or sixteen years of age, he opened an academy on his own account in Ayr; but not liking the profession of teaching, he soon discontinued it, and resolved to try his fortune in some way or other in England. While this notion occupied his mind, it happened that a commercial gentleman called one afternoon at his father's little inn for refreshment; and seeing the young man walking on crutches, he kindly inquired into the cause of his lameness. His mother, after answering the stranger's interrogatories, said that, notwithstanding his lameness, he had a strong desire to push his fortune in England; to which the traveller replied, that if he should come to his place (in Yorkshire) he would do what he could for him. Encouraged by this promise, and by the hope of future success in life, our young adventurer took his seat one night on a carrier's cart as it passed his father's door for Glasgow. He had no companion save his crutches; and his pecuniary means were remarkably limited. After three weeks' journey, he reached Yorkshire with only one shilling and twopence halfpenny in his pocket. Fortunately he soon found the gentleman who had called at his father's, and was immediately employed by him in an humble capacity, from which, by good conduct and industry, he rose to be the principal clerk in the establishment.

In the course of a few years Mr M'Christie commenced business for himself; but owing to the unexpected insolvency, principally of his employers, whose service he had but a short time quitted, and of others with whom he had transactions, he was soon involved in difficulties, and again rendered almost penniless. By this time he had acquired, during his leisure hours, a considerable knowledge of short-hand writing; and he now removed to London to seek employment as a reporter for the press. For a time, however, he met with little or rather no encouragement; but his persevering spirit never forsook him; and calling to mind his distinguished townsman, the late Sir James Shaw, he waited on that gentleman and made known his case to him, in the hope that the worthy baronet might use his influence in aiding him into a situation. Sir James, who received him kindly, could not at the time assist him into employment, but in the most delicate manner presented him with a sovereign, to meet, in some measure, his immediate necessities. By the help of this little gift, which he husbanded "with miser care," he was enabled to persevere a little longer in search of occupation. At length, when taking notes one day in the Court of Chancery, whither he had gone to practise, he was engaged by a solicitor to report a case of importance which was about to come before the court. For this work, which he accomplished in a satisfactory manner, he received upwards of five pounds, which was then to him a little fortune. From this time he daily rose into notice and reputation as a reporter, and was soon, and for many years, considered to be one of the most expert and perfect short-hand writers and best parliamentary reporters in London, being long employed by the *Times*, and other leading newspapers. We may remark, that considerably before this time he had ceased to walk on crutches, having got an ingenious invention for his leg, by which he was enabled to walk without difficulty, or very much appearance of lameness. He was employed to furnish reports of the principal medical lectures in London for the *Lancet*, all of which were much admired for their accuracy. While thus engaged, he also became a medical student, and in 1829 obtained his diploma from the Royal College of Surgeons, London. He now practised as a surgeon, at the same time acting as a parliamentary reporter, and likewise studying for his degree of doctor of medicine. We may mention, as honourable to Mr M'Christie, that about this period he again waited on Sir James Shaw, and requested him to name a charity to which he might hand over the sovereign he had so kindly given him when he came to London. This greatly gratified Sir James. He was also much rejoiced to hear of Mr M'Christie's progress, and urged him to renew his visits; and from that time till the esteemed baronet's death, they were the best of friends.

But it would require more space than our limits afford to

trace at length Mr M'Christie's varied and interesting career. Suffice it to say, that unweariedly persevering in his onward course, he obtained his degree of M.D. in 1833; after which he studied the law of England for five years, at Lincoln's Inn, and became a barrister-at-law. It may be stated, as an instance of the confidence placed in his ability as an advocate, that, in 1845, he received the sum of one thousand guineas as a retaining fee, besides other fees and expenses, to go to Ceylon, to conduct a case (in which he completely succeeded) for the recovery of a large estate in that island.

Mr M'Christie, as we have said, was Revising Barrister for the city of London. He was first appointed to the office in 1842, by the late Lord Chief-Justice Denman of the Queen's Bench, and subsequently by the late Lord Chief-Justice Campbell. "In 1857," says the *Law Times*, in an article on his death, "he again undertook a mission to Australia. It was one of the utmost difficulty and importance; and, after great bodily suffering and fatigue, he returned successful, but so injured in health and constitution as to remain an invalid until his death, which took place on the 7th December, 1860, at his residence in Great James Street, Bedford Row, London."

Professor Johnston was born at Paisley in 1796, but when very young came with his parents to Kilmarnock. He was the son of Mr James Johnston, a weaver's agent, mentioned in a preceding Chapter as presiding at the Dean Park meeting in 1816. Young Johnston displayed an early taste for literature; and when attending the classes of the late Rector Thomson in the Kilmarnock Academy, he produced various little essays, some of which were printed in Thomson's *Miscellany*, at that time the only periodical in the locality through which our young literary aspirants could find publicity for their productions. After going through the usual preparatory course, he entered the University of Glasgow with the view of qualifying himself for the church. At this time he had many pecuniary difficulties to contend with; but he struggled on with uncommon ardour, supporting himself in a great measure by teaching privately. He also taught during the college vacations; one of which, that of 1822, he spent in Kilmarnock, instructing a number of young men in English composition. At length he became a preacher of the gospel; but his mind had a strong bias to geological and chemical studies, which soon led him, we believe, to relinquish the clerical profession. He afterwards opened a school at Durham; and in 1833 he was honoured with the readership in chemistry and mineralogy in the university of that city. He was also, in 1843, appointed chemist to the Agricultural Society of Scotland. The *Athenæum*, to which we are indebted for some of these particulars, says of his productions: "Without enumerating them fully, we may refer to the *Lectures on Agricultural Chemistry and Geology*, and to the *Catechism* of the same sciences, as the more celebrated of his works in this department. Of the latter, thirty-three editions have been published in this country alone. It has been translated into nearly every language of Europe, and has been sown broad-cast in America. . . . Amongst his less professional productions, the *Notes on North America* should be mentioned with respect. But the most attractive of his compositions is the *Chemistry of Common Life*. It is also the most recent. In addition to these publications the Professor contributed occasionally to the *Edinburgh Review*, and frequently to *Blackwood's Magazine*." Professor Johnston died at Durham in September, 1855.

CHAPTER XXIV.

> Whosoever loves not picture is injurious to truth and all wisdom of poetry. Picture is the invention of Heaven—the most ancient and akin to Nature. It is of itself a silent work, and always of one and the same habit; yet it doth so enter and penetrate the inmost affection as sometimes it overcomes the power of speech and oratory.
>
> BEN JONSON.

IN the department of painting Kilmarnock has produced several individuals who have attained considerable eminence. The most distinguished of these was the late James Tannock. He was born at Grange Street in 1784, and evinced a talent for painting at an early period of life. In 1803 he went to Edinburgh and became a student of Nasmyth, then one of our principal landscape painters, and well known as the only artist to whom the poet Burns sat for his portrait. Mr Tannock afterwards practised for nearly two years in Paisley, and while there his talents attracted admiration. The celebrated poet Tannahill makes honourable mention of a portrait of Burns which he painted for the Kilbarchan Burns's Anniversary Society:

> "I'm proud to see your warm regard
> For Caledonia's dearest bard;
> Of him ye've got sae gude a painting,
> That nocht but real life is wanting.
> I think yon rising genius, TANNOCK,
> May gain a niche in fame's high winnock;
> There, with auld Rubens placed sublime,
> Look down upon the wreck of time."

After leaving Paisley Mr Tannock prosecuted his art for some time in Irvine, Greenock, and Stirling; and among those who sat to him in the latter town was the celebrated Mrs Grant of Laggan, author of *Letters from the Mountains*, &c. In 1810 he repaired to London and became a student of the Royal Academy, then presided over by Benjamin West. At the same time, in order to obtain some knowledge of the human frame, he attended the Anatomical Lectures of Sir Charles Bell, with whom he formed an acquaintance, and who introduced him to several persons of distinction. Soon after this time he entered himself as a student of the British Gallery. Among the eminent individuals with whom he became acquainted in London, were John Galt, the novelist, Miss Benger, the writer of the *Memoirs of Mary Queen of Scots*, and George Chalmers, the author of *Caledonia*, whose portrait he painted, and whose friendship and patronage he afterwards enjoyed.

Another eminent person who patronised Mr Tannock in London was the late Sir James Shaw, a full-length likeness of whom he executed in 1817, and presented, as stated in Chapter XVII, to the magistrates of Kilmarnock, to be placed in the Council Chambers. It is a fine work of art, and might be compared favourably with many celebrated paintings.

Mr Tannock's works, some of which, we believe, have been honoured with a place in the National Portrait Gallery, London, are generally characterized by a chasteness of execution and a truthfulness of delineation, that bespeak the true artist. Benjamin West, on seeing one of his portraits, thus wrote of it: "It is nature itself; it is the man sitting before you; he [Mr Tannock] is a man of genius. The manner of relieving the figure by the yellow chair, and the management of the back-ground, prove him so."

Mr Tannock's portraits of Burns, of which he painted a considerable number, are fine life-like productions. One of these, in the possession of Mr John Smith, bookseller, Kilmarnock, deserves special notice. It was taken from Nasmyth's portrait (the only one, as we have said, for which Burns sat), and is an exact copy of it in every way. It is exceedingly beautiful, full of animation, and highly finished; and it was the artist's own favourite among his various portraits of the bard. Another work of Mr Tannock, which displays a high order of excellence, is a half-length likeness of his father. To use the words of West quoted above, "it is nature itself; it is the man sitting before you."

Mr Tannock, during the greater part of his artistic career, resided in London, but usually spent a portion of each summer with his friends in Kilmarnock, where he died on the 6th May, 1863. As an artist he was modest and unassuming, and as a man amiable and intelligent.

Mr William Tannock, brother of the preceding, also possesses considerable talent as an artist. At his house in Grange Street, a picture-gallery was established some years ago, and is still open for the inspection of the public. The pictures were carefully selected in London by Mr James Tannock during his long residence in that city, and chiefly consist of pieces by the old masters of the Dutch and Flemish schools, among which are several by Wouvermans, Berghem, and other leading painters. One of the most prominent pictures in the collection is the "Nativity," attributed to Gerard Honthorst; the light on the surrounding figures, proceeding from the infant Saviour, having a most splendid effect. There is also in the collection a half-length picture of the "Virgin and Child," attributed to Vandyke, a large painting, by Rubens, of the "Garden of Love," with many other important works, comprising specimens of various schools, to the number of nearly two hundred; and presenting, we may truly say, an object of interest unequalled in this part of the country.

In 1831 a number of amateur artists, natives of Kilmarnock, and others located in the town, formed themselves into a society, under the name of the "Kilmarnock Drawing Academy;" their principal object being the improvement of each other in painting, either in oil or water colours. They rented an apartment in Cheapside Street, where they exhibited their pieces, and where each member was at liberty, at all times, to study the art. The institution, though it existed only for two or three years, had, in some measure, the effect contemplated; for the members, by frequently meeting together, reading artistic publications, and remarking on the merits or demerits of their own and other productions, gradually advanced in a knowledge of the art. The progress of the young painter is greatly facilitated by his having a variety of good paintings to copy; but, in this respect, the Academy displayed "a beggarly account of empty boxes." The attention of the public, however, was latterly directed to this fact by the editor of the *Kilmarnock Chronicle*, who threw out a hint to the more opulent classes to encourage the members, by lending them, for imitation, such paintings of merit as they might have in their possession; and Mr John Ingram of Haugh Holm, author of the *Angel of Hope*, took up the subject, and through the medium of the press called upon the gentlemen of the town and neighbourhood to patronise the young aspirants after artistic honours. He also proposed, as a means of attracting attention to the institution, that a public exhibition of paintings be got up in the Academy. Preparations for carrying the plan into effect were immediately made by the members; but the cholera at this time broke out in the town; and the minds of all classes being wholly engrossed with the subject of that awful calamity, the plan of collecting the pictures was abandoned, and the society soon afterwards ceased to exist.

The more prominent of the members, who were twelve in number, were Messrs William Macready, James Douglas, Thomas Barclay, and John K. Hunter.

Mr Macready rose to considerable eminence as a teacher of drawing. Indeed, we may safely affirm that he had no superior, or rather, we would say, no equal in the west of Scotland. His pencillings were greatly admired. A dilapidated castle or old baronial tower—a group of cattle on some verdant mead—a rural cottage shaded by venerable trees—rocks, hills, valleys, and streams; in short, whatever was poetic and beautiful in external nature, he depicted with a true and skilful hand. He died, after a very short illness, on the 16th October, 1854, aged forty-six.

Mr James Douglas resides, we believe, in Edinburgh, and follows the art of portrait-painting. In imitating the old masters, and retouching and repairing ancient pictures, he is said to be very successful.

Mr Thomas Barclay became skilful in pattern-drawing. He now resides in Glasgow, and is noted for his superior carpet designs.

The most remarkable individual, perhaps, who was connected with the Kilmarnock Drawing Academy, is Mr John K. Hunter. He is known among the lovers of the art in the west of Scotland as the "Kilmarnock Cobbler," from his having been bred in this locality to the trade of shoemaking. Amid difficulties that would have chilled the ardour of many minds, he has untiringly struggled on in his career, and has now attained a respectable position as a portrait-painter. His life, indeed, if truly narrated, would afford another instance of the fact that no obstacle, however great, can long impede the advancement of resolute perseverance and genius. He was one of the founders of the society just alluded to, and no member displayed a warmer interest in its prosperity. The greatest number of pictures ever exhibited at one time on the walls of the institution-room was forty-five, sixteen of which were his productions. These he found time and means to execute, though under the necessity of toiling hard at the trade of shoemaking for the support of a family of eight children. "Visit the Academy during the daylight," said the Kilmarnock newspaper of that time, "and you will find the shoemaker a devoted student of Titian; and at night go to his dwelling, and you will find him the hard-working son of Crispin; instead of delineating with a pencil the divine features of the human face, he is beating out the soles of a pair of shoes with his hammer—labouring to support a wife and family."

Mr Hunter, in 1838, removed to Glasgow, where he still resides, and prosecutes the profession of portrait-painting.

Our meed of praise is also due to the late Mr William Fleming, house and sign painter, though he was not a member of the Drawing Academy. His talent was of a general cast. Portraits, landscapes, and figure-pieces he painted with a rapidity somewhat surprising. His likenesses of the public characters or oddities of the district, several of whom he selected, were true to nature; and of his ability in this branch of art, his portrait of the eccentric *Tam Reyburn*,* though it had to be executed by stealth, may be named as a fair specimen. Mr Fleming died of consumption in 1837, in the thirtieth year of his age.

At the present day there are several rising artists in Kilmarnock, among whom may be named Mr Alexander S. Mackay, Mr John Curdie, and Mr James M. Mackay. Mr A. S. Mackay confines himself to portrait-painting, and has

---

* This individual, whose portrait had the honour of appearing in the *Illustrated London News*, was commonly called "The Ayrshire Hermit." He was proprietor of the small farm of Holmhead, or, as it was sometimes denominated, "The Ark," on the banks of the Irvine, about three miles east from Kilmarnock. Here he resided, and having lost a lawsuit respecting a road which he claimed to his house, he made a solemn vow that he would neither shave his beard, crop his hair, nor change his clothing till he got the right for which he contended. This alleged right he never obtained; and as he kept his vow most religiously, his hair and beard became enormously long and matted, and his clothes so patched and darned that scarcely a piece of the original could be discovered. He died in 1843, aged about seventy-three years.

produced various pictures, remarkable for truthfulness and beauty. Mr Curdie pursues the delightful walk of landscape-painting. Some of the sweet, sylvan nooks by our own streams—the Marnock and the Irvine—as well as some of our picturesque old ruins, he has delineated with a freshness of colouring and a delicacy of touch that are truly admirable. Mr J. M. Mackay, though less experienced than the others—being yet but a young man—has also executed some pleasing pictures.

Another Kilmarnock artist of considerable promise was the late Mr James B. Reid. Though comparatively young, he painted various pieces graphically representing domestic scenes of Scottish life. In the prosecution of his art he removed to Edinburgh, where he died in November, 1863, aged twenty-six years.

In conclusion, we may say, the study of the painter is one of the noblest character—one that peculiarly deserves encouragement; for his works, like those of the poet, have a humanizing influence on the public mind: they tend to lead it from the grovelling scenes of life to the study of the sublimities and beauties of nature; and, in other respects, are powerful auxiliaries in advancing the cause of civilization and general refinement.

CHAPTER XXV.

"The simple Bard, unbroke by rules of art,
He pours the wild effusions of the heart;
And if inspired, 'tis Nature's powers inspire—
Hers all the melting thrill, and hers the kindling fire."

BESIDES the poetical writers already mentioned, three others remain to be noticed, who have obtained some distinction in that department of literature. These are—John Ramsay, author of *Woodnotes of a Wanderer;* Marion Paul Aird, author of the *Home of the Heart;* and Alexander Smith, author of the *Life Drama, City Poems,* &c.

Mr Ramsay was born in Kilmarnock in 1802, and in early life was taught the art of carpet-weaving. One of his first productions was the little poem, entitled *Lines to Eliza.* It originally appeared in the *Edinburgh Literary Journal,* accompanied with some laudatory remarks by Henry Glassford Bell, Esq., the talented editor of that periodical. Encouraged by the commendation of so competent a critic, Mr Ramsay continued to cultivate his poetic talent, and in 1836 published his poems in a collected form. Since that period they have gone through seven editions of one thousand copies each.

Mr Ramsay's muse, unlike that of many of our minor poets, is bold and versatile. The descriptive, the pathetic, the humorous, and the satirical, flow in turns from his pen; and in thought and expression he is often forcible. His *Address to Dundonald Castle* is, in many passages, pleasingly picturesque, and shows that he has gazed upon that venerable ruin with the contemplative eye of a poet. *Eglinton Park Meeting,* however, is perhaps his most masterly poem. The rambling nature of the subject allows him to indulge in various moods; while no small scope is afforded for satirical sallies, and for portraying the ludicrous—a style of writing in which he is sometimes pretty successful. The happiest of his productions in the more homely vein is the *Sports of Fastern's E'en in Kilmarnock.* There is a dash of sly satire about it; and some of the more prominent worthies who used to figure on the race-ground are "hit off" with considerable truth and ability. Several of Mr Ramsay's smaller poems also display the characteristics of a vigorous poetic mind.

Marion Paul Aird, author of the *Home of the Heart and other Poems*, was born in Glasgow, but since her infant years has been resident in Kilmarnock. Her progenitors belonged to Ayrshire, and occupied respectable stations in society. In her juvenile years she displayed a talent for drawing, and, it is said, delineated miniatures of her young companions with considerable fidelity. Her education, though not superior, was sound and substantial. With books and flowers she held early fellowship; nor were the former of that frivolous cast which often attract the attention of young females; for historical and biographical works were her favourites.

Trifling circumstances have often been the means of awakening the latent spark of genius; and the slightest hint or suggestion to a gifted mind not unfrequently facilitates the dawning and expansion of intellect. It was thus with the subject of our sketch. She was requested by a companion, who first directed her attention to the delightful study of poetry, to write some verses on a certain subject. Unconscious that nature had endowed her with the spirit of poesy, she touched the lyre, and thus produced her first effusion. Humble, no doubt, it was; but the finer sensibilities of the heart were now awakened; and since that period, her hopes, her joys, her affections and her sorrows, have been breathed forth through the blissful medium of song. The first of her productions that saw the light was printed in the *Kilmarnock Journal*, in the summer of 1838; but her name as a poetess was unknown to the public till it was announced at a banquet given to Dr Bowring, towards the close of the same year. Some verses from her pen were read on that occasion; and she was honoured with a poetical reply by the learned and talented doctor. In 1846 her first work was published, under the title of the *Home of the Heart and other Poems*, and was favourably received by the public.

The *Home of the Heart*—the leading poem in the volume—contains several beautiful passages. Like some lucid streamlet, it occasionally flows in gentle simplicity, often in attractive beauty, and sometimes in graceful dignity, and breathes, as it glides along, the most tender and devotional feeling. Several of the other pieces, such as *Our Early Days, Summer Emblems*, the *Auld Kirkyard*, and the *Herd Laddie*, though not marked with the masterly touches of genius, are sweetly-delineated pictures, and are evidently the conceptions of a mind alive to all that is beautiful, tender, and virtuous. In 1853 Miss Aird issued a second volume, consisting of pieces in prose and poetry, and bearing the title of *Heart Histories*. Like her first work, it met with considerable patronage. She has since published another work, under the title of *Sun and Shade*.

Alexander Smith, author of the *Life Drama, City Poems*, &c., was born at Kilmarnock on the 31st December, 1830, in a little thatched house near the foot of Douglas Street. His father, a native of the neighbouring village of Old Rome, was then a pattern-drawer in one of our printfields. He removed, in 1833 or 1834, with his family to Paisley, where the subject of our notice received the rudiments of an English education; after which he returned with his father to Kilmarnock, and was sent to work as a *putter-on* in a printwork belonging to the late Bailie Geddes. In the course of a short time he again went to Paisley, and at last removed to Glasgow, where he commenced the study of the classics, which, however, he soon relinquished, and entered on the business of a muslin designer.

In boyhood he was an ardent admirer of the beauties of nature; and many of the glowing pictures which he has given in his works were no doubt drawn from the recollection of early scenes. The following lines, for example, were suggested by the remembrance of the fine sea-view from the hills of Dundonald, which had excited his admiration when a boy:

> "I stood afar upon the grassy hills,
> I saw the country with its golden slopes,
> And woods, and streams, run down to meet the sea.
> I saw the basking ocean skinned with light.
> I saw the surf upon the distant sands
> Silent and white as snow. Above my head
> A lark was singing 'neath a sunny cloud,
> Around the playing winds."

But though early impressed with the charms of nature, it was not till he was sixteen or seventeen years of age that he began to give expression to his thoughts through the medium of verse, or even to manifest the slightest interest in the works of the poets. His poetic genius, however, appears to have expanded rapidly, or rather, as a friend has happily said, "it seems to have burst into summer all at once;" for before he had attained the age of twenty he had written the greater part of the *Life Drama*—a work of considerable length, and abounding in beautiful and striking passages. The *Life Drama*, we may state, originally appeared in the *Critic* in 1852, and created an unusual interest in literary circles. Published also in a separate form, it has had a very extensive circulation. According to *Chambers's Journal*, 10,000 copies were sold at home, and 30,000 abroad.

In 1854 Mr Smith applied for the Secretaryship of the

Edinburgh University; and though there were many other distinguished competitors, he succeeded in obtaining the situation, the duties of which he is said to discharge in a very able and satisfactory manner.

In 1855 he wrote a number of sonnets on the Crimean war, some of which are highly spirited. They were printed in a volume along with others by Dobell, the author of *Balder* and *The Roman.* Mr Smith also issued a work in 1857, entitled *City Poems*, and though less startling than the *Life Drama*, it is more remarkable, perhaps, for true feeling and genuine poetry. He has since published another poetical production, under the name of *Edwin of Deira*, and also a volume of essays, entitled *Dreamthorp.*

In vocalists, as well as in poets, Kilmarnock and its neighbourhood have been somewhat prolific since the days of Burns. It would seem, indeed, that the Genius of Song, that threw her "inspiring mantle" over the Bard of Coila, still lingered amongst us, and that they sprang up, under her influence, like so many wild flowers under the genial sunshine.

The most distinguished of our singers is the far-famed Templeton. He was born in the adjoining village of Riccarton, and is the youngest son of a family remarkable for their vocal capabilities. When about ten years of age, his eldest brother, who was then a celebrated teacher of music in Edinburgh, perceiving that he possessed great sweetness and power of voice, sent for him to that city, where, under his tuition, he rapidly improved. His subsequent career is well known. After being for some time the conductor of the choir of a church in Edinburgh (during which time he taught in the most respectable families), he went to London, and studied "under approved masters." He then commenced as a theatrical singer at Worthing; and his fame having extended to Brighton, he was engaged there; and made a successful "hit."

Mr Templeton was afterwards engaged at Drury Lane, and

called forth the flattering compliments of Mrs Wood and the celebrated Braham, both of whom were then performing in the same theatre. So great, indeed, was the advance which Templeton had by this time made, and so highly was he thought of by Braham, that that gentleman predicted his future success. "Templeton," said Braham, "if you have an *eye* to your pocket, add an *i*, and Italianize your name; be called Templeton*i*, and you will rival Rubini, *high* as he ranks." The celebrated Tom Cooke, too, out of compliment to his extraordinary abilities, used to call him "The tenor with the additional keys." In 1833 he attracted the admiration of Madame Malibran; and in his interviews with that gifted and accomplished vocalist, he received many useful suggestions. She inspired him with confidence in his own talents; and after performing with him at Covent Garden and Drury Lane for two seasons, she presented him with a jewelled ring, as a tribute of respect for his genius. In 1836-37 he made his first professional tour in Scotland, Ireland, &c., in which he met with unprecedented success. In 1842 he visited Paris, and had the satisfaction of finding his fame as firmly established, and his talents as much appreciated, in that city as in his native land. The celebrated Auber, Duprez, and Bordona, paid him the greatest respect. In the following year he was again engaged for Drury Lane theatre, where, in the opera of *La Favorite*, he gained additional laurels.

Soon after this period Mr Templeton added a new charm to his musical entertainments—that of introducing his favourite solos with lectures, in which he displays considerable powers of elocution, and an intimate acquaintance with the histories of our most celebrated lyrical poets and composers. In 1844 or 1845 he paid a professional visit to America, where he met with that general attention and respect which his genius merits, and which have always been shown him in his native country.

To these brief notices a short account of Duncan Macmillan, "the Ayrshire Ventriloquist," as he has been denominated, may be appropriately added. The art or gift, of which he is possessed in an eminent degree, is not unworthy the consideration of the philosophic mind. It shows the varied powers, peculiarities, and beauties of the human voice, and the wonders that man, when so gifted, is capable of performing; and it affords intellectual gratification and rational amusement of a singularly interesting kind. It is not our part, however, to give a dissertation on ventriloquial science, and we shall, therefore, proceed with the subject of our sketch.

Duncan Macmillan was born at Kilmarnock, in the beginning of the year 1817. The talents for which he has become so remarkable were manifested in early life. When at school, he made himself conspicuous, and frequently gave offence, by mimicking the voices of his master and class-fellows. The peculiarities, too, of some of the more noted individuals in the locality were made the subjects of his vocal imitations; as an instance of which we may mention, that one old woman exclaimed to another who was making complaints about his tricks, "Deed, he's an unco callan, Duncan; but ye needna compleen, for he acts us a'." But our juvenile ventriloquist did not long confine himself to mere imitations. He soon made attempts at vocal deception, and was so felicitous in his performances, that, before he had reached the age of fourteen, his fame had spread over a great part of Ayrshire. Even at that time it might be said of him, in the words of Hudibras, that

> "He had an odd promiscuous tone,
> As if he'd spoke three parts in one,
> Which made some think, when he did gabble,
> They'd heard three labourers of Babel,
> Or Cerberus himself pronounce
> A leash of languages at once."

About the same period several of the nobility and gentry

of the county, anxious to witness a display of his powers, honoured the young aspirant after ventriloquial renown by inviting him to their residences. Among these was the noble proprietor of Loudoun Castle. To that princely mansion, therefore, our hero repaired; and, in the presence of the Marquis and Marchioness of Hastings and a select party, he was so successful in displaying the wonders of the human voice, that his noble hosts, and others of the company, believing he was destined to attain great eminence in the art, ventured a prediction to that effect—a prediction which has been literally verified. At length Mr Macmillan, who had been dependent for support on one of our local trades, which was little calculated to advance his pecuniary interests, resolved to practise the art as a profession. A desire also to see the world, to mark the peculiarities of men and things, strengthened the resolution; and these he has evidently noted with the eye and mind of a true observer; for, in his public entertainments they are portrayed and imitated with a fidelity and humour truly astonishing. Wherever he has professionally appeared, the greatest success has attended his polyphonical and gastriloquial displays. His lectures, too, on the history of the art, and the lively original anecdotes which he relates, give a zest to his performances; and, together with his unparallelled talents in imitation and vocal illusion, have won for him a name that will not speedily pass away.

CHAPTER XXVI.

Outrageous as a sea, dark, wasteful, wild.
MILTON.

As we have already shown, it has been the fate of Kilmarnock to be visited at various periods by fearful calamities. But the most disastrous of these, at least in the destruction of property, was the inundation of the town on the morning of the 14th July, 1852. There exists, indeed, no record, so far as we are aware, of such an event having previously occurred in the locality.*

The weather, for some time before the occurrence, was unusually warm and oppressive; and though the more observing of the inhabitants expected that such intense heat would probably be followed by a thunder-storm, yet no one ever dreamed that a flood so mighty in its strength would rise so instantaneously, and lay waste in its course fields, bridges, mills, dams, houses, gardens, and orchards.

Early on the morning of the calamity thunder of unusual loudness was heard rolling over the town; and as it continued it increased in depth and solemnity till its peals became terrific. At short intervals the lightning flashed so vividly as to appal the stoutest hearts. The rain, too, poured in copious floods, swelling the Kilmarnock Water to such an

---

* We have heard it stated that, at one time during the latter half of last century, the Kilmarnock Water rose to such a height that the road at *Haw's Well* (which many must still remember, and which took its name from Robert Haw or Hall, whose residence was near it) was rendered unpassable. At a later period Glencairn Square and the adjoining streets were twice flooded by the rising of the Irvine and Kilmarnock Waters, and once by the overflowing of the Irvine alone.

unprecedented height as to lead to the belief either that the reservoir at Lochgoin had burst its banks, or that a waterspout had fallen on the moors above Fenwick, where the rivulets that feed the river take their rise.* Such, however, was not the case; for, on these places being visited on the following day, no trace of such occurrences could be discovered. But those residing in the moors had never witnessed so dreadful a morning, even in the bleakest and wildest season of the year. In the words of Milton,

> "The thickened sky
> Like a dark ceiling stood."

The peals of thunder and the gleams of lightning were frequent and fearful; and the rain rushed down so impetuously that the very windows of heaven appeared to be opened.

Thus copiously supplied, the different branches of the Kilmarnock Water—particularly the Croilburn and the Craufurdland—were soon greatly increased in volume, and rolled on in awful strength, washing the soil from many fields, forcing in many places new channels for themselves, and bearing upon their brown, turbulent bosoms large planks of timber, trees, and other evidences of their desolating power.

To note minutely all the ravages committed by the inundation would be a difficult task; we shall, therefore, only endeavour to record the more prominent—following the course of the destruction, and basing our description on the testimony of witnesses, or on personal observation.

At the farm of Hairshaw Mill, situated on the Croilburn, a little above its junction with the Craufurdland, the power

* The Kilmarnock Water is formed by the confluence of various rivulets, the principal of which have different local designations, but are generally known by the names of the Borland, the Craufurdland, and the Croilburn (see page 11). The two former have their sources in Kingswell Moor, about eight or nine miles from Kilmarnock. The latter rises in the same tract of moorland, to the south-east of Lochgoin, and joins the Craufurdland about a mile below Waterside Mill. The Borland, or, as it is sometimes called, the Fenwick Water, was not so remarkably swollen on the morning of the inundation as the other two.

of the torrent was very remarkable. Part of a field, planted with potatoes, was so scooped out and filled with water as to appear like a loch; and at the back of the ruins of an old corn-mill, near the farm-house, a pool about eight feet deep was formed in the bed of the stream. A stone about six tons in weight, that had lain there from time immemorial, was borne away; and hundreds of ponderous boulders were scattered about. At several places along the edge of the stream the banks were so broken down, that the water-course was made three times broader than it was before the flood. A holm, belonging to the same farm, which had been known to yield fifty-five bolls of potatoes in one year, was so overspread with stones that we scarcely could believe that it ever had been arable. Hardly a green leaf could be seen on it to tell that vegetation had formerly been there. It resembled the rough bed of some dried-up river. Two stone bridges, we may add, that spanned the Croilburn, were completely demolished.

The first great havoc committed on the Craufurdland Water was at Mr Alexander's carding and spinning mill, about two miles above Fenwick. The dam was swept away, and the water rushed into the mill, filling it to the depth of six feet six inches, and lifting from their places various pieces of machinery, one of which was about two tons in weight. The height of the water at the bridge beside the mill was sixteen feet. The strength of the current was here so great that a stone, which was lying near the same spot, and which was supposed to be ten tons in weight, was carried away.

The torrent swept on in its resistless course, flooding some fine fields of grain, and washing down large portions of the banks. Dalraith Bridge, a strong stone structure, was borne off. At Raith Mill, part of a garden was destroyed; and several trees that had stood the "pelting of the pitiless storm" for many years, were torn from their roots as if they had been mere saplings. At Sandbed Spinning Mill, then occupied by Mr J. Raeburn, bonnet-manufacturer, the destruction was immense. A boiler belonging to the work, about a ton and a half in weight, was lifted by the current and carried as far down as Craufurdland Castle. A fine orchard was entirely laid waste. Here the flood rose even above the walls of some of the cottages, though, fortunately, the inmates had been roused from their slumbers by the peals of thunder that preceded the inundation, otherwise loss of life might have ensued.

In tumultuous fury the river hastened onward, lashing the woody banks behind Craufurdland Castle, and uprooting trees, or laying bare their old fantastic roots.

The next great damage was at Assloss, the property of John Parker, Esq. Here the flood broke into a fine holm, partly planted as an orchard, overspreading it with vast masses of stones, some of which were a ton in weight. Farther on, it laid waste another piece of land, planted with fruit trees and bushes. It then burst open a door leading into the principal garden, through which it rushed, breaking down a large portion of the garden-wall.

Near Dean Castle, the Duke's Bridge, a neat wooden erection, was borne away entire; and here the water must have risen to a great height, as we observed it had wreathed the upper branches of some large trees with many weeds. Gaining strength by the accession of the Borland Water, a little below this point, the flood now assumed a still more formidable aspect; rushing on, it drove away portions of the banks as if they had been wreaths of snow, and in its fury tore up massive stones, tossing them about like so many pebbles.

The Bonnet-maker's Dam and Sluice were next wrested from their foundations; and the bed of the river opposite the foot of the Dark Path was deepened several feet.

The Kilmarnock Foundry Dam was next demolished; and the scene which the foundry houses presented was awful in the extreme. At the back of the work the river winds somewhat abruptly; and this circumstance, together with the rising ground on the opposite side, tended in some measure to increase the rush of the water towards the houses. Fortunately, some of the occupants, like those in other places, had been kept awake by the rolling of the thunder; others had heard the sound of the approaching deluge, and gave the alarm. Considering the great and rapid rise of the water, which was about ten feet deep at the manager's residence, it is truly wonderful that many lives were not lost. As it was, the inmates were in great peril, many of them, among whom was a lady with an infant clinging to her breast, having to flee for safety in their night garments through the muddy waters, which were rushing in at every door.*

The inhabitants of the Townholm, the street leading to the Foundry, were in a similar state of danger. Panic-struck by a visitation so little expected, many of them abandoned their houses and property, and hurried to the higher grounds in the vicinity, in a state of utter despair. One man and his wife, unable to get out of their house, were obliged to mount upon a table, and even there, were several feet in water. In the same room, a bed, on which a child was sleeping, was lifted from its position and floated. The child cried, but soon fell into a sound slumber, and remained in that state, dry and unhurt, during the continuance of the flood.

* We may mention that, after the inundation, the shaft of an old coal-pit, *cradled* with stone and of a circular form, was discovered in the bed of the river, at the back of the Foundry. Considerable surprise was created by its appearance in such a situation, where no work of the kind could be wrought with safety. There is an old tradition, however, which the discovery seems to confirm, that the water at one time ran in a different direction, namely, to the east of the Foundry; and the probability is, that the pit would be sunk at that period.

We may likewise state, that about a hundred years ago, according to another tradition, while eight or nine men were employed in a pit at Townholm, in the same locality, water burst suddenly upon them from an "old waste," and only one escaped with his life. This story also has apparently been confirmed; for several skeletons and antique implements of labour, which were no doubt those of the drowned individuals, were found in March, 1863, in an "old working," at the place alluded to.

The woollen factory of the Messrs Laughland, Roxburgh, and Gilchrist, which is situated in this locality, received considerable injury. A large quantity of goods was destroyed; and the machinery likewise was greatly damaged; even the iron frames of the windows were shivered to pieces.

Some idea of the strength of the current may be formed from the fact that, at this quarter, a huge boiler was lifted from its site in Mr Donald's hook-work, and borne down the public street, which was here flooded to the depth of five feet. Buoyant as some light canoe, it sailed along, adding to the intense sublimity of the scene, yet filling the spectators with horror, as they naturally conceived that it would be fearfully destructive to everything with which it might come in contact.

The next scene of destruction was the property of Mr Thomas Cuthbertson, carpet-manufacturer, Craighead. The garden-wall was laid prostrate; the garden itself was converted into a ruinous waste; and much valuable property, of various kinds, was destroyed or swallowed up in the wide vortex of waters. At this place, a scene of awful interest was exhibited, the incidents of which we will endeavour to relate as we heard them from the lips of one of the sufferers, Alexander Pettigrew.

Pettigrew and two other individuals, named James Bruce and William Campbell, proceeded to Mr Cuthbertson's stable, in which the water was three or four feet deep, with the view of saving two horses. Campbell succeeded in getting one of them away. Bruce endeavoured to rescue the other; and Pettigrew, who was engaged keeping open the stable-door, began to think he was long in accomplishing his object, and hastened to assist him. While they were loosing the horse from its stall, the garden-wall, at a short distance, gave way; and an additional body of water, about seven feet deep, rolled down upon them. Bruce at this moment had hold of the horse; but the rush of the torrent separated them. He then endeavoured to gain the wall of the next house, which he reached and clung to, unable to go farther.

By this time Pettigrew had seized the horse, and was able to keep himself above the water by clinging to its neck. In this position he was driven about for the space of ten minutes. At last, seeing no likelihood of saving himself by means of the horse, which seemed unwilling to leave the spot, he began to despair, when a long-bodied cart drifted towards him. Inspired with fresh hopes, he instantly raised himself from the animal, and, with one desperate effort, sprang upon the cart, thinking it would serve as a little bark to bear him out of danger. But his weight coming suddenly on it forced it against the door of the cart-shed, which made it bound back again in the direction of the current coming from the garden. Again it made for the shed, and again struck the door, forcing it open. Pettigrew, still holding by the cart, which was now rapidly entering the opening it had made, perceived that the opposite gable had by this time been carried away, and that he would be borne into the main current behind. With great presence of mind, or rather, perhaps, in the madness of despair, just as the cart was entering the building, he tore a slate or two out of the roof at the top of the door, and got hold of a slate-nail with the forefinger of his left hand. The cart, too, on which his feet still rested, was delayed in its course by his legs pressing against the eaves of the house; and, fortunately, at this moment he seized the lead of one of the skylight windows with the other hand, and raised himself to the roof, where he sat with the water within a few feet of him.

Pettigrew now turned his thoughts upon poor Bruce, whom he observed standing by an outhouse, about seven yards from the spot where he had last seen him. A range of buildings adjoining now gave way, carrying with them the side wall of the house on which Pettigrew was sitting; fortunately, the roof had a connection with another house—the only one left entire within his reach. Still his position was perilous in the extreme; but with a fortitude that never forsook him, he hastened to the more secure roof, and remained there, with the waters rolling wildly about him. Bruce was still where Pettigrew had last observed him; but he soon saw him lifted by the waters and borne along to a short distance till he came in contact with a pump, which he clasped with his arms. The window of a greenhouse now drifted towards him, and by means of it he raised himself to the top of the pump. Pettigrew shouted to him to get on the roof of a house at hand; but he had scarcely said the words when the house was swept away. Bruce continued to stand by the pump, grasping it and the window-frame as the only means now left him of support; but, alas for the frailty of man's hopes! a large fruit tree, which had been torn from the garden, was swept towards him by the ruthless current, and, with one fell stroke, it forced him away, blasting the expectations of many anxious onlookers, who could render no assistance. All hope, however, was not yet gone; for, still alive, he was carried a little below the bend of the river, where, with the grasp of death, he clung to a growing tree, reviving the almost extinguished hopes of the spectators. Pettigrew shouted to him to climb the tree; and Mr Cuthbertson's son and others repeatedly threw a rope to him; but the awfulness of his position seemed to have deprived him of all energy and sense of recollection; for, though the rope fell within a few feet of him, he was unable to avail himself of the advantage thus afforded; and, in a short time, he was swept away. After the water had somewhat abated, his lifeless body was found at the corner of Green Street.

Pettigrew's position was still awfully perilous, as he had no way of escape from the frail tenement on which he sat, and around and against which the waves were beating in great fury. Casting his eyes up the water, he saw the large boiler already mentioned, which seemed the evil genius of the flood, tumbling towards him: he trembled for the consequences; for he thought that one stroke of it against the house might shiver it to atoms, and ingulf him in the yawning deep. For a moment it paused, as if planning his instant destruction; then, as if moved by mercy, it floated to the west of him, and made its way down the river.

Pettigrew remained on the roof till the flood had subsided, when he descended in a state of great exhaustion. The horse which he and the unfortunate Bruce had ventured their own lives to save, was borne down by the current, and afterwards found dead.

Farther down the stream, a house formerly used as a glue-work, at Townhead Bridge, was levelled with the ground; but the bridge itself withstood the power of the torrent—the parapets being all that were destroyed. The large boiler, after pressing a short time against the arch, went crushing beneath it, and came bounding out at the other side with fearful velocity.

Messrs Brown, Merry, and M'Gregor's printwork (now Mr Higginbotham's), immediately below the bridge, was deeply inundated, and the loss which they sustained was very great. A wright's shop in connection with the work was so sapped that it fell into ruins a short time after the waters had abated. Almost the whole of the wall which enclosed the ground on the opposite side of the river was also driven away. A little farther down, the dam of the Messrs Blackwood's mill became almost a total wreck; and large pieces of the solid rock behind it were dashed down the channel. At Ladeside there was considerable havoc; and the lives of the inhabitants were so endangered, that many had to force their way out by the back windows to the higher grounds in Soulis Street. The public works situated between Ladeside and the Flesh Market Bridge, namely, Mr Crooks's tanwork, Messrs Gregory and Thomson's carpet factory, and Mr Wilson's woollen mill (now Mr Somerville's), sustained very great damage. A dye-house, in the same locality, belonging to Messrs Brown and M'Laren, carpet-manufacturers, was entirely swept down. The Academy was much flooded; and the wall behind it, with its iron railing, was thrown about in fragments. Immediately below the Academy, at the house next the Corn Exchange Buildings, the water was six feet seven inches above the level of the street. The house of the late Mrs Finnie, on the other side of the river, was completely deluged; and Mrs Finnie herself was in great danger, but was rescued by the noble exertions of two individuals named Gray and Richmond.

We come now to the Flesh Market Bridge, situated nearly in the centre of the town; and here, perhaps, life and property were in greater danger than at any other place along the whole course of the river. This bridge, which was built in 1770,* is connected with a range of other bridges running behind it, on which the Council Chambers, the Police Cells, and other houses are erected. The arch, or rather arches, of these structures are somewhat flat, giving to the passage beneath the appearance of a confined tunnel. At the mouth of this passage the water gathered to a great height, overturning the walls along the river, and the parapet of the bridge, and rushing into Green Street, Waterloo Street, the Cross, Guard Lane, Market Lane, and thence down King Street. Most of the inhabitants being in bed, the alarm created by the cry, "The water is flooding the town!" was beyond all description. Men, women, and children started from their slumbers, and, almost in a state of nudity, ran in all directions seeking the more elevated spots; while others, terror-stricken, were unable to move from their position. As if to add to the horror of the

* The bridge adjoining, on which the Flesh Market was situated, was built in 1779.

scene, the large boiler before spoken of floated into Waterloo Street, striking and injuring the walls of some of the houses. For a short time it was turned round and round by the eddying waters, and was again borne back into the river and dashed against the bridge, which many thought would fall to pieces before it. At last, on the water subsiding a little, it went crushing beneath the arch, emitting, as it disappeared, the most terrific sounds. It ultimately rested at a short distance below Sandbed dam. The furniture and other goods belonging to various shopkeepers in Waterloo Street were either carried away or rendered almost useless. Life itself was in great peril. One family, unable to escape by the doors of their house, began to knock the back out of a wall-press, with the view of finding a way through a neighbour's rooms; and what is rather curious, and shows the despairing state into which many were thrown, that same neighbour was, at the very instant, using similar means on the other side of the wall, in order to escape through their apartments. At last, by their united efforts, the wished-for passage was effected. Still the means of escape had to be sought. Ultimately, one of the party forced out a back window, and leapt upon a stair on the opposite side of the court. He then secured a plank, which he laid from the stair to the window, and by this temporary bridge the others escaped in safety.

As we stated above, the Council Chambers and the Police Cells are erected on one of the bridges, and fears were entertained that these might give way. In the cells were twenty-one prisoners, male and female; but, fortunately, the keeper, Mr Geddes, was early apprised of the rising of the water, and, by praiseworthy exertions, succeeded in rescuing them. The prisoners were conducted to the new Court-house in St Marnock Street; and so perilous was their way down King Street, that three of them were nearly swept away. As an evidence of the danger the bridge was supposed to be in, we may mention that Mr Hamilton, town-clerk, hurried through the flooded streets to the Council-house, and brought away all the valuable papers.

The Cross was covered with an entire sheet of water; and all the shops, particularly those in Regent Street and Cheapside, were less or more inundated. So violent was the rush of the torrent from Waterloo Street into the Cross, that some of the shop-doors were burst open; and at the Old Bridge behind Victoria Place, the water boiled up in a fearful manner, taking away the back wall of a dwelling-house, and flooding Bank Street to the base of the Low Church steeple. At Sandbed Street, the iron-railed wall running along the river, and a considerable portion of the wall of the garden behind the Union Bank, were overthrown. The wooden bridge also, leading from Sandbed Street to Nelson Street, was completely carried off; and at the same place, the workshop of Mr George Connell was laid in ruins.

A large cistern, which had been borne down from the dyework of Messrs Brown and M'Laren, was driven into one of the lanes diverging from King Street to Sandbed Street; and here a considerable piece of the causeway was scooped out, evincing the resistless power of even the side-currents of the flood.

To those who could look upon it without thoughts of danger, King Street presented a noble spectacle. It was converted into a broad river, which rolled along in sullen grandeur, carrying upon its waves trees, planks of timber, tubs, casks, chairs, and other articles; but its very murmur seemed to proclaim that the town was destined to be swept away. In one or two places stones were torn from the pavement; and a lamp-post near Dr Paxton's house (now Mr J. Alexander's) was laid prostrate as if it had been a reed. So rapidly, indeed, did the torrent sweep along, that two men were borne off their feet, and narrowly escaped being drowned. They were extricated by the active exertions of the late Mrs David Brown, and some others.

To particularize the merchants whose shops and cellars were flooded along King Street would be invidious, as a vast quantity of goods belonging to all, from the Cross downward, was greatly damaged or destroyed. The appearance of Titchfield Street was similar to that of King Street. Douglas Street was perhaps more flooded than either, as not only the water coming from Titchfield Street, but that from the main river, at the west end, rushed into it, creating much alarm, and putting life itself in danger. A little below this spot the wooden bridge at West Shaw Street was borne away; and several gardens in the vicinity were greatly injured. In that of Mr James Stevenson the water was two feet six inches deep. The property of the late Mr Templeton, shawl-manufacturer, likewise suffered materially. The pillars of the gate leading to the house were overthrown, and the house itself flooded to a considerable depth before the inmates could effect their escape. In the same locality, the nursery grounds of Messrs Dreghorn and Aitken were deluged to a considerable extent. Even below the junction of the river with the Irvine, where the water had greater scope, the crops in several holms were greatly damaged.

Such is a brief outline of the ravages committed by the flood on the memorable morning of the 14th of July, 1852. We may add that the torrent continued in all its fury from about four o'clock till six, after which it gradually subsided, exposing to the eye, at the various places we have mentioned, the melancholy spectacle of wreck and ruin.

The following table shows the height to which the water rose in the principal streets. At the suggestion of Councillor Hugh Reid of Pleasantfield, and with the permission of the late Provost Cumming, marks were chiseled on the walls of the houses specified, to point out the heights, and to serve as a slight memorial of the dread calamity:

	"Ft.	In.
"Depth of the water at Mr Caldwell's Foundry, Townholm,	5	2
Mr J. Porteous's House, Townholm,	5	3
Mr Neill's House, Townholm,	7	4
Railway Bridge at Ladeside,	6	11
Mr Mackie's House, corner of Green Street,	6	7
Corner of the House opposite Mr Mackie's,	6	5
Mr Ferguson's Shop, Flesh Market Bridge,	5	6
Corner of Flesh Market, at foot of Guard Lane,	6	0
Guard Lane at King Street,	2	11
Corner of Waterloo Street at the Cross,	4	3
Nailer's Close at the head of the Cross,	2	3
Mr Finnie's, ironmonger, Regent Street,	0	10
No. 2, Portland Street,	1	7
Foot of Strand Street,	3	3
Back Causeway at King Street,	3	2
No. 41, King Street,	2	0
Mr Archibald M'Kay's Shop, 124, King Street,	1	9

"The water extended to No. 25 in Regent Street; to the Exchange Buildings in Portland Street; to No. 12, on the opposite side of Portland Street; and to No. 18 in Bank Street."

Immediately after the inundation, the magistrates and others appointed a committee "to ascertain the extent of the damage," and their report was as follows:

"First—The estimated value of the whole property, heritable and personal, within the Parliamentary bounds, destroyed by the late flood, is £15,000.
"Second—The whole number of families who have sustained loss is 221.
"Third—Of this number, 99 families are of the poorest class, and totally unable to withstand the loss of clothing, furniture, and damage to their dwellings.
"Fourth—The estimated value of the loss of these 99 families is about £300."

A subscription was opened under the auspices of the Provost, Magistrates, &c., for the relief of the poorer sufferers, and the sum subscribed was £550 2s. The Duke of Portland, the Marquis of Titchfield, Sir John Shaw of London, and Lord Eglinton, were the principal donors.

In closing our narrative of the flood, we cannot refrain from expressing our approbation of the resolution which the magistrates adopted for preventing rubbish being thrown into the river. The necessity of keeping it at all times free of every obstruction is sufficiently apparent, especially when we consider that "any given quantity of rain," to use the appropriate words of Sir Thomas Dick Lauder, "must now produce a much greater flood than it could have done before the country became so highly improved. Formerly the rain-drops were either evaporated on the hillside, or were sucked up by an arid or spongy soil before so many of them could coalesce so as to form a rill. But when we consider the number of open cuts made to dry hill pastures—the numerous bogs reclaimed by drainage—the ditches of enclosure recently constructed—and the long lines of roads formed with side-drains and cross conduits, we shall find that, of late years, the country has been covered with a perfect net-work of courses to catch and to concentrate the rain-drops as they fall, and to hurry them off in accumulated tribute to the next stream." It may also be stated, as a proof of the great extent to which the country is now drained, that, according to evidence given before a committee of the House of Lords in 1846, the tiles made in this district for the Duke of Portland alone, during the years 1825 and 1826, amounted in number to 59,204,385. Seeing, then, that the land is so much drained, and that the effect of such drainage is to render the rise of the streams more rapid and more extensive, we think our authorities cannot be too active in adopting every reasonable means for facilitating the safe flow of the river through the town.

Many of our townsmen had reason to congratulate themselves on their providential escape on the morning of the inundation. The suddenness of the occurrence—the early hour at which it happened—and the terrible force with which the water rushed into the town—all conspire to awaken our wonder that many lives were not lost. Had the Flesh Market Bridge, and those in connection with it, given way, the channel of the river, in all likelihood, would have been choked up—the various streets would have been flooded to a far greater degree—and the loss of life as well as of property might have been immense.

CHAPTER XXVII.

> Books, we know,
> Are a substantial world when pure and good;
> Round these, with tendrils strong as flesh and blood,
> Our pastime and our happiness will grow.
> WORDSWORTH.

IN a moral and intellectual point of view, the inhabitants of Kilmarnock are not inferior, we believe, to those of any other town in Scotland. The number and efficiency of the schools, the enlightening and refining tendency of the public libraries, and the elevating efforts of the various literary and scientific associations, have done much to improve their taste and talents.

The most important of our literary institutions is the Kilmarnock Library. It was founded in 1797, by a few of the more wealthy inhabitants of the town and neighbourhood. In 1811 it consisted of eight hundred and forty volumes; and in 1862 the number had increased to upwards of three thousand. In that year it was largely augmented by the addition of the libraries, previously distinct, belonging to the Philosophical Institution and the Kilmarnock Athenæum; so that it now numbers about six thousand volumes, comprising nearly two thousand separate works. Apart from their numbers, many of these, in the departments of history, natural and experimental science, and mental philosophy, are highly valuable; the departments of fiction and general literature are largely furnished with well-selected works; and altogether the institution is one of which the town has just reason to be proud.

We have already had occasion to mention, in a previous

Chapter, that, in accordance with the will of the late Robert Crawford, Esq., the yearly interest of about £1900 will, on the death of an annuitant, fall to the Kilmarnock Library. This valuable legacy, available exclusively for the purchase of books, was bequeathed on the condition "that the entry-money shall not exceed ten shillings, and that the annual subscription shall not exceed five shillings." This munificent bequest will not only serve as an enduring and honourable memorial of Mr Crawford, but will continuously secure large additions to this already extensive library; while the further reduction of the annual subscription, already as small as the maximum fixed by Mr Crawford, and the complete abolition of the entry-money, already effected, will make it more and more accessible to the public at large.

The Philosophical Institution was formed in 1823, for "the promotion of *general*, and more particularly of *scientific* knowledge." The society sought to attain its aim by the formation of a library and a museum, the holding of stated meetings for experiment and discussion, the delivery of lectures by members and by distinguished scientific professors, the organizing of *conversazioni* for more familiar and popular addresses on scientific subjects, and the providing of philosophical diagrams and apparatus. Except that the library has been, as stated above, merged in the Kilmarnock Library, the various objects of the Philosophical Institution are still, from season to season, vigorously prosecuted.

In October, 1847, this institution opened a public exhibition of models, relics, manufactures, paintings, &c., in the hall of the Crown Hotel, for the purpose of bringing the association more prominently before the community; and though no expense was spared to make the display in every respect worthy the attention of the enlightened and the curious, a considerable sum of money was realized, and the number of members more than doubled. The exhibition, it may be added, did great credit to the taste and activity of the committee of management. Everything calculated to amuse and instruct seemed to be gathered together; and, what is creditable to Kilmarnock, several of the models and specimens of manufactures, paintings, &c., which were much admired, were native productions.

The Kilmarnock Athenæum was instituted in 1848, for the purpose, as expressed in its rules, of promoting "the social and intellectual improvement of the inhabitants, more especially of the youth and working classes, by the providing of a first-class reading-room, the maintaining of a library, and the adopting of such other means as are usually employed by similar institutions for the furthering of these ends." The reading-room of this association, largely supplied with the most ably-conducted newspapers, and with the leading magazines and other periodicals, has been always popular and flourishing. The library (the establishment of which was facilitated, and the annual increase of which largely augmented, by the munificence of Sir John Shaw*) soon became extensive and valuable, and is now amalgamated, as mentioned above, with the Kilmarnock Library.

The rooms in which the business of these three important and popular societies is carried on form part of the Corn Exchange Buildings recently erected. The Athenæum reading-room is large and elegant, and its appliances are of the most comfortable and convenient description. An adjoining room, even more spacious and very tastefully fitted up, contains the Kilmarnock Library, and serves for the meetings of the Philosophical Institution. The three societies, though they have effected a harmonious junction of their libraries, are

* It should be mentioned that, since the amalgamation of the libraries, Sir John Shaw still continues his fostering kindness to the Athenæum, and that his donations are now applied in such a way as to render the benefit of the reading-room more accessible to "the youth and the working classes," for whose advantage more especially the institution was originally designed.

distinct in administration, and offer their advantages either singly, or in any combination that may be desired. The separate terms of yearly subscription at present are: for the Kilmarnock Library, five shillings; for the Philosophical Institution, two shillings; and for the Athenæum reading-room, seven shillings; but the Library and Athenæum together may be taken for ten shillings and sixpence; and membership in all three associations is secured by an annual payment of twelve shillings and sixpence.

Another institution worthy of notice is the Kilmarnock Philharmonic Society. It was formed in 1845, for the purpose of concentrating the vocal and instrumental talent of individuals belonging to the town, and for the practising of the higher classes of sacred music. It consists of about seventy ladies and gentlemen, and every facility is given for the admission of others possessing the necessary capabilities. Though associated chiefly for mutual improvement, they have given several public concerts, the proceeds of which have been devoted to benevolent purposes. Thus they not only extend beyond the sphere of the society those higher influences which peculiarly belong to choral harmony, and which tend to ameliorate the moral and social feelings, but also alleviate in some degree the wants and necessities of the poorer classes of the community. At one of these concerts, given in April, 1848, and conducted by Mr Adam Boyd, Handel's celebrated oratorio, *Judas Maccabœus*, was brought before the public for the first time in Ayrshire; and the masterly manner in which it was executed awakened in all present the ecstatic emotions which that sublime composition, when skilfully performed, is so eminently calculated to inspire. It may be added that, in consideration of the disinterested services of the society, a complete set of part-books of Handel's oratorio, *Joshua* (value ten guineas), was presented to them by the Provost, Magistrates, and other influential gentlemen. The oratorios of *Joshua*, the *Messiah*, *Samson*, by Handel, and the *Creation*, by Haydn, have since been brought out with great success.

Besides these institutions there are in the town two Masonic Lodges, and a Society of the Independent Order of Oddfellows.

The oldest of our Masonic Lodges is the Kilmarnock Kilwinning St John's, No. 22. It is also one of the oldest existing lodges in Ayrshire originally holding of Mother Kilwinning. It was instituted in 1734. The unfortunate last Earl of Kilmarnock, as stated at page 92, was one of its originators,* and was its first Right Worshipful Master. Besides the Earl of Kilmarnock, a number of influential gentlemen were connected with the lodge in its early years. Among these were Sir David Cunningham of Corsehill, Thomas Boyd of Pitcon, Alexander Montgomery of Coilsfield, Peter Cunningham of Bourtreehill, Charles Dalrymple of Langlands, Robert Paterson, town-clerk, William Park, surgeon, and James Muir, Master of Arts. The Earl of Errol also, as already mentioned (see page 92), was a member and Right Worshipful Master of the lodge in 1761. Among the members at a later period were William Parker, banker, Thomas Samson, the hero of the well-known *Elegy*, Gavin Turnbull, the poet, and John Wilson, the printer of the first edition of Burns's poems. Burns also was connected with the lodge,

---

* The following letter, signed by the earl and others, was addressed at the formation of St John's to the Mother Lodge of Kilwinning:

"BRETHREN,—We return you humble and hearty thanks for the honour you have done us, in sending your Worshipful Master and Warden to constitute a lodge here dependent upon yours. We shall always acknowledge our Mother Lodge with all due fealty and submission in after calls and assisting her poor's box, as far as is due from a grateful daughter to so worshipful and ancient a mother. Meantime we have sent three pounds to your box by your Worshipful Master, as an acknowledgment of the favour you have done us, and the duty we owe you.

"KILMARNOCK, Master.
"RO. PATERSON, Senr Warden.
"WM RANKIN, Junior Warden."

having been enrolled an honorary member in the autumn of 1786 (see page 163). The present Right Worshipful Master is John Steven, Esq., writer.

The St Andrew's Lodge, No. 126, was instituted in 1771. Its first Right Worshipful Master was Mr Thomas Boston, who appears from the minutes of the lodge to have been frequently appointed to that office. The lodge has continued to prosper and to hold regular meetings from its formation to the present time. The present Right Worshipful Master is Hugh Shaw, Esq.

In 1767 another Lodge was formed in the town, and called the St Marnock; but it does not now exist. Its last meeting was in 1818. The first Right Worshipful Master of St Marnock was William Park of Langlands, surgeon. In 1770 that office was held by William, Earl of Glencairn. The Rev. Mr Mutrie of the Low Church was chaplain; and among the honorary members were the Honourable John Cunningham, brother to the Earl of Glencairn, James Dalrymple, Esq. of Orangefield, &c.

There was, we may add, another Lodge in the town, called the St James Nethertonholm Kilmarnock, but it has not existed for a number of years.

The Loyal St Marnock Lodge of Odd-fellows was instituted 1st January, 1841, and numbers about six hundred members. Since its formation to the present time, it has continued to be popular and prosperous, and has effected much good as a benefit society. It dispenses annually as "sick gift" and "funeral gift" a sum varying from £300 to £400; and its funds amount to upwards of £6000. It is worthy of remark, that while many friendly societies have ceased to exist during the last twenty or thirty years, this institution, by judicious and economical management, continues to be prosperous, as we have said, and bids fair to be as beneficial in years to come as it has been in those that are past.

CHAPTER XXVIII.

"——— Our lot is given us in a land
Where busy arts are never at a stand;
Where nought eludes the persevering quest
That fashion, taste, and luxury suggest."

HAVING now narrated the principal matters connected with the history of Kilmarnock, we will conclude our labours by adverting to some of the more recent improvements, and by noticing such buildings, trades, &c., as have not been formerly mentioned, or seem to require a further description.

The town consists of about sixty-two streets and eighteen lanes. Among the streets recently formed, Portland Terrace, and those adjoining, are conspicuous. They are adorned with handsome villas; and, from the pleasantness of the situation, the town will, in all likelihood, extend in that direction.* Many neat and beautiful residences have also been built within the last few years in other places of the burgh, particularly in London Road, Dundonald Road, Witch Road,†

---

* In 1783 a plan for enlarging the town was drawn out at the request of the Earl of Glencairn, by which it appears that a new road was to be made from the farm-house of Wardneuk to High Street. A street was also to be formed from Beansburn to the Blind or Dark Path. Another was to run in a line from High Street to Dean Castle; and a new Cross was to be formed where these streets were to intersect each other. We know not why the plan was abandoned.

† This, though now a handsome street, was a wild, *eerie-like* spot at a comparatively recent period, and probably obtained its name in dark superstitious times, when such places were peopled with ghosts or goblins by the imaginations of the credulous. We have heard it said that it was called Witch Road, from being the path by which those charged with witchcraft in the olden time were led from the town to suffer punishment at the Gallows-knowe; but this is not supported by any sufficient

2 o

and Hill Street, all of which give ample evidence of a prevailing taste for the elegancies and refinements of life.

Bonnieton Square, in the neighbourhood of the Railway Station, has also been lately erected, and, though beyond the Parliamentary boundary, may be considered as forming part of Kilmarnock. It was built for the accommodation of the artizans and others employed at the railway works, and consists of twenty-three houses or buildings, which are occupied by about ninety-two families. Its situation is extremely pleasant, from the view of a considerable part of the surrounding country which it commands. At the extensive railway workshops, in the neighbourhood of the Square, is a plain but handsome clock tower; and a small gas-work supplies the whole of the premises. A library has been established for the use of those employed at the works.

authority; and, fortunately for the honour of Kilmarnock, it never was the scene, so far as we have been able to learn, of such revolting exhibitions as the torturing and burning of old women for witches, whose principal crime was their wrinkled appearance, their extreme poverty, their weakness of mind, or, what is still more probable, their superior intelligence. It appears, however, from *Wilson's Guide to Rothesay*, that Janet M'Nicol, who was "strangled to death at the Gallows-craig" of that place, in 1673, for " the vile and abominable crime of witchcraft," had resided in the neighbourhood of Kilmarnock for twelve years, "maintaining her wicked practices." But Janet seems to have avoided the notice of the ecclesiastical authorities here, as no mention is made of her, so far as we have observed, in the Kirk Records of that period. According to Sir Walter Scott and others, Mr Mitchell [? Michael] Wallace, minister of Kilmarnock, sanctioned, along with other clergymen of the county, the burning of witches at Irvine, in 1613.

It appears also from the *History of the Witches of Renfrewshire*, that "the Laird of Kilmarnock" was one of the commissioners appointed to inquire into the case of Christian Shaw, a girl of eleven years of age, who was supposed to have been bewitched about the year 1696. Seven persons, according to the *Domestic Annals*, were charged as her tormentors and put to trial. Six were found guilty, and five of them, among whom was the celebrated "Maggie Lang," were hanged and burned on the Gallowgreen of Paisley, 10th June, 1697. The sixth, a John Reid, escaped public execution by hanging himself in his cell; and the belief was that he had been "strangled by the devil." It is rather curious, that some of the victims confessed their guilt at their trial and at the place of execution.

Christian Shaw, who was a daughter of John Shaw of Bargarran in Renfrewshire, was married, about the year 1718, to a Mr Miller, parish minister of Kilmaurs. At his death, which occurred about 1725, she returned to Bargarran, and afterwards introduced the manufacture of white stitching thread into the west of Scotland.

The appointment in 1846 of an additional Sheriff-Substitute for the county, whose residence and court are at Kilmarnock, has given an importance to the town beyond what it formerly possessed. Along with this parish, the following have been assigned as his district, namely: Ardrossan, Beith, Craigie, Dalry, Dreghorn, Dunlop, Fenwick, Galston, Kilbirnie, West Kilbride, Kilmaurs, Largs, Loudoun, Mauchline, Riccarton, Stevenston, and Stewarton. The first criminal or jury court cited for the Kilmarnock district was held on the 21st September, 1847.

For the better accommodation of the Sheriff, as well as that of the Magistrates, Commissioners of Police, &c., a new Courthouse was erected in St Marnock Street in 1852, and has since been made more convenient for public purposes by several alterations. The first court held in it was on the 5th May of the same year, and was presided over by the present Sheriff, Thomas Anderson, Esq.

But the most important feature, perhaps, in the recent progress of Kilmarnock is Duke Street, which runs from the head of the Cross to Green Street. It promises, from the beautiful buildings already erected in it, to be one of the finest streets of the town. It was opened for public traffic on the 25th November, 1859, on which occasion the civic authorities, headed by Provost Finnie, walked along it in procession, accompanied by a large number of the inhabitants. In the following year another improvement was effected, by the formation of Union Street, in the upper quarter of the town.

At the present time (1864) another new street, we may state, is about to be formed. It will run in a direct line from Langlands Brae, near the Railway Station, to the Courthouse in St Marnock Street. It will intersect Dunlop Street, College Wynd, and Nelson Street; and by opening up these antiquated and confined places, it will be highly beneficial in a sanitary point of view, and will also improve, in no small degree, the appearance of that quarter of the town. This new line of street, we may mention, was projected some years ago by the Town Improvement Trustees, who are now enabled to proceed with the undertaking through the praiseworthy liberality of John Finnie, Esq. of Bowdon Lodge, Manchester—a native of Kilmarnock—who has advanced the requisite funds, and guaranteed the trustees against all pecuniary loss.

Among the buildings erected during the last few years, the Corn Exchange, situated at the corner of what was formerly called the Low Green, deserves particular notice. It was built in 1862, from designs by James Ingram, Esq., architect, and has a magnificent appearance. It is two storeys in height, and covers an area of one thousand six hundred and two square yards. Its frontage extends one hundred and thirty-six feet along Green Street, and ninety-two feet along London Road. The building, the style of which is Italian, is adorned with a tower which rises to the height of one hundred and ten feet, and is called the Albert Tower, in remembrance of the late Prince Consort. On the front of the tower the Kilmarnock Arms are sculptured, and a fine wreath representing fruits and flowers hangs gracefully over them. Above this is an ornamental projection, on which, in *bass-relief*, are the words—"The earth is the Lord's, and the fulness thereof." Immediately above the inscription are three clock dials, one of which facing the north will, we believe, be illuminated. Eight Corinthian pillars and a small dome which they support, complete the tower.

The under storey of the building, facing the two streets, is rusticated, and is occupied with commodious shops. The upper storey, in which are the Athenæum reading-room, the Kilmarnock Library-room, the Registrar's office, and the office of the Inspector of Nuisances, is beautified by large windows with circular arches and projecting keystones. On eleven of these keystones heads have been sculptured, one of which, at the window beneath the tower, represents the late Prince Consort, that on the left, the late Lord Clyde, and that on the right, our respected townsman, Sir John Shaw, Bart. The other figures are merely fanciful. On the balustrade at the top of the walls are also some finely-executed vases, which, with the heads alluded to, add considerably to the beauty and grandeur of the edifice.

Behind the shops is a large hall for the business of the Corn Exchange and other public purposes. Its main entrance, above which is a small stone balcony supported by carved trusses, is at the corner of the building facing Duke Street. The hall, which is eighty-four feet long, fifty-one wide, and fifty-one from the floor to the ceiling, is truly beautiful, and affords accommodation for upwards of twelve hundred persons. At one end, which is circular, is a light but handsome gallery, and at the other a platform on which one hundred and thirty individuals can be conveniently seated. The ceiling, which is elegantly constructed, and from which the light is principally admitted, has a pleasing appearance, and so also have the side windows. One of these, which is richly stained, and which was designed and executed by Mr R. C. Robertson, strikes the visitor as exceedingly beautiful. It is divided into compartments, on each of which is an appropriate emblem. Another object that attracts attention is an elegant clock, of the most approved construction, which is placed on the east wall. It is the workmanship of our townsman, Mr John Cameron, who presented it to the Exchange Company.

The Athenæum reading-room, which fronts Duke Street, and the Kilmarnock Library-room, which fronts Green Street, are also fine spacious apartments. They are both well lighted and tastefully furnished. On the wall of the former is a handsome spring time-piece, around the dial of which is the

Kilmarnock Coat of Arms carved in wood. It was presented to the Exchange Company by the makers, Messrs Breckenridge and Son.

In connection with the building, and situated at its south end, is a spacious market for the sale of butter, eggs, and other farm produce. It measures eighty-one feet in length and sixty-four in breadth. It is covered with a substantial roof, from which it is lighted, and has two entrances from Green Street, and two doors that lead into the hall.

The building, which cost upwards of £6000, belongs to a joint-stock company, with the exception of the market and three of the shops in Green Street, which are the property of the town. The Albert Tower was built by public subscription, and cost about £600.

This noble edifice was opened on the 16th September, 1863, when the Kilmarnock Philharmonic Society, conducted by Mr Andrew Fyfe, gave two high-class musical festivals in the hall. The composition selected for performance was Handel's sublime oratorio, *Judas Maccabæus*, which was skilfully executed. These concerts were followed on the succeeding night by a ball; and on the day after, an inauguration dinner took place, at which Provost Crooks acted as chairman, and Sir James Fergusson, M.P., as croupier.

In 1841 the population of the town and parish was 19,956, and on the 31st March, 1851, it was 21,283. Since that time many new tenements have been erected; and the population of the town and parish in 1861 was 23,551. In 1851 the number of inhabited houses in the town was 1375; separate occupiers, 4230; males, 9119; females, 10,079. Of these, 10,870 were born in Kilmarnock; 5761 in other places of Scotland; 195 in England; 2313 in Ireland; 2 at sea; and 57 in the colonies and foreign parts. The attendance at seventeen of the churches on the 31st of March, 1851, was, forenoon, 5665; afternoon, 6354. The population of the

Parliamentary burgh, which includes part of Riccarton, was, in the same year, 20,913.* The Parliamentary and municipal constituency was 681; and in 1861 it was 730. In 1856 the total rental of the burgh and parish of Kilmarnock, including railways, was £56,364 8s.; and the corporation revenue was £604.†

The following statistical tables have been kindly furnished us by James S. Gregory, Esq., registrar, by whom they were drawn up:

CENSUS STATISTICS OF THE PARISH SINCE 1801.‡

Census.	Population.	Increase.	Increase ℔ cent.
March 10, 1801,	8,079	—	—
May 17, 1811,	10,148	2,069	25.6
May 28, 1821,	12,769	2,621	25.8
May 29, 1831,	18,093	5,324	41.7
June 7, 1841,	19,956	1,863	10.3
March 31, 1851,	21,283	1,327	6.6
April 8, 1861,	23,551	2,268	10.6
		15,472	

An average increase of 257 ℔ annum for the last 60 years.

* The Parliamentary boundary is thus described in the *Reform Act for Scotland:* "From the point at which Kilmarnock water joins the river Irvine, in a straight line to a point on the Irvine road which is distant 350 yards to the west of the point at which the same leaves Grange Street, thence in a straight line to the point at which the road to Hillhead leaves the Kilmaurs road, thence in a straight line through the summit of the Bonfire-knowe to the Kilmarnock water, thence in a straight line to the bridge over the mill-burn on the Mauchline road, thence down the mill-burn to the point at which the same joins the river Irvine, thence in a straight line to the Bellsland bridge on the road from Riccarton to Galston, thence in a straight line to the point called Witch-knowe at which two roads meet, thence in a straight line to the bridge over the Maxholm burn on the Ayr road, thence down the Maxholm burn to the point at which the same joins the river Irvine, thence down the river Irvine to the point first described."

† According to a petition of the magistrates, to the Lords of Session regarding the Town Green, in 1777, the annual revenue of the town at that time was only seventy pounds. "The whole public revenue of Kilmarnock at present," says that document, "does not exceed £70 sterling per annum; of this there is exhausted about £66 by necessary annual expenses; so that there does not remain above £4 per annum to be employed on any emergent public purpose or improvement."

‡ As stated at page 4, the number of inhabitants, in 1547, in the parish, which

TOTAL SUMMARY OF POPULATION AT CENSUS 1861.

	Males.	Females.	Total.	Increase.
Burgh of Kilmarnock,	9,942	10,756	20,698	1,500
Landward of Parish,	1,443	1,410	2,853	768
Parish of Kilmarnock,	11,385	12,166	23,551	2,268
Parliamentary Burgh,	10,890	11,724	22,614	1,701

SYNOPSIS OF ANNUAL REGISTRATIONS, &c.

Year.	Population: 1 ℔ cent on Census 1851.	Births: Rate ℔ An. of Population.		Deaths: Rate ℔ An. of Population.		Marriages: Rate ℔ An. of Population.		Total Rate ℔ Annum of Population.		Illegitimate Rate of Total Births.	Twins.	Stillborn.	Average Age at Death.	
			1 in		1 in		1 in		1 in	1 in			Yrs	Mos
1855	22,147	842	25	559	38	180	119	1581	14	59	14.3	4	41	24	6
1856	22,368	918	23	592	36	211	100	1721	13	75	12.2	4	38	21	1
1857	22,592	970	23	578	39	203	114	1751	13	76	12.7	8	40	23	3
1858	22,818	911	25	556	41	173	132	1640	14	77	11.8	4*	34	25	0
1859	23,046	1042	22	556	41	218	105	1816	12	86	12.1	9	30	24	4
1860	23,276	909	25	685	34	231	100	1825	12	79	11.5	11	50	24	9
1861	23,551	1007	23	591	39	202	116	1800	13	88	11.0	13	30	27	8
1862	23,791	992	24	576	41	169	140	1737	13	85	11.0	14	37	26	5
1863	24,029	910	26	635	37	192	125	1737	13	75	12.0	6	32	23	7
Average of 9 years,		944	24	592	38	197	116	1734	13	77	12.0	8	37	24	5
1863, in Scotland,		1 in 28		1 in 43		1 in 140				1 in 10					

Kilmarnock is still, as it has long been, the seat of various important manufactures, though some of its old trades, such as shoemaking, have considerably declined. In 1831, according to published documents, the annual value of the boots and shoes made was about £32,000, and so late as 1837, about £50,000. It must now be far below that sum; for the number of shoemakers at present employed scarcely exceeds

then included that of Fenwick, was little more than 1400; and in 1668 the population of the town is supposed to have been about 600 (see page 173). Dr Webster states that the number of inhabitants in 1763 was nearly 5000, and in 1792, 6776. He refers, we presume, to the population of the town.

* In the year 1858 there was one triplet.

two hundred. Muslin weavers also have decreased considerably in number. Bonnet-making is still carried on pretty extensively. Carpet-weaving is likewise one of our principal manufactures. There are five factories in the town, in one of which, that belonging to Gregory, Thomsons, and Company, Brussels are now wrought with steam power. The annual value of the carpets produced in 1837, was estimated at £150,000. In the same year the shawls made and printed were valued at £230,000, and the leather manufactured, at £45,000. This trade, including the departments of tanning, dressing, &c., is still carried on to a considerable extènt. Besides these, which may be considered the staple trades of Kilmarnock, there are many others, among which may be enumerated—iron-casting, engine-making,* carpet machine-making, woollen machine-making, wool-spinning, gun-making, coach-making, and letter-press printing. Agricultural implement-making is also carried on at Beansburn, in the immediate neighbourhood of the town; and the superiority of the articles usually manufactured, has won for their maker, Mr Andrew M'Kerrow, a more than local celebrity. The making of water meters, too, has been lately introduced. The works, which are situated in Townholm, were opened in 1854. We may remark, that the meter here manufactured, which bears the name of Kennedy's Patent Water Meter, is ingeniously constructed, and is principally used by large manufacturing establishments, and by water companies. A factory for the weaving of cotton cloth by steam power has also been recently established by T. and J. Ferguson. It is situated on the banks of the Kilmarnock Water, at the foot of West Netherton

---

* "We may mention that, in 1816, a locomotive engine, the first of the kind started in Scotland, was tried [here]. It was intended to convey coal to Troon from the Duke of Portland's colliery; but, from its defective construction and ill adaptation to flat rails, it only drew ten tons at the rate of five miles an hour."—*New Statistical Account.* This engine, which we remember having seen, was of very rude appearance compared with those now in use.

Street. Since its erection in 1854, it has been considerably enlarged.

The following facts, collected from the uncontradicted evidence of witnesses from Kilmarnock, on behalf of the Glasgow, Dumfries, and Carlisle Railway Bill, before a committee of the House of Lords in 1846, afford a pretty full idea of the commercial, manufacturing, and agricultural interests of Kilmarnock and its neighbourhood:

		Value.
English Goods in all branches of drapery brought annually to Kilmarnock,	300 tons	£100,000
Ironmongery from England,	700 ,,	60,000
Refined Sugar from London,	500 ,,	
Leather and Trimmings for Boots and Shoes from England,	100 ,,	
Seeds of all kinds from England,	100 ,,	
Materials for Printworks from England,	3000 ,,	
Value of the same when manufactured,	......	400,000
Grass Seeds sent to England,	1300 ,,	
Leather and Skins sent to London,	500 ,,	
Carpets sent to England,	400 ,,	120,000
Military and other Bonnets,	......	16,000
Tea from London,	1000 chests	
Porter from London,	500 hhds.	
Draining Tiles, each one foot in length, made for the Duke of Portland in 1825 and 1826,	59,204,385	
Purchased for the Duke from other tileworks,	1,000,000	
To be made during the year 1846,	2,000,000	

The prosperity of Kilmarnock is also promoted by the numerous coal-works in the neighbourhood.* So extensively, indeed, is the coal trade now carried on, that clusters of miners' cottages, like so many little hamlets, appear in all directions round the town. The large iron-works, too, commenced some years ago at Hurlford, have given a bustling appearance to the locality round the old village of Crooked-

---

* One of our first coal-works, we believe, was in the neighbourhood of Dean Castle, at least we infer this from the following minute in the Town's Books: "15th June, 1736.—The town gives £30 sterling to aid the coal-work at Dean, on the same terms as the other subscribers, in consideration that it will be of great benefit to the town."

holm, at which, it may be mentioned, a handsome place of worship, in connection with the Free Church, was lately erected.

The commercial interests of the town are greatly facilitated by six banking establishments, namely, a branch of the Union Bank of Scotland, one of the Commercial Bank of Scotland, one of the Bank of Scotland, one of the Royal Bank of Scotland, one of the National Bank of Scotland, and one of the Clydesdale Bank. There is also a Savings Bank. The Union Bank, in Bank Street, and the Royal Bank, in Portland Street, are large new erections, and truly ornamental to the town in an architectural point of view.

From the circumstance of two railways running from the town, namely, one to Glasgow, with branches to Ayr, Troon, Irvine, &c., completed in 1843, and one to Cumnock, Dumfries, Carlisle, &c., completed in 1850, we may safely predict that Kilmarnock will rapidly increase in commercial importance, and continue to be, as it has hitherto been, the greatest emporium for all kinds of business in Ayrshire.

Among the improvements recently effected in the town, the introduction of water by means of pipes deserves particular notice. The Company, to whose enterprise we are indebted for this important convenience, was formed in 1850. The works, including settling reservoir, storage reservoir, filters, distributing basin, and main and distributing pipes, cost upwards of £20,000. The settling reservoir and the storage reservoir are on the estate of Rowallan, the property of the Marquis of Hastings. The former, which is at Gainford, in the parish of Fenwick, covers nearly three acres of ground. The latter, which is at North Craig, about two miles from Kilmarnock, covers, with its embankments, &c., twenty-five acres, and contains upwards of sixty-five millions of gallons. The works are constructed on the gravitating principle; and the distributing basin, at North Craig, is at an elevation of about two hundred and forty feet above the Cross of Kilmarnock. The main pipes, therefore, being always fully charged, an abundant supply of water can at all times be had for extinguishing fires, or for other useful purposes. In a sanitary point of view also, the water thus introduced must be highly beneficial; for the great quantity used, even for domestic purposes, cannot fail to carry off many impurities through the various sewers and drains of the town, and thereby promote the health of the entire community.

We had occasion in a former part of our work, to speak of the patriotic spirit displayed by the volunteers of Kilmarnock in 1715, when an attempt was made by the friends of the Stuarts to place the old Pretender on the throne of Britain. The Kilmarnock men were then among the first who marched to Glasgow to defend it against the rebel forces. In the early part of the present century also, when the war raged between France and Britain, two volunteer regiments were formed in Kilmarnock for local protection. The same patriotic ardour seems to prevail among our townsmen at the present time. Towards the close of 1859, when the movement was made throughout the country for the better protection of the nation, they were the first in Ayrshire who enrolled themselves as volunteers. In November of that year a corps was formed under the name of the "1st Company Ayrshire Rifle Volunteers." In April, 1860, the "9th Ayrshire (2nd Kilmarnock) Rifle Volunteers" was instituted; and in May following, another company, called the "5th Ayrshire Artillery Volunteers, Kilmarnock," was also formed.

The First Company of Ayrshire Rifles, on its first establishment, was officered by James Hunter Picken, Esq. of Hillhouse, captain; Robert Railton, Esq., carpet-manufacturer, lieutenant; **Thomas Bishop Andrews**, Esq., writer, ensign; Hugh Hutchison Smith, Esq., surgeon; and the Rev. Thomas Ramage, chaplain. On the resignation of Captain Picken,

Mr Railton was promoted to be captain, Mr Andrews to be lieutenant, and John Dickie, Esq., Junr, seedsman, received his commission as ensign. Mr Ramage resigned, and was succeeded by the Rev. Alexander Hamilton, A.M., the present chaplain. The corps numbers about seventy men.

The Ninth Company of Ayrshire Rifles, on its first establishment, was officered by James Young Deans, Esq. of Kirkstyle, captain; James Wilson, Esq., banker, lieutenant; John M'Millan, Esq., chemist, ensign; John Borland, M.D., surgeon; and the Rev. John Symington, chaplain. On the resignation of Mr Wilson, Henry Hay Norie, Esq., banker, was appointed lieutenant; and on the resignation of Mr M'Millan, John Montgomery, Esq., engineer, became ensign, since whose resignation the office has remained vacant. About the same time Mr Deans resigned his commission, whereupon Mr Norie was promoted to the captaincy, and James Smythe Taylor, Esq. of Moorfield, was appointed lieutenant. The corps numbers about ninety-six men.

The Fifth Company of Ayrshire Artillery, on its first establishment, was officered by David Rankin, Esq., postmaster, captain; James Meikle, Esq., writer, first lieutenant; George Morison, Esq., merchant, second lieutenant; Alexander Marshall, M.D., surgeon; and the Rev. Daniel Vere Thomson, chaplain. Mr Meikle has resigned, and been succeeded by James Wilson, Esq., banker. The corps numbers about one hundred men.

Respecting the state of the poor, a few words may be said. In consequence of the influx of strangers for several years past, the number of paupers has considerably increased. At present, 1864, the annual assessment levied for their support is about £5000.* The salaries of the various officials, includ-

---

* The amount of money laid out for the poor about the beginning of last century, is shown by the following extract from the Session Records: "The sum of Disbursements to the poor, from the 15th of June, 1701, to the 22nd of June, 1705, extends to

ing those of the medical attendant and the collector, are paid, of course, from the same fund, and amount to about £400. There are nine hundred and eighty-seven registered paupers on the roll; but, including casual poor and dependants, about two thousand five hundred and fifty are relieved yearly. Of these a considerable number are natives of Ireland. It may also be stated, that as disease occasionally prevails to a considerable extent among this class of the community, the necessity of erecting a fever hospital has been long admitted. On this subject an able report, written by James Aitken, M.D., was read at a meeting of the Board, in March, 1848, from which it appears that upwards of £1200 had then been received in bequests and donations for that object.

Besides the Parochial Board, there are several institutions for relieving the distress of the infirm and the indigent; the more prominent of which are the Male and Female Benevolent Societies. Various legacies have also been bequeathed for the same object by humane individuals, among whom we may mention the late Dr Hunter of London, the late William Parker, Esq., London, the late Sir James Shaw, and the late William Paterson, Esq., Ayr. The gentleman last named also left a valuable annuity for promoting the interests of education in the town, by aiding deserving young men in the prosecution of their studies at the seminaries of learning in Kilmarnock, and thereafter at any of the universities in Scotland.

A few remarks may also be made relative to the rural part of the parish. In 1792 a society was instituted here for promoting the progress of agriculture; and since that period great improvements have been made on the land round the

---

Two Thousand Seven Hundred Eleven pound, Five Shilling, Eight pennies, Scots money. Distributed by William Fulton as Kirk Treasurer for the aforesaid space." At this rate, the annual expenditure for behoof of the poor did not amount to more than £56 9s. 9d. of English money.

town. Not a few fields that, in our own remembrance, were overspread with broom, whins, thistles, or rushes, and consequently of little value, are now in a high state of cultivation, and yield abundant crops.* The wretched-looking farmhouses, too, of former years, have given place to others of a genteel, commodious, and comfortable kind; and even the cottars' dwellings, with their little gardens, have an air of neatness and cleanliness, at once delightful to the eye and creditable to the taste and industry of the occupants. As a natural result of the enterprise and diligence which have effected these improvements, the condition of the tenantry has been greatly ameliorated; so much so, that many of them enjoy not only the necessaries, but the elegancies and luxuries of life—a state of things which contrasts strangely but agreeably with what existed so late as 1778, when, according to Aiton, only two families in the country part of the parish could entertain their friends with a cup of tea.

The parish is eight or nine miles in length, and about four in breadth.† The principal landowners are His Grace the

---

* Aiton, writing about 1811, says: "The whole arable land in the parish of Kilmarnock was set, about 1763, at between 2s. 6d. and 3s. per acre. It would now be set at *twenty* times that rent. The farm of Silverwood," he continues, "of seventy-three acres in extent, was rented for nineteen years prior to 1776, at £5 in money and five bolls of meal, and is now set at near £200."

According to the statement of a descendant of a Mr John Lang, who had a lease of the farm of Rumpie from the last Earl of Kilmarnock, the annual rent of it, per acre, was only half-a-crown, which was to be paid in hens and chickens! The greater part of the farm, which consisted of about forty acres, is now comprised in the lands of Holms.

† The following description of the boundary of the parish of Kilmarnock, based upon one that was issued when the present system of registration came into operation, will be found nearly as correct as is possible, consistently with brevity: From the point where the Moorfield burn falls into the river Irvine, a little below Cambuskeith Mill, up and along the river in an easterly direction, to the High Milton (including the High Milton Mill and Armsheugh); then, north-east, as far as Sneddonhall (including Blackshill and High and Laigh Russia); then west along the Moscow road (having the estate of Darwhilling on the north); then to the farm of Walston; then keeping parallel to the road (both sides of which are in the parish) to the point of junction with the Craufurdland road; then along the Craufurdland road (one side of which, with the houses on the south side of the

Duke of Portland, the Marquis of Hastings, John White, Esq. of Grougar, William H. Craufurd, Esq. of Craufurdland, William Dunlop, Esq. of Annanhill, and John Parker, Esq. of Assloss. The seats of the three last-mentioned gentlemen, and Mount, the residence of Mrs Guthrie, are the more prominent in the parish.

Craufurdland Castle, which is about three miles from the town, in a north-east direction, is a structure of great antiquity, part of it having been built prior to the days of William the Conqueror.* It is situated on the summit of a steep bank, overlooking Craufurdland Water. This stream and Fenwick Water, both of which rise on the neighbouring moors, flow for several miles on each side of the estate, and uniting at the Dean Castle, take the name of Kilmarnock Water, which joins the Irvine a little below the village of Riccarton. In the vernal season of the year, the romantic bank on which Craufurdland Castle is situated is covered with a beautiful sheet of yellow daffodils, indigenous to the soil. On this delightful spot the late Mrs Craufurd of Craufurdland used to assemble yearly, on the second or third Saturday of April, about seven or eight hundred children, who were all supplied with a large bouquet. Some years the floral display is so luxuriant, that half as many more children might carry off its golden honours. It is still customary, we believe, for the

---

bridge, is in the parish); then along the bridge, and through the gatehouse (of which the one end is in the parish, and the other in that of Fenwick); then (across the Kilmarnock water and through the lands of Dalmusternock) to Craigspout; then north-west (including part of the farm of Meiklewood, and traversing Fenwick moor) to the farm of Redden; then south by Rowallan (including Rowallan Mill, Little Mosside, Meikle Mosside, Tannahill, Toponthank, Wardneuk, Onthank, and Little Onthank) to the Stewarton Roadend on the Kilmaurs road; then still southwards along the road to the farm of Hillhead; then south-west (past the Bonnieton farm) to the farm of Springhill; then to the burn at the Moorfield tilework; then along the course of the burn to Old Gatehead, across the Dundonald road at the Thirdpart Kilns, to the point first described.

* Statement communicated to the author by the late Mrs Craufurd of Craufurdland.

boys and girls of Kilmarnock to go to Craufurdland Castle for their wild lilies or glens; and few days of the year are better known by them than *glen Saturday*, as they justly term it. In the immediate vicinity of the castle are some beautiful avenues, and a fine wood-skirted loch, to which we alluded when speaking of the game of curling. The proprietor, William Houison Craufurd, Esq., is the lineal descendant of the Houisons of Braehead—a name that will long be associated with Scottish story.

Rowallan Castle, three miles north-west from the town, on the banks of the Carmel, is also of considerable antiquity. It was long the residence of the Barons of Rowallan, the names of some of whom occupy prominent places in the history of our country. In the troublous times of the Church of Scotland, conventicles were held in one of the apartments of the house, which still bears the name of the *Auld Kirk*, and in which are preserved two *kirk stools* belonging to that period. It is chiefly famous, however, for being the birth-place of Elizabeth More or Mure, first wife of Robert the Second, king of Scotland, who, as the historical reader is aware, lived and died in the neighbouring castle of Dundonald. The blood of the ancient family of Rowallan has, consequently, mingled with that of the greater portion of the royal families of Europe.

Rowallan Castle was also the paternal residence of Sir William Mure, author of the *True Crucifixe for True Catholikes*, &c. He was born about the year 1594, and was nephew, by the mother's side, of Alexander Montgomery, author of the once popular poem of *The Cherrie and the Slae*. The poetical talent of Sir William, like that of many other poets, displayed itself at a very early period of life; one of his compositions having been printed in the *Muse's Welcome*, a poetical garland got up in honour of King James's visit to Scotland in 1617. His pieces consist of the *True Crucifixe for True Catholikes*, published in 1629; various other poems; and a version of the *Psalms* of David. The learned Principal Baillie, when a commissioner, in 1643, to the Westminster Assembly, who were then engaged in examining various versions of the *Psalms*, with a view to select a proper one for the Church of Scotland, thus spoke of Sir William's in one of his letters: "I wish I had Rowallan's *Psalter* here, for I like it better than any I have yet seen;" and the committee appointed to revise that of Rous, which was adopted, and which was first used publicly at Glasgow in May, 1650, are said to have been "instructed to avail themselves of the help of Rowallan's."

The poems of Sir William are marked by a pure religious feeling, and for delicacy of conception and execution, have been compared by some writers to those of his illustrious contemporary, Drummond of Hawthornden. Though much inclined to literary studies, he performed, on several occasions, a public part on the theatre of life. He was a member of the Parliament which met at Edinburgh in 1643, for the ratification of the Solemn League and Covenant. In the following year he acted in a military capacity for the Parliamentary interest, was wounded at Long Marston Moor, and, in a few weeks after, was engaged at the storming of Newcastle. It is said that his taste in arboriculture and architecture was considerable; that many of the noble trees that wave their broad shady branches round Rowallan Castle, were planted under his auspices; and that he "reformed the whole house exceedingly." He died in 1657. The estate of Rowallan now belongs to the noble family of Loudoun.

Several other beautiful mansions, though beyond the parish, are within view of the town, such as Caprington Castle, Fairlie House, Treesbanks, and Bellfield, all of which, with their woody pleasure-grounds, add to the beauty of the surrounding country.

APPENDIX.

I.

CHARTER AND INFEFTMENT BY JAMES VI
IN FAVOUR OF
THOMAS, LORD BOYD, IN LIFE RENT, AND ROBERT, MASTER OF BOYD, IN FEE;
DATED 12 JANUARY, 1591.

[THE interest of the Charter, of which the following is an abridged translation, lies mainly in the fact that it is the document by which the town of Kilmarnock was erected into a Burgh of Barony.]

"JAMES, by the grace of God, King of Scots, to all good men of his whole realm, cleric and laic, Greeting:

"Know that we, now after our completed age of twenty-five years, have given, granted, and disponed, and by our present Charter have confirmed, to our well-beloved cousin, Thomas, Lord Boyd, in free-holding or life-rent, for all the days of his life, and to Robert, Master of Boyd, his eldest son and heir-apparent, in fee heritably, and to his heirs male and of entail respectively and successively underwritten, all and sundry the lands, lordship, and baronies respectively after-specified, with their castles, towers, forts, manors, gardens, orchards, mills, multures, fishings, outsets, parts, pendicles, breweries, woods, yearly rents, tenant-holdings, free holdings, servitudes, advowsons, donatives, and patronages of churches and chapelries of the same, and with all and sundry their pertinents, lying in the bailiwick of Cunningham, and under the sheriffdom of Ayr: which all and sundry foresaid lands, lordship, &c., with their &c., belonged heritably aforetime to the foresaid Thomas Lord Boyd, held by him and his predecessors immediately from us and our most noble progenitors as Princes or Seneschals of Scotland; and which he, at Holyroodhouse, by his lawful procurators and by his letters patent, by stick and staff, as the manner is, simply and purely, resigned into the hands of us, as his Lord Superior of the same, together with all right, title, &c., which he has had, has, or in any way shall be able to have, and renounced all claim for the future for ever, in consideration of this our new Infeftment, of the tenor following:

" We, for good, faithful, and gratuitous service performed and paid to us and our most noble progenitors by the aforesaid Thomas, Lord Boyd, and his predecessors in times past, and for certain sums of moneys in name of composition paid into our treasury, and for other reasonable causes and considerations moving us, do, of our certain knowledge and our own motion give and grant anew, and for ourselves and our successors for ever confirm, to the said Thomas, Lord Boyd, in &c., and to the said Robert, Master of Boyd, his &c., and to his heirs, &c., all and whole the foresaid lands, lordship, &c., along with all right, title, &c., which we for ourselves, our predecessors or successors, as Kings or Princes of Scotland, have had, have, or in any manner shall be able to have or claim, to them or any part of them, their rents, &c.: renouncing, disclaiming, exonerating, disponing, and transferring the same totally, from us and our successors to the aforesaid Thomas, Lord Boyd, and Robert, Master of Boyd, &c., along with all action, right, &c: and in like manner renouncing for ourselves and our successors all actions of non-entrance, error, &c., and other processes whatsoever, raised or threatened by us, our predecessors or successors, or any of us, our treasurers or advocates in our names, against the aforesaid Thomas, Lord Boyd, &c., concerning the said lands, lordship, &c.:

" And further, we, for the causes above-written, do anew erect, unite, annex, incorporate, and create, all and sundry the aforesaid lands, lordship, baronies, with their aforesaid pendicles, and other things above specified, with their castles, &c., into a free lordship and free barony, to be called in all time coming the lordship and barony of Kilmarnock: and we also will and grant, and for ourselves and our successors decree and ordain, that the Castle and Manor of Kilmarnock shall be the principal messuage of the said lordship and barony; and that the single sasine by the aforesaid Thomas, Lord Boyd, and his son, &c., at the principal messuage, shall be now, and in all time coming, a sufficient sasine for all and sundry the lands, lordship, baronies, &c.:

" Further, we, in consideration of the special love and favour which we bear and have towards the aforesaid Thomas, Lord Boyd, and in consideration of the policies - and buildings in The Kirktown of Kilmarnock, lying under the said barony and our aforesaid sheriffdom, do, for the convenience and entertainment of our lieges frequenting the same, by the tenor of our present charter, infeu, erect, and create and make the said town, called The Kirktown of Kilmarnock, and the lands of the same with their pertinents, into a free burgh of barony for ever, to be called in all time coming the burgh or town of Kirktown of Kilmarnock: and we give and grant to the inhabitants and indwellers of the said burgh, present and future, plenary power, faculty, and free power of buying and selling, in the same, wine, wax, cloth, woollen and linen, broad and narrow, and other merchandises whatsoever; and of having and holding in the said burgh bakers, brewers, butchers, venders of flesh and fish, and all other tradesmen belonging to a free burgh of barony: and we also grant that there may be free burgesses in the foresaid burgh; and that they, with consent of the said Thomas, Lord Boyd, the said Master of Boyd, his son, &c., may have the power of annually electing for the future bailies and officers for the ruling and governing of the said burgh; and that the said burgesses and inhabitants of the same may have and hold a market-cross and a market weekly on the Sabbath-day [Saturday], and a free fair annually on the twentieth day of the month of October, to last for eight days of the same; with plenary power to the foresaid Thomas, Lord Boyd, and his son aforesaid, and &c., to assign and locate in feu-firm his lands adjacent to the aforesaid town of Kilmarnock, in whole or in part, into burghal divisions, for buildings or houses to be erected on the same, with all the tholnies,* customs, privileges, and liberties, pertaining or in any way able to pertain in future to the free fair and free burgh of barony, in same manner as, and as freely as, any burgh under our kingdom is infeued by us or our predecessors:

"All and whole the aforesaid lands, lordship, and barony of Kilmarnock, with their castle, &c., to have and to hold, to the aforesaid Thomas, Lord Boyd, &c., and to the aforesaid Robert, Master of Boyd, &c., and to the heirs male of his body lawfully begotten; whom failing, to Thomas Boyd, his brother-german, and the heirs male, &c.; whom failing, to Adam Boyd, likewise his brother-german, and the heirs male, &c.; whom failing, to any other heirs male of the body of the said Thomas, Lord Boyd, to be as yet lawfully begotten at any time preceding his death, and to the heirs male of their bodies lawfully begotten; whom failing, to Robert Boyd of Badinhaith, brother-german of the said Thomas, Lord Boyd, and the heirs male, &c.; whom failing, to Adam Boyd of Penkill, and the heirs male, &c.; whom all failing, (which God forbid!) to the nearest lawful heirs male whatsoever of the said Thomas, Lord Boyd, bearing the names and arms of Boyd; to wit, the aforesaid burgh or town of Kirktown of Kilmarnock, from us and our successors as Princes and Seneschals of Scotland, in a free burgh in barony, and the aforesaid remaining lands, &c., in a free lordship and free barony, &c., throughout all their straight boundaries, old and divided, as they lie in length and breadth, in houses, buildings, woods, plains, moors, marshes, roads, paths, waters, ponds, streams, meadows, pastures, and pasture-lands, mills, multures, and their appurtenances, fowlings, huntings, fishings, peat, turf, coals, collieries, minerals, mines, pigeons, pigeon-houses, workshops, distilleries, breweries, and broom, woods, groves, and thickets, firewood, timber, quarries, stone, and lime; with courts, decrees, amercements, escheats, &c., of the said courts; with gallows, pit, sok, sak, thole, thame, infang-thief, outfangthief, pit and gallows; with common pasture, free entrance and exit; with free forests in all places where there are and have been woods within the foresaid lands, with privilege of forest courts, amercements and escheats of the same; and wraik, wert, wair, and venison; with all and sundry the privileges of a free barony and free forests; and with all and sundry the other liberties, commodities, profits, conveniences, and just pertinents whatsoever, whether not named or named, whether under the earth or upon the earth, far and near, pertaining, or in any manner able rightly to pertain in future to the aforesaid lands, lordship, &c.: freely, quietly, plenarily, entirely, honourably, well, and in peace, in like manner and as freely, in all things and through all things, as the said Thomas, Lord Boyd, and his predecessors held and possessed the same from us and our successors† as Princes and Seneschals of Scotland, before the resignation aforesaid:

"There being paid therefrom annually by the aforesaid Thomas, Lord Boyd, during his life, and after his death by the said Robert, Master of Boyd, his &c., and by his heirs male, &c., to us and our successors as Princes, &c., the rights and servitudes due and wonted to us and our successors before the said resignation, according to the tenor of the ancient infeftment of the same:

"In witness whereof, &c., Witnesses, &c., at Holyroodhouse, the twelfth day of the month of January, in the year of our Lord M.D.XCI, and of our reign XXV."

---

* "Tholonium," the liberty of buying and selling on one's own ground, or the right of charging "Toll" for such liberty.

† So in the original.

II.

KILMARNOCK LANDS.

IN the year ——, the Earl of Kilmarnock feued out to the Magistrates, Town Council, and community of Kilmarnock, by a feu disposition, "All and Haill the Green called Barbadoes Green, and —— acres of land or thereby lying and at the back of our Wards in Townend; and All and Haill Three Acres of Land or thereby with the green ground betwixt and the Water and Craigs therein, with the Stone Craig called the Broadford, and little Isle, or piece of green ground within the Water at the foot of the Willie Wand Wheel,*—and all and haill the piece of ground on which the Meal Market is now built.

"BOUNDARIES.—*Barbadoes Green*, by the Water of Kilmarnock on the east and south-east, the old Water going with a part of the lands called Langlands, on the south; the lands underwritten at the back of the Wards feued out by the said Town with the said Ward, and the yeard of Thomas Smith, weaver, on the west, north, and north-east parts.

"And All and Haill these —— acres of land, or thereby, with the houses situated thereon at the back of our said Wards, presently possesst by Robert Mitchell, &c.; by the said Green, called Barbadoes Green, the lands called Langlands, on the east, with Longhouse Yeard and the remainder of Lang's Lands, formerly possesst by Robert Andrew, on the south; the high-way to Ayr on the west and north-west; and us, the said Earl of Kilmarnock, our Wards presently possesst by Charles Dalrymple and Robert Mitchell, in the north and north-east parts.

"*Townhead Property*.—All and Haill these two acres of land, or thereby, at Stepends and Stone Craig Holm, presently possesst by Margaret Boyd, widow, and her sub-tenants, with the green ground thereto adjacent betwixt and the Water; bounded by the lands presently possesst by Robert Connell, in Little Dean, on the east; the lands possesst by William Taylor in Braehead, on the south; the Water of Kilmarnock, on the north and west parts.

"All and Haill that acre of land, or thereby, presently possesst by Margaret Thomson, widow, with the Stone Craig therein, and the Stone Craig called the Broadford, and little Isle, or green ground, betwixt the Waters at the foot of the Willie Wand Wheel; bounded by the lands now feued out to John M'Leslie and the Dean Mains, on the north and east; and the Water of Kilmarnock and the lands on the east side thereof; and the said two acres of land immediately disponed on the east and south; the lands of John Gemmell, stationer, on the west; and the high-way to Glasgow, on the north parts."

The *remaining lot* is the piece of ground on which the Meal Market is now built.

The Town of Kilmarnock paid for these several subjects £3650 Scots, and pay also a yearly feu rent of £7 Scots.

---

* "Willie Wand" signifies a rod of willow, and "Wheel," a whirlpool or eddy. "The Willie Wand Wheel," therefore, may be rendered "the whirlpool or eddy of the stream at which willows grow."

APPENDIX. 303

III.

THE TOWN GREEN, AND THE RIGHTS AND TITLES OF THE BURGH.

ABOUT the year 1772 or 1773 considerable discontent prevailed among a number of the inhabitants, in consequence of certain acts of the Town Council regarding the feuing of portions of the Town Green for building purposes. So frequent and serious, indeed, were the bickerings, or rather riotous proceedings, which the scheme of the Council occasioned, that soldiers had to be called into the town to restore order and tranquillity. The ground proposed to be feued was the side of the lower green, running from the old school-house to the angle opposite David's Lane (now part of the site of Duke Street), and thence along the London Road as far as the river. The Green then measured eighty-seven falls, of which twenty-four were to be feued. A Mr James Wilson, merchant, and others, "called in question the powers of the Magistrates and Council, in the police or administration of the property of the burgh," and the case went before the Lords of Council and Session in 1774, when the Lord Ordinary pronounced the following interlocutor: "The Lord Ordinary having considered the memorials, finds, That the right of property of the green in question is only vested in the magistrates, as trustees and administrators for the benefit of the community; finds it sufficiently proven, by the tack produced, and by the narrative of the act of council, that the manufacturing inhabitants have always had the use of this ground for the purposes of bleaching, drying, &c. Finds that the magistrates may, by fencing the ground or other proper means, render it more useful for those purposes; and, though granting feus may increase the public revenue, under the management of governing persons, yet it is neither a proper nor a just act of administration, to alienate this piece of ground, which the inhabitants have always occupied and used for the purposes of industry and manufactures in the village; therefore suspends the letters *simpliciter*, and decerns." The dispute was again brought before the same Court, but how it was ultimately settled we are not aware; it would appear, however, that Mr Wilson and his adherents were the successful parties, as the ground alluded to was long unoccupied with buildings.

The following extracts from the Petition of the Magistrates and Council we give for the sake of their historical interest:

"The suspenders have given a very erroneous state of the way and manner in which this green was acquired; particularly, they have averred, that there was a contribution made by the inhabitants, whereby it was acquired from the Earl of Kilmarnock, and vested in the community long before there were any magistrates existing.

"In order to obviate this, it will be proper to give your Lordships a more particular deduction of the rights and titles of this burgh. By disposition, dated 14th October, 1690, William, then Earl of Kilmarnock, and William, Lord Boyd, his son, set forth, 'That Robert Rodger, Matthew Hopkins, and Hugh Wallace, merchants in Kilmarnock, had, for themselves, and in name and behalf of the town and inhabitants of Kilmarnock, made payment to the said Earl and his son of the number of fifty guineas of gold, and were likeways content, and had agreed, for the Earl's profit and utility, to ware out and expend the haill necessary depursements that his Lordship should be at in erecting the said town of Kilmarnock into a burgh-royal: Therefore, the said Earl and his son, not only consented and gave power to the forenamed persons, to procure the said burgh of barony to be erected into ane burgh-royal, upon their own proper expences in manner foresaid, with reservation to his Lordship of the right of property thereof, and his privilege of chusing the magistrates thereof on leets to be offered to him, and of the haill other privileges that may be suitable to his right and interest, at the sight, and by the advice of his honourable friends, by whose advice the said erection is to be made, and no otherwise; but also, sold and disponed to, and in favours of the said Robert Rodger, Matthew Hopkins, and Hugh Wallace, for themselves, and in name and behalf of the said town, inhabitants, and community of Kilmarnock, the haill common-goods and customs of the said burgh and barony, heritably and irredeemably, to be uplifted and disposed of by them and the said community, for upholding the tolbooth, for furnishing of coals and candle to soldiers, and other public uses of the said burgh. And as the said Matthew Hopkins, Robert Rodger, and Hugh Wallace, had advanced the foresaid sum for the said community, and are to advance the expences of the said erection: Therefore, the said Earl, for their security, assigned them in and to the foresaid customs and common-goods, ay and while they should be completely paid and reimbursed by the said community and inhabitants of Kilmarnock, of the foresaid sum advanced by them, and of whatever sums they should happen to advance upon the foresaid account, with annual rent from the time of advancing.'

"The intention of getting this town erected into a royal burgh proved abortive; it had, however, the effect of altering altogether the government and constitution of the burgh of Kilmarnock. For, about two years afterwards, a magistracy and town council were constituted for the better administration of the affairs of the burgh;* and the management of the town being put on this footing, and John M'Leslie and Robert Paterson being elected baillies, Rodger, Hopkins, and Wallace wanted to be reimbursed of the money they had advanced to the Earl on account of the disposition 1690. The two baillies, with Charles Dalrymple, writer, and William Morris, apothecary in Kilmarnock, did for themselves, and in name and behalf of the town and inhabitants, make payment to the saids Messrs Rodger, Hopkins, and Wallace, of the balance then resting of the foresaid fifty guineas, on which occasion the saids Messrs Rodger, Hopkins, and Wallace, executed an assignation, bearing date the 27th May, 1696, whereby they assigned the aforesaid persons in and to the aforesaid common-goods and customs to be used and disposed of by them, and the said community, for the ends and purposes aforesaid; and as they had advanced the said sum paid to Hopkins, Rodger, and Wallace, for the town, they were on that account assigned in and to the said common-goods and customs for their security, ay and while they should be reimbursed of the same.

"Afterwards, by a deed, bearing date 5th November, 1700, William, Earl of Kilmarnock, with consent of his curators, did, upon the narrative of the foresaid disposition in 1690, and in consideration of the sum of £3650 Scots then advanced to him by Robert Wright and William Morris, then present baillies, and Matthew Duncan, treasurer, for themselves, and in name and behalf of the council and community of the said town, and their successors in office, baillies, treasurer, and community of the said town, and also, in corroboration of the said disposition 1690, above recited, by his father and grandfather, sold, disponed, and in feu-farm let and demitted in favours of the said Robert Wright and William Morris, then present baillies, and Matthew Duncan, then treasurer of the said burgh, and their successors in office, baillies, treasurer, and council and community of the said town, all and

* See note, page 8.

haill the said common-goods and customs of the said burgh of barony, comprehending therein *the common greens of the said town*, shops under the tolbooth thereof, the weights, pecks, and measures, the tron and weights thereof, and the customs of the fairs and weekly markets, and all the customs belonging to the said burgh of barony, as the same are presently possessed by the said baillies and council, and have been in use to be possessed by them and their predecessors, ever since the date of the foresaid disposition made and granted by the said Earl's grandfather and father, to them; and also, gave liberty to the said baillies, treasurer, and council, and their successors in office, to build a meal market, &c., and to exact, uplift, and receive the customs and casualties that should be found due in law for the same. The *reddendo* of this feu-right is, £7 Scots yearly, and upholding the tolbooth and bridge, furnishing coal and candle to soldiers, and other public uses of said burgh; and in this disposition, the set of the town is again modelled, and new regulations made anent the chusing of the baillies, and is confirmed by the Earl after his majority, by ratification on the back thereof.

"And, on the 28th February, 1704, a disposition was executed in favour of the magistrates and town council, the occasion whereof was, that Hugh Hunter and James Thomson, then present baillies, James Smith, treasurer, Jasper Tough, Robert Hodgeart, Robert Wright, late baillies, William Sloss, William Breckenridge, William Fulton, John Harper, Andrew Dick, William Baird, Matthew Duncan, Matthew Hopkins, Benjamin Thomson, James Cathcart, and John Adam, then present counsellors, having, for themselves, and in name and behalf of their successors in office, baillies, treasurer, counsellors and community of the said town, made payment to the said John M'Leslie and Robert Paterson, late baillies, Charles Dalrymple and William Morris, of the sum of £   , which completely satisfied and paid them of the foresaid sum advanced and paid by them to the saids Rodger, Hopkins, and Wallace, and resting annualrents: Therefore, the saids John M'Leslie and Robert Paterson, Charles Dalrymple and William Morris, sold, transferred, and disponed to, and in favours of the said James Thomson and Hugh Hunter, baillies, James Smith, treasurer, and remanent counsellors of the said town of Kilmarnock, and their successors in office, baillies, treasurer, and counsellors, of the said town, for themselves, and for the use and behoof of the magistrates, council, and community of said burgh, the foresaid right and disposition by the Earl, to Hopkins, Rodger, and Wallace, and their disposition to M'Leslie, Paterson, Dalrymple, and Morris, together with the haill common-goods and customs of the said burgh and barony, and that heritably and irredeemably, &c., with full power to the saids Hugh Hunter, James Thomson, baillies, James Smith, treasurer, and remanent counsellors above-named, and their successors in office, baillies, treasurer, and counsellors of the said town, to intromit with, &c."

In reference to the Green the petitioners afterwards say: "As for the way in which this green was acquired, your Lordships will be informed, that the price paid for it, in particular, was twenty-four guineas; and that was part of a sum of £800 Scots, borrowed from John Luke, merchant in Glasgow, upon bond, by the magistrates and council, and which bond was afterwards satisfied and paid, by money borrowed by the magistrates and council for that purpose, upon credit of the town's funds. And, as to a story of a contribution made by the inhabitants, at that time, for the purchase of this green, and that by the money contributed, it was purchased accordingly; this has been boldly averred by the suspenders, but is altogether without foundation. There was, indeed, a contribution made among the inhabitants about that time; but that was a contribution for quite a different purpose; it was a contribution for raising a stipend for a second minister, and the money contributed was applied accordingly. . . . In those days, it [the Green] was an entire piece of ground, and very fit for pasture, or other uses, being really what its name imported, covered with green swaird. But about the year 1759, a bridge was built over the river of Kilmarnock, about the middle of that part of the river which encompasses one side of the green; and a road was made through the green to that bridge, and a cross one along the side of the town, between the town and the green, in order that every part of the town might have free access to the road leading by the bridge. This is, by much, the most public inlet to Kilmarnock: It is the road to Edinburgh, with which place they have a good deal of intercourse and communication; and it is likewise the road to Dumfries, through which channel they receive many of their raw materials of manufacture, which are the produce of the south of Scotland, or the north of England."

It may be added that where the Green Bridge is now erected there was formerly a ford, which was usually crossed by foot passengers when coming into or leaving the town in that direction.* But the principal outlet towards the London Road was, we believe, by Back Causeway, and thence up the precipitous brae called Tankardha'—a name which tradition affirms was given to it in consequence of a number of tinkers having had their workshops or dwelling places there in the olden time.

IV.

THE KILMARNOCK COAT OF ARMS.

IN the *Peerage of Scotland* the Arms of the Kilmarnock family are thus described: "Azure, a fess chequé, argent and gules; *Crest*, a dexter hand, couped at the wrist, erect, pointing with the thumb and the two next fingers, the others turning down; *Supporters*, two squirrels proper; *Motto*, CONFIDO, I trust." On the lower scroll,

---

* A somewhat humorous anecdote is told of a Galston farmer in connection with this ford. He used to come by it almost every Sabbath to the Church of Kilmarnock accompanied by a female servant; and with more selfishness than gallantry he generally ordered her, when the stream was swollen, to carry him across on her back, which she always did with seeming good humour. The farmer, who was a bachelor, thinking, no doubt, that it would be wise to secure such a one as a helpmate for life, at length asked her in marriage. She consented; and on the day of the marriage ceremony, which was to be performed in Kilmarnock, they bent their steps as usual by the ford; and the water happening to be swollen at the time, she again, at his request, took him on her back and bore him to the other side. When they returned to the same place after the nuptial knot was tied, he again gave her the hint to help him across. "Na, na, lad," she exclaimed, "I'll begin wi' ye as I mean to end; I was only your servant when I carried ye, but noo I'm your lawfu' wife—I'm your equal, lad; I'll be maistered nae langer, sae ye maun just strip your shoon like mysel', and toddle through the water on shanksnaigle." How the farmer looked the reader may judge.

however, of various prints of the arms, such as the one here given, the word *Goldberry* usually appears; but of its real meaning we have met with no explicit explanation. We ventured an opinion regarding it at page 20; and, since that part of the text was written, we find that a similar one is given in Robertson's *Ayrshire Families*. Many of the mottoes on the armorial bearings of our ancient nobility had their origin in some particular war-cry, or singular heroic deed. The word in question, therefore, may have been adopted, as we formerly said, in commemoration of the bravery of Sir Robert Boyd, who

according to tradition, when engaged at the battle of Largs, attacked and defeated, with a little band of fearless followers, a strong detachment of Norwegians, at a place called *Goldberry*, or *Goldberry Hill*, a few miles south of the main scene of action.

The oldest extant representation of the Arms of any of the Boyd family, of which we have been able to obtain any account, is a Seal of Robert, first Lord Boyd, preserved among the "Tweeddale Charters." The document to which it is appended, and to which Sir Robert Boyd (not yet ennobled) seems to have been a witness, is a "Precept of Seisin" for infefting Sir David Hay of Yester, Knight, in the fourth part of the lands of the Baronies of Yester, &c., in excambion for the lands of Teling in Forfar; and it bears date the 10th January, 1451. The arms are as follows: Couché, a fess chequé; *Crest*, on a helmet with mantlings, a dexter hand, with the two last fingers turned down, issuing from a coronet of three points; *Supporters*, two squirrels; *Legend*, SIGILLUM ROBERTI BOYD DE KILMARNO.

The accompanying engraving, from a seal attached to a document of Robert, Lord Boyd, in 1460, represents the ancient armorial bearing of the family. It will be found to resemble very closely the one just described; and the only material difference in the legend is, that the latter has "DN" (for *dominus*, lord), which does not occur in the earlier. It has neither the motto CONFIDO, nor the word *Goldberry*; but, as will be observed, it has a coronet and helmet below the dexter hand. For this cut we are indebted to John Fullarton, Esq. of Overtoun. It was executed for Pont's *Topography of Cunningham*, lately printed for the Maitland Club.

The Kilmarnock Burgh Seal is similar to the Arms of the Boyd, save that it wants the coronet and helmet, as well as the two squirrels. Around the Shield are the words, SIGILLUM COMMUNE BURGI DE KILMARNOCK, and beneath it, VIRTUTE ET INDUSTRIA.

V.

THE FURNITURE OF DEAN CASTLE IN 1611.

As we have given in Chapter II, a somewhat minute description of the various apartments of Dean Castle, it may be interesting to our readers to know the style in which they were furnished two hundred and fifty-three years ago. This is shown by the following list, which we copy, with the explanatory notes, from the *Scottish Journal* for September, 1847. The list was taken from a document among the Boyd papers, bearing date 25th July, 1612, and is as follows:

"Twa cowpis of siluer, every ane of thaim vechtain ten unce of siluer; ane lang carpet, half worset half selk; ane schort carpet for the chalmer buird; ane lang greine buird claithe, the lenthe of the haill buird; twa schort greine buird claithis for |the chalmer buird; four cuschownis of tripe veluet;* four cushownis of carpet ruche vark; thrie sehewit cuschownis of the forme of cowering vark; four cuschownis of ruishe vark; twa lang buird claithis of flandiris damais; saxteine seruietis† of damais; ane lang dornick‡ buird claithe; ane lang damais towell; ane cower buirde claithe of small lynyng; ane dusoun of dornick seruiettis; ane braid dornick towell; twelf lang lyning buird claithis; four dosun and ane half of lyning seruietis; fywe buird claithis of grit lynyng; fywe dosoun of round lynyng seruietis; aucht towellis of roun hardine; four drinking claithis, twa thairof sewit with selk, and the vthur twa plaine; twa lynyng drinking claiths; ane copbuird claith; ane down bed; aucht feddir beddis, with aucht bowsteris effering thairto; auchteine codis, pairtlie filed with downis and pairt with fedderis; auchteine pair of dowbill blankettis; fywe coweringis of ruishe vark; ane fair rallow caddow;§ sevin houshauld coweringis; saxtein pair of lynyng scheittis; twa pair of heid scheittis of small lynyng, schewit with quhyet vork and perling; twa pair of heid scheittis schewit with black selk; ane pair of plaine heid scheittis; sax pair of heid scheittis; ten codwairis‖ of small lynyng, schewit with black selk; sax codwairis of small lynyne unschewit; ane stand of stampit crambassie** vorset courteinis, with ane schewit pand effering yrto; ane stand of greine champit curteinin, with ane pand effering yrto; ane vther stand of gray champit†† vorset courteinis, vith ane pand effering yrto; ane stand of greine pladine courtainis, with the pand effering yrto; ane stand of quhyet schewit courteinis; ane pair quhyet vowen courteinis, with the pand effering yrto; seventie pewdir plaitis; ane dusoun pewdir trunchoris; ten coweris of pewdir; sevinteine saisceris; two new Inglis quart stowpis; twa new quart flacownis; thrie ale tyne quart stouppis; twa ale tyne quart flacownis; ane tyne pint stoup; twa new chalmer pottis; four new tyne chandilleris; fywe grat brassin chandilleris; ane grit morter of brass, and ane iron pester; twa tyne bassings, with ane lawer of tyne; five grit brass panis; thrie meikle brassin pottis, and ane lytill brassin pot; twa iron pottis; aue grispan of brass, and ane pair of grat standard raxis; fywe lang speittis; ane grit iron tank; ane meikill frying pan, and aue grit masking fatt; thrie gyill fattis;

---

* Tripe veluet—an inferior kind of velvet. † Seruietis (servitis)—table napkins.
‡ Dornick—a species of linen table-cloth.
§ Rallow caddow—a kind of streaked or rayed woollen cloth.
‖ Codwairis—pillow-slips. ** Crambassie (crammasy)—crimson.
†† Champit—having raised figures.

APPENDIX. 309

twa meikill barralls; four lyttill barralls; ane burnest, and twa grit iron chimnays; twa pair of taingis; ane chalmer chimnay; twa lang hall buirds; thrie furmis; ane schort hall buird; twa chalmer buirdis; twa chyiris of aick; ane copbuird of aick; sax buffet stuillis; ane meikill bybill;* twa meikill meill gurnells of aick; thrie cofferis; twa grit kistis of aick for keiping of naipperie; four less kistis; and ane candill kist; twa stand bedis of aick."

VI.

CLEANING THE STREETS IN 1735.

In this year the first scheme, we believe, of a systematic kind for cleaning the streets of the town was put in operation by the magistrates and members of council; and the fact is worthy of record, as it shows, in some degree, the progressive improvement of the period; for nothing, perhaps, is a greater indication of civilization among a people than habits of cleanliness. The following document respecting the matter we insert for the satisfaction of the curious:

"The Bailies of Kilmarnock subscrybing recommend a voluntary contribution among the neighbourheod for cleaning the causeys and public strelt at the mercat place how oft occasion requyres—to be paid yearly to the person that shall undertake the same. And as it is proposed that the toun council be at one half of this charge, the neighbourhood are only to defray the other half, appoynts John Hunter, merchant, to make tryal herein, and get the first year's allowance from these concern'd and report. Given at Kilmarnock this twenty-ninth of October, 1735 years.

"Ja. Dow.
"Rot Paterson.

"William Gilchrist sixe pence pd. Baillie Robb sixe pence pd. William Thomson three pence pd. John Wilson two pence pd. John Broun two pence pd. Alexr Mason, two pence pd. Thomas Broun two pence pd. John Parker on penie. robart Jamson on penie. Robert Hunter Junior 9 pence pd. William Smith twopene pd. William Bankhead two pence pd. George Mitchell three pence pd. Thomas Findlay 2 pence. hew gutrie 2 pns pyed. John Glen four pnc pd. William Parker four pence. William Steuart, thre pence. Adam Greg, two pence pd. William Moris 2d. pd. Mathew Hopken 1 p. paid. William Richmont 2d. pd. James Allan 2 pd. Bailli Paterson 4d. John Dickie 2d. pd. James Simpson 2d. pd. adam dickie 2 pns pyed. Rot Kerr 3d. pd. moungo borland 2 pns pd. william hunter on penie pyd. Matt. Miller tuo pence. James Adam two penc pyed."

The expense incurred yearly by cleaning the streets about the year 1763 is shown by the following extract from the Town Treasurer's Book: "Pd Wm Robinson for clating the streets from Lamass, 1763 to 1764, 6s. & a grape Shaft 4d." Another extract or two may be made, showing that matters of cleanliness were not less attended to about ninety years ago than at the present day: "Oct. 1780, Paid for advertising Removing Dunghills, 1s!" "Paid officers and Drummer for advertising the Inhabitants to sweep their chimneys every 3 months, 1s."

---

* This "meikill bybill" [bible] is the only book, it will be observed, that is mentioned in the inventory.

VII.

"THE RED STEUART."

TIMOTHY PONT, when noticing the more remarkable matters connected with Kilmarnock, says: "Item: not far from Kilmarnock, in ye midell of ye river Iruin, was the Read Steuart slaine, after he had receaved a Responce from a vitch yat he should not perrish nather in Kyle or zet in Cuninghame, the said river being the merch betwext the two, and being in nather of them."

The "Red Steuart," according to Crawford, quoted in the Notes on Pont, was "Sir John Stewart of Dundonald, a natural son of King Robert the Second," and was "commonly called the Red Stewart from his complexion." Of his fate, however, a somewhat different account is given by Crawford. After stating that "King James the First, his nephew, conferred the honour of knighthood" on him, "at the solemnity of his coronation, anno 1424," he says: "But the same year, James Stewart, son of Murdoch, Duke of Albany, upon his father's imprisonment, accompanied with a number of outlaws, came to the town of Dumbarton, set it on fire, and surprised Sir John Stewart of Dundonald, whom he killed, with several others."

VIII.

"RABBLING THE MINISTER."*

THE following curious particulars regarding the rabbling of the Rev. Robert Bell, parson of Kilmarnock, about the year 1689, are given in Stephen's *History of the Church of Scotland*. It appears that an account of the affair was written by Mr Bell himself, in whose words it is chiefly related by Stephen:

"Mr Bell having been requested by his neighbour minister at Rickerton to celebrate the marriage of two persons at that church, in the minister's necessary absence, as he was walking thither, he was seized by two armed men, who came from a great party which he saw at some distance. One of them, as he came near to him, presented a musket at his head; whereupon he told him he was his prisoner, and would go where he had a mind to carry him. He having recovered his musket, placed Mr Bell betwixt himself and his companion in arms; in this posture he was brought to the minister of Rickerton's house, where he was commanded to pull off

---

* "Rabbling the ministers," as the rude treatment which the curates met with in 1689 was called, took place in various localities in Ayrshire; and in Glasgow an affray of the kind occurred at which even blood was shed.—*(See Chronicles of Saint Mungo.)* Macaulay, when alluding to these disorders, says: "In justice to these men [the rioters] it must be owned that they had suffered such oppression as may excuse, though it cannot justify, their violence; and that, though they were rude even to brutality, they do not appear to have been guilty of any intentional injury to life or limb." According to the same authority, such tumultuous proceedings were condemned by the more sober portion of the Covenanters.

APPENDIX. 311

his hat, calling him rogue and rascal at the same time, and otherwise treating him very rudely. . . . From this house the minister was carried prisoner to Kilmarnock. . . . When they came to the bridge, they met the whole of the aforesaid party returning from the market-place, where they had compelled the church-officer to deliver up the keys of the church. They then discharged, by way of proclamation, the minister, whom, in an opprobrious manner, they called the *curate* of Kilmarnock, from all intromission with the benefice and casualty of the church, or the least exercise of the ministerial function. . . . From this place they carried him back to his house, and there compelled him to deliver into their hands the *Book of Common Prayer* of the Church of England. After this, they led him as a prisoner, bareheaded, betwixt four files of musketeers, through a great part of the town unto the marketplace, where the whole party, which appeared to be about the number of two hundred, was drawn up in battalia. They were armed with firelock muskets, and pistols. The market-crosses were large, upright shafts placed on a flight of circular steps. On the uppermost step these rude guards placed Mr Bell, with two of their number, one on each hand, and others ranged themselves downwards on the other steps. They called for fire, when one of their commanders made a speech to the people, whom curiosity in some, and malignity in others, had collected round the cross. After this, another of their commanders, taking the *Book of Common Prayer*, read the title of it, and, elevating his voice very high, told the people 'that in persuasion of the aforementioned League and Covenant, they were now publicly to burn this *Book of Common Prayer*, which is so full of superstition and idolatry;' and then throwing it into the fire, and blowing the coals with a pair of bellows, and catching it from amidst the flames, he fixed it on the point of a pike, and lifted it up amidst the shouts of the conspirators, 'Down with prelacy, idolatry, and superstition of the churches of England and Scotland!' They afterwards cut the skirt of Mr Bell's gown with a sword, and ultimately dismissed him as 'an ignorant, obdurate curate and malignant.'"

IX.

FASTERN'S E'EN.

In the spring of 1858, an attempt was made to revive the old holiday of Fastern's E'en; and amusements, consisting of foot-racing, pony-racing, leaping, &c., "came off" that year in a field to the east of the town. The sports, however, were continued for only two or three seasons, when they were again given up.

As further illustrative of the origin of Fastern's E'en, and of the way in which it was observed in early times, we give the following from the *Kilmarnock Journal* of the 6th March, 1836:

"The Scottish name of this day is much older than the English one; for, according to Jamieson (learned in ancient lore), Shrove-Tuesday is not to be found in Anglo-Saxon. In that language, *Faesten* signifies to fast; and, consequently, *Fasten's E'en*, or *Fastern's E'en*, is the evening before the fast. In the German, it is called *Fastnacht*, and *Fastel-abend;* in the Danish, *Fastel-aun;* and in the Belgic, *Vasten-avond:* the words, *abend, aun,* and *avond,* signifying *evening* in these languages, as *nacht* does *night* in German. In ancient days, when the Catholic religion was dominant in

Britain, this feast was observed with many ceremonies and sports. Being the day immediately preceding the *Fast* of Lent, the 'haill inhabitants,' from 'the old country gentleman, all of the olden time,' down to the menial servant, thought themselves entitled to indulge in every kind of extravagance and madness. Accordingly, in old authors, we have accounts of pancake feasts—matches at football—throwing at the hen—thrashing the hen—throwing at cocks—shying at cocks—'preparing of bacon meat, and the making of savoury black puddings for good cheer—besides domestic feasting and revelry, with dice, cardplaying, and an immensity of mumming.' This, too, was the apprentices' holiday; and, in the words of an old author, 'men and boys all ate and drank, and abandoned themselves to every kind of sportive folly, as if resolved to have their fill of pleasure before they were to die.' Crowdie is mentioned by Sir F. M. Eden *(State of the poor)* as a never-failing dinner on this day with all ranks of the people in Scotland, as pancakes are in England. ' A ring,' says he, ' is put into the basin or porringer of the unmarried folks, to the finder of which, by fair means, it was an omen of marriage before the rest of the eaters.' In Stewart's *Popular Superstitions of the Highlands*, the observances of Fastern's E'en are minutely recorded. He says that the ring is put into the crowdie or brose, made of ' the bree of a good fat jiggot of mutton.' This, with plenty of other good cheer being despatched, the *Bannich Junit*, or ' sauty bannocks,' are brought out. They are made of eggs and meal, mixed with salt, to make them ' sauty '—they have a ' charm ' in them which enables the *finder* to *find out* his future wife; and he to whom it falls is sure—if not already married—to be married before the next anniversary. The *Bannich brander*, or ' dreaming bannocks,' then find a place in the feast. They contain a ' little of that substance which chimney-sweeps call soot;' and on baking them the baker must be as mute as a stone; for one word uttered by him would destroy the whole charm. Each person gets one—slips off quietly to bed—lays his head on his bannock, and expects to see his sweetheart in his sleep."

X.

PROGRESS OF THE TOWN SINCE 1816.

The following brief account of the progress of the town since 1816, has been written from memory, but will, we believe, be found nearly correct:

To begin at the head of the town: There were then no houses at Beansburn, except a little row of thatched cottages, some of which are still there. The Townholm, which is now nearly filled with buildings, was then a corn-field. The only houses near it were the old Foundry buildings at the head of the field, and a little cottage which still stands at the foot of it. The road to the Foundry went round by Tam's Loup, and thence along the edge of the water. Various buildings, especially public works, have likewise been erected at the head of High Street and in Menford Lane. Dean Street was not so large as it now is. There were no houses in Witch Road, and none in Hill Street, save one or two where Witch Road joins it, and an old tollhouse and another building which stood at the head of what was then called "Kilmaurs Brae." Neither was there a single dwelling where Buchanan Street, India Street, and Henrietta Street branch off from Hill Street, or where Park Place or

Montgomery Street stands. Several of the houses in Wellington Street were not then built. The site of Henderson Church was a garden stocked with old fruit trees, and the site of the houses near it, on the east side of Portland Street, was also garden ground attached to the houses in Back Street. Union Street, in the same quarter, was opened up only about two years ago. West George Street, at the head of which was a bowling-green, was not formed till after 1819; neither was East George Street. Langlands Street, West Langlands Street, North Hamilton Street, Kadikoi Place, and Bonnieton Square occupy ground which was then under the tillage of the husbandman, and considered by the townspeople as in the country. The most of the houses in Morton Place, including the Observatory, and also the whole of those in Park Street and Park Lane have been built since that time.

To return to Portland Street: The George Inn was not erected, and there were some empty steadings between it and the Cross. The Cross also has a more spacious and improved appearance by the recent opening of Duke Street and the erection of its elegant buildings. The most of the villas and houses in London Road are comparatively modern. King Street itself—our principal street—was not completed for some time after 1816. About 1818 a weaver's shop and a few old rickety structures stood on the Sandbed side of it, near the present Bridge Lane, and on the other side some fens were unoccupied. St Marnock Street, St Marnock Place, Dundonald Road, Portland Terrace, South Hamilton Street, and Grange Terrace are all modern, and at the time to which we refer, there was no building in that direction except Kilmarnock House and its offices, and a few little huts or cottages which stood between the policies of the mansion and Kilmarnock Water, and where the celebrated Haw's Well was situated (see note, page 260).

The additions which have been made to the town on the east of King Street are no less remarkable. Mill Lane, or "Between the Dykes," as it was then called, from two tall hedges with which it was enclosed, had no houses in it except a smithy, a barn, and one or two old structures which stood near the site of the present Reformed Presbyterian Church, where we recollect seeing the spinning of thairm carried on in our boyhood. Clark Street was then without a single house, and was the site of gardens or a nursery. The populous street called Robertson Place, together with Welbeck Street, was not formed, and no habitation was in that direction save the house of the late Mr James Hamilton, gardener, which stood on the rising ground near Mr Dick's park. The ground on which Fowlds Street stands was a nursery, possessed by Mr Fowlds, whose name it bears. The site of Princes Street and part of that of Queen Street were in the same nursery. St Andrew's Street, or the "Back Road," as it was termed, is in a great measure a new street, and at the time of which we speak, two tall forest trees, probably the remains of some ancient plantation, grew at the head of it, near the foot of King Street. Bentinck Street is comparatively modern; so is West Netherton Street; and in East Netherton Street several new houses have been erected. In short, so numerous are the additions which have been made to Kilmarnock since about the year 1816, that it may now be considered an entirely new town compared with what it was at that period.

APPENDIX.

XI.

CLUBS.

The earliest of our literary Clubs, of which we know any particulars, was the Forensic Society. It was instituted about 1831, and continued to meet weekly for several years. At each meeting an original paper on some important subject was read; after which a debate ensued on the sentiments it contained. Several of the members, we may mention, afterwards rose to some distinction as authors, &c. Among these may be named Mr James Paterson, the publisher of our first Kilmarnock newspaper, and author of the *Families of Ayrshire*, &c.; F. G. P. Neison, author of *Vital Statistics*, &c.; the late Hugh Craig; and the late Dr John Taylor of Ayr: all of whom we have already had occasion to notice. Dr Taylor was perhaps the leading member of the club. As an extempore speaker he had few equals. He was fluent in expression, impassioned in delivery, and never failed to impart a charm by the freshness and beauty of his ideas, and by his finely rounded sentences.

The Burns Club, which still exists, was formed in January, 1855, and, like other societies bearing the same name, was established in honour of our great national poet, Robert Burns. One of its objects is to hold quarterly meetings for social intercourse and the reading of such original papers as any of the members may be pleased to produce. Its chief aim, however, is to meet annually for the celebration of the birthday of the poet.

The Kilmarnock Medical Club was instituted in 1856, and consists of the various medical practitioners residing in the town and its neighbourhood. It was formed, we understand, at the suggestion of Dr Paxton, with the design of affording the members an opportunity of meeting together for the discussion of subjects connected with the profession, and also for cultivating a friendly feeling with each other. The club meets quarterly; and in the winter season each member in rotation gives an annual entertainment to the others in his own house. By this friendly union of the medical men the public is much benefited, as they are always ready to act in good accord when their joint services are required. The presidency of the club is decided by seniority. Donald M'Leod, M.D., is honorary secretary.

We may state that there are seven medical men at present in the town, namely, Drs Aitken, Paxton, Borland, Thomson, M'Leod, Marshall, and Smith, by whom, we believe, some of the most difficult operations in surgery have been performed with marked success.

Another society, called the Kilmarnock Eclectic Club, though it has not met for some time past, may also be briefly noticed. It was formed in 1857, in order "that persons of liberal tastes and studies," as expressed in its rules, "might have opportunities of meeting together socially, and of enjoying the benefits which such intercourse, under judicious regulations, necessarily confers." The producing of papers is not imperative; but able, though short, original articles are frequently read on some branch of art, science, literature, or antiquities. Alexander Smith, author of the *Life Drama*, &c., the Rev. P. Hately Waddell of Glasgow, and Horatio M'Culloch, the celebrated landscape-painter, are honorary members of the club.

XII.

THE SNOW-STORM OF SATURDAY, 3RD MARCH, 1827.

This remarkable snow-storm, which occurred, as stated above, on Saturday, the 3rd of March, 1827, will be long remembered in this locality. In several places of the town the snow was about twenty feet deep; and some of the country roads in the vicinity were so filled up, that the tops of the tall hedges with which they were skirted could scarcely be discerned. Unfortunately, too, the storm proved fatal to one of our townsmen, Mr John Brown, shoemaker. He was a passenger in the Telegraph coach from Glasgow to Kilmarnock; and on its being arrested near Drumboy Hill, he, along with the driver and two fellow-travellers, left it to seek assistance at Logan's Well Inn, when he lost his way, and perished amid the trackless snow. The county newspaper of the time thus describes the occurrence: "It began to snow about 9, A.M., and continued without intermission for nearly twenty-four hours. Towards evening a strong east wind arose, and the rising drift speedily shut up the roads, and put a stop to travelling. The coaches were all arrested eastward. The Ayr Telegraph for Glasgow, which left Kilmarnock with six horses, came to an anchor between the two Fenwicks; that for Ayr lies at the foot of Drumboy Hill. The Regulator is somewhere about Logan's Well; the Kilmarnock coach, the Britannia, near the Mearns; and the English coach, about Mauchline. The Telegraph coach from Glasgow seems to have encountered the greatest difficulties. On her being stopped at Drumboy Hill, the guard joined the five inside passengers in the coach, whilst the driver and three outsides resolved to proceed to King's Well, about a mile and a half distant, to procure assistance; and the driver accordingly, after many deviations, reached the inn with some of the horses. Such was the war of the elements, that no aid could be given at this time, and the six people remained in the coach. About midnight two of the outside passengers, after floundering about for six hours, came again in their wanderings upon the coach, which they at first mistook for a house, and were taken in greatly exhausted; and here till next day did those eight remain in great distress, and half suffocated by the snow drifting over them to the depth of four or five feet. The third passenger, Mr John Brown, shoemaker, Kilmarnock, was not, however, even so fortunate. He missed both his way and his fellow-travellers, and sank beneath the shelter of the shapeless drift. His body was found on Monday, and brought to Kilmarnock in the evening."

Regarding the effects of the storm in Kilmarnock, the same authority says: "Our streets on Sunday morning presented a novel appearance. Deep snow, wreathed in all directions, covered every thing. The churches remained vacant; and those meeting-houses which did attempt public worship were thinly attended. People were employed to cut foot-paths—clearing the streets being out of the question. The snow lay in wreaths in some places to the height of from twelve to twenty feet. There has been no snow-storm here like the present since 1795."

We may add, that the Regulator coach, mentioned above, which left Glasgow for Kilmarnock with six horses, also encountered great difficulties. It got only about a hundred yards beyond Logan's Well Inn, when the horses were floundering in wreaths of snow of about five feet in depth. Fortunately, however, they were extricated from their perilous position, and the coach was dragged backwards to the inn. The Rev. Dr George Smith, of the Low Church (now of the Tolbooth

Church, Edinburgh), was one of the passengers, and though anxious to get to Kilmarnock, where he was to preach the next day, he was compelled to remain till Monday in Logan's Well house. As another instance of the unusual nature of the storm, we may state, that when the Doctor looked out of his bed-room window in the morning, he was much struck by seeing the back court filled with snow to the eaves of the outhouses, and the post-gig sticking up on the top of a huge wreath at a short distance from the inn.

XIII.

THE CHURCHYARDS.

A NUMBER of human bones was discovered in 1860, in the lane adjoining the Low Church, when workmen were forming a drain. Others, with the remains of a coffin, were afterwards found at the rebuilding of a house in Bank Street. From these discoveries it has been inferred, that the Low Churchyard extended at one time to the edge of the river, and also over the ground now occupied by Low Church Lane. This old graveyard has not been used since about 1850; and St Andrew's cemetery, which was opened about the end of 1837 or the beginning of 1838, is now the common place of sepulture. The burying-ground of the High Church, and that of St Andrew's Church which was laid off in 1856, are private property, and available only to those to whom the respective lairs belong. From the 23rd August, 1843, to the 15th July, 1864, the interments in three of the cemeteries, namely, the Low Churchyard, St Andrew's burying-ground, and St Andrew's Church burying-ground, amounted to twelve thousand and eighty.

XIV.

EXTRACTS FROM THE OLD KIRK RECORDS.

THE following entries from the Kirk Treasurer's Books show the nature of the disbursements to the poor in the olden time:

"1692.—To Bessie Miller, to buy blankets to her, £1 Scots."

"1692.—To Robt Barr, for making Bessie Miller's grave, two shilling, and fortien shilling of charity, £2 13s. 4d. Scots."

"1703.—To Jean Gray, in Walstoun, to bind ane old bible, 7s. Scots."

"1704.—To John Gillies, a poor man from Lochwhingoch, 6s. Scots."

"1711.—Given to a stranger at the Kirk door, 8s. Scots."

"1712.—Given to John Miller's child for a Psalm book, 4s. Scots."

"1712.—Given to John Wylie to help to pay his coffin, £2 8s. Scots."

"1712.—Given to a paralatick man, a stranger, 15s. Scots."

"1713.—For a dead coffin to Margaret Fulton, £1 16s. Scots."

"1713.—To a lame seaman, by ye 2 ministers app., 18s. Scots."

"1714.—To Baylie Moris, for drugs to the poor Lad's arm that was cut off, £10 1s. 1d. Scots."

"1714.—To Baylie Tough, upon ye same account, £6 16s. Scots."

"1714.—To the poor Lad himself, the remainder that was left, £12 6s. Scots."

"1716.—To ane old man, ane 118 years of age on precept, 12s. Scots."

"1755.—To Mr Adie, for teaching poor scholars for three months, £5 19s. Scots."

"1759.—To a Coat for James Boyd, 9s. 4d. sterling."

A few other entries relative to other matters may be given:

"1697.—To Baylie Paterson, for going doun to ervin and giving drink money to the founders of the bell, £9 8s. Scots."*

"1697.—For bringing the bell out of ervin, £1 9s. Scots."

"1699.—To William Thomson, at the Session's desire, to buy a horse, £6 Scots."

"1699.—To pay half a galloun of ale, at the raising of stones to the minister's dyke, 10s. 8d. Scots."

"1717.—To Jock Nickol, for cutting doun ye hemlock in Kirkyard, 6s. Scots."

"1733.—From Adam, an Irishman, for all the bad coin got from the former treasurer, and some a cumnock man got, £10 15s. Scots."

"1751.—To cash collected publickly for the sufferers by the fire in the Gorbals of Glasgow, £192 Scots."

XV.

THE JUGGS.

The following extracts, the first of which is from the Kilmarnock Kirk Records, and the others from the Records of the "New Kirk of Kilmarnock" (see page 134), show the character of the offences for which individuals were sentenced by the ecclesiastical courts to droe penance in the juggs:

"June 4, 1646.—The Qlk day compeired Andro M——, and is ordained, with the advyse of the Presbetrie, to satisfie; who, instead of his willingnes to obey the presbeytrie order, in face of the Session, cursed Janet M——; for the which the Session ordaines him to be put *presentlie* in the *joggs*, and upon the Saboth next to acknowlege that his offence in the publick place, and pay fortie shillings of penaltie."

"Jany 15, 1645.—The qlk Day compeared David W——, being accused, confessed his scandalous carriage of cursing in the Kirk on the Sabboth Day, ye people being convened, and thurfor is ordained to stand in the *jogges* and in the Kirk upon ye public place."

"Feby 9, 1645.—The qlk day compeared Bessie R——, and for her gross miscarriage and upbraiding of ye Session from off ye public place of repentance, and being found guilty, with confession of her fault, is ordained to stand in the *joges* two hours before sermon the nixt Lord's Day, and to appear two several Days before the congregation on ye publick place to give satisfaction."

---

* This was no doubt the old bell mentioned at page 10. It appears from this entry to have been founded at Irvine.

XVI.

LIST OF THE MAGISTRATES, TREASURERS, PROVOSTS, AND CLERKS OF THE BURGH OF KILMARNOCK, FROM 1695 TILL 1863.

[It has been stated (page 8) that for about one hundred years from the date of the original Charter of 1591, the Burgh was governed by a Baron-Bailie.* The names of those who held that office we have not been able to discover; but we find mention made of Robert Rodger, treasurer, in 1690, and Matthew Hopkin, treasurer, in 1694.

In the following list, the Treasurers, Town-Clerks, and Provosts, though holding office for several years, are mentioned only under the dates of their appointments. The names of those in the list, who are understood to be alive at this date (July, 1864), are marked thus, a.]

1695—John M'Leslie
    Robert Paterson
    Patrick Alexander, clerk
    William Moris, treasurer.
1696— . . . .
1697—Robert Paterson.
1698—Robert Hodgeart
    Jasper Tough
    Matthew Duncan, treasurer.
1699—Robert Hodgeart
    Robert Wright.
1700—Robert Wright
    William Moris
    William Fulton, treasurer.
1701—Jasper Tough
    William Moris.
1702—Jasper Tough
    Hugh Hunter.
1703—James Thomson
    Robert Wright.
1704—Hugh Hunter
    James Thomson
    James Smith, treasurer.
1705—Robert Wright
    William Baird.
1706—Robert Hodgeart
    William Baird
    Adam Dickie, treasurer.
1707—Robert Hodgeart
    William Moris.

1708—Jasper Tough
    Matthew Hopkin
    Benjamin Thomson, treasurer.†
1709—Hugh Hunter
    James Thomson
    Robert Paterson, clerk.
1710—James Thomson
    Matthew Duncan
    James Wilson, treasurer.
1711—Robert Wright
    William Moris.
1712—William Moris
    Benjamin Thomson
    William Gilmour, treasurer.
1713—James Thomson
    Robert Wright.
1714—Adam Dickie . . . . . .
    David Brown & Son, treasurers.
1715—William Moris
    Adam Dickie.
1716—William Moris
    Mungo Muir
    John Dickie, treasurer.
1717—Mungo Muir
    Adam Dickie.
1718—Mungo Muir
    Adam Dickie
    William Findlay, treasurer.
1719—Adam Dickie

---

* Before the passing of the Burgh Reform Bill, the town was governed by two Bailies, a Treasurer, and sixteen Councillors. It is now governed by a Provost, four Bailies, a Treasurer, and ten Councillors. The police department is managed by fifteen Commissioners, elected by the ratepayers, who are such as pay three pounds or upwards of yearly rent. The Provost, Bailies, Town Treasurer, and Baron-Bailie, are also Commissioners *ex officiis*.

† Up to about sixty years ago, the town treasurers received a salary of £6 13s. 4d. Scots money—equal to 11s. 1¼d sterling. In 1710, Benjamin Thomson, treasurer, enters in the book his salary in these quaint terms: "To my Dear bought cellary for 2 years as yr parson had 0013. 06. 08."

APPENDIX.

1719—Jasper Tough.
1720—Jasper Tough
　　William Baird.
1721—William Baird
　　Adam Boyd.
1722—Adam Boyd
　　Mungo Muir.
1723—Mungo Muir
　　Adam Dickie.
1724—Adam Dickie
　　James Wilson.
1725—James Wilson
　　John Glen
　　Fergus Alexander, treasurer.
1726—John Glen
　　Mungo Moor.
1727—Mungo Moor
　　Alexander Brown
　　John Morton, treasurer.
1728—Alexander Brown
　　Adam Dickie.
1729—Adam Dickie
　　Alexander Cunningham
　　James Clarke, treasurer.
1730—Alexander Cunningham
　　Adam Boyd.
1731—Adam Boyd
　　Adam Dickie
　　Hugh Campbell, treasurer.
1732—Adam Dickie
　　William Gilchrist.
1733—William Gilchrist
　　Mungo Moor
　　John Lymburner, treasurer.
1734—Mungo Moor
　　Adam Dickie.
1735—Adam Dickie
　　James Rae
　　Robert Hunter, treasurer.
1736—James Rae
　　James Wilson.
1737—James Wilson
　　William Gilchrist.
1738—William Gilchrist
　　Mungo Moor
　　James Paterson, treasurer.
1739—Mungo Moor
　　John Dickie
　　Robert Paterson, } joint clerks.
　　William Paterson, }
1740—John Dickie
　　John Wilson.
1741—John Wilson
　　William Gilchrist
　　William Hunter, treasurer.
1742—William Gilchrist
　　James Paterson.
1743—James Paterson
　　John Dickie.
1744—John Dickie
　　George Mitchell.
1745—George Mitchell
　　James Paterson.

1746—James Paterson
　　William Gilchrist.
1747—William Gilchrist
　　John Wilson
　　John Murchlan, treasurer.
1748—John Wilson
　　George Mitchell.
1749—George Mitchell
　　John Lymburner.
1750—John Lymburner
　　John Dickie
　　David Brown, treasurer.
1751—John Dickie
　　George Mitchell.
1752—George Mitchell
　　James Wilson.
1753—James Wilson
　　William Gilchrist.
1754—William Gilchrist
　　George Mitchell
　　David Hunter, treasurer.
1755—George Mitchell
　　Robert Paterson.
1756—Robert Paterson
　　William Thomson
　　John Hunter, junr, treasurer.
1757—William Thomson
　　John Parker.
1758—John Parker
　　John Lymburner.
1759—John Lymburner
　　William Muir
　　William Gregory, treasurer.
1760—William Muir
　　James Wilson.
1761—James Wilson
　　John Wilson.
1762—John Wilson
　　John Lymburner
　　John Hamilton, treasurer.
1763—John Lymburner
　　David Brown.
1764—David Brown
　　John Parker.
1765—John Parker
　　John Wilson.
1766—John Wilson
　　Hugh Parker
　　Thomas Baird, treasurer.
1767—John Parker
　　James Wilson.
1768—Hugh Parker
　　John Wilson.
1769—John Wilson
　　John Hunter
　　William Paterson, clerk.
1770—William Gregory
　　James Wilson
　　John Guthrie, treasurer.
1771—John Parker
　　Hugh Parker.
1772—Hugh Parker
　　John Gemmell.

1773*—John Parker
    David Hunter
    James Meuros, treasurer.
1774—David Hunter
    Hugh Parker.
1775—Hugh Parker
    John Hunter.
1776—John Parker
    James Meuros.
1777—John Parker
    John Gemmell
    William Cumming, treasurer.
1778—John Gemmell
    David Hunter.
1779—David Hunter
    John Parker.
1780—James Wilson
    Dr William Hamilton.
1781—Dr William Hamilton
    William Smith.
1782—William Smith
    William Cumming
    James M'Lean, treasurer.
1783—William Cumming
    John Parker.
1784—John Parker
    James Wilson.
1785—James Wilson
    William Cumming.
1786—William Cumming
    John Parker.
1787†—John Parker
    Alexander Fowlds.
1788—Alexander Fowlds
    William Parker
    John Muir, treasurer.
1789—William Parker
    Thomas Greenshields.
1790—Thomas Greenshields
    John Parker.
1791—John Parker
    John Glen, Assloss
    John Smith, treasurer
    William Brown, clerk.
1792—John Glen
    William Parker
    James Gregg, } joint clerks.
    William Brown,}
1793—William Parker
    Thomas Greenshields.
1794—Thomas Greenshields
    Alexander Fowlds.
1795—Alexander Fowlds
    John Muir
    John Wilson, treasurer.
1796—John Muir
    John Smith.
1797—Captain William Dunlop
    Alexander Fowlds
    James M'Lean, treasurer.
1798—Alexander Fowlds
    Robert Borland.
1799—Robert Borland
    William Parker.
1800—William Parker
    Alexander Fowlds
    William Brown, treasurer.
1801—Alexander Fowlds
    William Gregory.
1802—William Gregory
    Thomas Greenshields.
1803—Thomas Greenshields
    Robert Borland.
1804—Robert Borland
    John Wilson, bookseller.‡
1805—John Wilson
    William Parker.
1806—William Parker
    Robert Borland.
1807—Robert Borland
    William Brown
    Robert Thomson, treasurer.
1808—William Brown
    Thomas Greenshields.
1809—Thomas Greenshields
    James M'Lean.
1810—James M'Lean
    William Brown.
1811—William Brown
    John Andrew
    John Thomson, treasurer.
1812—John Andrew
    Robert Thomson.
1813—Robert Thomson
    Thomas Greenshields.
1814—Thomas Greenshields
    James M'Lean.
1815—James M'Lean
    John Andrew.
1816—John Andrew
    John Thomson
    James Porteous, treasurer.
1817—John Thomson
    William Brown.
1818—William Brown
    Thomas Greenshields.
1819—James Porteous
    John Fulton
    James Thomson, treasurer.
1820—John Fulton

* This year, the Right Honourable James, Lord Kilmaurs, was one of the Councillors.

† In consequence of no commission having been received this year from the Superior, Miss Scott, the Council elected the magistrates. The Leit was read at Dean Castle.

‡ The printer of the first edition of Burns's Poems.

APPENDIX. 321

1820—John Thomson
    John M'Cubbin, treasurer.
1821—William Brown
    Thomas Greenshields
    Archibald Finnie, treasurer.
1822—Thomas Greenshields
    James Porteous.
1823—James Porteous
    William Wallace.
1824—William Wallace
    William Rankin.
1825—William Rankin
    William Cumming.
1826—William Cumming
    Archibald Finnie
    John Colvil, treasurer.
1827—Archibald Finnie
    Thomas Greenshields.
1828—Thomas Greenshields
    Ebenezer Smith.
1829—Ebenezer Smith
    James Crooks.
1830—James Crooks
    Matthew Strang.
1831—Matthew Strang
    William Rankin.
1832—Archibald Finnie
    John Colvil
    Matthew Brown, treasurer
    George Douglas, } joint clerks.
    a Alex. Hamilton,
1833—JOHN ANDREW, Provost
    Thomas Morton
    a Hugh Wilson
    George Young
    Hugh Craig
    Matthew Gilmour, treasurer.
1834—JAMES REED, M.D., Provost
    William Geddes
    George Young
    a Hugh Wilson
    Hugh Craig.
1835—William Geddes
    Hugh Craig
    Matthew Brown
    a Thomas Mack
    George Paxton
    Robert Bunten, treasurer.
1836—Hugh Craig
    George Paxton
    John Brown
    a Thomas Mack
    Robert Cumming, treasurer.
1837—ARCHIBALD FINNIE, Provost
    George Paxton
    John Brown
    a Thomas Neil
    a Hugh Wilson
    Robert Blackwood, treasurer
    a Robert Crooks, treasurer.
1838—John Brown
    a Thomas Neil
    a Hugh Wilson
    Robert Cumming.

1839—*a* Hugh Wilson
    Matthew Strang
    a Thomas Gregory
    Hugh Reid.
1840—WILLIAM BROWN, Provost
    Matthew Strang
    a Thomas Gregory
    Hugh Reid
    John Brown
    a John Dickie, treasurer.
1841—MATTHEW STRANG, Provost
    a Robert Crooks
    Hugh Reid
    James Blackwood
    John Brown.
1842—John Brown
    a Robert Crooks
    James Blackwood
    a Hugh Wilson.
1843—James Blackwood
    a Hugh Wilson
    John Brown
    George Young.
1844—JOHN BROWN, Provost
    a Hugh Wilson
    George Young
    a John Dickie
    Robert Cumming
    a William Taylor, treasurer
    a John Thomson, treasurer.
1845—Robert Cumming
    a James Donald
    a John Dickie
    a William Taylor.
1846—*a* John Dickie
    James Blackwood
    a James Donald
    Robert Cumming
    a James S. Gregory, treasurer.
1847—ROBERT CUMMING, Provost
    a James Donald
    a John Dickie
    a John Watt
    a Thomas Mack.
1848—*a* John Watt
    a James S. Gregory
    Captain Speirs
    a Thomas Mack
    a John Torrance, treasurer.
1849—Captain Speirs
    a Thomas Mack
    Andrew Aitken
    John Howie.
1850—Andrew Aitken
    John Howie
    a John Torrance
    a David Rankin
    a James Brown, treasurer.
1851—Andrew Aitken
    a David Rankin
    a John Watt
    Hugh Craig.
1852—*a* JAMES DONALD, Provost
    a John Watt

2 U

1852—*a* Thomas Mack
    a George M'Laren
    a James Laughland
    a James Wilson, treasurer.
1853—*a* John Watt
    a Thomas Mack
    a James Laughland
    a George M'Laren.
1854—*a* Thomas Mack
    a John Dickie
    a William Taylor
    a James Laughland.
1855—*a* JOHN DICKIE, Provost
    a Hugh Wilson
    a James Brown
    a George M'Laren
    a James Laughland.
1856—*a* Hugh Wilson
    a George M'Laren
    a James Laughland
    a Thomas Mack
    a Alexander Brown, treasurer
    a Peter Sturrock, treasurer.
1857—*a* James Laughland
    a Thomas Mack
    a Archibald Finnie
    a John Watt.

1858—*a* ARCHIBALD FINNIE, Provost
    a Thomas Mack
    a John Watt
    a Thomas Cuthbertson
    a John Crooks.
1859—*a* John Watt
    a Thomas Cuthbertson
    a John Crooks
    a Andrew Barclay
    a John Bicket, treasurer.
1860—*a* John Crooks
    a Hugh Wilson
    a James Brown
    a William Mitchell.
1861—*a* JOHN CROOKS, Provost
    a Hugh Wilson
    a James Brown
    a William Mitchell
    a William Simpson.
1862—*a* Hugh Wilson
    a William Mitchell
    a William Simpson
    a John Bicket
    a James Watson, treasurer.
1863—*a* William Simpson
    a John Bicket
    a Hugh Wilson
    a William Mitchell.

INDEX.

Academy, erection of, 143; document deposited in the foundation of, 144; first teachers of, 144; present ditto, 145-6.
Academy, Drawing, &c., 248.
Academy, "E. U." Theological, 157.
Adam, John, teacher, 136.
Adam, R. P., of Tour, 186 *(note)*.
Adie, James, teacher, 138.
Agricultural Society, 294.
Agriculture, state of, 295.
Aird, James, of Milton, covenanter, 45.
Aird, Marion P., poetical writer, 253-4.
Airth, David, teacher, 135.
Aitken, James, M.D., 186 *(note)*, 294.
Aitken, Rev. James, 105, 223.
Albany, Duke of, 23.
Albert Tower, 284, 286.
Alexander III grants lands to Sir Robert Boyd, 20.
Alexander, James, teacher, 135.
Alexander, Jean, murder of, 188-9.
Andersonne, Johne, teacher, 134.
Andrews, T. B., A.V.R., 292.
Architectural Erections, ancient (A.D. 1600), 9; modern, 284.
Arran, Countess of, prisoner in Dean Castle, 15; marries Lord Hamilton, 32.
Arran, Earl of, *see* Boyd, Thomas, (5).
Athenæum reading-room, 277, 285.
Auber, artiste, 257.
Ayr Advertiser, extracts from, 176, 189, 191 *(note)*.
Ayrshire Examiner, 215.
Ayrshire Miscellany, 192, 243.
Ayrshire Reformer, 214.
Ayrshire Volunteer Artillery, 5th Co., 293; Rifles, 1st Co., 292, 9th Co., 293.
Ayrshire Wreath, 216.

Baird, Thomas, trial of, for sedition, 203; death of, 204.
Balmerino, Lord, trial of, for treason, 75.
Bank, the first, in Kilmarnock, 4.
Banks, the present, 291.
Bannockburn, the 3rd Sir Robert Boyd at the battle of, 21.
Barbour, quoted, 2.
Barclay, Thomas, artist, 249.

Bathgate, Rev. William, 158.
Beaton, John, periodical writer, 215.
Beattie, Dr, his character of the Earl of Errol, 91.
Bell, the old church, 10.
Bell, B. R., first sheriff-substitute, 185.
Bell, Sir Charles, 246.
Bell, Henry Glassford, 252.
Bell, Rev. Robert, 132.
Benevolent Societies, 294.
Benger, Miss, authoress, 246.
Bequests, list of old charitable, 131 *(note)*; modern benevolent, 294.
Berghem, artist, 247.
Birthdays, Kings', 107.
Black, Rev. Davidson, 158.
Blair, Bryce, engineer, 236.
Blind Harry, quoted, 21.
Bonnet-makers' Records, extracts from, 36 *(note)*.
Bonnieton Square, 282.
Bordona, artiste, 257.
Borland Water, 11; source of, 261 *(note)*.
Borland, Dr John, his services in visitations of Cholera, 212; presentations to, 213; surgeon to the 9th A.V.R., 293.
Boston, Thomas, free mason, 280.
Boswell, James, his description of Slains Castle, 90.
Bouverie, Honourable E. P., 208.
Bowie, John, sculptor, 55.
Bowl-playing, 115.
Bowring, Dr John, 208; banquet to, 254.
Boyd, Adam, musician, 278.
Boyd Family, origin of, 19.
Boyd, Alexander (1), son of Sir Thomas (4), superintends the training of James III, 29; accused of treason, 29; tried, 30; executed, 31.
Boyd, Alexander (2), son of Robert (4), First Lord Boyd, succeeds, 32, "Baillie and Chamberlain of Kilmarnock," 32.
Boyd, Allan, killed at the siege of Perth, 23.
Boyd, Charles, 2nd son of the last Earl of Kilmarnock, 90.
Boyd, James (1), son of Sir Robert (3), 22.
Boyd, James (2), son of Thomas (5), Earl of Arran, lands and lordship restored to him, 32, slain, 32.

Boyd, James (3), Eighth Lord Boyd, character of, 37; gives a grant to the Parish School, 134.
Boyd, Sir Robert (1), at the battle of Largs, 19; grant of lands to, 20, tradition regarding him, 20, death of, 20.
Boyd, Sir Robert (2), joins Wallace, 20; at Loudoun Hill, at the Castle of Ayr, at the siege of York, 21.
Boyd, Sir Robert (3), joins Bruce, 21; at Bannockburn, 21; grant of lands to, 22.
Boyd, Robert (4), First Lord, 29, Lord of Parliament and Lord Justiciary, 29, ambassador to England, 29, accused of treason but acquitted, 29, constituted regent, 29; marries his eldest son to the King's sister, 30, accused, cited before Parliament, flies to England, 30; condemned and outlawed, 31, death of, 31.
Boyd, Robert (5), Third Lord Boyd, estate and honours restored to, 32, at the battle of Glasgow, 32; served heir to James, son of the Earl of Arran, 33; death of, 34.
Boyd, Robert (6), Fourth Lord Boyd, at Langside, 34, one of the commissioners to England, 34, death of, 34; epitaph, 35.
Boyd, Spencer, 183 *(note)*.
Boyd, Sir Thomas (1), made prisoner at the battle of Durham, 22.
Boyd, Sir Thomas (2), *Dominus de Kilmarnock*, kills Neilson of Dalrymple, 23.
Boyd, Sir Thomas (3), Lord of Kilmarnock, a hostage for the ransom of James I, 23, imprisoned for wasting the "crown rents," 23, death of, 23; tomb of, 6.
Boyd, Sir Thomas (4), slays Stewart of Darnley, 24, killed in revenge, 24.
Boyd, Thomas (5), son of the First Lord Boyd, marries the King's sister, 30, made Earl of Arran, 30; embassy to Denmark, 30; machinations against him, 31; dies at Antwerp, 32.
Boyd, Thomas (6), Fifth Lord Boyd, a "pass" to allow him to travel, 35 *(note)*.
Boyd, Thomas, of Pitcon, 279.
Boyd, William, abbot of Kilwinning, 24.
Boyd, William, First Earl of Kilmarnock, *see* Kilmarnock, Earl of.
Boyd, William, Second Earl, *see* ditto.
Boyd, William, Third Earl, *see* ditto.
Boyd, William, Fourth Earl, *see* ditto.
Boyd, William, called Lord Boyd, son of last Earl, anecdotes of, 74, 91; letter to Col. Cranfurd, 86; recovers the lands, 89, sells them to the Earl of Glencairn, 89; succeeds to the carldom of Errol, 90; revisits Kilmarnock, 91, death of, 91; R. W. M. of St John's Lodge, 279; letter of, to the Lodge, 92 *(note)*.
Boyd, Rev. Zachary, 3 *(note)*.
Braham, artiste, 257.

Breakanridge, Thos., schoolmaster, 136.
Breckenridge & Son, 218 *(note)*, 223, 286.
Brien, Rev. John T., 226.
Brodie, Rev. Neil, 223, 224.
Brown, Rev. Adam, 221.
Brown, William, teacher, 146.
Brown, William, manufacturer, 161.
Burgh Records, extracts from, 8, 74 *(note)*, 95 *(note)*, 98 *(note)*, 107 *(note)*, 112 *(note)*, 115 *(note)*, 137, 138 *(note)*, 183 *(note)*.
Burgh School of Kilmarnock, origin of, 137, salary of the teacher of, 137; minute of Council regarding, 138 *(note)*, teachers in, 138-143, merged in the Academy, 143.
Burlaw, Laws of, 108 *(note)*.
Burns, Gilbert, 161.
Burns, Robert, his poems first issued from the Kilmarnock press, 160, "Wee Johnnie," 160 *(note)*; Kilmarnock patrons of, Tam Samson, &c., 161; quotations from, 90, 96, 162, 165, 167; H. M. of St John's Lodge, 163, 279; alehouses frequented by, 163; Centenary celebration, and principal speakers at, 186 *(note)*, widow and children of, befriended by Sir James Shaw, 232 *(note)*; portraits of, in the Town Hall, 185; in Kilbarchan, 245; by James Tannock, 246.
Burtt, Rev. John, poetical writer and divine, biographical sketch of, 196-7.
Busbie Castle, described, 33 *(note)*.

Caledonian Mercury, extracts from, 123, 125, 128.
Calico-printing introduced, 209.
Cameron, John, 285.
Campbell, Alex., periodical writer, 215.
Campbell, George, 235 *(note)*.
Campbell, John, Lord Chief Justice, 243.
Campbell, Rev. Dr John, 222.
Campbell, Rev. John, 222.
Campbell, Rev. Peter, 150, 225.
Canal from Riccarton to Troon contemplated, 168 *(note)*.
Carnegie, Rev. ——, 45.
Carpet-weaving, introduced, 95; present state of, 289.
Carrick, John D., periodical writer, 214.
Carts, first used, 95.
Chalmers, George, quoted, 99.
Chambers, quoted, 73, 84 *(note)*, 173.
Chancery, Court of, 242.
Chartist Agitation, 208.
Cholera, 210, first appearance of, 210, first victims of, 210; temporary hospital, 211; number of deaths from, 212, place of interment, 212, predisposing causes, 212; second visitation of, 213, number of deaths, 213, temporary hospital, 213, erection of permanent hospital, 213, third visitation of, 213, number of deaths from, 213.

Clerk's Lane Church, 151, first ministers of, 151; present state of, 158.
Coal-works, the first, 290 (*note*).
Cock-fighting, 111.
Coila Repository, 192.
Coins, ancient, found, 41 (*note*).
College Wynd, early buildings in, 3, school in, 3, last teacher in, 3 (*note*).
Colquhoun, John C., 208.
Connell, Dr James, teacher, 145.
Constituency, parliamentary and municipal, 287.
Cooke, Tom, artiste, 257.
Corn Exchange Buildings, 277; description of, 284-6, ceremonies at opening of, 286.
Council Chambers, erection of, 184; tragic incident in the police cells, 185; portraits in the Town Hall, 185, 246.
Court-house, erection of, &c., 283.
Covenant, and Covenanters in Kilmarnock and neighbourhood, 38, Ross and Shields, their heads set up at Kilmarnock, 38; their monumental inscription, 39; Finlay shot by order of Dalziel, 40, cruelties of the garrison of Dean Castle, 40; the Highland Host, 41; six natives of Kilmarnock transported, 43, sufferings of these and others in the Greyfriars' Churchyard, 43; on board ship, 44, five of these lost at sea, 44, their monumental inscription, 44; James Aird of Milton, 45, James Robertson, from Stonehouse, 45; John Finlay of Mulrside, 46, their dying testimonies, 46; Jasper Tough, surgeon, 47; John Nisbet tried and executed, 48; his monumental inscription, 49; Captain Paton, 51-55; tragical occurrence at Little Blackwood, 56; prisoners carried to Newmilns, 57; ordered to be shot, but rescued, 58; concluding reflections, 59.
Craig, Archibald, at the Dean Park radical meeting, 201; presides at the Morton Place radical meeting, 205; apprehended, 206, emigrates to America and becomes a preacher, 206 (*note*), death of, 206.
Craig, Hugh, 208.
Cranfurd, Colonel J. W., 85.
Cranfurd, W. H., of Craufurdland, 296.
Cranfurd, Mrs W. H., 296.
Craufurdland Castle, 296.
Craufurdland Loch, 116, 279.
Craufurdland Water, 11; source of, 261 (*note*).
Crawford, Robert, sketch of, 216; will of, 276.
Croilburn Water, source of, 261 (*note*).
Cromarty, Earl of, trial of, 75.
Crookedholm, Free Church at, 291.
Crooks, Provost John, 286.
Cross, Soulis, 25-6.

Culloden, battle of, 72; rejoicing in Kilmarnock on the victory at, 74 (*note*).
Cunningham, Sir David, of Corsehill, 279.
Cunningham, Honourable John, 280.
Cunningham, Rev. John, 96.
Cunningham, Matthew, schoolmaster, 135.
Cunningham, Peter, of Bourtriehill, 279.
Cunningham, W. C. S., of Caprington, 223.
Curdie, John, artist, 251.
Curling, game of, 115; historical and descriptive sketch of, 117.

Dalrymple, Charles, of Langlands, 279.
Dalrymple, James, of Orangefield, 280.
Dalziel, cruelties of, 39; his estimate of Captain Paton, 55 (*note*).
Dean Castle, situation, 11, derivation of the name, 11; appearance, 12, tradition regarding its ancient surroundings, 12, architecture of, 12, time of its erection, 12, visited by Grose, 12 (*note*); described by Pont, 13, original note by Mr Fullarton, 13, general description, 13-15, traditions regarding, 15, historical associations of, 15; the grounds round it, 16, partly destroyed by fire, 16; garrisoned during the persecution, 40, 50.
Deans, James Y., of Kirkstyle, 293.
Denman, Lord Chief Justice, 243.
Dickie, John, junior, A.V.R., 293.
Dickinson, Rev. John, 222.
Dobell, Sydney, poetical writer, 256.
Douglas, James, 249.
Douglas, Gavin, 31 (*note*).
Dowie, Johnnie, 163.
Drum, the Warning, 113.
Ducat Tower at Newmilns, attacked by Covenanters, 58.
Duke Street opened, 283.
Dun, William, teacher, 138.
Duncan, John, schoolmaster, 143.
Dundonald Road, 281.
Dunlop, Sir John, portrait of, in Town Hall, 185; elected M.P., 208.
Dunlop, William H., of Annanhill, 296.
Duprez, artiste, 257.

Earthquake felt at Kilmk, 178 (*note*).
Eddie, ——, teacher, 138.
Edinburgh Literary Journal, 252.
Eglinton, Earl of, portrait of, in Town Hall, 185.
Elegy on Tam Samson, incidents connected with the origin of, 164.
English traveller, anecdote of, 172.
Errol, Earl of. *see* Boyd, William (4).
Evangelical Union, 157.
Evangelical Union Academy, 157.
Evangelical Union Church in Clerk's Lane, 157-8, in Winton Place, 158.
Ewart, Charles, Sergeant in Scots Greys, 187; French eagle taken by, 188, promotion of, and public dinner to, 188, his death, 188.

INDEX.

Fairs, 106.
Falkirk, battle of, 72.
Fastern's E'en, observances at the celebration of 110-11; tumult on, 112 (*note*).
Fees, school, in 1676, 135.
Fenwick, disjunction of, from Kilmarnock parish, 5 (*note*), 131, first Kirk Session at, 131; humorous anecdote regarding a minister of, 125 (*note*).
Ferguson, Sir James, M.P., 286.
Fever Hospital, 294.
Fillans, James, sculptor, 227.
Findlay, ——, teacher, 235 (*note*).
Findlay, covenanter, 57.
Findlay, John, of Waxford, 237.
Findlay, Rev. Dr Robert, professor, sketch of, 237.
Findlay, William, 237.
Fine Arts, 245-51.
Finlay, covenanter, 40.
Finlay, John, of Muirside, 46.
Finnie, Provost Archibald, 186 (*note*), 283.
Finnie, John, of Bowdon Lodge, 284.
Fires, Kilmarnock destroyed by, 173, contributions for relief of sufferers, 173; thirty-two houses destroyed, 175, subscriptions for relief of sufferers, 175.
Fleming, William, artist, 250.
Flood of 1852, atmospheric phenomena preceding it, 260; effects at Hairshaw Mill farm, 261; Mr Alexander's spinning mill, 262; at Assloss, 263, at Dean Castle, 263; at the Foundry and the Townholm, 264; at the factory of Messrs Laughland & Co., 265, at Craighead, 265; between Townhead Bridge and foot of Green Street, 268; in Waterloo Street, 270, at the Town Buildings and Police Cells, 270; at the Cross, 271, and in King Street, &c., 271; table, shewing the height of the flood at certain principal points, 273, value of property destroyed, 273, subscriptions for relief of the poorer sufferers, 273, concluding remarks, 273-4.
Forrester, Paul R., teacher, 145.
Foster, Rev. James, attends the Earl of Kilmarnock before and at his execution, 79; describes his behaviour, 81-3.
Franck, English traveller, at Kilmarnock, 6; his description of the town, 7.
Free Henderson Church, 224.
Free High Church, 224.
Free High Church Schools, 147.
Free Masons, St Andrew's Lodge, 280.
Free Masons, St James's Nethertonholm Lodge, 280.
Free Masons, St John's Lodge, notice of, 279, letter of, to Mother Kilwinning, 279 (*note*); Earl of Kilmarnock first R.W.M., 92 (*note*); Earl of Errol, R.W.M., 92 (*note*); song addressed by Burns to, 162; lodge-room of, 163, extract from minutes, 163.

Free Masons, St Marnock Lodge, 280.
Free St Andrew's Church, 224.
Funerals attended by women, 114, church-bell at, 114 (*note*).
Fyfe, Andrew, musician, 286.
Fyfe, Wm Wallace, periodical writer, 215.

Gallows-knowe, 150.
Gallows-knowe Church, *see* United Presbyterian, Portland Road.
Galt, John, novelist, 246.
Gardiner, Maria, 95.
Gas Company, 209.
Gemmell, John, covenanter, 56.
Gibson, John, periodical writer, 215.
Gillespie, Mr, of London, 223.
Glasgow Field, battle of, 32.
Glasgow Mercury, quoted, 97 (*note*).
Glencairn, Family of, 89 (*note*).
Glencairn, Earl of, presents Rev. William Lindsay to the 2nd Charge of the Low Church, 120; presents Rev. James Mackinlay to ditto, 129; opens a new line of street, 149; R. W. M. of St Marnock Lodge, 280.
Glover, Jeanie, song writer, 170.
Glovers, 111 (*note*).
"Gold Berry," probable origin of, 20.
Goldie, John, 161; notice of, 165; works of, 166-7; proposes a canal to Troon, 167; death of, 168.
Gordon, Sir John Watson, 186.
"Goudie's Bible," anecdote regarding, 166 (*note*).
Graham, John, A.M., biographical sketch of, 138; appointed schoolmaster of Kilmarnock, 140, removes to London, 140; sale of his furniture, 141, opens a school at Pancras Wells, 141, commits forgery, 141; tried and imprisoned, 142, further forgeries, 142, apprehension and execution, 142.
Graham, Mrs John, passes the forged notes, 142, tried and condemned, but recommended to mercy, 142.
Graham, John, teacher, 145.
Graham, Rev. John, 226.
Grant, the Misses, teachers, 147.
Grant, Mrs, of Laggan, 246.
Gregory, James S., Registrar, statistical tables by, 287-8.
Gregory, William, of Virginia, letters from, 3 (*note*), 10 (*note*), 183 (*note*).
Grougar School, 146.
Gunnyon, Wm, teacher, 146, 186 (*note*).
Gunpowder, explosion of, 176.
Guthrie, Mrs, of Mount, 296.
Guthrie, Rev. William, of Fenwick, ordination of, 131; curling stone of, 118, monument of, 118.

Hall, Wm, worsted shawl printer, 209.
Hamilton, Rev. Alex., A.M., 151, 293.
Hamilton, Dr, 161.

INDEX.   327

Harkness, Alex., schoolmaster, 145-6.
Harvey's *Life of Bruce*, quoted, 22.
Harvey, Rev. Alexander, 220.
Haw's Well, 260 (*note*).
Hastings, the Marquis of, 296.
Henderson, Andrew, teacher, 143.
Henderson, William (1), teacher, 138.
Henderson, Wm (2), teacher, 143-5, 240.
Henderson Free Church, 224.
High Church, erected, 101, cost of, 101, subscriptions, 101, a Chapel of Ease, 101; change in the management, 102, parochialized, 102; ministers, 103-5.
Highland Host, list of losses by, 43 (*note*).
Hill, Rev. John, 222.
Hill Street, 282.
Hodgeart, Barbara, 237.
Hodgeart, Robert, 237.
Home, Reverend and Honourable, 83, 86.
Honthorst, Gerard, artist, 247.
Howie, Isobel, of Lochgoin, courageous act of, 52.
Hudibras, quoted, 258.
Hunter, John K., artist, 249.
Hunter, Dr Wm, London, his bequest, 294.
Hunter, author of the *Scoffing Ballad*, 128.

Independent Church, 221.
Inglis, Captain, letter to the Laird of Rowallan, 50 (*note*); sends for an order to shoot the prisoners at Newmilns, 58.
Ingram, James, architect, 222, 284.
Ingram, John, poetical writer, 248.
Iron-works, Hurlford, 290.
Irvine Presbytery, records of, 6 (*note*).

Jacobite Lyric, 64.
Jaffray, Rev. Robert, 150.
James V restores estates and honours to the Boyds, 32.
James VI grants a passport to fifth Lord Boyd, 35 (*note*).
Jameson, Rev. ——, at the execution of the Earl of Kilmarnock, 83.
Jamieson, Rev. David T., 157.
Jamieson, William, teacher, 144-5, 240.
Johnson, Dr Samuel, 90.
Johnston, Alexander, 208.
Johnston, George, of Redburn, 227.
Johnston, Professor James F. W., 243; his works, 244.
Johnston, James, 201, 243.
Johnston, Robert, architect, 218.
Jonas, Rev. Edward J., 226.

Kennedy, John, poetical writer and teacher, biographical sketch of, 197-9.
Kennedy's Patent Water Meter, 289.
Kilmares, William, Lord, 96.
Kilmarnock, Baron, 92.
Kilmarnock (1), Earl of, creation of, 37; grants of a charter to, and to the town,60.
Kilmarnock (2), Earl of, 60.
Kilmarnock (3), Earl of, gives a grant to the town, 60; loyalty of, 62, serves with his men in the royal army in 1715, 62; in Glasgow, 63; in the Highlands, 64, his death, 64.
Kilmarnock (4), Earl of, 64, his interest in the town, 64; marriage, 65; loyal to the house of Hanover, 65, joins the Pretender, 65; his zeal for the cause of Charles, 66, tradition regarding, 66; at Falkirk, 71; at Culloden, 72; prisoner, 74; trial, 75; condemned, 77, petitions in his favour, 77; his appearance at the trial, 78; behaviour after his sentence, 79; execution, 84, old prints of the execution, 84 (*notes*); interment, 85; letter to his factor, 87; to his son, 89; a free mason, 92; (*note*), 279.
Kilmarnock (4), Countess of, 65; at Callander House, 71; death of, 86; extract from her testament, 87.
Kilmarnock Annuals, 216.
Kilmarnock Athenæum, 277; subscription to, 278.
Kilmarnock Building Company, 210.
Kilmarnock Chronicle (1), 213.
Kilmarnock Chronicle (2), 215.
Kilmarnock Church, 99; a collegiate charge, 131; *see* Low Church.
Kilmarnock Cross, execution at, 48; site of a corn-mill, 93; of a curling pond, 116.
Kilmarnock Drawing Academy, 248.
Kilmarnock Herald, 215.
Kilmarnock House, description of, 17; modern uses of, 18; Reform meeting at, 207.
Kilmarnock Journal, 214.
Kilmarnock Library, 275; the room, 277, 285; subscription to, 278.
Kilmarnock Mirror, 192.
Kilmarnock Standard, 216.
Kilmarnock Water, its ancient name, 11 (*note*), how formed, 11, 261 (*note*); old course below Waterside, 18; extraordinary rise of, 260 (*note*); old coal-pit in the present bed of, 264 (*note*).
Kilmarnock Water Company, 291.
Kilmarnock Weekly Post, 216.
Kilwinning, monastery of, 2; to it belonged the tithes, &c., of the church of Kilmarnock, 99.
King Street opened, 184.
Kings' birthdays, 107.
Knockinlaw, antiquities found at, 28 (*note*).

Lady's Walk, 18, 86.
"Laird of Kilmarnock," 282 (*note*).
Lamont's *Diary*, extract from, 174.
Landowners in the parish, 296.
Land, value of, 295 (*note*).
Landreth, Rev. Peter, 216.
Langside, battle of, 34.
Landsborough, Rev. David, 225.
Largs, battle of, 20 (*note*).
Lauder, Margaret, 120.

INDEX.

Laurie, John, of Isles, 162.
Lawson, Rev. George, 151.
Lawson, Rev. John, 219.
Lee, Thomas, teacher, 145, 234.
Lennie, Rev. George, 221.
Leighton, John, periodical writer, 215.
Leslie, Rev. James, 133; death of, 123.
Libraries, *see* Kilmarnock Library.
Limont, Rev. ———, 220,
Lindsay, of Pitscottie, *Cronicles*, quoted, 24.
Lindsay, Rev. James, 151.
Lindsay, Rev. William, presented to 2nd charge, 119; opposed, 120; call, 121; call rejected by Presbytery and Synod, 121; appeal to the General Assembly, 122; his admission ordered, 122; opposed, particularly by Town Council, 123; settlement, 124; *Scoffing Ballad* on the settlement, 125.
Little Blackwood, encounter at, 56.
Livingstone, Anne, Countess of Kilmarnock. 65; anecdote of, 71.
Locarts, lords of Kilmarnock, 2.
Lochgoin, 51 (*note*), encounter at, 51.
Locomotive Engine, the first in Scotland, 282 (*note*).
Logan, William C., teacher, 145,
London Road, 231.
Longevity, remarkable instances of, 114.
Lord's Supper, celebration of, at Mauchline Muir, 131.
Loudoun Hill, battle of, 21.
Low Church, Boyd's Epitaph in, 35; description of, 99; patronage of, 100; uproar in, at the disputed settlement, 124; ministers of before the Revolution, 130; since then, 133; fatal catastrophe in, 176; list of the persons killed, 180 (*note*); subscriptions for sufferers, 183; panic in, 178 (*note*); time of erection of, 180, rebuilding of, 183, discovery of human bones, 183 (*note*).
Low Church Bell, 10.
Low Church Steeple, 10.
Lowe, Rev. A. H., 222.

M'Arthur, printer, 159.
M'Christie, Thomas Y., biographical sketch of, 240-3.
M'Dougall, Rev. William, 220.
Macfee, John, 209.
Macfie, Rev. Daniel, 223.
M'Gill, Rev. Dr, 155
Macindoe, Rev. Dr Peter, 221.
Macintosh, Rev. John C., 222.
Mackay, Alexander S., artist, 250.
Mackay, James M., artist, 251.
M'Kerrow, Andrew, 289.
Mackinlay, Rev. Dr James, notice of, 129, death of, 129; grave of, 165.
Mackinlay, Rev. James, yr, 129.
Maclaren, Alexander, at the Dean Park meeting, 201; apprehension and trial of, 203; death of, 204.

Maclaughlan, Rev. John, 225.
M'Michael, Rev. Dr N., 238
Macmillan, Duncan, ventriloquist, notice of, 258.
M'Millan, John, A.V.R., 293.
Macnaught, Rev. Daniel, 219.
M'Nicol, Janet, "Witch," 282 (*note*).
Macready, William, artist, 249.
Maggie Lang, "Witch," 282 (*note*).
Magistrates, first appointed, 8 (*note*); manner of their appointment, 60.
Mail-coach, the first, 95 (*note*).
Main, Rev. Thomas, 224.
Malibran, Mme, artiste, 257.
Marches, Riding of the, 109.
Marshall, Alexander, M.D., 293.
Martin, Rev. Thomas, 224.
Mary Queen of Scots, 34.
Masonry, *see* Free Masons.
May-pole, 115 (*note*).
Meal Market 69.
Meikle, James, A.V.A., 293
Menteith, James, schoolmaster, 136.
Miller, Hugh, his account of Rev. John Russell, 104.
Miller, James, murder of, 189; monument to, 191.
Miller, Dr John, labours during cholera, 212; presentation to, 213.
Ministers of the parish, or Low Church, before the Revolution, 130; since the Revolution, 133.
Ministers of the High Church, 103-5.
Miser's Funeral, 194 (*note*).
Mitchell, David, 204 (*note*).
Montgomerie, Robert, schoolmaster, 136.
Montgomery of Lainshaw, 33
Montgomery, Alexander, of Coilsfield, 279.
Montgomery, Alexander, poetical writer, 35 (*note*)
Montgomery, Hugh, of Eglintoun, kills the son of the Earl of Arran, 32.
Montgomery, Johanna, tomb of, 6.
Montgomery, John, 293.
Montgomery, Sir Niel, of Lainshaw, murdered, 33.
Moor, Dr James, 16; his cabinet of medals, 17 (*note*); intercedes for Earl of Kilmarnock, 77.
Moore, Dr William, 161.
More, Elizabeth, wife of Robert II, 297.
Morison, George, A V.A., 293.
Morison, Rev. Dr James, his theological views, 156; suspended by the Presbytery, 157, institutes the "E.U." Church, 157, is translated to Glasgow, 157.
Morton, teacher, 143.
Morton, Thomas, 234; biographical sketch of, 235-7.
Mowat, Rev. Matthew, 33 (*note*), 130; first Moderator of Fenwick Kirk Session, 131.
Mowbray, Sir Philip de, 2.
Muir, James, A.M, 279.

INDEX.

Muir, Robert, 161, Gilbert Burns's opinion of, 161.
Murdoch, Robert, schoolmaster, 136.
Murdoch, Right Rev. Dr, 225.
Mure's *Hist. of Rowallane*, quoted, 28 (*note*).
Mure, Elizabeth, *see* More.
Mure, Mungow, of Rowallane, 25 (*note*).
Mure, Thomas, " Doctor," 135.
Mure, William, of Rowallan, poetical writer, 297-8.
Mutrie, Rev. John, 128, 133.
Mylne MSS., extract from, 19 (*note*).

Nasmyth, artist, 245, 246.
National Portrait Gallery, 246.
Nelson, Francis, accountant, 238-40.
New Farm Loch, 116.
New Mill, 93.
Newmilns, rescue of Covenanters at, 58.
New-year's day, celebration of, 112, murder on, 112; rational observance of, 113.
Nisbet, John, executed at the Cross, 48; his epitaph, 49.
Norie, Henry Hay, A.V.R., 293.

Observatory, 234.
Odd-fellows, St Marnock Lodge of, 280.
Oliphant, Rev. James, 103, 124.
Original Seceders' Church, 226.
Osburne, James, schoolmaster, 135.
Oswald, Richard, 96.

Parish of Kilmarnock, extent of, 295, boundary of, 295 (*note*).
Parish School, about 1642, 134, early teachers of, 134; teachers after the Revolution, 136, Burgh School added, 136; state of, in 1764, 138; later teachers of, 144; situation of, 144 (*note*). *See* Academy.
Parishioners, number of, in 1547, 4; 287 (*note*).
Park, William, of Langlands, 279, 280.
Parker, John G., of Assloss, 296.
Parker, Major William, associated with Burns, 161, 162, 163; volunteer, 187, 207; free mason, 279.
Parker, Wm, of London, his bequest, 294.
Parliament establishes a school in each parish, 134.
Parliamentary Burgh, population, 287, boundary, 287 (*note*) constituency, 287.
Parochial Board, offices of, 18. *See* Poor.
Paterson, Boyd, 87.
Paterson, Jas, periodical writer, 213, 215.
Paterson, J. C., periodical writer, 215, 216.
Paterson, M. T., 87.
Paterson, Wm, of Ayr, his bequests, 294.
Paterson, Mr, of Braehead, 161, 279.
Paterson, William, of Paterson, 223.
Paterson, Wm, C., periodical writer, 215.
Paton, James and Mrs, of Little Blackwood, 56.

Paton, Captain John, of Meadowhead, sketch of his sufferings, 51-55, his execution, 55, monumental inscription, 55.
Patrick, Sandy, his " public," 163.
Peacock, Christian, murder of, 188.
Penney, Rev. W. W., 226.
Philharmonic Society, 278.
Philosophical Institution, 276, terms of subscription, 278.
Picken, James H., of Hillhouse, A.V.R., 292, 186 (*note*).
Picture Gallery, Mr Tannock's, 247.
Pipe's Brae, 109.
" Pit and gallows," right of, 150 (*note*).
Pont, Timothy, his description of Cunningham, quoted, 2, 6, 26.
Poor, support of, 293 ; amount of, beginning of last century, 293 (*note*) ; salaries of officials, 293.
Popish priest, appointment of, in 1547, 100.
Portincross, Castle of, 22 (*note*).
Portland, Duke of, 100, 296.
Portland Street opened, 186.
Portland Terrace, 281.
Prince Charles, *see* Stuart.
Prince Consort, 284, 285.
Prince of Wales, celebration of his marriage, 109 (*note*).
Pringle, Lucky, her " public," 163.
Printing, Letter-press, first introduced, 159 ; first iron press, 213.

Radicals, meetings of, at Dean Park, 201; at Morton Place, 204; attempted rising of, 206, apprehension of leaders, 206; chartist agitation, 208.
Railton, Robert, A.V.R., 292.
Railway to Glasgow, Dumfries, &c., 291.
Ramage, Rev. Thomas, 221, 292.
Ramage, Rev. William, 220.
Ramsay, John, poetical writer, 252.
Rankin, David, A.V.A., 293, 162 (*note*), 186 (*note*).
Rankine, rhyming blacksmith, 85 (*note*)
Recreations, out-door, &c., 109.
Reform, Parliamentary, *see* Radicals.
Reform Bill, 207, meetings in support of, 207, speakers in support of, 207.
Reformation, ecclesiastical arrangements consequent on, 129.
Reformed Presbyterian Church, 220.
Reid, James, innkeeper, 108 (*note*).
Reid, James B., artist, 251.
Reid, John, "wizard," 282 (*note*).
Reid, Michael, 15 (*note*).
Reyburn, Tam, 250 (*note*).
Riot at settlement of the Rev. William Lindsay, 124; trial and sentence of the ringleaders, 128.
Ritchie, Rev. Dr David, 133.
Ritchie, Rev. Dr John, 156.
Rob Roy, 64.
Robertson, James, martyr, 45.

Robertson, Rev. James, 102; ordination of, 152, style of preaching, 152; anecdotes of, 153-5, death of, 155.
Robertson, Rev. John, 96, 129; grave of, 165.
Robertson, John R., periodical writer, 215.
Robertson, Rev. Patrick W., 224.
Robertson, R. C., 285.
Robertson Place erected, 210.
Roger, Robert, innkeeper, 207, ascends in a balloon, 207 (note).
Roman Catholic Chapel, 225.
Roman encampment, 26.
Roman Well, 26 (note).
Rose, James, teacher, 146.
Ross, John, martyr, 38.
Rowallan Castle, 297; side school at, 146.
Rowat, Rev. James, 131, his bequest, 131 (note).
Royal Academy, 246.
Rubens, artist, 247.
Rumple, farm of, 295 (note).
Russell, Alexander, periodical writer, 215.
Russell, Rev. John, character of, 103; anecdote of, 104, institutes the first Sabbath school, 104, Hugh Miller's account of, 104-5.

Sabbath school first proposed, 104.
Saint Andrew's Church, 223.
Saint Columba, 2.
Saint Crispin's Society, 109.
Saint Marnock, era of, 1.
Saint Marnock's Church, 222.
Samson, Charles, 162.
Samson, Thomas, 161, the epitaph on, 161; a free mason, 163, 279; death of, 165.
Scott, Sir Walter, 57 (note), 188, 282 (note).
Scott, Miss, 100.
Scots Statesmen, Staggering State of, quoted, 29 (note).
Schools, *see* Academy, Burgh School, Parish School.
School in College Wynd burned, 3, 174.
School, East Shaw Street, 147.
School, Female, of Industry, 148.
School, Free, 147.
School, Holm Mission, 148.
School, the Wife's, 240.
Schools, Free Church, 147.
Schools, Nelson Street, 148.
Schools, Parochial Board, Ragged and Reformatory, 18, 148.
Schools at Grougar and Rowallan, 146.
Schools, Private or Adventure, 146.
Secession Church at Gallows-knowe, 149; disruption in, 150, removed to Portland Road, 150.
Session Records, extracts from, 9, 114 (note), 118 (note), 120, 121, 122, 133 (note), 135, 136, 137, 178 (note), 183 (note).
Sharpshooters, Volunteers, 187.
Shaw, Christian, bewitched, 282 (note).

Shaw, Hugh, free mason, 280.
Shaw, Sir James, biographical sketch of, 230; personal appearance of, 232, moral character of, 232, interest in the family of Burns, 232; kind acts of, 175, 241, 242, 246; his portrait in the Town Hall, 185; his statue at the Cross, 227.
Shaw, Sir John, 233; his donations to the sufferers by the Flood, 273; to the Athenæum, 277.
Shaw, John, of Bargarran, 282 (note).
Sheelin-hill, 93.
Shepherd, James, schoolmaster, 143.
Sheriff, appointment of a local, 283, his district, 283.
Shields, John, martyr, 38.
Shovel-board, 118 (note).
Silk manufacture, 97.
Silverwood, farm of, 295 (note).
Skellat-bell, 114.
Smeaton, Rev. Mr, 151; wide congregation of, 166 (note).
Smiddieraw, 94 (note).
Smith, Alexander, poetical writer, 254-6.
Smith, Alexander, A.M., schoolmaster, 146, 186 (note).
Smith, Dr Adam, 139.
Smith, Hugh H., A.V.R., 292.
Smith, James, schoolmaster, 136, 138.
Smith, John, 246.
Smith, Messrs, Windyedge, 223.
Soulis, Lord, killed by a Boyd, 25, monument and inscription, 25; traditionary story of, 26-8.
"Soulis, Auld," his adventures at the battle of Falkirk, 69.
Spooner, Rev. Ernest, 226.
Sprot, John, schoolmaster, 186.
Stage-coach, the first in Scotland, 95 (note).
Statistical Tables, 287-8.
Statue of Sir James Shaw, situation of, 229; erection of, 227, articles deposited in foundation of, 227; description of, 229; inauguration dinner, 228.
Sterling money first mentioned, 135.
Steven, John, free mason, 280.
Steven, Rev. William, 221.
Stevenson, James, teacher, 146.
Stewart, Alexander, of Darnley, kills Sir Thomas Boyd, 24.
Stewart, Allan, of Darnley, killed by Sir Thomas Boyd, 24.
Stewart, Rev. Charles, 223.
Stewart, John, schools established by, 148.
Stuart, Prince Charles, raises his standard in Scotland, 65; guest of Earl of Kilmarnock at Callander House, 66; imposes contributions on Glasgow, 68.
Sturrock, John, writer, 186 (note).
Suicides, 182 (note).
Surgeons, Royal College of, 242.
Sykes, Colonel, 239.
Symington, Rev. John, 220; A.V.R., 293.
Synod of Fife, extract from records of, 173.

INDEX.

Tannahill, Robert, poetical writer, 245, quotation from, 245.
Tannock, James, artist, biographical sketch of, 245-7.
Tannock, William, artist, 186, 247.
Taylor, James S., of Moorfield, A.V.R., 293.
Taylor, Dr John, 214.
Templeton, John, vocalist, biographical sketch of, 256.
Thieves' Hole, 39, 98.
Thomson, Rev. Daniel V., 133, 223, 227; A.V.A., 293.
Thomson, Captain James, periodical and poetical writer, biographical sketch of, 193-5.
Thomson, John, schoolmaster, 136.
Thomson, John, surgeon, 186 (note).
Thomson, Rev. John, 223.
Thomson, William, schoolmaster, 143, 144, 240, 243.
Thomson, Rev. William, teacher, 145.
Thomson, ——, teacher, 240.
Tinnock, Nanse, her "public," 163.
Tontine Buildings, erection of, 191.
Torrance, John, writer, 186 (note).
Tough, Jasper, surgeon, 47.
Town Records, see Burgh Records.
Town Council, enactments by, against drunkenness, &c., 8, 9.
Town-house, old, 97; bell of, 98.
Town Improvement Trustees, 284.
Trade, Board of, 236.
Trades, early, 7,
Trades, processions of, 109.
Trinity Episcopal Church, 225.
Trower, Right Rev. Dr W. J., 225.
Turnbull, Gavin, poetical writer, biographical notice of, 168; a free mason, 163, 279; quotation from, 166.

Union Street opened, 283.
United Presbyterian Church in King Street, 218-20; in Portland Road, 150; in Princes Street, 157.

Vandyke, artist, 247.
Volunteers, in 1715, 62, 63, 64; in 1745, 66; in the French war, 187, 193; in 1860, 292.

Walkinshaw of Scotston, 84, 85.

Wallace, James, builder, 225.
Wallace, Rev. Michael or Mitchell, 130; sanctions witch-burning, 282 (note).
Wallace, Rev. Thomas, 225.
Walpole's Letters, extracts from, 75, 77, 79 (notes).
Ward, Rev. John, 222.
Warning Drum, 113.
Weavers' Charter, 37 (note).
Watt, Patrick, martyr, 43.
Wedderburn, Rev. Alexander, maltreated by the Highland Host, 42; death of, 43, 132; further notice of, 43 (note).
"Wee Johnnie's" epitaph, 160 (note).
Weir, Andrew, teacher, 145.
Weir, Rev. Robert, 222.
Wellington Street opened, 186.
Wellington Street Free Church, 151.
West, Benjamin, criticism on James Tannock, 246.
White, James, martyr, 56; monument and epitaph, 57.
White, John, of Grougar, 296.
White, Major, 46.
White, ——, radical reformer, 202.
Wife's School, 240.
Wildbore, Rev. R., 226.
Wilkie, Rev. Robert, notice of, 130 (note).
Williamson, General, attends the Earl of Kilmarnock before execution, 81.
Willox, John, periodical writer, 215.
Wilson, Rev. David, 156.
Wilson, James, A.V.A., 293; 186 (note).
Wilson, John, notice of, 159, works printed by, 159; a free mason, 163, 279; his epitaph, 160 (note).
Wilson, Matthew, periodical writer, 215.
Witchcraft, executions for, 281 (note).
Witch Road, 281.
Wodrow, quoted, 39, 43 (note), 47, 133 (note).
Wood, Mrs, artiste, 257.
Worsted shawl-printing introduced, 209; statistics of, 210.
Wouvermans, artist, 247.
Wright, Rev. William, 131; death of, 133 (note).
Wyllie, Daniel, teacher, 147.

Young, Robert, schoolmaster, 135.
Young, Rev. William, 224.

KILMARNOCK:
PRINTED BY SMITH BROTHERS, KING STREET.

www.ingramcontent.com/pod-product-compliance
Lightning Source LLC
Chambersburg PA
CBHW030326240426
43673CB00040B/1286